The Crime Laboratory

Case Studies of Scientific Criminal Investigation

The Crime Laboratory

Case Studies of Scientific Criminal Investigation

By James W. Osterburg

Second Edition

Clark Boardman Company, Ltd., New York, New York 1982

Third Printing, July 1986

Library of Congress Cataloging in Publication Data:
Osterburg, James W.
The crime laboratory.

(Law & society)
Includes index.
1. Crime laboratories. I. Title.
II. Series.
HV8073.083 1981 363.2'56 81-7694
ISBN 0-87632-364-6 AACR2

With appreciation and affection, this book is dedicated to Robert F. Borkenstein, Joseph D. Nicol, Charles E. O'Hara, and Ralph F. Turner, colleagues who contributed to my professional growth as a criminalist, and to the Charles E. Redfield Foundation, Inc., which has a worthy history in support of law enforcement progress.

Foreword

Criminal justice as an academic area of study has come a long way since this book was first published in 1968. Earlier, as Dean of Faculties of John Jay College of Criminal Justice, I was pleased to support the research and didactic testing of **The Crime Laboratory** from a discretionary fund at my disposal. Following publication, it was recognized by criminalists in the academic community as a sound scholarly text which set standards for a work of its kind.

Today there is an even greater need for books that encourage and portray the intelligent and thorough utilization of physical evidence in criminal investigation. Supreme Court decisions and jury expectations relative to police performance have made physical evidence more significant. Indeed, there are attorneys I am aware of who are awaiting the right case in order to suitably raise the issue that poorly conducted crime scene investigations, in which physical evidence is present but not recognized, collected, and analyzed, constitute denial of due process and is a constitutionally reversible error. The criminal investigator who masters the content of this book and applies its principles will not be guilty of such negligence in his professional conduct.

The second edition of **The Crime Laboratory** extends the number of case exercises and adds a new section of laboratory exercises. The laboratory work will provide "hands-on" experience, supplying the very same practical knowledge which is acquired by students of the more traditional physical sciences in their laboratories.

Donald H. Riddle
John Jay College
City University of New York

Contents

Table of Text Figures

Science is nothing but developed perception, integrated intent, common sense rounded out and minutely articulated.

George Santanyana, The Life of Reason, V, 1905.

Preface to First Edition

The family, church, and school, among other influences, appear to be less effective social control devices than in former years. The problems that arise from this decreased influence are becoming, more and more, matters to be dealt with through the law. Indeed, criminal law especially is burdened by the decline in authority of the other institutions. The adaptation of science to the needs of the law seems an obvious step that must be employed to assist in the administration of justice. However, with the exception of medicine, only in recent times has science been enlisted to enlighten the problems of investigation and proof in criminal law. Even today there is at best a minimum usage of science for this purpose.

Much of crime laboratory work is based upon a comparison of crime scene clues with similar evidence whose origin is known. The acquisition of the latter is almost hopeless if the police are required to seek such standards in the presence of the suspect's counsel, and the implementation of the Escobedo and Miranda decisions makes it quite possible that counsel will be present more often in the future. Probably very few attorneys would advise a client to provide voluntarily the necessary comparison evidence if it would tend to incriminate him. Rather, as Justice Jackson stated in Watts v. Indiana, "any attorney worth his salt will tell the suspect in no uncertain terms to make no statements to police under any circumstances." Furthermore, any attorney who believes a client to be guilty might very well warn him not to cooperate with the police in any manner whatsoever. This is an area of conflict between the needs of science and the requirements of the law. A satisfactory resolution is imperative if truth and justice are not to become victims of this confrontation.

One of the major reasons for the minimal use of science as an aid in the enforcement of criminal law is the lack of suitable educational material for those who have a primary responsibility, the police who arrive first at the scene of a crime. If the crime scene is not protected properly, and if the physical evidence is not recognized, collected, and preserved, then science through the crime laboratory—regardless of its staff and equipment—can be of little assistance in the administration of justice.

This book, then, is intended to serve the needs of five broad audiences:

1. The inquisitive police officer or detective who wishes to improve his understanding of scientific evidence through self-study.
2. The police recruit or neophyte detective who is studying criminal investigation as part of an inservice police academy training program.
3. The college student who is taking an introductory course in "The Crime Laboratory."
4. The legal profession, especially law students, defense attorneys, prosecutors, and judges who are concerned with the use and meaning of physical evidence in court.
5. Legislators and civic-minded citizens who are interested in the problems of justice in our changing society.

It has been assumed in the writing of this text that no equipment or laboratory facilities are available to the reader. Although no special laboratory equipment is needed to use the book, it is even more valuable in a course where such apparatus is available. For example, the material in this text may serve to supplement the work in the laboratory in which simplified field procedures such as the development of fingerprints, the benzidine test for blood, the use of detective dyes or thief-detection powders, and so on, are taught.

It is my belief that a significant appreciation of the potential of physical evidence is best acquired through an exposure to real laboratory cases. To this end, actual police cases were obtained from the widest possible spectrum of law enforcement: federal, state, county, and municipal agencies. In all, some thirty or more agencies cooperated in one way or another. I was unable to employ all of the cases submitted, largely because of duplication. The cases which were selected were chosen for their teaching suitability, their interesting nature, and their variety. The case material treated in this book is not so unusual as to be unique; rather, it is more or less commonplace for those areas utilizing progressive law enforcement procedures. On the other hand, there are still many sections of the country in which the material will appear unbelievable, since in such areas almost no use is made of scientific measures for clue development. To a not inconsiderable extent this is true even for agencies that have a crime laboratory convenient to them. Paraphrasing the horse and water aphorism—you can lead an investigator through a laboratory but you can't make him use it. Effective supervision, of course, can change this outlook; however, many police supervisors have had little professional education in police science or in crime laboratory work, so that reform through this source is presently limited. There is also a tendency, especially for those who learned investigation through apprentice training, to think of seeking laboratory aid as a last resort when there is no further opportunity for glory and self-aggrandizement through a personal coup leading to the solution of the case. At this stage, natural considerations of self-protection against possible criticism assert themselves and the services of the laboratory are sought, since "It looks good to have it in the record that the laboratory was called." Of course, at this point it is too late, for the crime scene has been irrevocably altered. Readers of this text should be able to evaluate how laboratory services are being employed in their jurisdiction and to insist, if their position permits, upon necessary improvements. When investigators routinely make intelligent use of the crime laboratory, as they do in our more competent departments, we can expect that better proof or disproof of criminality will be made available for use in court.

The thesis upon which this book is based is simple. The development of the educated police officer requires that an opportunity be provided for him to scrutinize a wide variety of typical, and a few atypical, examples of physical evidence. Thus, the usual as well as the unusual will come within the focus of study of those in the first echelon of the investigative process—the officer first at the scene of the crime and the field detective.

Since this text is a pioneering effort to portray realistically some aspects of laboratory work, some faults may become apparent to users. In order to minimize this unhappy possibility, the manuscript was used in tentative form for several semesters. College students at Indiana University and the University of California at Berkeley, police officers of the New York City Police Department attending the John Jay College of Criminal Justice of the City University of

New York, and law enforcement personnel attending Phoenix College, Arizona (a two year program) and the Corning Community College, New York, assisted in the evaluation of the manuscript. In addition, persons lacking any police experience were asked to read the text and perform the exercises unaided. Difficulties brought to light in this fashion were corrected in order to avoid quandaries for homestudy readers. I also asked many of my academic colleagues as well as friends still working actively in criminalistics to criticize the manuscript. Numerous suggestions were offered; of course, many were accepted but some were rejected. For all of its faults as well as its virtues, I acknowledge full responsibility.

James W. Osterburg
1968

Preface to Second Edition

Revising **The Crime Laboratory** for this second edition entailed a number of considerations, the most obvious being how to improve upon a text that already has an established place in crime laboratory courses. First, an effort was directed toward supplying additional case exercises. Also, in response to the requests of numerous instructors, "hands on" laboratory exercises have been added. These new case exercises have been included to round out the discussions and to introduce new areas of development in the field of criminalistics.

Second, the materials have been reorganized to facilitate student reading, and the case exercises rearranged and renumbered to allow for easy reference. Theoretical discussions of each area of concern are confined to one section of the book. The case exercises themselves appear in a separate section, along with instructions and practical guidelines to aid the student in analyzing each problem. Another adjustment which users of the first edition may notice is that the illustrations included in the text and the exercise sections have been recoded to simplify reference.

Third, this edition, unlike the first, does not contain expert solutions for each case exercise. Only those cases for which the solutions serve as learning tools to pinpoint fundamental principles and processes have been retained. The rationale behind this change is that expert solutions are not and never have been incorporated into the book as mere answer keys, grading the student's analysis of a case as simply correct or incorrect. This would defeat the essentially didactic purposes of this book. The instructor is now afforded the opportunity to use the case exercises for which no solutions are provided in the text as a means of testing student progress. Solutions for these cases are furnished in the new Instructors Manual.

It is hoped that these basic changes will not only aid the instructor in teaching the course, but also will bring the student closer to mastering the fine points of criminal investigation.

James W. Osterburg
1981

Acknowledgments

The research and writing of this text and the acquisition of case material required numerous trips to various laboratories and agencies. Considerable expense was involved, and without the financial assistance of the Charles E. Redfield Foundation, Inc., this book would not have been possible. In addition, I should like to mention the encouragement of Charles E. Redfield prior to the writing of the book and to express my appreciation for the many kindnesses extended by him during its writing.

The opportunity for student testing of the case material was provided by the John Jay College of Criminal Justice in two ways: by underwriting the costs of lithographing the significant case photographs, and by using the text in mimeographed form for teaching its students, who are largely members of the New York City Police Department. This assistance was made possible by the late President Leonard E. Reisman and Dean Donald H. Riddle of the John Jay College of the City University of New York.

Many persons, including students, have offered comments on the book after reading it in mimeographed form. In particular, Professors Robert F. Borkenstein and Louis Sattler, and Dr. Charles Kingston were most helpful in their critical commentaries. Professors Paul L. Kirk, R. F. Turner, P. Murphy, Mr. P. Rajeswaran, Mr. Herbert L. MacDonell, and my colleagues at Indiana University, Professors L. E. Brown, R. A. Myren (now Dean of the School of Justice at The American University, Washington, D.C.), and H. J. Trubitt made suggestions that improved the text.

The persons listed below assisted in identifying or contributing appropriate case material or helped in obtaining other suitable illustrations for the first edition:

Attorney-General Laboratory, Ontario, Canada: H. Ward Smith, D. M. Lucas, V. Krcma, and R. C. Nicol

Burma National Police: U Sein Hla Aung and U Hla Baw.

Chicago Police Department: Daniel Dragel and Claude B. Hazen.

Cincinnati Police Department: Stanley R. Schrotel and Robert J. Roncker.

Columbus Police Department (Ohio): Lloyd Shupe.

Dansville Police Department (New York): James E. Bradley.

Federal Bureau of Investigation: J. Edgar Hoover and Ivan Conrad.

Illinois Bureau of Criminal Identification and Investigation: Joseph D. Nicol.

Indiana State Police: Charles Davis.

Laboratories for Scientific Criminal Investigation, University of Rhode Island: Harold C. Harrison.

Los Angeles Police Department: Ray Pinker.

MacDonell Associates, Inc.: Herbert L. MacDonell.

Michigan State Police: Charles Meyers.

Minnesota State Bureau of Criminal Apprehension: Wilkaan Fong.
New York City Police: John Berryman, Henry Guttenplan, Joseph McNally, and Xavier Olivo.
New York State Police: J. N. Cesaro.
North Carolina, State Bureau of Investigation: Harry M. Smith.
Office of District Attorney, County of Santa Clara, California: Lowell W. Bradford.
Office of District Attorney, Pittsburgh-Allegheny County: Charles McInerney.
Painted Post Police Department, New York: Richard Boyle.
Philadelphia Police Department: Edward Burke.
St. Paul Police Department, Minnesota: Ted Elzerman.
San Francisco Police Department: John F. Williams.
Santa Ana Police Department, California: J. A. Kearns.
Sheriff, San Bernardino County, California: Anthony Longhetti.
Sheriff's Department, Orange County, California: W. J. Cadman.
Sheriff's Office, Los Angeles County, California: Clifford Cromp.
Sheriff's Office, Kern County, California: G. Bahnsen.
Texas Department of Public Safety: J. D. Chastain.
Toledo Police Department, Ohio: Ted B. Kwiatkowski.
U.S. Army, Criminal Investigation Laboratory, Ft. Gordon, Georgia: Travis W. Parker and Hillyard O. Medlin.

The individuals named below furnished additional case material and/or solution to an exercise for the second edition:

Burma National Police: U. Sein Hla Aung and U. Hla Baw
Columbus Police Department, Ohio: Lloyd Shupe*
Highland Park Police Department, Illinois: Donald J. Verbeke
Michigan State Police: Charles Meyers* and Lonnie L. Smrkovski
New Jersey State Police: Clinton L. Pagano
New York City Police: Joseph P. McNally* and Edward Palmer*
Office of District Attorney, Pittsburgh-Allegheny County: Charles McInerney*
St. Paul Police Department, Minnesota: Ted Elzerman*
San Francisco Police Department: John Williams*
Santa Ana Police Department, California: J. A. Kearns*
Sheriff's Department, Contra Costa County, California: Duayne J. Dillon
Sheriff, San Bernardino County, California: Anthony Longhetti
Forensic Science Consultants: Joseph D. Nicol, Robert D. Olsen, and T. Dickerson Cooke,* Institute of Applied Science, Chicago.

Several journals were helpful also. I gratefully acknowledge the cooperation of the publisher of Law and Order, William C. Copp, and its editor, Lee E. Lawder, in permitting numerous articles which first appeared in that publication to be used in this text. The permission granted by the Military Police Journal to use the "ear case" is acknowledged and I am grateful to its editor, Major Gary A. Sorenson, for his cooperation. Two other sources of

*Affiliation at time case material was received but is no longer with the department indicated.

ideas, the Journal of Forensic Sciences and the Journal of Criminal Law, Criminology and Police Science deserve special mention, and permission to quote from them is appreciated.

Little, Brown and Company was most cooperative in permitting the use of several paragraphs from The Science of Judical Proof 3rd ed. rev. and enl., 1937, by John H. Wigmore. The Federal Bureau of Investigation, U.S. Department of Justice, and its Director J. Edgar Hoover were most gracious in permitting the reproduction in its entirety of their publication entitled "FBI Suggestions for Handling of Physical Evidence."

An author is often dependent upon many people and organizations for many things. It is impossible to thank all of them by name; however I should be ungrateful if I failed to single out Joan Huntington for her editorial assistance, enthusiasm, and general cooperation in the production of the manuscript. The library of Indiana University was invaluable to me; Miss Betty LeBus, Librarian of the Law School, and Mrs. Janet Horton, Librarian of the Undergraduate School Library, were particularly helpful and deserve special mention. Mrs. James M. Osterburg (nee Elizabeth Johnstone) also contributed her artistic talents in the execution of Introductory Exercise A. Mr. William Dellenbeck of the Institute for Sex Research of Indiana University assisted in some of the photographic problems that arose while writing this book.

Aristotle could have avoided the mistake of thinking that women have fewer teeth than men by the simple device of asking Mrs. Aristotle to open her mouth.

Bertrand Russell

Part 1

General Principles

1

The Crime Laboratory's Role in Investigation

The present chapter endeavors to provide an understanding as well as a realistic appreciation of the role of the police crime laboratory in the investigative process. Stated briefly, through the scientific examination of evidence, the crime laboratory is able to assist the practical detective by:

Linking the crime scene or victim to the criminal.
Establishing a crime element.
Corroborating or disproving an alibi.
Inducing admissions or confessions.
Exonerating the innocent.
Providing expert testimony in court.

Police crime laboratories were established in the United States in the early 1930s. Sufficient experience is now available to assess their role in the criminal investigative process. Most clearly the evidence demonstrates that the crime laboratory is seldom able to determine — on the basis of laboratory work alone — the identity of the perpetrator. This remains the task of the field investigator. His job is not threatened by the laboratory; however, it may well be threatened in the future if he fails to use the laboratory when it may be of assistance to him. The restrictive influence of Supreme Court decisions on long-accepted investigative practice makes it imperative that leads and tools which may have been neglected in the past be used now to the fullest extent possible. The laboratory is one such tool.

Neglect of the laboratory may be attributed to many reasons.

1. Lack of knowledge as to how the laboratory can aid the criminal investigator.
2. Unfamiliarity with the more esoteric varieties of clue material. This may result in some crime scene evidence not being preserved for examination.
3. Failure to collect physical evidence. This may be caused by a fear of cross-examination on some technical, legal, or scientific requirement that may be overlooked. This manifestation of uncertainty and lack of confidence is the result of inadequate training and experience. Many detectives, especially in important cases, become cautious and decide to let an expert handle this matter for them. There is usually some delay before the expert is able to arrive at the crime scene. During this period the exigencies of the situation may shift, the investigator's attention is directed elsewhere, and there is a good chance that the evidence will be lost forever.
4. Overrepresentation of laboratory capabilities. Misinformed instructors who therefore are quite ignorant of the real functions of a laboratory are often guilty of this. Unfortunately, when the laboratory is unable to deliver the results which detectives have been led to expect, many of them become disillusioned with it. They soon abandon it altogether except for token use in hopeless

cases where "it looks good in the report."

5. Inconvenience. This arises when there is no local laboratory to which a detective may deliver physical evidence rapidly and easily, or when a report of laboratory results can not be obtained quickly for further investigative use.

The first four reasons should grow less significant as the knowledge made available in this text becomes part of the general education of criminal investigators. Allocation of resources to increase the number of universities offering courses in criminalistics and to obtain the scientific instruments necessary to equip crime laboratories will take care of the fifth reason.

Linking Crime Scene and Criminal

The classical illustration of this laboratory function is the development of latent fingerprints at the crime scene. Other examples are the following: a gun found in the possession of a suspect and a fatal bullet are connected by examination under the comparison microscope; a shoeprint on a piece of paper found at the scene of a safe burglary is tied to the heel or sole impression made from a suspect's shoe; the hand printing on the "stick-up" note given to the bank teller is shown to be that of a person answering the description provided by eyewitnesses. A term useful in describing this important laboratory role is *associative evidence.* Given the examples above, the term is self-explanatory. A more elaborate explanation of its meaning and some of the principles involved in developing associative evidence in the laboratory are discussed in Chapter 3.

The examples cited are common operations in the crime laboratory. It is in the area of unusual clue material, in which the method of establishing an association between criminal and crime scene or victim has yet to be developed, that the need for and value of the well-educated, imaginative, and enthusiastic laboratory worker become apparent. The intriguing challenge of the nonroutine case often stimulates such a person to apply his experimental and photographic ingenuity, making possible the incriminating linking of associative evidence. Physical evidence sometimes available in hit-and-run cases falls into this category. The almost countless ways in which a person may leave a trace of contact with the vehicle are well known to the motor vehicle accident investigator. Proving that it was this vehicle and this person that were in contact often taxes the resourcefulness of the crime laboratory worker.

In many ways case work for the detective and research work for the academician are similar. As the late Paul L. Kirk, a distinguished criminalist, said in a letter to the author, in both areas ". . . only the questions are reasonably clear, but neither the answers nor the means of obtaining them are known at the beginning."

Establishing a Crime Element

In order to prove that a crime has been committed, every concept contained in each clause in the penal law describing that crime must be proved. For many situations the detective is able to achieve this goal through the complainant, eyewitnesses, or the defendant; however, technical matters require laboratory assistance. Thus, the laws governing contraband, such as narcotics or guns which are shown to be in working order, are applicable only when the substance or object in question is demonstrated to be that proscribed by law. Alcohol, whose manufacture, distribution, or sale are governed by numerous regulations, must be shown to be present in the substance that has been seized. If the chemist is unable to determine alcohol in the liquid, perhaps owing to its subsequent conversion into acetic acid because of the existence of suitable conditions and sufficient delay before delivery to the laboratory, a necessary *element* of the crime has not been established and the case will have to be dropped.

Corroboration of an accusation is necessary in some crimes, particularly those involving various sex laws. Thus, the demonstration of a seminal stain on some object as car upholstery or female undergarments may be sufficient to confirm the details described by the complainant. An admission that a particular type of weapon was used in the crime may be corroborated through an examination of a bullet recovered from the crime scene. This is true even though the bullet may also be so damaged that it cannot be compared with test bullets, or the gun was discarded by the criminal and cannot be located.

Although intent is often inferred from the behavior of a criminal in the commission of a crime, it may be established also through the technical examination of evidence. Arson is a crime in which the setting of fire sometimes may be shown by the laboratory to be intentional and deliberate. If considerable effort and extremely diligent care are required to start and sustain a blaze in its early stages, the resulting fire can only be considered as one which was willfully started. A subsequent explanation by an accused that the fire started accidentally is unlikely to be regarded as credible by a jury.

Checking an Alibi

When a suspect under investigation offers an explanation or alibi concerning physical evidence in a case, the laboratory is often able to prove or disprove the statement. For instance, a stain resembling blood in physical appearance is accounted for as having been produced by a raw steak which accidentally fell and touched the clothing while a person was acting as chef for a cookout. The laboratory determination that beef blood, human blood, or both are present in the stain can have significantly different outcomes for the individual offering such an alibi. Whether a person was possibly acting in self-defense may at times be shown by determining the distance between victim and gun muzzle at the time of the shooting. When overlapping breakage patterns in window glass have been caused by two bullets discharged from opposite sides of the window, laboratory examination may often establish which bullet was fired first. Although other examples of the examination of physical evidence and the possible interpretations that may be placed upon the results could be given, these examples should suggest the real possibilities and significance of clue material examined in the crime laboratory.

Inducing Admissions or Confessions

One of the several conditions necessary to obtain a confession from a suspect is to have evidence against him which is understood by him and which he believes is incriminating. Physical evidence obviously has demonstrative qualities which make it especially valuable for this purpose. Thus, when possible, performing a test in the presence of a suspect and coupling it with an explanation of its meaning often results in an admission or confession. A wife who attempted to poison her husband by the addition of tincture of iodine to his drink quickly unburdened herself by confessing to the misdeed when a simple chemical test with starch solution was performed in her presence. The nonspecific benzidine test for suspected blood stains has had similar "miraculous" results when the significance of the appearance of a blue or blue-green color was discussed with the detective within hearing of the suspect. The lie detector has its greatest value as a scientific aid when a confession is induced by showing the chart record and discussing with the suspect the meaning of the irregularities in the blood pressure, pulse, respiration, and electrodermal measurements made during the test.

Exonerating the Innocent

Protection of the innocent from misinterpretation of evidence, especially physical evidence, is an important laboratory function. Although the checking of an alibi in some ways accomplishes the same result, it should be noted that the laboratory serves this purpose by other means. For example, an employee of a financial institution may identify a suspect as the passer of a forged negotiable document; however, competent examination of the writing on the document may prove the suspect could not have written the questioned document and that the visual identification by the employee-witness was erroneous.

In another case, a homicide seemed to be one that would be solved easily, owing to the many circumstances pointing to the suspect. His explanation of an apparent blood stain as that of animal origin seemed to be but one more lie, or at best a weak explanation of its source. The laboratory report that the stain was indeed animal blood was disconcerting to the detectives, but it caused them to reexamine the entire case in order to be sure they had not prejudged the individual.

Providing Expert Testimony

Even though most criminal cases do not ultimately go to trial, it is nevertheless necessary that all laboratory personnel be prepared to qualify as expert witnesses in those areas in which they perform laboratory examinations. It is unfortunate that there always seem to be police chiefs who believe that by *fiat* they can make a laboratory expert just as they make a detective a homicide expert or a patrolman a traffic expert. Under the American system of justice, a judge determines whether a person is an expert after the qualifications of the individual (i.e., education, self-training, and experience) have been stated in open court or stipulated by defense counsel.

In addition to technical qualifications, a good expert witness must have knowledge of court rules and procedure. He must be able to testify effectively by being able to explain technical material in such a way that the average juror is able to understand the matter under discussion. This is always a difficult task and doubly so when it is attempted in the tense atmosphere of the court room.

Conclusion

When detectives have an accurate and realistic understanding of the assistance the laboratory can give to them, when they have truly grasped the principles involved in the recognition, collection, and preservation of evidence, and if laboratory service is readily available to them, then science, technology, and criminal investigative practice will have joined hands in furtherance of the administration of justice.

Suggestions for Further Reading

Cadman, W.J. "How to Get the Best from Your Crime Laboratory," *The Police Chief* 45 (2), 64-70 (1978).

Ceccaldi, P.F. *La Criminalistique.* Paris: Presses Universitarires de France, 1962.

Cole, David. "The Police — The Scientist — The Coroner," *The Police J.* 4, 382-389 (1979).

Gazey, S.P. "Laboratory Design For Forensic Science," *J. Canadian Soc. of For. Sci.* 8, 132-142 (1975).

Keefe, J.F. "Forensic Sciences Services and the Criminal Justice System," *J. For. Sci.* 3, 673-680 (1979).

Kirk, P.L. *Crime Investigation.* 2nd ed. Edited by J.I. Thornton. New York: Wiley, 1974.

———, and Bradford, L.W. *The Crime Laboratory: Organization and Operation.* Springfield, Ill.: Thomas, 1965.

Nickolls, L.C. *The Scientific Investigation of Crime.* London: Butterworth, 1956.

O'Brien, K.P. and Sullivan, R.C. *Criminalistics: Theory and Practice.* 3d ed. Boston: Allyn and Bacon, 1980.

O'Hara, C.E. and Osterburg, J.W. *An Introduction to Criminalistics.* Bloomington, Ill.: Indiana University Press, 1972.

Saferstein, R. *Criminalistics: An Introduction to Forensic Science.* Englewood Cliffs, N.J.: Prentice-Hall, 1977.

Serrill, M.S. "Forensic Sciences: Overburdened and Underutilized," *Police Mag.* 1, 382-389 (1979).

Svensson, A., Wendel, O., and Fischer, B. *Techniques of Crime Scene Investigation.* 3rd ed. New York: Elsevier, 1981.

Turner, R.F. *Forensic Science and Laboratory Technics.* Springfield, Ill.: Thomas, 1949.

Walls, H.J. *Forensic Science: An Introduction to Scientific Crime Detection.* 2nd ed. New York: Praeger, 1974.

2

Crime Scene Search for Physical Evidence

Whether a police agency has its own laboratory or uses another agency's facilities, the problems of recognition, collection, and preservation of physical evidence remain the same. The difficulties inherent in any crime scene investigation are the subject of this chapter. The following areas of concern must be carefully understood if the investigator is to make maximum use of the crime laboratory:

1. Recognition of physical evidence.
2. Collection and preservation of physical evidence.
3. Legal aspects involved.
   a. Identification of physical evidence — recording and marking physical evidence.
   b. Custody of physical evidence.
4. Scientific aspects involved.
   a. Prevention of change in physical evidence — containers and tools.
   b. Obtaining comparison specimens — background materials and sufficiency of sample.

Recognition

Any serious discussion of the *recognition* of physical evidence at a crime scene must consider widely differing capabilities among individual investigators. In departments where the laboratory staff personally examines the crime scene, the only important limitation is rooted in the breadth of scientific education, resourcefulness, and imagination of the person conducting the search. A police chief has the right to expect that the laboratory man know where any physical evidence may be sent for examination if it is beyond the equipment of the laboratory or scientific training of the staff to handle.

Sophistication in the recognition of physical evidence can be achieved only through education and experience. At present, many chiefs place most reliance on the experience factor. No doubt much can be learned in due course through actual crime scene search work; however, the possibility for the loss of some physical evidence will always exist because its recognition, in terms of laboratory potential, is not learned through on-the-job training alone. This experience must be supplemented, or better, preceded by formal scientific training, if an examination of the crime scene is to be of maximum investigative value.

On the other hand, any experienced, practical investigator is not likely to overlook obvious clue materials. Blood, spent bullets or cartridges, paint chips, fingerprints, and the like are sufficiently well-known even to detectives of limited training. More likely to be overlooked are odorless accelerants at arson crime scenes, glass slivers present in trouser cuffs or imbedded in rubber heels, fibers and other debris present on clothing, evidence to determine the direction of the impacting force that broke a window glass, evidence to determine if a lock was picked, and other more esoteric clue materials.

To insure the recognition of physical evidence, though experience is helpful, there is no substitute for scientific education. This does not imply that all investigators must be scientists. Rather it suggests that each department should have some scientifically trained personnel available who can assume responsibility for the crime scene search, at least in major cases.

Collection and Preservation

Much dull, drawn-out, descriptive material purporting to discuss this subject has been printed. Essentially, the problem is quite simple if a few fundamental ground rules or guidelines are thoroughly understood. There are two major sets of principles, one legal and the other scientific, that govern the collection and preservation of physical evidence. Each has its own special considerations.

Legal Aspects

Of particular importance from the legal standpoint are the problems of identity and custody.

Identity

The discoverer of any physical evidence must be able to identify each piece of evidence as being the piece that he found in a particular place at the crime scene. Ordinarily two procedures are employed to accomplish this—*recording* the crime scene and *marking* the particular evidence involved.

Recording

The general methods for recording at the crime scene are photographs, sketches, and notes.

Photographs

In addition to general photographs covering the crime scene, photographs of specific items of evidence should also be taken. The aims of all these photographs are to enable a person not present at the crime scene to understand better what the situation was when first called to the attention of the police, to see the relationship between items of investigative interest at the time the scene was under examination, and to review the scene in the light of developments which occurred during the investigation that followed.

Sketches

If it is not possible to obtain photographs, sketches can aid the investigator, at least in minor cases. More important, sketches should be used to supplement, not supplant, photographs. The great value of a sketch over a photograph is that of selectivity. Only the important aspects of the crime scene need be included. Unimportant details that distract attention should be omitted. For coverage of large areas, overview sketches permit easy comprehension of a complicated route taken by a perpetrator.

Notes

Some details are better recorded by notes than by photographs or sketches. Convenience also may dictate their use. Thus, each item of evidence, its location, identification mark (see below), and further descriptive particulars are investigative details readily recorded in a notebook. Information such as time of arrival at the scene, who was present, witnesses interviewed, and similar facts are obviously best recorded in this fashion.

Marking Evidence

A unique mark placed directly on the evidence is probably the most reliable means of identification; however, some objects are difficult or impossible to mark directly. When evidence consists of a hard (metal) object, a liquid, or a powdered material such as a narcotic, a tag can be securely attached or a container (box or envelope) can be used and sealed; then the tag or container is marked for identification.

The identification mark necessary for legal purposes can be as simple as an initial, badge number, or other mark made in a unique manner. However, if space is sufficient, as with a tag or container, the defendant's initials, location where the evidence was obtained, date, and case or arrest number might be added. Essentially the problem is that of being able to state unequivocally that this item and no other is the one found by the investigator. If it can also be connected to the defendant by placing his initials on it, this is even better—but not necessary.

Of course, on many occasions a defendant (or even a suspect) is not known at the time the evidence is discovered, so that there are other reasons why much evidence never has this information marked on it. The major requirement then is that the investigator must mark the evidence in some permanent fashion so that he will be able to identify it positively as the evidence found and explain the circumstances concerning its acquisition at any time in the future.

Custody

The legal profession requires that possession of physical evidence be accounted for from the time of its discovery until it is offered as evidence in court. This is referred to as *chain of custody* or *continuity of possession.* If it can be shown that the evidence was not held continuously by a responsible person or persons, or stored in some safe location with limited access except to authorized individuals, the defense attorney is likely to succeed in barring its admission. Keeping the number of persons handling the evidence to a minimum is therefore desirable. This implies direct delivery of evidence to the laboratory by the investigator rather than by a messenger. The United States Mail, United Parcel Service, or Air Express delivery are permissible for distant laboratory facilities.

Scientific Aspects

The scientist in the crime laboratory requires all possible steps be taken to prevent change in evidence. If some change is beyond complete control (as in biological materials, for example), then it should be minimized by taking all possible necessary precautions. In order to examine crime scene evidence, the crime laboratory scientist often requires comparison material, i.e., specimens of known origin or exemplars from a known source. The special advisements necessary to achieve these ends are discussed below.

Prevention of Change in Physical Evidence

In the collection and preservation of evidence, one should proceed with the idea that only one opportunity is available to perform the job. Failure to collect and preserve physical evidence present at the crime scene eliminates the possibility of laboratory support. For the investigator, to the extent the laboratory might have been able to provide such assistance if available physical evidence had been submitted for study, this is an opportunity lost forever.

Physical evidence may undergo change or modification in many ways:

1. Loss by leakage such as of a fine powder, through a small hole or rip in an envelope.
2. Evaporation or seepage of liquid from an unstoppered or semiporous container.
3. Contamination, chemical or bacterial, caused by the use of unclean containers.
4. Mixture, through the mingling of evidence from various sources when a common container is used.
5. Alteration, by the unwitting addition of a new crease or fold in a document, tear or cut in a garment, and so on.

In general the steps which tend to minimize or eliminate the above changes are as follows:

1. Use suitable, intact, complete containers.
2. Use clean, fresh containers.
3. Maintain the integrity of each individual

specimen by using separate containers.
4. Handle the evidence as little as possible.

Biological specimens, such as blood and seminal stains in an undried state on fabrics or a crime weapon, are for most cases best preserved by permitting them to dry naturally in (room) air away from direct heat and sunlight.

Containers

The following are examples of clean, suitable containers readily available in most communities:

1. Bags
   a. paper
   b. plastic
2. Boxes
   a. pill (drug store type)
   b. shoe
   c. large cartons
3. Envelopes
   a. regular mail
   b. brown manila, metal-clasp
   c. transparent plastic
4. Other containers
   a. plastic
      (1) used to dispense pills by druggist
      (2) used to store leftovers in refrigerators
   b. glass
      (1) Mason jar with lid
      (2) bottle with stopper
   c. cans

It is more efficient, of course, to acquire these items in advance of their use rather than to attempt to locate them when the investigator's major attention should be directed to the crime scene search.

Tools

It is fairly obvious that from time to time some means are required for separation or removal of evidence from its setting, e.g., a seminal stain on automobile upholstery, a tool mark on a safe door, a broken ornament on an automobile, and so on.

Among an almost endless variety of tools that might be carried, the following general types will be found most useful:

1. Cutting implements
   a. scissors
   b. scalpels
   c. saws (metal and wood)
   d. compound-action metal snips or shears
2. Gripping devices
   a. tweezers
   b. pliers
   c. assorted wrenches
3. Other basic tools
   a. screwdrivers (small to large)—regular and Phillips types
   b. hammer
   c. pry bar

Obtaining Comparison Specimens

In obtaining samples to be used as the basis of comparison with some questioned item of physical evidence, all variables should be eliminated or controlled if possible. Thus, for a spurious check written with a ballpoint pen, a suspect who upon request is willing to supply specimens should be asked to write on a check form using a ballpoint pen. A pencil, liquid ink pen, crayon, plain or lined paper, and so on, are differences that should not be introduced by the investigator. With a little care, diligence, and understanding of this principle he can eliminate such variances.

The box of cartridges used by a criminal to load a gun should be obtained, if possible, for any firearms tests that are to be made. This is important when the distance is to be determined between the gun muzzle and the object struck at the time the weapon was discharged. While distance-to-object tests can be made with cartridges from another source, it is desirable to use the same source when available. This is an application of the principle of the control of variables. It seeks to keep all conditions as close as possible to the original insofar as they may be determined and duplicated.

Background Material

In the collection of physical evidence (such as a stain) present on an object it is also desirable to obtain a sample of the object close to the area bearing the evidence stain. Thus, in a case involving automobile paint on a bicycle alleged to have been struck by a car it is necessary, under this principle, to obtain a "pure" bicycle paint sample. By "pure" is meant bicycle paint uncontaminated with automobile paint, and vice versa. Of course, the evidence samples are obtained from the car in those areas where the bicycle paint was transferred to it and from the bicycle in those areas where the car paint was transferred to it. Fabric containing a blood stain should be removed in one piece or, if this is not possible, cut so that some unstained area is available for examination.

The purpose of obtaining background material is to determine if there is anything present on it that might contribute to, or interfere with, the scientific examination of the stain itself. Detergents or perspiration on an undershirt could interfere with or yield misleading results concerning the grouping of a blood stain on the garment.

Sufficiency of Sample

There is a tendency among investigators to be over optimistic concerning the ability of the scientist, using modern instrumental methods of analysis, to analyze small traces of physical evidence. In addition, when the clue material is uncommon, the investigator tends to obtain an insufficient amount of the comparison material needed in order for the scientist to establish the experimental conditions for the analysis. Accordingly, a large representative sample of comparison material is required if the analyst is to be able to examine critically the small quantity of clue material found at the crime scene. Although it is not possible to control the amount of clue material (a few drops of blood, some small specks of paint or glass, and so on), it is nearly always possible to control the amount of comparison material obtained. This should be secured in generous amounts. For example, several milliliters of blood or 1.0 grams of paint would be minimum quantities for comparison specimens.

Detailed Recommendations

Part 3 contains a reprint of a Federal Bureau of Investigation pamphlet entitled *Suggestions for Handling of Physical Evidence.* It contains specific details that are helpful in implementing the handling and the transmission of various types of physical evidence to a laboratory. These explicit recommendations are particularly useful when evidence must be sent through the mail or by United Parcel or Air Express. It is helpful to read this material in light of the general principles discussed in this chapter. The reader will notice how well the general and specific details complement each other.

Suggestions for Further Reading

Cato, B.H. "The Preservation of Scientific Evidence in the Courts — Improving Its Effectiveness," *For. Sci. Soc. J.* 14, 93-98 (1974).

Goddard, K.W. *Crime Scene Investigation.* Reston, Va: Reston, 1977.

Grant, J. "The Collection of Forensic Evidence from the Forensic Scientist's Point of View," *For. Sci. Soc. J.* 14, 177-182 (1974).

Kirk, P.L. *Crime Investigation.* 2d ed. Edited by J.I. Thornton. New York: Wiley, 1974.

MacDonell, H.L. "Preserving Bloodstain Evidence at Crime Scenes," *Law and Order* 25(4), 66-69 (1977).

Nickolls, L.C. *The Scientific Investigation of Crime.* London: Butterworth, 1956.

O'Hara, C.E. and Osterburg, J.W. *An Introduction to Criminalistics.* Bloomington, Ind.: Indiana Unisity Press, 1972.

Saferstein, R. *Criminalistics: An Introduction to Forensic Science.* Englewood Cliffs, N.J.: Prentice-Hall, 1977.

Smith, H. Ward. *Laboratory Aids for the Investigator.* Ontario: Attorney General's Office, 1962.

Svensson, A., Wendel, O., and Fischer, B. *Techniques of Crime Scene Investigation.* 3rd ed. New York: Elsevier, 1981.

Turner, R.F. *Forensic Science and Laboratory Technics.* Springfield, Ill.: Thomas, 1949.

Walls, H.J. *Forensic Science: An Introduction to Scientific Crime Detection.* New York: Praeger, 1974.

3

Laboratory Processing of Evidence: Significant Concepts

Among the many questions asked in the crime laboratory, two kinds constantly occur. The first: "What is this substance? Is it a narcotic, an alcoholic beverage, a seminal stain, human blood?" The second involves inquiries such as: "Is this the fingerprint of John Jones?" "Was this shoe impression made by this shoe?" "Did this gun fire this bullet?" "Is the paint on the jimmy the same as the paint on the door that was pried open?" These two types of questions — as to evidence identification and individualization — are basic to resolving crimes. But before the investigator can even begin to unravel the mysteries presented by the evidence in hand, it is of the upmost importance that he or she understand:

1. The nature of identification, identity, and individualization.
2. The meaning of associative evidence.
   a. What is meant by the critical examination of physical evidence.
   b. How characterizing details are revealed — special process, contrast, optical methods, and instrumental methods.

The Nature of Identification, Identity, and Individualization

Answering the question "What is this substance?" requires, quite simply, that the identification of the substance be determined. "Is the crime scene evidence uniquely related to a suspect or an object in his possession?" — the second question — requires that a relationship establishing an identity between the two objects (finger and impression, gun and bullet) be determined, i.e., that an individualization be made. *Identification* is the process of placing an entity in a predefined, restricted class; establishing an *identity* or *individualization* is an extension of this process and refers to the evaluation of the combination of conditions that uniquely characterize an entity.

These seemingly abstract ideas may, perhaps, be more clearly understood by an illustration. Suppose a library user finds a page of a book on the floor of the library. He takes it to the librarian, who may almost immediately make an identification from the subject matter. Let us say it is quite obviously a mathematics book. If the page is intact and the book title present, she can move its identification further along. She now knows the page is from a book titled *Mathematics*, but the identity of the particular book from which the page came has still not been determined. If, upon examination of the first copy of the book located on the library shelf, it is noted that the page bearing this number is missing, it might be stated: "An identity has now been established." While the layman might agree that it has, the legally trained person and the crime laboratory worker will definitely disagree. There may be other copies of the book in the library in which the same numbered page is missing. Other possible explanations also exist which preclude the possibility of an identity based on this evidence alone. What then is necessary to demonstrate or prove the page came from a specific book?

If the page had been removed in such a way that the torn edge was irregular and a jigsaw-type fit exists between the torn edges, a serious argument for identity, i.e., one-to-one correspondence or uniqueness, could be made. However, if the page had just dropped out or had been very smoothly torn or cut, or if the torn edge of either part had been seriously damaged or perhaps missing, the jigsaw-fit idea is no longer applicable. To establish identity between the page and a particular copy of the book now becomes more difficult.

Some rare book librarians assisted by scientific specialists, some crime laboratory workers, some questioned document examiners—these are the persons who might have the equipment and the capacity to examine the details upon which such an identity must rest.

The number of details required and the similarity between them necessary to establish an identity cannot be stated with certainty. Statistical considerations, related experiences, scientific "taste," and so on are the guidelines governing the formation of an opinion after evaluation of the details. The reader of this text will have a better appreciation of the problem after completion of the case exercises in Part 4.

The Meaning of Associative Evidence

Crime laboratories have existed in the United States for approximately a half century. Experience during that time has shown that the development of *associative evidence* is one of the major services provided by the laboratory for the criminal investigator. Unfamiliar to law scholars, associative evidence is nevertheless a useful term to describe one of the principal functions of the crime laboratory, and signifies that some connection or association has been established between crime scene and criminal. This is accomplished by examination of physical evidence located at the crime scene and apparently similar evidence located on the person of the suspect, his clothing, or in his home or automobile.

In order to establish a unique connection, i.e., an identity between crime scene and suspect, the tangible evidence common to both must not only be examined but also evaluated. The question of the location of such evidence and attendant issues is treated in Chapter 2. The problem of the examination and evaluation of physical evidence is discussed below.

The Critical Examination of Physical Evidence

It has been said that no two things are exactly alike. This premise is undoubtedly true if methods are available for full disclosure of ultraminute differences. Thus, no two fingerprint impressions left by a finger are exactly alike if the examination of the details of the ridge lines is pursued to an ultrafine degree. Yet, it is fairly common knowledge that two fingerprint impressions can be identified as having a common source (one finger) with little likelihood existing that they were made by two different fingers. This identity is based on an examination of gross details of the ridge lines of the fingerprint impression. Note that while it is gross details of the ridge lines that concern us, these same details with respect to the fingerprint pattern are in fact viewed as minute details. When one is able to observe a sufficient number of the same characterizing details in the same relative location in two fingerprint impressions, a conclusion of a single source of common origin is justified.

In the United States it is generally accepted that any combination of twelve characterizing details are sufficient to associate or connect a fingerprint impression with a particular finger. The various ridge details may be described as follows:

Name	*Visual Appearance*
1. Ending ridge (including broken ridge)	1.
2. Fork (or bifurcation)	2.
3. Island ridge (or short ridge)	3.
4. Dot (or very short ridge)	4.
5. Bridge	5.
6. Spur (or hook)	6.
7. Eye (enclosure or island)	7.
8. Double bifurcation	8.
9. Delta	9.
10. Trifurcation	10.

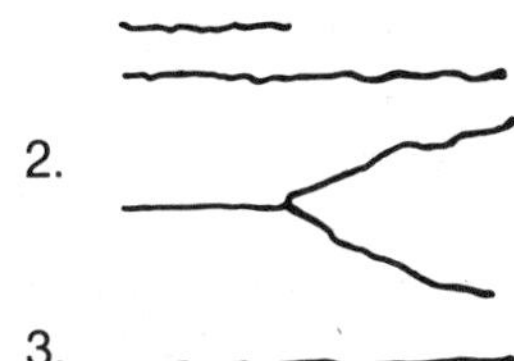

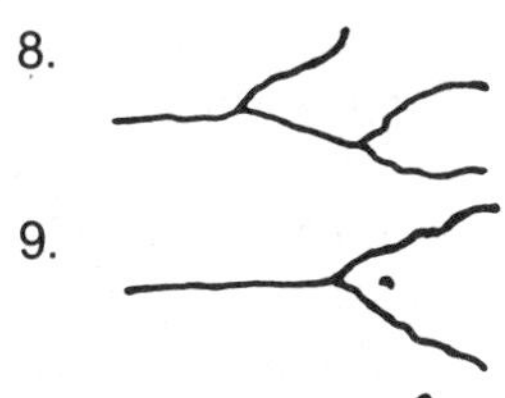

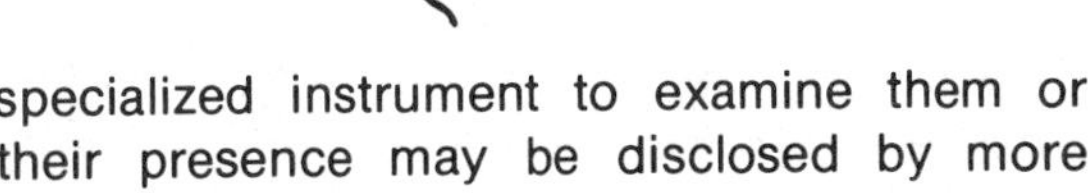

The ridge details are listed here in the relative order of frequency with which they are found in fingerprints. The ending ridge is the most common; the trifurcation the least common.

Associative evidence, then, is developed through crime laboratory work. When methods exist for revealing details that characterize the material and when standards for the evaluation of these details have been established, the development of associative evidence will be a completely objective process.

How Characterizing Details Are Revealed

For forensic purposes, details which serve to characterize may vary from macroscopic to microscopic in size. They may require a specialized instrument to examine them or their presence may be disclosed by more simple means.

Visual examination is sufficient to detect details of macroscopic size. The irregular cracked edge of a broken headlight lens located at the scene of an automobile accident, the torn piece of paper used in writing a threatening note, the ripped irregular edge of the adhesive tape employed to bind a victim, the shoe impression left by a burglar on papers scattered by him at the scene—these are a few examples of clue materials in which macroscopic details are readily discernible.

Special Process

Occasionally, a special process is required to

develop detail. Etching gun metal to restore a serial number which was deleted deliberately is an example. Although the detail in the outline of the number may be visible for a few moments only, patience will often be rewarded in reconstruction of the whole serial number as each individual number makes an ephemeral appearance over the course of several hours. The development of fingerprints may also be considered as a special process.

Contrast

The development of contrast is another method of making macroscopic details visible. Contrast may be achieved through controlled illumination, including not only ordinary artificial (tungsten) light, but also more esoteric varieties, as X-ray, ultraviolet (black light), and infrared light. Thus, to reveal indented writing on an under page of a paper pad, side (or oblique) illumination is employed to create a shadowy outline of the writing; "soft" X-rays can disclose informative details, which are not otherwise discernible, of a gunpowder pattern on dark clothing; the stained hands or clothing resulting from contact with otherwise invisible thief-detection powder are clearly visible in ultraviolet illumination; and infrared film, filter, and illumination are used to disclose obliterated writing. In another fashion, powder applied to the surface to be processed for fingerprints can be successful only when the color selected is based on securing contrast with the main background color of the object to be examined.

Optical Methods

Small details are disclosed through inspection of an enlarged image. An optical method is employed to provide the desired magnification —usually 2X to 25X, although 100X to 400X are necessary also. Fingerprints are examined at 3X to 5X, bullets at 10X to 20X, blood cells at 50X to 100X, crystalline derivatives of narcotics at 100X to 200X, and spermatazoa at about 400X. Such enlarged images are often achieved through use of a microscope; however, the lens of a camera may also be employed to produce images from 2X to about 20X to 25X in the photomacrograph. Further magnification of the negative in a photographic enlarger does not yield additional detail. Scientists refer to disclosure of detail as *resolution.* The value of many laboratory instruments rests upon their power of resolution.

In the crime laboratory a specially designed microscope, known as the *comparison microscope,* is particularly useful in the development of associative evidence. Essentially this instrument permits a direct comparison (side by side in a split field in the eyepiece) of crime scene evidence (the fatal bullet) with a test bullet deliberately fired and carefully recovered in order to preserve the barrel markings of the gun through which it was discharged. This microscope is also useful in the examination of tool marks, fingernails, or any other evidence in which a series of lines, or *striations,* inherent in the evidence must be compared under magnification of about 25X or less. For some evidence such as a shovel used in suitable soil (e.g., clay), these striated marks are visible to the naked eye and they may be compared by superimposition of photographs taken of the questioned earth-shovel mark and test-dig marks made in similar soil with a suspected shovel.

Instrumental Methods

The senses of the investigator may be extended through the application of instrumental physics and chemistry and the resolution of the minutiae present in the clue materials. The details that characterize a material are sometimes reproduced by the instrument as a photograph but more often as a curve plotted, usually automatically, on graph paper. For example, the spectrograph and X-ray diffraction camera can yield results in the form of a series of lines on a photographic film; the infrared recording spectrometer, the ultraviolet spectrophotometer, and the lie detector yield curves on graph paper. It is beyond the scope of the present volume to discuss these methods further.

Quite recently a new method of examination of physical evidence—neutron activation analysis—has been under intensive investigation by research workers. Two particularly stubborn, yet very important problems (hair identification and gunpowder primer residue removed from a person's hands or cheeks by warm paraffin), appear to be yielding to research efforts using atomic piles as the neutron source for activation analysis. In this method the qualitative and quantitative details of chemical trace element composition in the physical evidence (hair or powder in the paraffin matrix) are now possible for amounts that defy analysis by other means. The sensitivity is so exceptional that this method of trace element analysis should make possible the definitive examination of many other clue materials. This will permit associative evidence comparisons and statements concerning identity which heretofore were impossible. A preliminary survey, with encouraging results, has been made of the following clue materials using activation analysis to characterize them: plastic, rubber, grease, wood, glass, paper, and soil. Obviously, the varying kinds and amounts of trace elements present, i.e., the qualitative and quantitative details, allow two specimens to be compared successfully or shown to be dissimilar.

Conclusion

As science improves in its ability to establish an identity between two clue materials, greater use will be made of the crime laboratory when the field investigator who is charged with the recognition and subsequent handling of physical evidence has a depth of understanding of the problems involved and of the aid it is able to extend to him. Such understanding is not the result of lectures or reading alone. In addition, practical laboratory exercises are required. These exercises must treat each problem separately, causing the field investigator to learn at first hand the limitations and difficulties confronting the scientist. Actual experience in simple crime laboratory techniques must be part of the training of the investigator of the future. Until this is achieved, society shall have to settle for second best. In an age of civilized society this is not good enough, particularly since the courts—especially those of the United States —are withdrawing the cruder techniques of yesterday from the practice permitted the modern detective.

Suggestions for Further Reading

Ceccaldi, P.F. *La Criminalistique.* Paris: Presses Universitaires de France, 1962. Pp 6-30.

Fong, W. "Criminalistics, Evidence, and Proof," in *Forensic Science: Scientific Investigation in Criminal Justice.* Edited by J.L. Peterson. New York: AMS Press, 1975. Pp 378-385.

Gaudette, B.D. and Keeping, E.S. "An Attempt at Determining Probabilities in Human Scalp Comparison," *J. For. Sci.* 19, 599-606 (1974).

Kind, S. "The Nature of the Process of Identification." *J. For. Sci.* 4, 1962 (1964).

Kirk, P.L. "Criminalistics," *Science* 140, 357-370 (1963).

———, "The Ontogeny of Criminalistics," *J. Crim. Law, Criminol. and Pol. Sci.* 54, 235-238 (1963).

———, and Kingston, C.R., "Evidence Evaluation and Problems in General Criminalistics," *J. For. Sci.* 9, 434-444 (1964).

Osterburg, J.W., et al., "Development of a Mathematical Formula for the Calculation of Fingerprint Probablities Based on Individual Characteristics," *J. Am. Stat. Assn.* 72, 772-778 (1977).

The foundation of law is not opinion but nature.

Cicero, De Legibus, ca. 50 B.C.

Part 2

Physical Evidence Traces

4

Traces of the Person

4.1 Fingerprints

Of all possible crime scene clues, fingerprints are the most familiar to the public as well as to the police. A belief commonly held is that the mere touching of an object deposits fingerprints on it. Actually, this is not true. The reason for this is that there are several conditions that must be met before even a fragmentary fingerprint is left behind. The factors controlling the deposit of fingerprints are as follows:

1. Condition of cleanliness of the fingertips.
2. Method of handling the object.
3. Method of releasing the object.
4. Suitability of the object for receiving fingerprints.

A. Cleanliness

The process of thoroughly washing and drying the hands removes the natural oils and perspiration usually present on them. In addition, grime acquired through touching numerous objects in the normal course of living is also washed away. Thus cleansed, the fingertips cannot deposit, upon touching an object, that admixture of material necessary for the development of fingerprints. Assorted colored powders chosen to provide contrast with the background, or chemical methods (iodine fuming, silver nitrate bath, or ninhydrin spray) are the means employed to make fingerprints visible. This is referred to as *latent print development*. Crime scene evidence must be processed to develop latent fingerprints that might be present.[1] Developed latent prints seldom show a complete pattern. Instead, only a portion of the whole print results. This is usually referred to as a *partial print*. The incomplete quality of crime scene prints is accounted for by the uneven distribution on the fingers of the natural oils, perspiration, and grime. Among other reasons, this unreliable distribution necessitates that a good recording medium as printer's ink and smooth white paper be used in taking fingerprints for record purposes. Soap and water are not the only means by which the fingertip substance may be removed. For example, handling porous material, as in adding pulverized diluent to heroin, results in the body secretions and grime being absorbed by the powders in the mixture. Of course, no fingerprints will then be left if a glassine envelope or other package is being filled with heroin or other narcotic. To the informed, the absence of fingerprints on narcotics packaging is thus to be expected. On the other hand, criminal lawyers often argue that their client did not handle the material since the state failed to prove that the defendant's prints were present on any of the packages. Such a charge often requires rebuttal testimony to explain why fingerprints were not found. Indeed, in some jurisdictions, evidence examiners probably spend almost as much time in the witness chair explaining why fingerprints were not obtained as they do in testifying about prints they do find.

Lawyers are not alone in the belief of ubiquity of fingerprints. The same sort of argument has been advanced by writers seeking to dispute the official version of some celebrated homicides. For example, two critical commentaries on the Sacco-Vanzetti case and the assassination of President Kennedy are based, in part, on the absence of the respective accuseds' fingerprints on pertinent items of evidence in each case.[2] For example, the importance placed on the fingerprint evidence by one critic is indicated in the following excerpt:

> Certainly, if Sacco's and Vanzetti's prints had been obtained from the murder car, the fingerprint evidence would have become the major, irrefutable item in the state's arsenal of proof. Obviously, Sacco's and Vanzetti's prints were not on the murder car. This is negative evidence, but logic does not stop here. There had been five men in the Buick . . . it is inconceivable that the fingerprints of some of those five would not have shown.[3]

Subsequently, the critic adds the following:

> It is possible that, by a freak of chance the prints of the cardinal two, Sacco and Vanzetti, might have been obliterated. But it is hardly conceivable that the prints of *all five* men whom Stewart's theory placed in the Buick would fail to show . . . .[4]

Relative to the Kennedy case, the following comment is made in an article critical of the Warren Commission concerning the absence of Oswald's fingerprints on some of the important evidence:

> Further, there were not fingerprints on the surface of the rifle, on the shells, or on the remaining bullet in Oswald's rifle. The famous palmprint was old, and on a part of the rifle only exposed when disassembled. According to the Commission, this rifle had to be assembled that day, loaded with four bullets, fired

rapidly, and hidden, without any fingerprints appearing on it. If they were wiped away by Oswald, when, and with what?[5]

When the reader has completed the next four sections of this chapter, he or she will be in a better position to evaluate the cogency of these arguments concerning the nonexistence of fingerprints as proof that neither Sacco, Vanzetti, nor Oswald were involved in the respective homicides. The following three sections assume that the necessary deposit materials is present on the fingers.

B. Method of Handling the Object

The firmness of pressure exerted by the fingers in handling an object affects greatly the quality of the latent impression. Holding an object too firmly results in the pliable ridges of the fingers being pressed flat so that the ridge detail is lost, rendering the print useless. Similarly, the superimposition of one print upon another makes the impression valueless. Superimposed latent prints are developed quite often on crime scene evidence.

Most people, when asked to leave their fingerprints by touching a piece of paper lying on a flat surface, will press so hard that the developed print is often quite useless as evidence. The pressure must be firm yet gentle. For example, a burglar removed a storm window instead of breaking the glass and probably carried it in his outstretched arms to the rear of the backyard. His fingers were pressed against the glass by the weight of the window. This is one of the few cases where the author found prints of all ten fingers at a crime scene. Apparently, gravity supplied just the proper pressure to leave an excellent set of fingerprints.

C. Method of Releasing the Object

The method by which an object is released can greatly affect the latent impression. For example, it is possible to destroy ridge detail by sliding the fingers along the surface of the object. A latent print left by this method is called a *smudge* when it becomes visible through processing (Fig. 4—1). In order to leave a reasonably good impression, the object must be released in clean-cut fashion without pullling along the surface.

D. Suitability of Object for Receiving Prints

Partial fingerprints are by far the most common type of fingerprint found at crime scenes. Generally they are incomplete owing to the method of touching and the suitability of the surface to record ridge details. Occasionally, however, it is the area of an object that limits the size of the imprint. Thus, crime scene technicians may overlook potential evidence because the surface area appears to be too small to record a sufficient number of ridge lines to permit establishing an identity. For example, the ignition key of an automobile, the trigger of a gun, the handle of a door, an electric light switch, and so on, are often not processed for fingerprints for this reason.

Fingerprints require a smooth surface so that important ridge details can be recorded rather than lost. Thus, kitchen appliances (such as refrigerators) and rear view mirrors in automobiles are especially suitable for receiving fingerprint impressions. Incredible as it may seem, safe manufacturers often employ a crinkled surface on their products. Safe burglars can move, push, or otherwise handle such safes with complete impunity since there is no possibility of leaving a useful print on such irregular surfaces.

The method of development can also influence the resultant print. For example, the Magna Brush (a proprietary device developed by H. L. MacDonell of Corning, New York) can be used to process facial tissue paper successfully. In other words, in the continuum of surface quality there are some methods of fingerprint processing which will work for a particular surface while other methods will not. Before Magna Brush, the surface of facial tissue would have been considered unsuitable for the development of fingerprints.

E. Processing and Comparison

Since fingerprints left at a crime scene are seldom visible they are called *latent* prints. Latent comes from the Latin verb meaning to lie hidden, to be concealed. In order to make a latent fingerprint visible it is therefore necessary to develop the print. This is done by processing an object with a powder (usually black or white) or by fuming (iodine), spraying (ninhydrin), or immersing (silver nitrate) the object. A fingerprint so developed must then be photographed in its original position and location, which is usually possible. It may then be removed (lifted) from the object upon which it was found, using transparent lifting tape available in wide rolls from police equipment supply houses. The lifted print is then pressed onto celluloid; so sandwiched between celluloid and lifting tape it is protected from damage.

Both photograph and lift must now be handled like any other piece of evidence (as described in Chapter 2). They must be submitted to a fingerprint expert who is asked to make a comparison between the lifted print and sets of fingerprints of possible suspects. These sets may be on file or they may be made expressly for this purpose. The expert is concerned with what Galton (ridge) details may be present, for the existence of such details in sufficient quantity forms the basis of establishing an identity.

Figures 4—3 and 4—4 present the types of Galton details or individual characteristics that are looked for and how they may be marked. Inked prints were chosen because of clarity of detail to illustrate the process of fingerprint comparison. In comparing a latent fingerprint with a known fingerprint the latent print is examined first. When an outstanding characteristic (or a cluster of characteristics) is observed in the latent print, the inked print is studied to determine if the same characteristic (or detail) can be found. Then another characteristic in the latent print is selected. Its distance from the first is determined by counting the number of ridge lines that separate the two. When the same kind of characteristic is found in the same location and separated by the same distance in the inked impression, both points are marked. This process continues until a sufficient number of characteristics, generally twelve or more, are discovered and marked. At this point an identity has been established between the latent and inked impressions. Since the person to whom the inked impression belongs is already known, it can be inferred that the latent print also belongs to that person.

4.1 Exercises 1, 2, 3 (p 173)

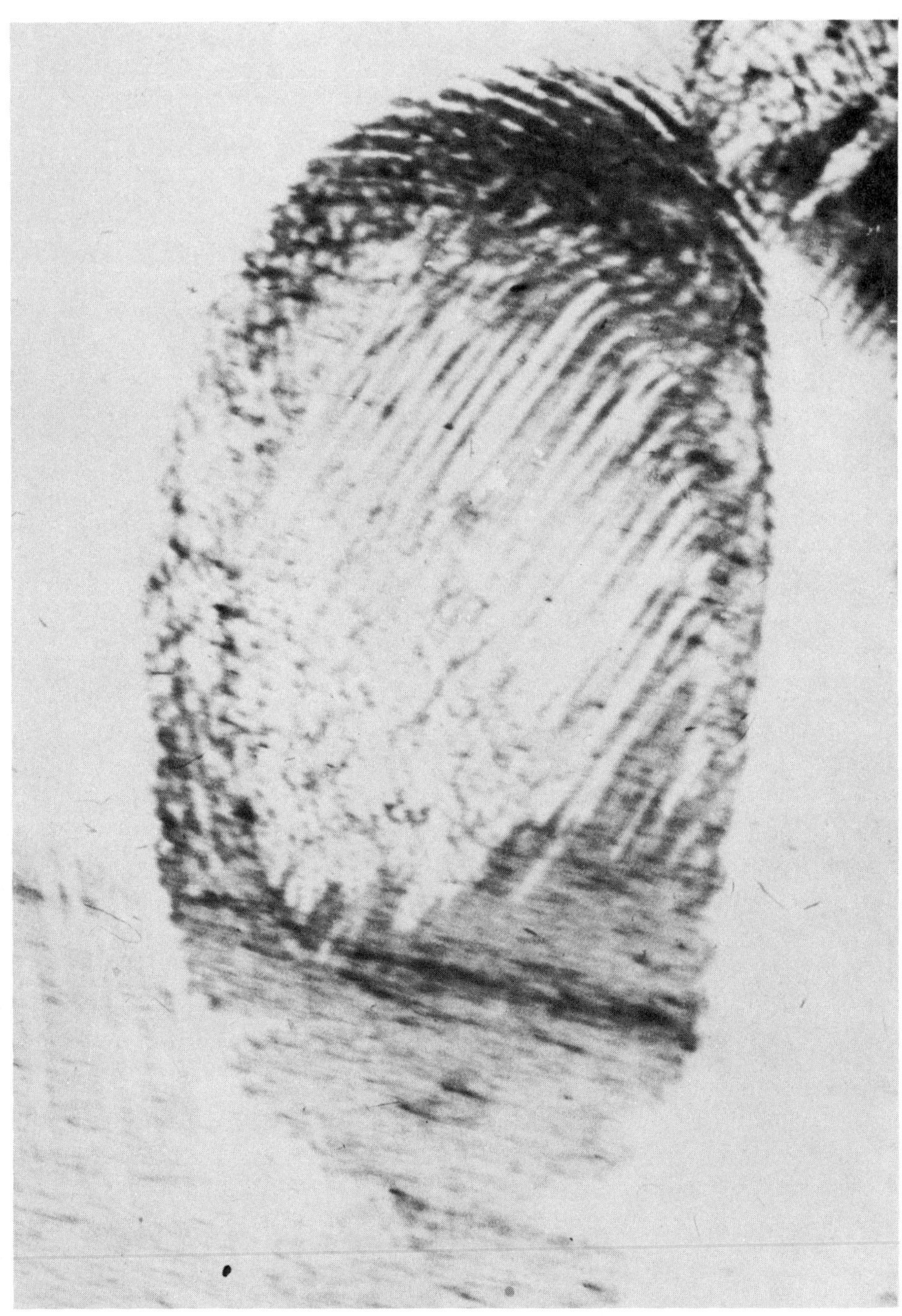

Fig. 4 — 1
A smudged fingerprint.
(Courtesy, New York City Police Department.)

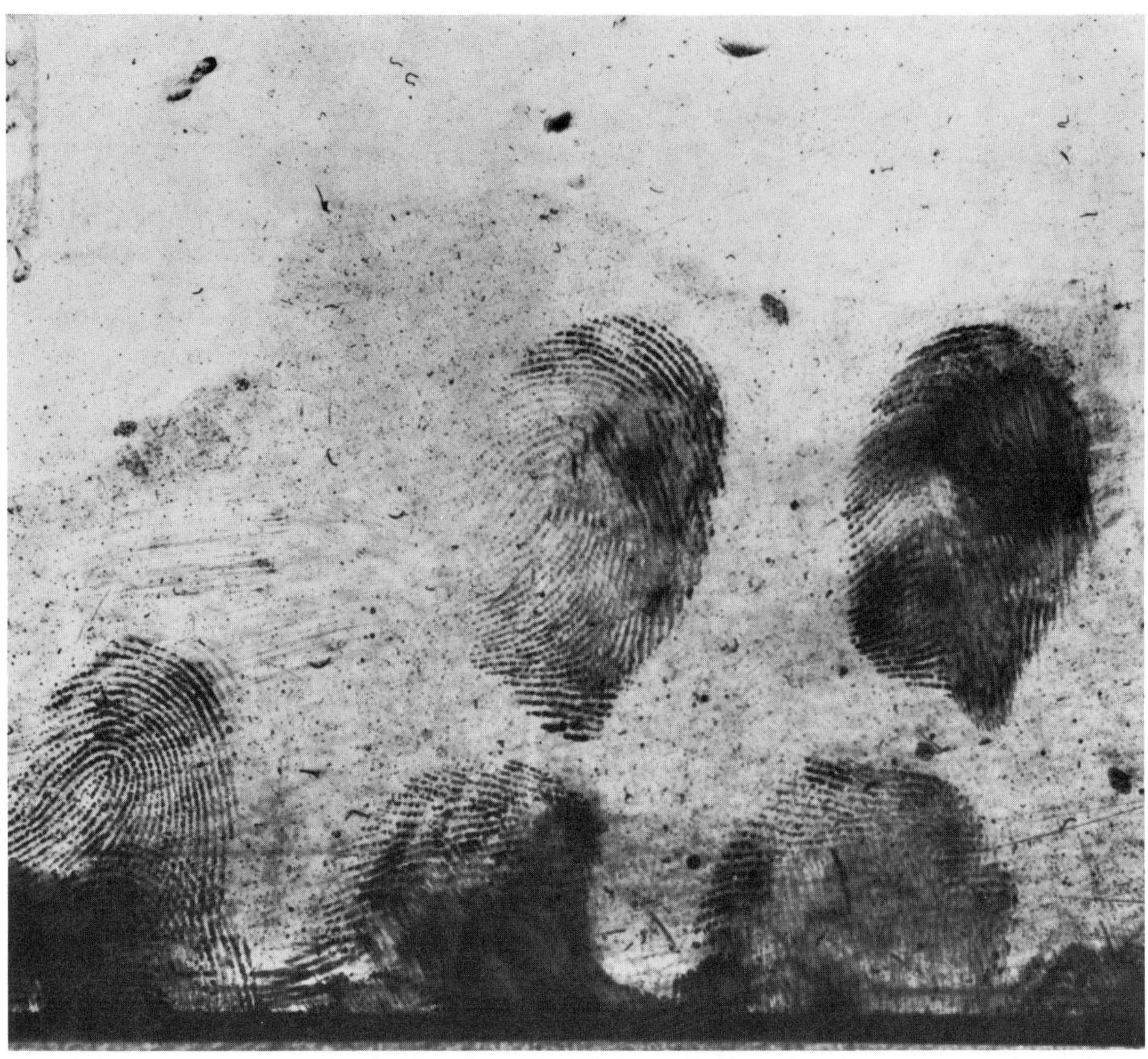

Fig. 4 — 2
Typical appearance of latent prints after processing.
(Courtesy, St. Paul Police Department, Minnesota.)

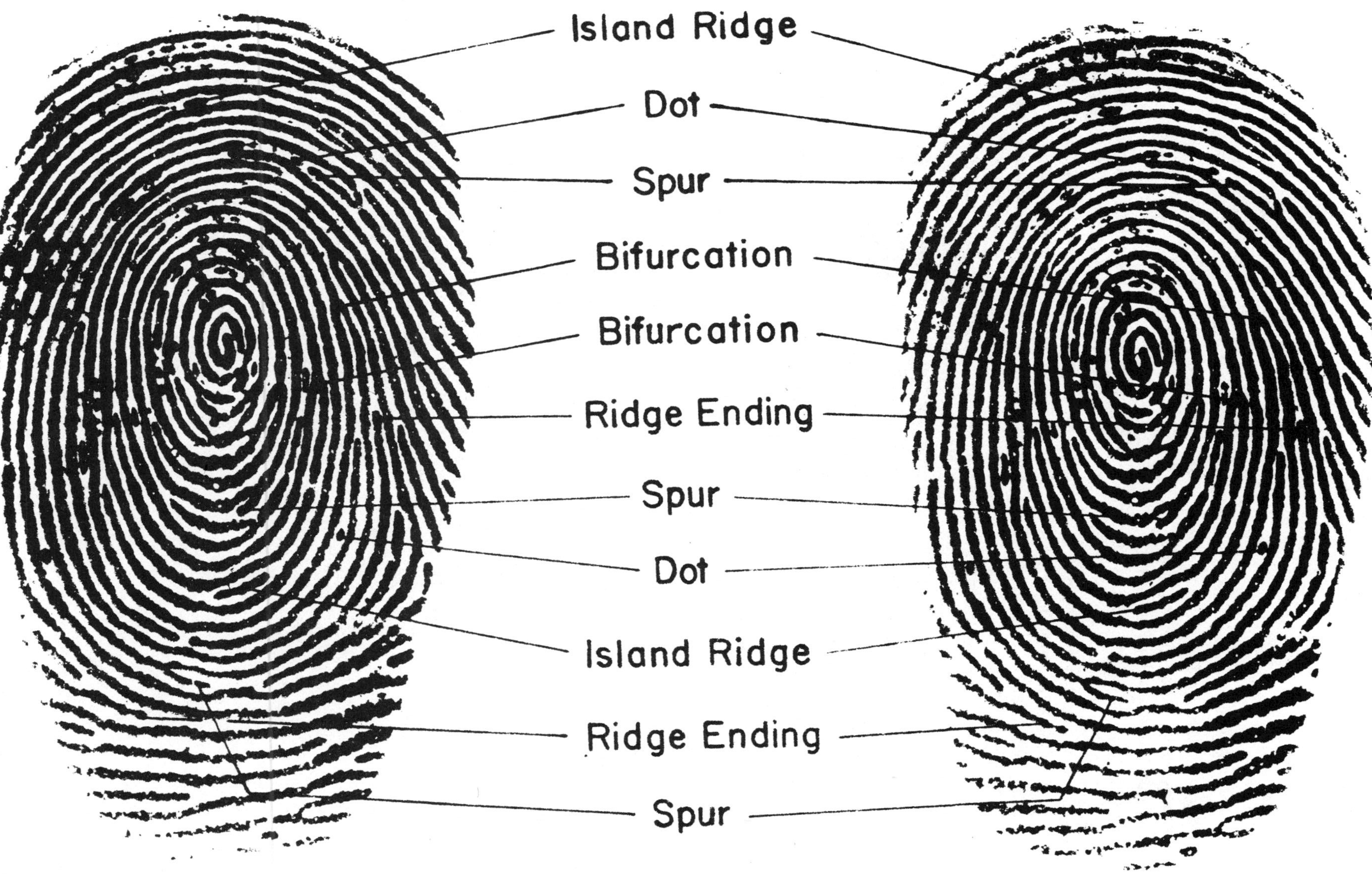

Fig. 4 — 3
Inked fingerprint.

Fig. 4 — 4
Inked fingerprint marked to show ridge details.
(Courtesy, Institute of Applied Science, Chicago.)

4.2 Palmprints

The friction ridges present on the palm of the hand are comparable to those on the finger tips. Both have the same types of characteristics: bifurcations, ridge endings, dots, eyes, and so on. Accordingly, the palmprint of a suspect can be as useful as his fingerprints in the development of associative evidence.[6] This fact is less well known than is the utility of fingerprints. The author is familiar with at least one homicide case in which considerable effort was required to educate and convince the prosecutor of the value of palmprints. An apparent obstacle for the uninformed is the lack of a palmprint file; however, when a suspect is apprehended through other investigative methods, it is possible to obtain his palmprint for comparison purposes. This action is similarly taken when a suspect has no fingerprint record. Palmprints are found less often than fingerprints. Leaning on an object such as a table top or the roof or door of an automobile can result in a palmprint. A low, glass partition, separating customer and teller in a bank, often provides a good surface for retaining a palmprint that may be left if the robber climbs over the partition.

Palmprints are not always as clear-cut as the one used in Case Exercise 4. For example, Fig. 4—5 is a partial palmprint found as a bloody imprint on a bedsheet at the scene of a homicide. Considerable experience is required to establish an identity in a case such as this where the evidence is fragmentary. The comparison must be made through careful study of the actual evidence. A study of the photographs alone of the evidence is not sufficient for the average student to reach a conclusion of identity. This illustration highlights the point that the actual evidence, rather than photographs of it, must be the final basis upon which a decision rests.

4.2 Exercises 4, 5 (p 173)

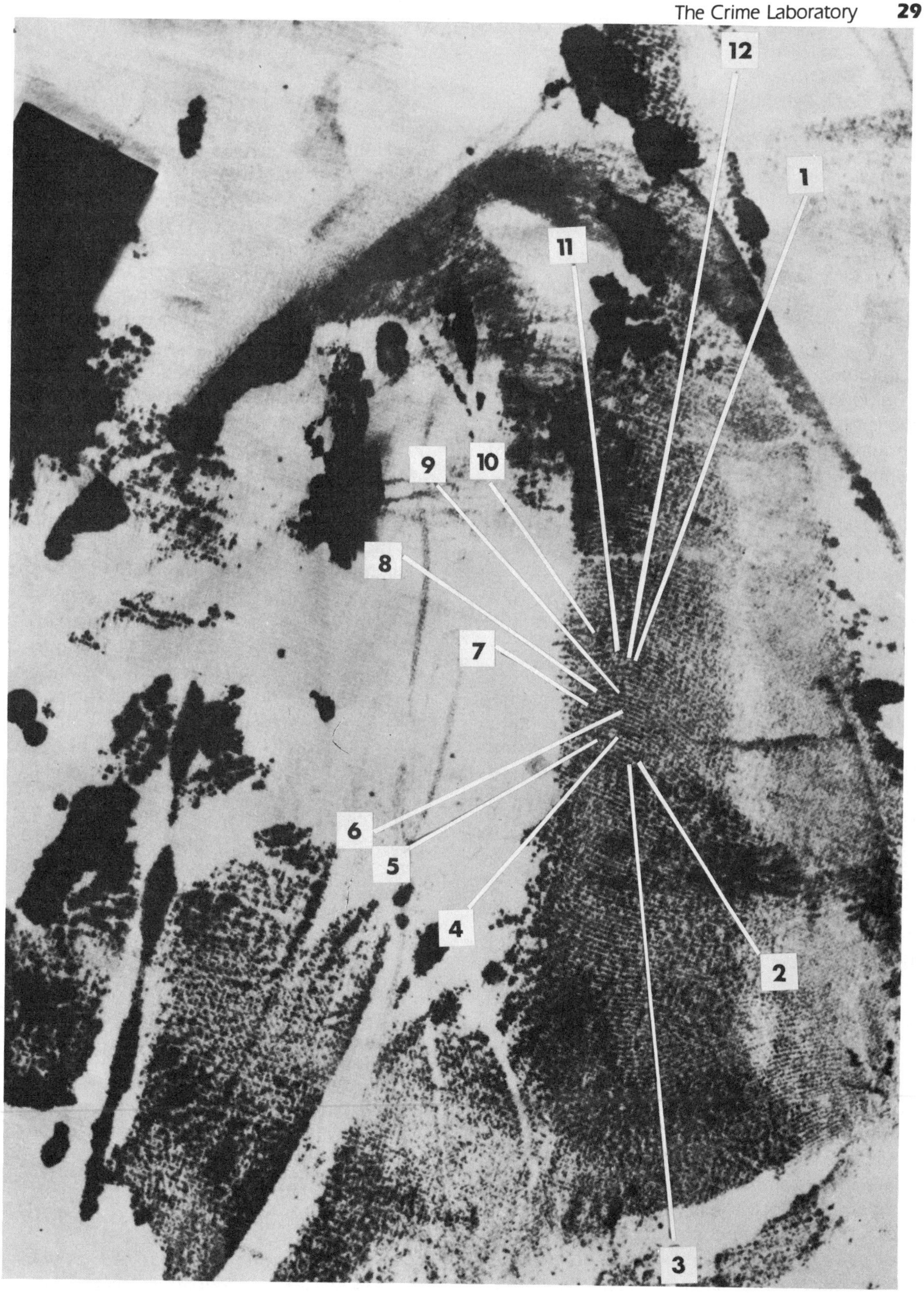

Fig. 4 — 5
A partial palmprint left in blood on a bedsheet at a homicide. *(Courtesy, Chicago Police Department.)*

4.3 Bare Footprints

Occasionally a criminal removes his shoes but not his socks in order to walk more quietly through a building; consequently, bare foot impressions are not often found at crime scenes. If they are present, the crime is often homicide (usually manslaughter) and has occurred in a residence at night. If the suspect is an occupant of the household, he may be barefooted and the impression may be visible in blood. The location of the bloody footprint, the story told by those involved, and other circumstances must be considered to determine the investigative and probative significance of the bloody imprint. In countries where shoes are not too common, footprints are more likely to be present at various crime scenes.

As with fingerprints and palmprints, the basis of soleprint individualization rests on the characteristics present in the friction ridges of the skin on the toes and sole of the foot.[7] In the case selected for Case Exercise 6 there is an interesting departure from the normal routine of establishing an identity of two prints through ridge details. In this case they were not present; instead, the sole seemed to be eaten away in places, a condition commonly associated with leprosy.

4.3 Exercise 6 (pp 173 -174)

4.4 Teethmarks

It is well known that the teeth can serve as a means of personal identification in multi-death disasters such as floods, airplane crashes, and conflagrations aboard ships.[8] In addition, teethmarks—rather than actual teeth, of course—are found as evidence in criminal cases. For example, it is not uncommon for a burglar to help himself to a snack from the refrigerator; butter, cheese, candy bars, and fruit have been partially eaten and discarded by burglars apprehensive about detection. Teethmark evidence is occasionally found in cases involving sexual assault and even in robbery cases. In some of these, the teethmark evidence may be satisfactory for establishing an identity with similar marks provided by a suspect.[9] During study of Case Exercise 7, observe that the known comparison marks were supplied by the victim rather than by the suspect. This exercise is an example of physical evidence which is taken from the crime scene rather than left at the scene; however, the principle is the same — the criminal and crime scene are linked together through associative evidence.

Consider the following case which illustrates the principle enunciated above:

> Two men kidnaped the manager of a large supermarket just after closing time at night. After placing him on the floor of the back seat of their automobile, they drove around until early in the morning. They then returned to the supermarket, forced the manager to open a safe and to give the money to them. He was next taken to a public park, tied to a tree and left there. A suspect's car was subsequently impounded. On the floor of the back seat of the car a pencil was found with teethmarks impressed in the wood. When questioned, the manager remembered that just prior to being kidnaped he had placed a pencil used by his bookkeeper in the handkerchief pocket of his coat. She had a habit of chewing on pencils. As a result of this information, the bookkeeper was requested by the investigator to bit a number of pencils in different positions in the normal manner in which she placed a pencil in her mouth.[10]

4.4 Exercise 7 (p 174)

4.5 Handwriting

Occasionally a crime is committed in which the only physical evidence available is documentary in nature. When it involves a felony that commands unusual public attention, special commitment of men and facilities may be called for. In such circumstances, the allocation of resources within the police agency and also from external sources such as the FBI, may permit the utilization of techniques that are too costly in the average case. A kidnaping is an example of such a situation.

When handwritten material is available in sufficient quantity in a criminal case, it may be analyzed for unusual writing characteristics that may serve to identify the writer. When no effort is made to disguise the writing, as is quite often true in a kidnap note, it is possible to search for similar writing among the public and quasi-public records which society requires for the conduct of its routine business. Several dozen to a few hundred investigators may be needed to search these records systematically. Sources of such routine writing would include applications for automobile operator's licenses, state license plates, marriage licenses, public utility services, signatures on election records, financial transactions, probation and parole records, and the like.

A. The LaMarca-Weinberger Case

Figure 4—6 is a photograph of an actual kidnap note. It was left for the parents of an infant who was abducted one afternoon while sleeping in a carriage in the backyard of his parent's house.[11] The solution of this, the LaMarca-Weinberger case, rested upon the detailed examination of the writing in the ransom note, followed by the study in the field of over two million public documents by a large force of investigators.

An expert document examiner selected writing characteristics present in the kidnap note which were outstanding from the viewpoint of recognition and identification. A photograph was specially prepared illustrating these unusual characteristics, and a copy was given to each field detective. After the significance of the writing characteristics was explained to the investigators, they were sent out to examine systematically numerous public documents for writing which had any characteristics resembling those depicted on the photograph furnished by the expert.

B. The Hauptmann-Lindbergh Case

It is interesting to contrast the LaMarca-Weinberger case with the Hauptmann-Lindbergh kidnaping. In the latter case, an even greater amount of writing — thirteen separate notes — was available.[12] In addition, a considerable amount of evidence indicated that the kidnaper was of German extraction and that he lived in the Bronx. A question that should arise in the inquisitive mind is: "Had the LaMarca-Weinberger technique been used, would the Lindbergh case have been solved sooner?"

It may be surprising to learn that a Treasury agent is reported to have suggested on three occasions that ". . . . we get a half-dozen bright young ladies to go through the Bronx licenses to check the ransom writing against the applications for licenses. The notes are written in so unusual a hand it should present no great problem to recognize similar handwriting."[13] However, instead of following this advice directly, another tactic was apparently used. Figure 4 — 7 is a reproduction of a circular that was distributed with the intention of identifying the kidnaper through his handwriting. Albert D. Osborn in commenting on this recalls that "The State Police even received one specimen written in Chinese. I saw it."[14]

A careful consideration of the flyer (Fig. 4—7) suggests that the strategy was not incorrect but was certainly less satisfactory than that of the Treasury agent. In retrospect, it is easy to criticize the expectation that individuals who were completely untutored regarding questioned document examinations would be able to recognize similar handwriting. An additional hazard was present in that this was a delegated responsibility but under no specific administrative control, so no systematic search was assured. These difficulties were avoided in the LaMarca-Weinberger case. The expertise of the FBI document examiner was sufficient to remedy the lack of training in handwriting recognition, and a methodical examination of a wide variety of public documents was undertaken under rigorous supervision. Hopefully, studying LaMarca's original note (Case Exercise 8, p 203) and then examining the expert's results presented in the Appendix (pp 400-402) will improve the practicing police officer-reader's ability to carry out future investigations involving handwriting.

4.5 Exercises 8, 9, 10 (pp 174-175)

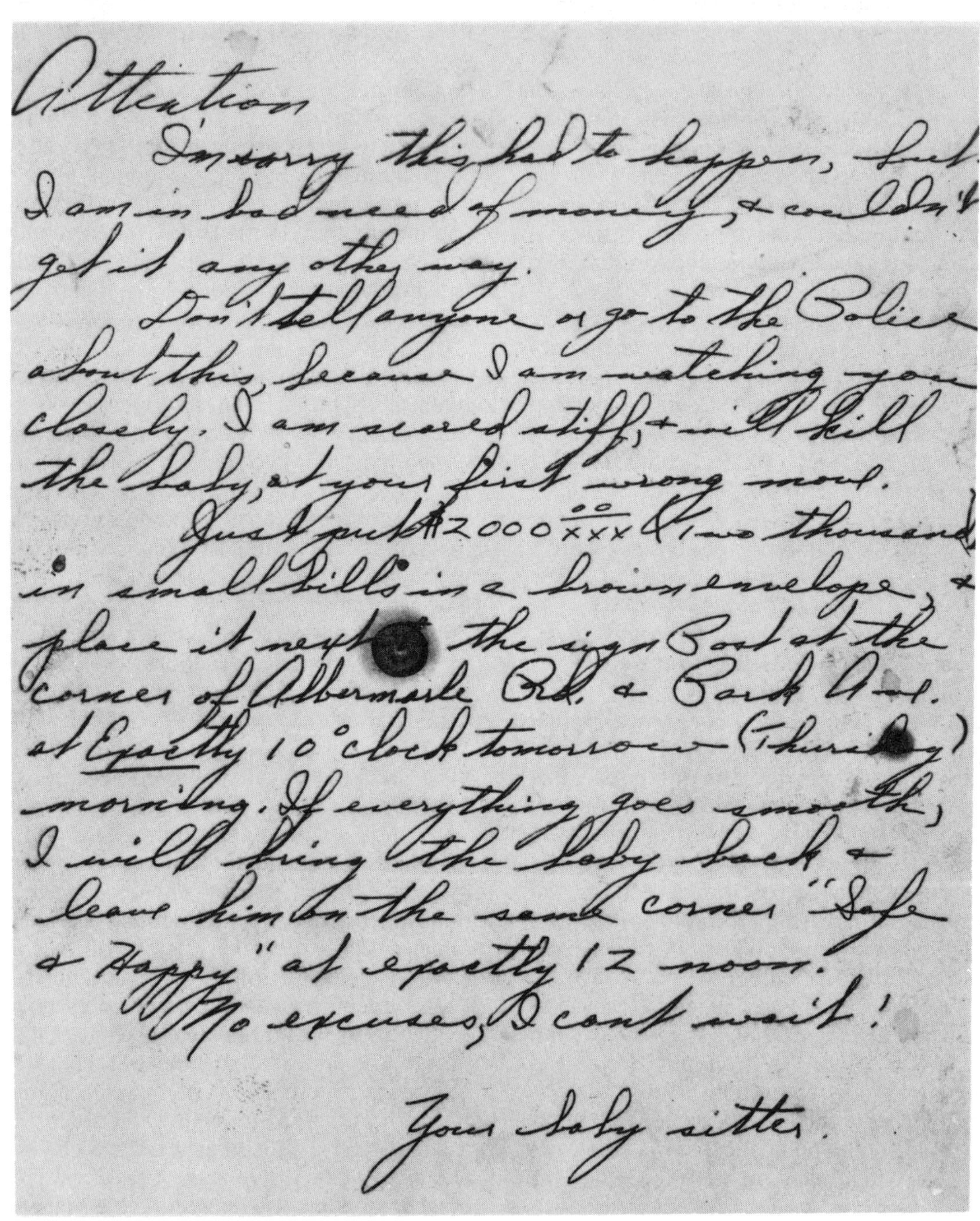

Attention

I'm sorry this had to happen, but I am in bad need of money, & couldn't get it any other way.

Don't tell anyone or go to the Police about this, because I am watching you closely. I am scared stiff, & will kill the baby, at your first wrong move.

Just put \$2000 00/xxx (two thousand) in small bills in a brown envelope, & place it next to the sign Post at the corner of Albermarle Rd. & Park Ave. at Exactly 10 o'clock tomorrow (Thursday) morning. If everything goes smooth, I will bring the baby back & leave him on the same corner "Safe & Happy" at exactly 12 noon.

No excuses, I can't wait!

Your baby sitter.

Fig. 4 — 6
Original ransom note in Weinberger kidnaping case.
(Courtesy, Federal Bureau of Investigation.)

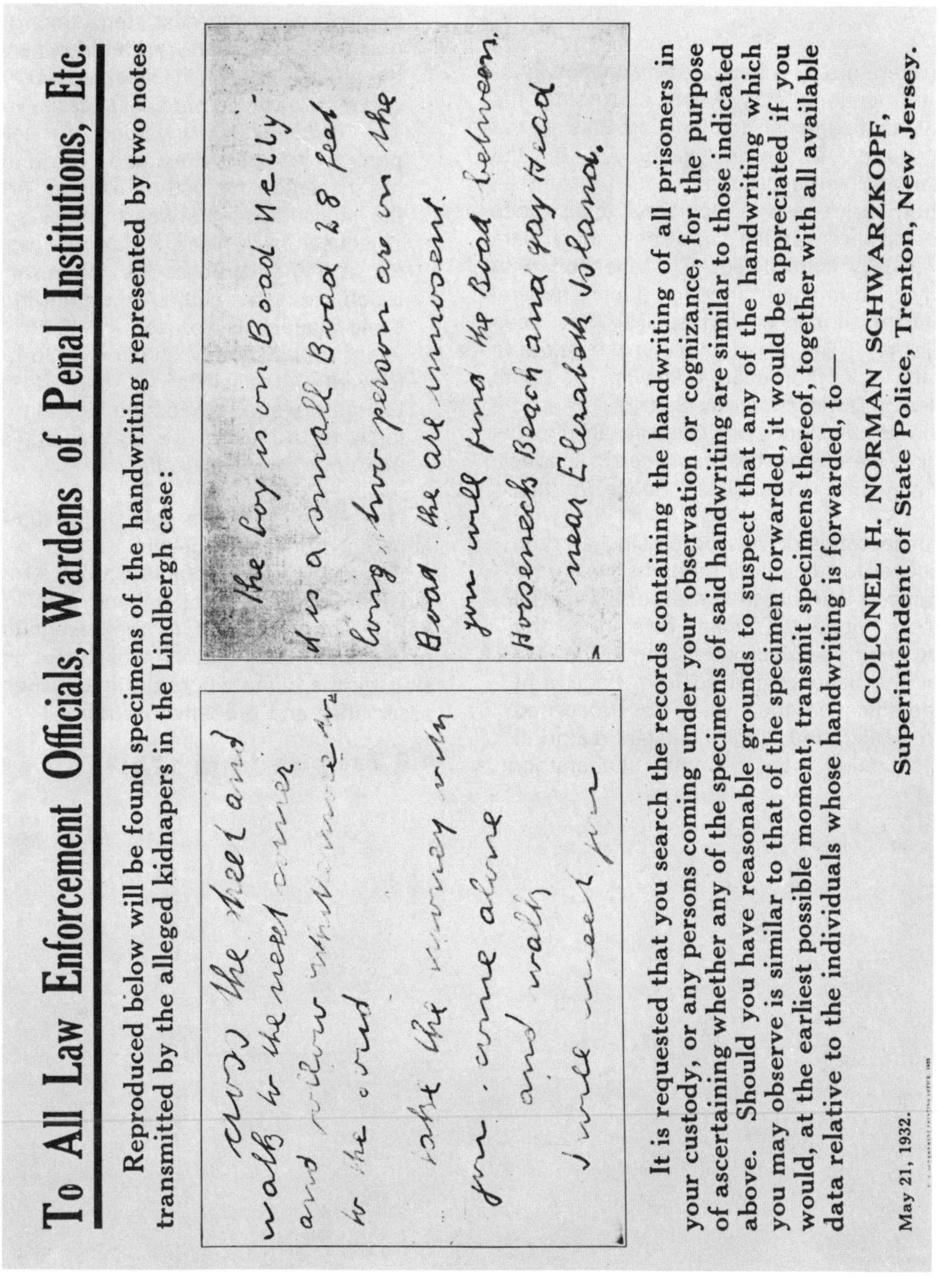

To All Law Enforcement Officials, Wardens of Penal Institutions, Etc.

Reproduced below will be found specimens of the handwriting represented by two notes transmitted by the alleged kidnapers in the Lindbergh case:

cross the street and
walk to the next corner
and follow Whittemore Ave
to the soud

take the money with
you. come alone
and walk
I will meet you

The boy is on Boad Nelly
it is a small Boad 28 feet
long. two person are on the
Boad. the are innosent.
you will find the Boad between
Horseneck Beach and gay Head
near Elizabeth Island.

It is requested that you search the records containing the handwriting of all prisoners in your custody, or any persons coming under your observation or cognizance, for the purpose of ascertaining whether any of the specimens of said handwriting are similar to those indicated above. Should you have reasonable grounds to suspect that any of the handwriting which you may observe is similar to that of the specimen forwarded, it would be appreciated if you would, at the earliest possible moment, transmit specimens thereof, together with all available data relative to the individuals whose handwriting is forwarded, to—

COLONEL H. NORMAN SCHWARZKOPF,
Superintendent of State Police, Trenton, New Jersey.

May 21, 1932.

Fig. 4 — 7
Circular distributed to law enforcement officials seeking specimens of handwriting similar to the writing present on two notes of the alleged kidnapers in the Lindbergh case.

4.6 Earprints

The literature of criminal investigation generally mentions ears when discussing the problem of personal identification. Ears are but one factor of several employed in the systematic, verbal description of a person (i.e., portrait parlé) used in a personal appearance file.[15] However, as the basis for identity, ears are usually considered in connection with newly born infants,[16] although a more general treatment of ear pattern analysis has been published.[17] The use of an ear in an attempt to identify an individual following a bomb explosion is described by Spitz.[18]

The circumstances involved in an unusual earprint identity are best explained in an article that appeared in the *Military Police Journal*:

> An investigator was processing a crime scene for latent fingerprints when he noticed that just to the left of a safe dial there appeared what resembled the outline of a human ear. Being fully aware of the benefits derived from fingerprint identification, the investigator proceeded to "dust" and "lift" the latent earprint. Contacting the Crime Laboratory (Fingerprint Section) by telephone, he inquired as to the next step. Among his questions was, "Can you identify a person by his/her earprint?" The answer was given, "We will do our best to assist you." The investigator forwarded the latent print to the laboratory and "earprinted" his suspects. The method used to "print" the individual's ears was to press some object such as a piece of glass against the ear and then process the glass with a brush, thereafter "lifting" the print in the same manner as he used in "lifting" the latent print. The investigator could have forwarded the pieces of glass to the Laboratory after processing; actually, the lifted record prints were excellent, and only the lifts were used.[19]

The alertness of the soldier-investigator is apparent from these details.

The case photographs in Case Exercise 11 illustrate how excellent training, intelligence, and imagination lead to the recognition of physical evidence and its subsequent conversion by the crime laboratory into evidence of associative and probative value.

4.6 Exercise 11 (p 175)

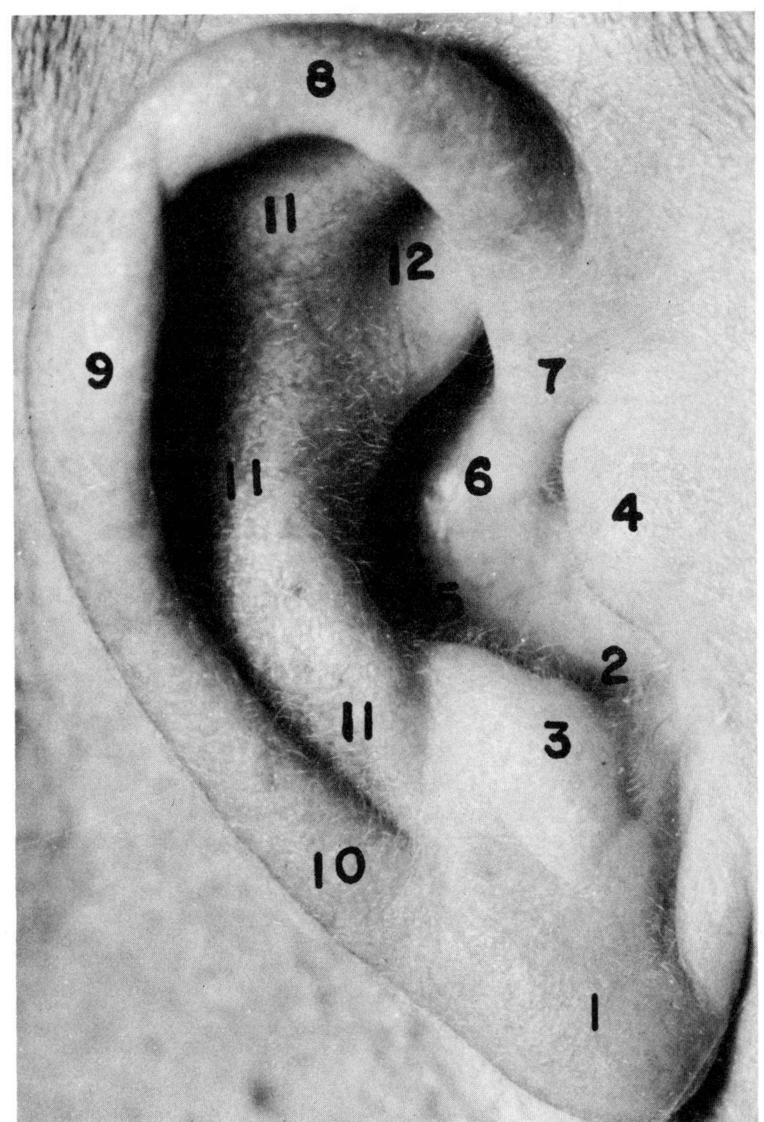

Fig. 4 — 8
Anatomical nomenclature of the ear.
(Courtesy, U.S. Army Criminal Investigation Laboratory, Ft. Gordon, Georgia.)

1. Lobule
2. Incisura Intertragica
3. Antitragus
4. Tragus
5. Concha
6. Crus of Helix
7. Start of Helix Rim
8. Upper Helix Rim
9. Helix Rim
10. End of Helix Rim
11. Antihelix
12. Triangular Fossa

4.7 Skin Patterns

The skin, in addition to the extremities — hands and feet, which have friction ridges — has folds (flexion creases and texture lines) that are random and form distinctive patterns.[20] Except when stretched, the skin of the forearm is especially rich in these designs. It is not uncommon to lay the forearm or side of the hand on countertops, tables, the divider that separates the bank teller from the customer, and so on. Processing a crime scene can occasionally produce an armprint as shown in Fig. 4—9.

4.7 Exercise 12 (p 175)

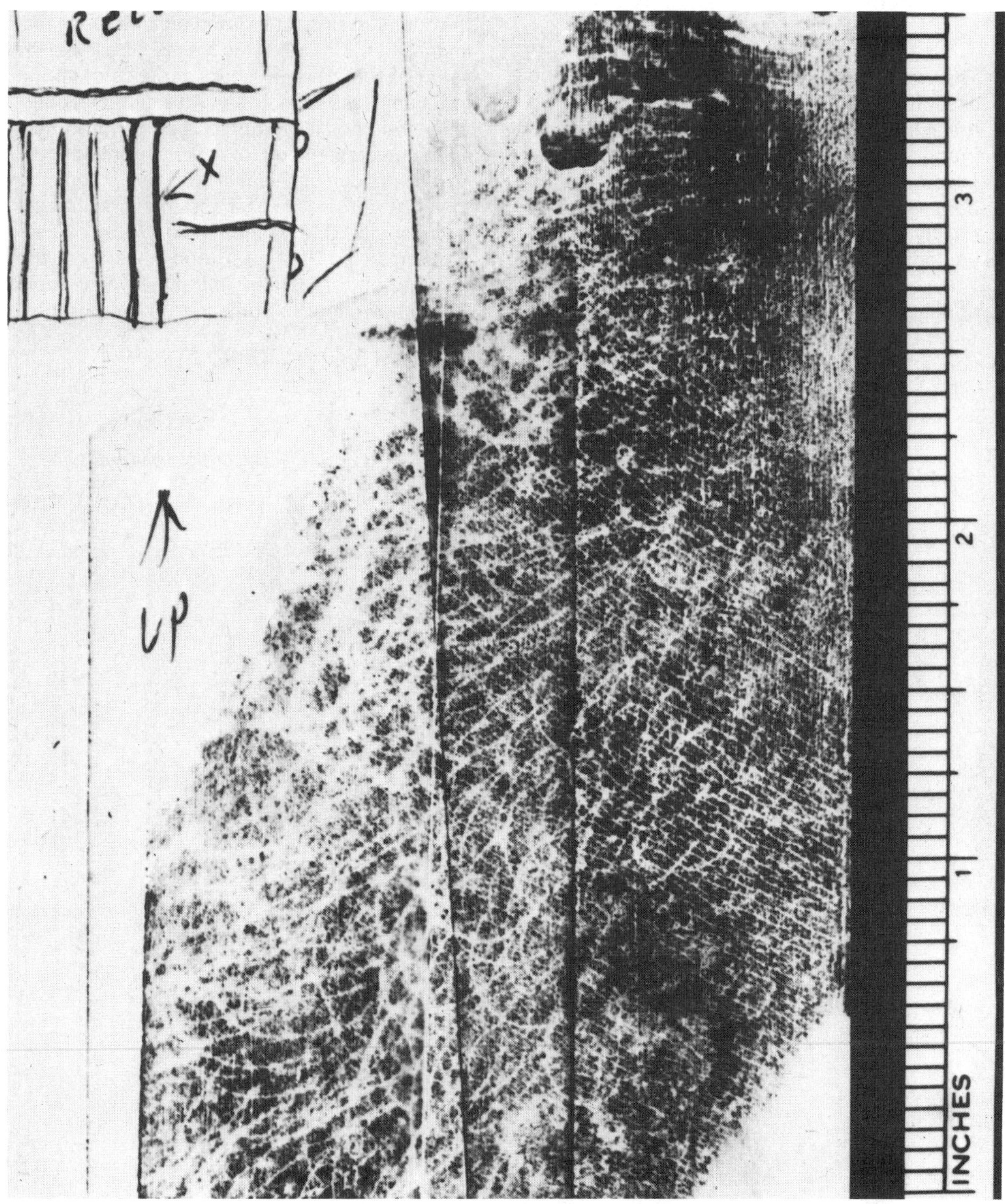

Fig. 4 — 9
Crime scene armprint (ca. 1:1)
(Courtesy, Sheriff's Department, Contra Costa County, California.)

4.8 Voiceprints

The voice is used in the planning and execution of many crimes, ranging from homicide, kidnaping, malicious destruction of property (bomb threats), and conspiracy to false reports and obscene telephone calls. To be useful the voice must be recorded on quality virgin magnetic tape using good equipment. When played back the questioned voice and a suspect's voice can be compared aurally. In addition, another comparison can be made by examining and comparing acoustic patterns of the two voices made by a sound spectrograph. This instrument converts the acoustic signal recorded on tape to a visual image (Fig. 4 — 10). This makes it possible for some of the physical characteristics of sound to be analyzed objectively. Although considerable training is required before one may appear as an expert in a voiceprint identity case, a reader of this text who has completed the thirty-three case exercises that precede the exercise for this section (see Order of Performance, pp 167-168) and mastered the recognition of details (minutiae) can apply such knowledge to voiceprint spectrographs.

4.8 Exercise 13 (p 175)

Unknown Speaker

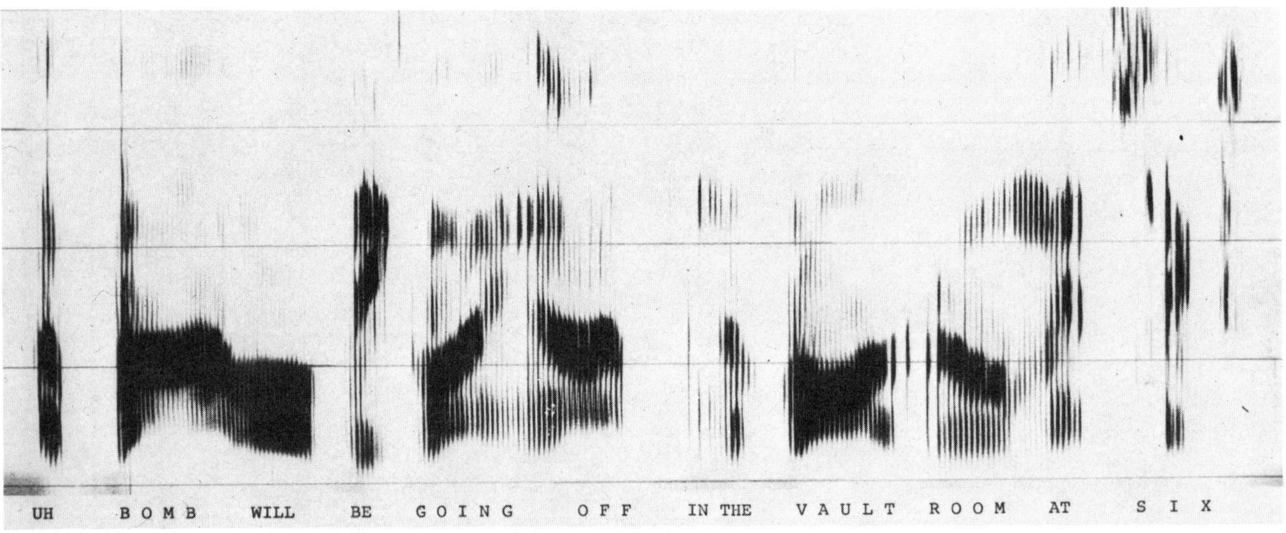

Fig. 4 — 10
Sound spectrum of unidentified speaker.
(Courtesy, Michigan State Police.)

4.9 Lip Impressions

Lip impressions are not common clues in criminal investigations. It is precisely for this reason that a lipstick exercise has been included in Chapter 4's case exercises. Few reminders are required to have a crime scene examined for fingerprints, blood stains, firearms evidence, and the like. However, it is the infrequently found trace evidence that is easily ignored owing to unfamiliarity with its potential. For example, cigarette butts can occasionally bear partial but usable lipstick impressions. Threatening letters sent by a disenchanted woman involved in a love-hate relationship have been "sealed with a kiss." An example of a lip impression on a document and useful for establishing an identity is given by Somerford.[21] Hit-and-run victims have been thrown by the impact in such a fashion as to leave a lip impression on the vehicle, usually the hood or fender. By comparison of a good lipstick impression on the vehicle with an exemplar taken from the female victim, it is possible to demonstrate that the car and victim were in contact.[22]

4.9 Exercise 14 (p 175)

References

Fingerprints

1. Kirk, P.L. *Crime Investigation*. New York: Interscience, 1953. Pp 391-401, 722-26.
   O'Hara, C.E. and Osterburg, J.W. *An Introduction to Criminalistics*. New York: Macmillan, 1949. Pp 77-102.
   Turner, R.F. *Forensic Science and Laboratory Technics*. Springfield, Ill. Thomas, 1949. Pp 54-69.
2. Popkin, R.H. "The Second Oswald: The Case for a Conspiracy Theory," *The New York Review* 3, July 28, 1966. P 20.
   Cook, F.J., "Sacco-Vanzetti: The Missing Fingerprints," *The Nation* 195, 442-51 (1962).
3. Ibid., p 450.
4. Ibid., p 451.
5. Popkin.

Palmprints

6. Scott, W.R. *Fingerprint Mechanics*. Springfield, Ill.: Thomas, 1951. Pp 22-27, 150-52, 423-24.

Bare Footprints

7. Wentworth, B. and Wilder, H.H. *Personal Identification*. Chicago: Fingerprint Publishing Association, 1932. Pp 132-54.

Teethmarks

8. Fischer, R.S., et al. "Techniques of Identification Applied to 81 Extremely Fragmented Aircraft Fatalities," *J. For. Sci.* 10, 121-35 (1965). Pp 123, 130-31.
9. Fearnhead, R.W. "Facilities for Forensic Odontology," *Med. Sci. and the Law* 1, 273-77 (1961). P 275.
   Nickolls, L.C. *The Scientific Investigation of Crime*. London: Butterworth, 1956. P 115.
10. Harrison, H.C., Assistant Director, Laboratories for Scientific Criminal Investigation, Kingston, Rhode Island. Letter dated September 1, 1965.

Handwriting

11. Tully, A. *The FBI's Most Famous Cases*. New York: Morrow, 1965. Pp 31-37.
12. Irey, E.R. and Slocum, W.J. *The Tax Dodgers*. New York: Greenberg, 1948. P 80.
13. Ibid., p 84.
14. Osborn, A.D., examiner of questioned documents. Letter dated April 16, 1959.

Earprints

15. Soderman, H. and O'Connell, J.J. *Modern Criminal Investigation*. 5th ed. Revised by C.E. O'Hara. New York: Funk & Wagnalls, 1962. Pp 74-76.
16. Falls, H.C., Fields, C., Warren, C.P., and Zimberoff, M. "The Ear of the Newborn as an Identification Constant," *Obstetrics and Gynecology* 16 (1), 98-102 (July 1960).
17. Iannarelli, A.V. *The Iannarelli System of Ear Identification*. Brooklyn: Foundation Press, 1964.
18. Spitz, W.U., Sopher, I.M., and DiMaio, V.J.M., "Medicolegal Investigation of a Bomb Explosion in an Automobile," *J. For. Sci.* 15, 537-552 (1970). P 549.
19. Medlin, H.O. "Earprint Identification Solves Crime," *Mil. Pol. J.* 16 (6), 10 (1967).

Skin Patterns

20. Dillon, D.J. "The Identification of Impressions of Nonfriction-Ridge-Bearing Skin," *J. For. Sci.* 8, 576-582 (1963).

Lip Impressions

21. Somerford, A.W. "Unique Document Problems" in Royal Canadian Mounted Police Proceedings of Crime Laboratory Seminar #5. Edited by Roy A. Huber. Ottawa, Canada: Queen's Printer, 1959. Pp 80-81.
22. Jones, L.V. *Scientific Investigation and Physical Evidence*. Springfield, Illinois: Thomas, 1959. Pp 145-146.

Suggestions for Further Reading

Fingerprints and Palmprints

Bridges, B.C. *Practical Fingerprinting*. 2d ed. Revised by C.E. O'Hara. New York: Funk & Wagnalls, 1963.

Crowell, J.R. "Unusual Latent Print Evidence," *Law and Order* 9, 14-16 (1979).

Donovan, T.J. "Latent Fingerprint Development Techniques," U.S. Postal Inspection Service

Crime Laboratory, Washington, D.C., *Int. Crim. Police Rev.* 330, 204-206 (1979).

Galton, Sir Francis. *Fingerprints*. Reprint ed. New York: Da Capo Press, 1965.

Grant, D. "Fingerprints in Unexpected Places," *The Pol. J.* (Brit.) 45, 66-68 (1972).

Lambourne, G.T.C. "The Use of Fingerprints in Identification," *Med. Sci. Law* 4, 217-224 (1979).

Midlo, C., and Cummings, H. *Fingerprints, Palms, and Soles*. New York: Dover Pub., 1961. Pp 3-119.

Olsen, R.D. *Scott's Fingerprint Mechanics*. Springfield, Ill.: Thomas, 1978.

Osterburg, J.W. "An Inquiry into the Nature of Proof: The Identity of Fingerprints," *J. For. Sci.* 9, 413-427 (1964).

Rhodes, H.T.F. *Alphonse Bertillon*. New York: Abelard-Schuman, 1956.

Wentworth, B. and Wilder, H.H. *Personal Identification*. Chicago: Fingerprint Publishing Association, 1932. Pp 114-54, 257-366.

Bare Footprints

Frankland, N. "Identification by Sole Print," *The Pol. J.* (Brit.) 44, 133-137 (1971).

Midlo C. and Cummings, H. *Fingerprints, Palms, and Soles*. New York: Dover Pub., 1961. Pp 120-132.

Scott, P. "The Case of the Great-Toe Print," *The Pol. J.* (Brit.) 26, 107-112 (1953).

Teethmarks

Dinkel, E.H. "The Use of Bite Mark Evidence as an Investigative Aid," *J. For. Sci.* 19, 535-547 (1974).

Goodbody, R.A., et al., "The Differentiation of Toothed Marks: Report of a Case of Special Forensic Interest," *Med. Sci. Law*. 16, 44-48 (1976).

Gustafson, G. *Forensic Odontology*. New York: Elsevier, 1966.

Hodson, J.J. "Forensic Odontology and Its Role in the Problems of the Police and Forensic Pathologist," *Med. Sci. Law*. 10, 247-251 (1970).

Levine, L.J. "Bitemark Evidence," *Dent. Clin. N. Am.* 21, 145-158 (1977).

Luntz, L.L. "The Use of Dentistry by Law Enforcement Agencies," *Fingerprint Ident. Mag.* 48, 6-16 (1966).

Schwartz, S.M. "Forensic Dentistry," in *Modern Legal Medicine, Psychiatry, and Forensic Science*. Edited by W.J. Curran, A.L. McGarry, and C.S. Petty. Philadelphia: F.A. Davis Co., 1980. Chapter 50.

Whittaker, D.K., Watkins, K.E., and Wiltshire, J. "An Experimental Assessment of the Reliability of Bite Mark Analysis," *Internat. J. For. Dent.* 3(7), 2-7 (1975).

Handwriting

Baxendale, D. and Renshaw, I.D. "The Large Scale Searching of Handwriting Samples," *For. Sci. Soc. J.* 19, 245-251 (1979).

Baxter, P.G. "The Training of Questioned Document Examiners," *Med. Sci. Law*. 10, 76-84 (1970).

Doulder, H.C. "Examination of a Document Case," *J. For. Sci.* 10, 433-440 (1965).

Fanciulli, J.S. "The Process of Handwriting Comparison," *FBI Law Enf. Bull.* 48(10), 5-8 (Oct. 1979).

Harrison, W.R. *Suspect Documents: Their Scientific Examination*. London: Sweet & Maxwell, 1958. Pp 288-348.

Hilton, O. *Scientific Examination of Documents*. Chicago: Callaghan, 1956. Pp 14-21, 136-150.

Muehlberger, et al. "A Statistical Examination of Selected Handwriting Characteristics," *J. For. Sci.* 22, 206-215 (1977).

_____. "Is There Any Place in Criminal Prosecutions for Qualified Opinions by Document Examiners?" *J. For. Sci.* 3, 579, 581 (1979).

O'Hara, C.E. and O'Hara, G.L. *Fundamentals of Criminal Investigation*. 5th ed. Springfield, Ill.: Thomas, 1959. Pp 823-837.

Osborn, A.S. *Questioned Documents*. 2d ed. Albany, N.Y.: Boyd Printing, 1929. Pp 25-38, 236-269.

Smith, T: "Determining Tendencies: The Second Half of a Classification System for Handwriting," *J. Crim. Law, Criminol., and Pol. Sci.* 55, 526-528.

Voiceprints

Anon. *On the Theory and Practice of Voice Identification*. Washington, D.C.: National Academy of Sciences, 1979.

Bunge, E. "Forensic Voice Identification by Computers," *Int. Crim. Pol. Rev.* 332, 254-270 (1979).

Koenig, B.J. "Speaker Identification. Part 1: Three Methods — Listening Machine and Aural-Visual," *FBI Law Enf. Bull.* 49 (1), 1-4 (Jan. 1980). "Part 2: Results of the National Academy of Sciences Study," *FBI Law Enf. Bull.* 49 (2), 20-22 (Feb. 1980).

Smrkovski, L.L. *Voice Identification*. East Lansing, Michigan: Michigan Department of State Police, 1976.

Tosi, O. *Voice Identification: Theory and Legal Applications*. Baltimore, Md.: University Park Press, 1979.

Lip Impressions

Suzuki, J. and Tsuchihasi, U. "Personal Identification by Means of Lip Prints," *J. For. Med.* 17, 52-67 (1970).

5

Wearing Apparel Traces

5.1 Shoeprints

Impressions of the sole or heel of a shoe are encountered from time to time in criminal investigations. Shoeprints may be left in loose earth, on paper, tile, linoleum, a wooden floor, or other surfaces. In all cases, a photograph of the impression is made first and then, if possible, a cast. A comparison test mark of the shoe suspected of having left the crime scene imprint is made and photographed. For the purpose of comparison, these photographs should be printed at least life size.

The comparison of the crime scene photograph with the known or test photograph is made by visual examination. The sections of the Introduction to Part 4 which discuss comparison characteristics and the interpretation of comparison details should be read at this point. When the two photographs are studied and the points of comparison identified, the question of the evaluation of data arises. The Introduction to Part 4 states that education, experience, and knowledge of the literature provide the basis for expert opinion. The literature search and empirical study recommendations in the following two sections furnish an opportunity to illustrate how some of the necessary experience can be gained and how a review of the literature may prove to be of assistance. The purpose of the research described in the following paragraphs is directed at developing an answer to a crucial question: "Are all crepe soles made by a certain machine identical?"

A. Literature Search

A search of the literature discloses some pertinent material.[1] Zmuda's article is a report of a study he made to determine the probability of design recurrence in crepe soles. In this study "nearly 200 crepe-soled shoes, over 100 consecutively cut soles and nearly 50 sole assemblies were examined.... However, no two crepe soles examined were found to be exactly alike."[2] The author then lists nine theoretical and practical reasons to account for this observation. Likewise, Speller lists five reasons why "the chances of finding two soles of plantation finished crepe rubber absolutely identical in pattern are extremely remote."[3]

B. Empirical Study

In addition to literature information as to why crepe soles differ, it is desirable that a person seeking to establish himself as an expert in this matter examine a large number of crepe soles. This may necessitate a visit to a wholesale footwear center or to plants where crepe rubber for soles is manufactured.

Obviously, it is not possible to examine all the crepe soled shoes that have been manufactured. This limitation is a commonplace occurrence for the crime laboratory worker when he is confronted with unusual types of evidence. The number of specimens he should examine is a difficult question to answer. The serious student might research this question through a study of sampling theory in the literature of statistics. If several hundred samples are available, they should be examined singly and with considerable care. Recurring individual characteristics, if any, should be noted particularly with regard to their location. Class characteristics should be expected to recur, but their location is not likely to be exactly the same on each sole. It is through such study that a person is able to present himself as an expert on the subject in court.

C. Crepe Sole Prints

Figure 5—1 represents an impression left by a burglar's shoe on a recently painted kitchen chair which was not quite dry. Figure 5—2 represents a comparison-test imprint made by the detective investigating the case. Normally the test impression is superior to the questioned (crime scene) imprint; however, in this case the investigator did not have the necessary technical knowledge to make a satisfactory test pattern. Indeed, it is usually better to bring the suspected evidence to the laboratory so that a more suitable test mark can be made. Another reason for doing this is that equipment adequate to reproduce a satisfactory imprint is seldom available to the field detective, especially at the crime scene.

In the case just mentioned, which is the subject of Case Exercise 1, the defendant, upon being placed in a cell, immediately destroyed the evidence by ripping the soles off his shoes and flushing the pieces down the toilet. Had the detective secured the shoes, not only would this untoward event have been prevented, but the shoe soles would have been available for use in preparing a better comparison specimen. The reason given by the detective for not taking the proper precautions was that in his previous seventy-five burglary arrests all of the prisoners pleaded guilty. Thus, his experience was such that he had little reason to change his policy and resort to the use of physical evidence. This type of investigative behavior was not satisfactory then, and certainly now it is inexcusable if the significance of the Supreme Court's decisions in several criminal cases is understood.

D. Sneaker Prints

In much of the United States sneakers are commonly worn as footwear by teenagers and young adults, especially those in the lower economic class who wear them as long as weather permits. Since these groups constitute a large proportion of persons charged with crime in recent times, sneakers emerge as an important potential source of physical evidence.

Fortunately, the sole design of sneakers varies considerably. This is significant in criminal investigation for two reasons: (a) the sole pattern, considered as a class characteristic, may be used to exclude a suspect or it may be used to center investigative interest on any person found wearing sneakers similar in sole design, and (b) defects in manufacture or those acquired through wear constitute individual characteristics, which are useful in the development of associative evidence.

The matter of "centering investigative interest" may be illustrated by referring to an actual case.

> This investigation involved a series of seven rape offenses. Following the second offense, a left footprint was found in the mud, photographed, and a plaster cast made. The fourth offense produced a right footprint which was found in the snow. It too was photographed and a plaster cast made. The two prints were of the same type of gym shoe, a type which later was found to be manufactured and sold only for export trade. After the arrest of the accused, it was learned that the shoes had been purchased overseas and brought back by one of his relatives. Investigation of one of the offenses revealed a latent fingerprint on a loosened porch light bulb. The print was processed but no match was made in the fingerprint file.
>
> Photographs of the shoeprint casts were prepared [Figs. 5 — 3 and 5 — 4] and a special bulletin sent out to all personnel. A patrolman operating in the affected area noticed a young man sitting on a porch with his feet up on the porch railing. The young man was wearing a pair of white gym shoes. On closer inspection, the patrolman observed that the tread design [Fig. 5 — 5] was the same as that in the bulletin he was carrying.
>
> When confronted with the evidence, the arrested party admitted his guilt. The investigation revealed that he had no previous record, was married, and the father of several children. Observation, aided by a wide distribution of data, paid off in all cases cleared by arrest.[4]

This case, which is the subject of Case Exercise 2, provides an excellent vehicle for a dialogue concerning the significance of the Mapp,[5] Miranda,[6] Rochin,[7] and Schmerber[8] cases relative to the acquisition of physical evidence.

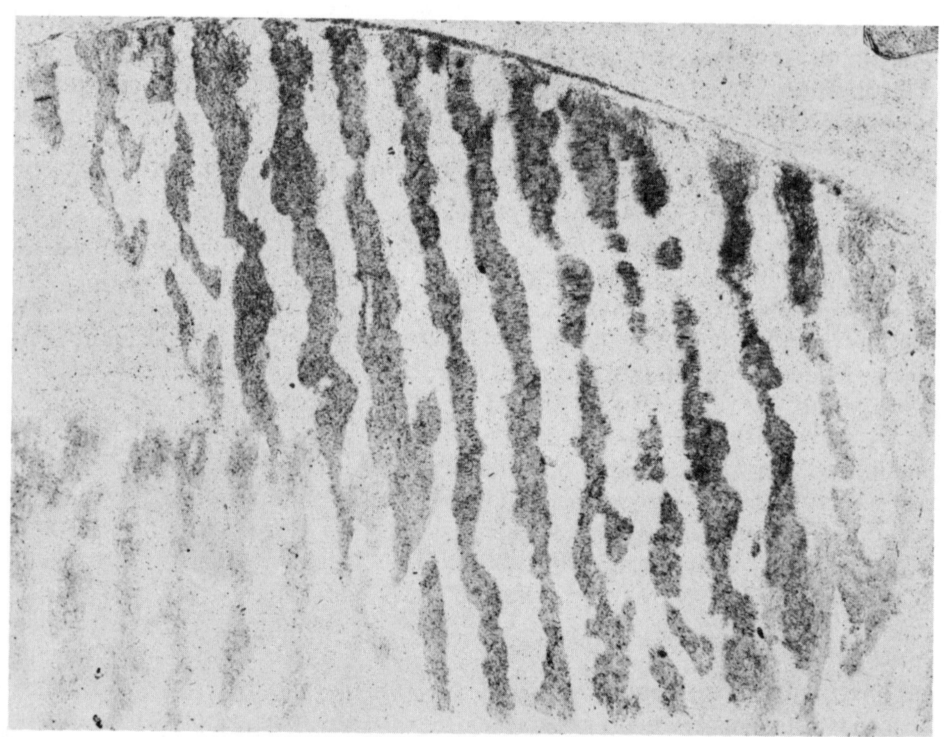

Fig. 5 — 1
Crepe sole impression left by a burglar on a recently painted chair.

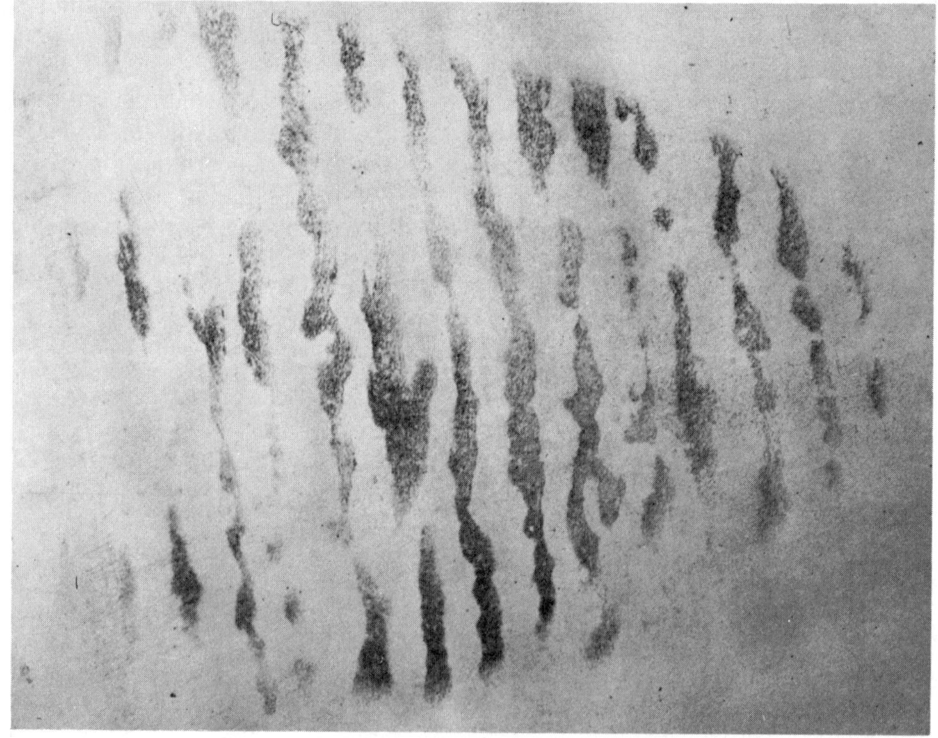

Fig. 5 — 2
Known impression made by detective using suspect's shoe.
(Courtesy, New York City Police Department.)

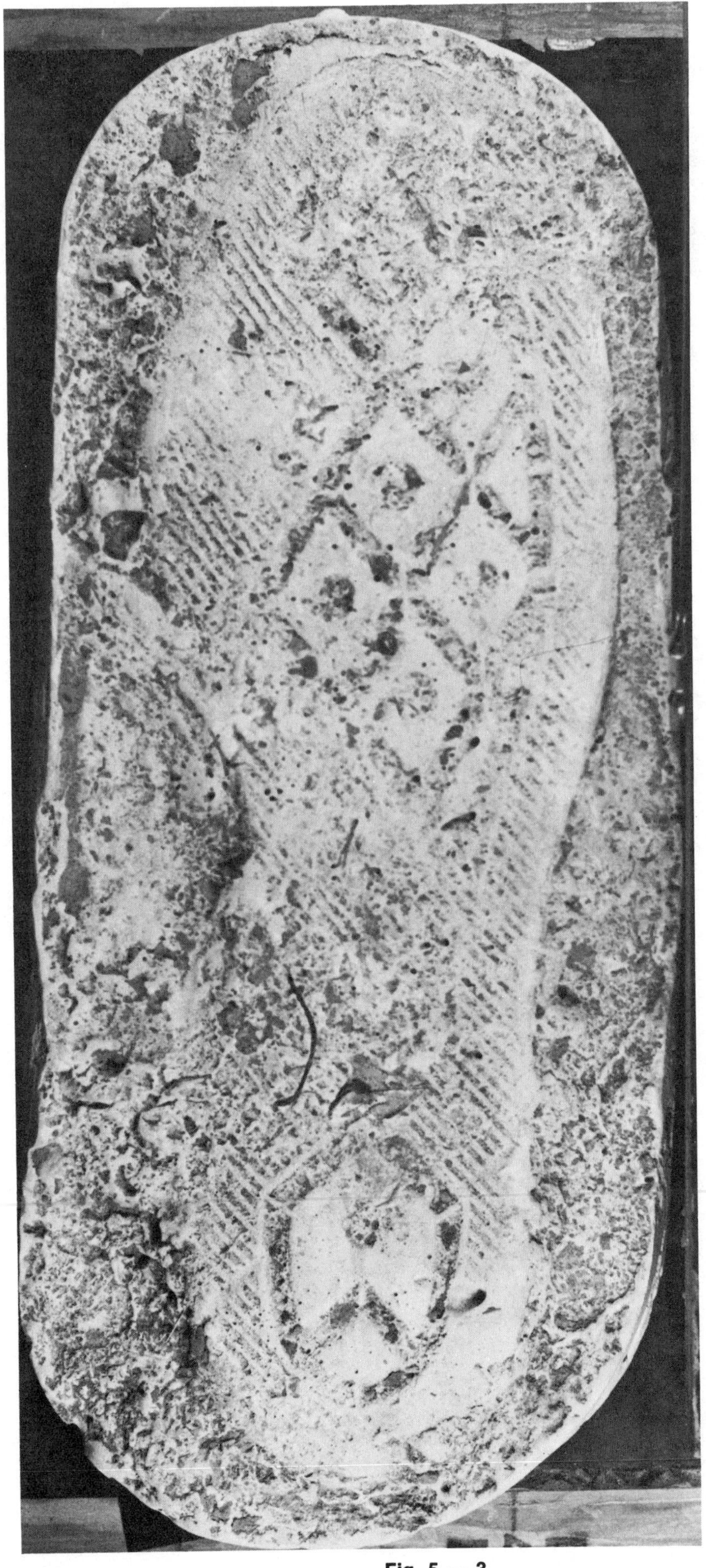

Fig. 5 — 3
Photograph of plaster cast of full shoeprint found in mud at scene in a rape case.

Fig. 5 — 4
Photograph (slightly enlarged) of plaster cast of a partial sole impression discovered in snow at crime scene in a rape case.

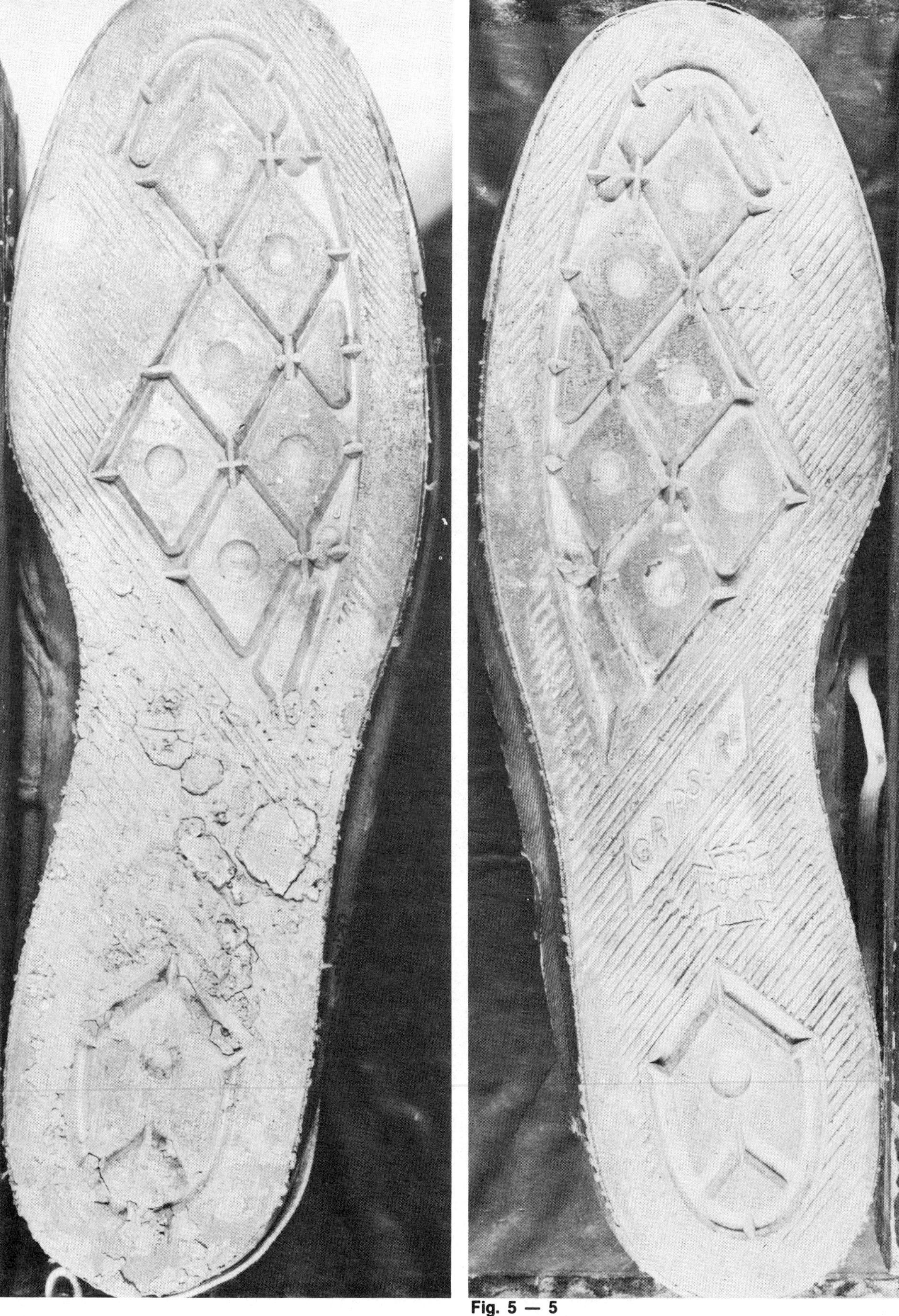

Fig. 5 — 5
Shoe soles observed by patrolman on post in response to department bulletin depicting crime scene imprints shown in Figs. 5 — 3 and 5 — 4. *(Courtesy, Cincinnati Police Department.)*

E. Heelprint Comparisons

With the rapid expansion of urban communities, more and more paved areas are to be expected and imprints in dirt are less likely to be left. Nevertheless, shoe impressions will still be found in cities. For instance, burglars are often careless when looting the premises. In their hasty search for hidden valuables, they often dump the contents of file cabinets, bureau drawers, and bookshelves on the floor. In moving amidst this debris, they may leave a shoeprint on some of the papers strewn about.

The area surrounding the point of entry into a building should be carefully examined, especially if a hole has been cut through the roof and dampness from rain or dew is present. In lowering himself into the room from the roof or in climbing through a transom, the burglar may step on a piece of paper and leave an imprint. Occasionally, previously undisturbed, dusty surfaces such as floors, file cabinet tops, or chair seats can retain a telltale mark.

The shape, size, and visibility of crime scene shoeprints depend on several factors:

1. Dirt or other materials present on the sole and heel of the shoe.
2. Condition of the recording surface, i.e., smooth, dusty, tacky.
3. Pressure exerted in leaving the imprint. This generally depends upon the weight of the person and the support given by the recording surface.

Similar comments are applicable to the test impression which must be made in order to determine if the shoe in question left the crime scene imprint. Natural variations in test impressions are shown in Figs. 5—6 through 5—9.

Occasionally an indistinct and only partially complete impression found at a crime scene may nevertheless prove to be of value to the investigator. For this reason, impressions of ostensibly poor quality should not be ignored. Figure 5 — 10 is a photograph of an apparently indistinct imprint that was left at the scene of a burglary in a bank building. Many detectives would not bother to preserve this heelmark because of its frail and fragmentary appearance. Figure 5 — 11 is a clear impression taken for comparison purposes. It was made by using fingerprint ink on the heel of the defendant's shoe. Figures 5 — 10 and 5 — 11 are the basis of Case Exercise 6.

Through the exposure of an investigator to a variety of laboratory experiences such as this, crime scene evidence, despite its poor outward appearance, will no longer be ignored or deliberately disregarded. Investigative supervisors who have been properly educated concerning the potential value of crime scene evidence will not tolerate the behavior of subordinates who are negligent or remiss about preserving such traces because of their seemingly poor quality.

5.1 Exercises 1, 2, 3, 4, 5, 6, 7 (pp 243-244)

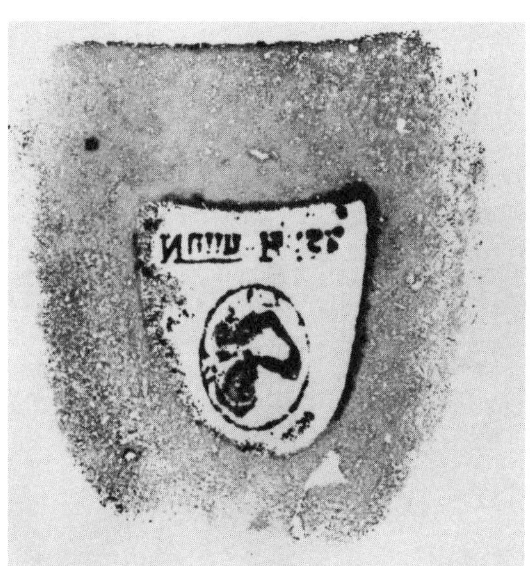

Fig. 5 — 6
Test impression made by wearing a burglar's shoe and stepping on a paper on the floor.

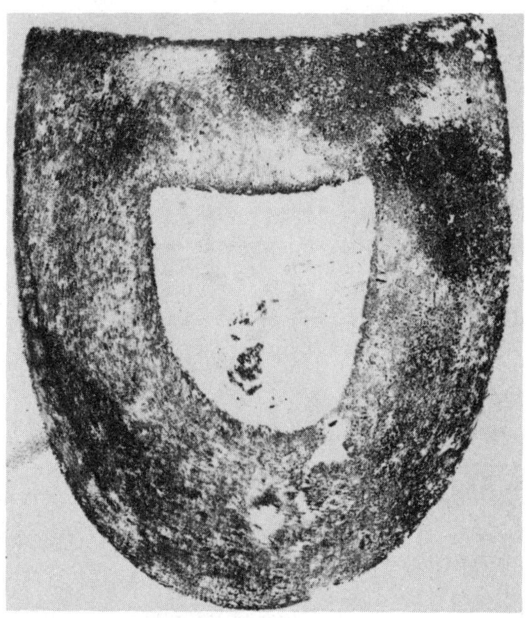

Fig. 5 — 7
Test impression of same shoe (Fig. 5 — 6) made by placing a piece of ordinary bond paper over the inked heel and pressing the paper surface into the heel with a clean roller.

Fig. 5 — 8
Test impression of same shoe (Fig. 5 — 6) made by inking the heel, placing a shoe tree in the suspect's shoe, and rolling the impression onto the paper as in walking.

Fig. 5 — 9
Test impression of same shoe (Fig. 5 — 6) made in same manner as in Fig. 5 — 8, illustrating the natural variation in the details obtained.
(Courtesy, Laboratory of Criminalistics, Office of District Attorney, Santa Clara County, California.)

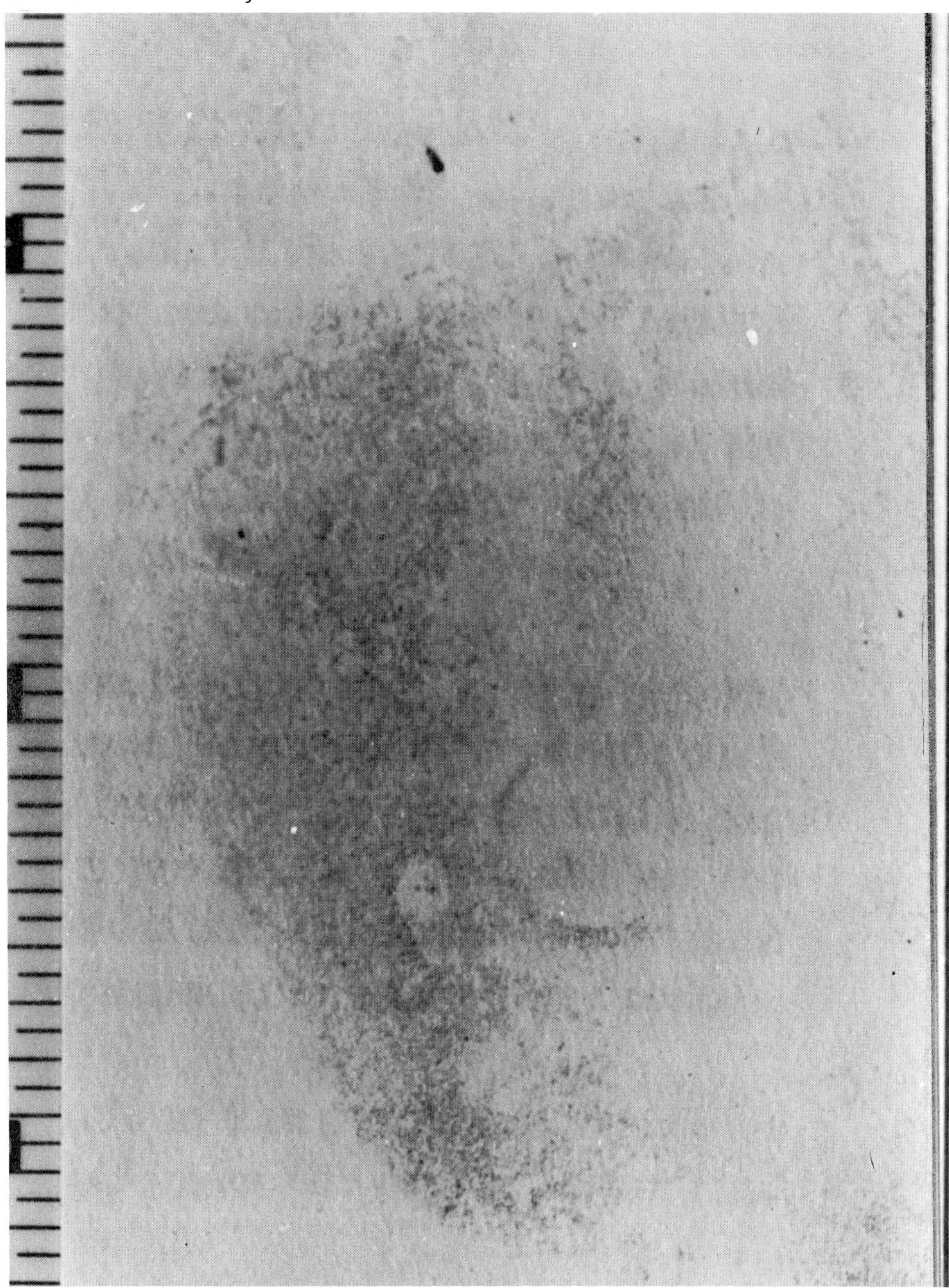

Fig. 5 — 10
An indistinct and partial crime scene heelprint.

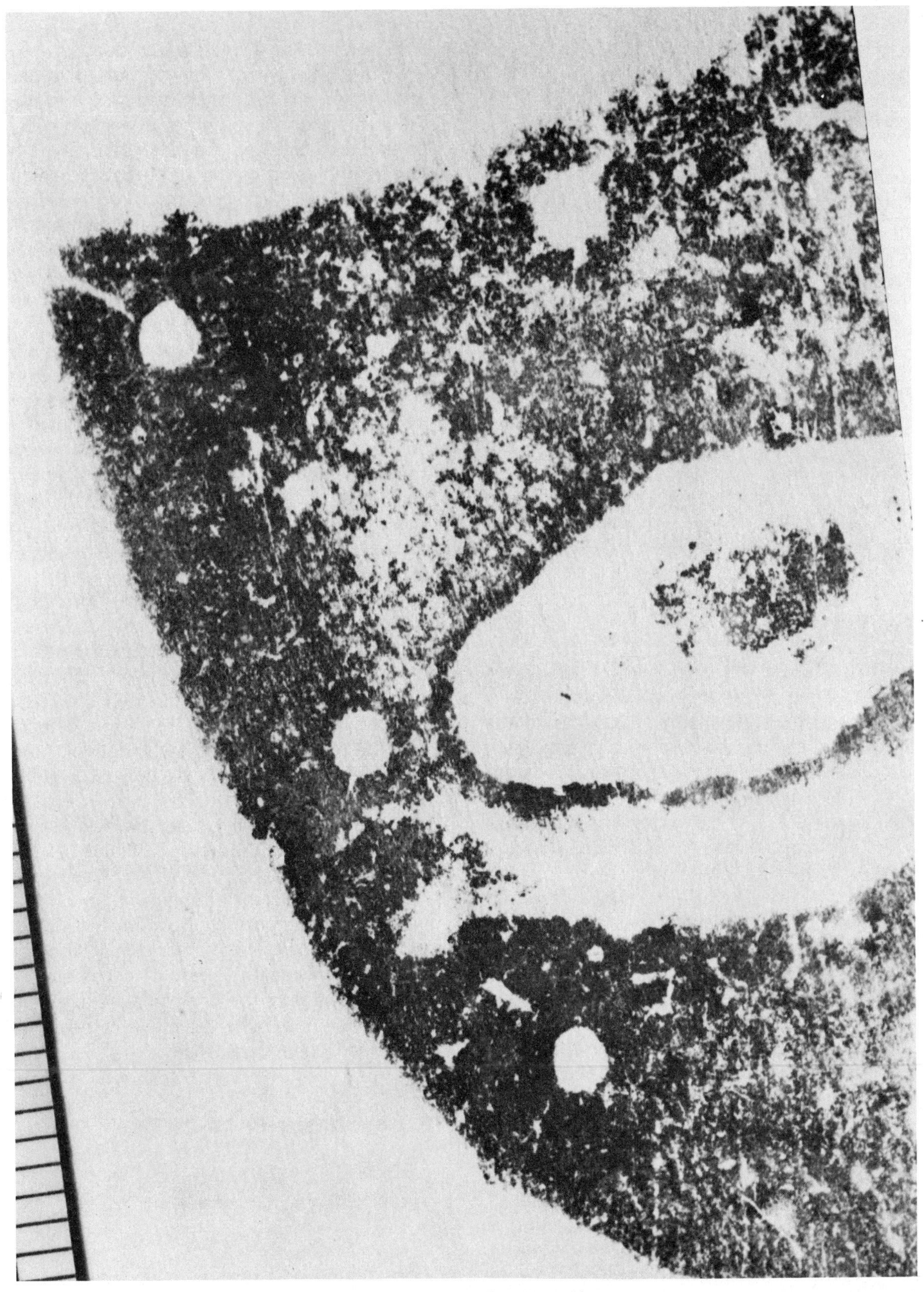

Fig. 5 — 11
Clear impression made of a suspect's heel for comparison purposes.
(Courtesy, Michigan State Police.)

5.2 Cloth: Weave Pattern and Stitching

In addition to footwear, the clothing worn by a perpetrator in the commission of a crime is a potential source of evidence. An even broader view can be taken, *viz.*, that cloth in some form is an important source of physical evidence in its own right.[9] Weave pattern, stitching, threadbare spots or holes, and fiber characteristics[10] — their nature, thickness, color in natural and ultraviolet light — represent aspects of textile fabrication that must be recognized as potentially useful in the development of associative evidence. In the case exercise for this section the stitching of a garment is of primary interest.

5.2 Exercise 8 (p 243)

5.3 Gloves

The possibility of leaving fingerprints behind is as well known to criminals as it is to the victims of crime. Considerably less well known, even to police personnel, is the fact that it is rather difficult to leave a good latent impression even intentionally of a single finger, and much less so for all fingers of one or both hands. Though hardly necessary, criminals often use a handkerchief to wipe surfaces they must touch while committing their crimes Gloves are sometimes worn to avoid leaving fingerprints.

The routine processing of a crime scene occasionally results in the disclosure of a glove impression. Undoubtedly, in some investigations, glove impressions have not been recognized as such by the inexperienced and untrained eye and consequently were overlooked as potential evidence. Partial glove impressions can also easily be mistaken for smudged fingerprints and ignored as such.

Another telltale print — that of the glove itself in the form of its cloth weave, stitching, or tattered condition — may be left instead.[11] When the glove has a defective weave or is worn through in spots, the impression has considerable potential as associative evidence.

Unfortunately, more often than not a glove imprint has insufficient characteristics to allow the definite conclusion that it was made by a particular glove and no other. On the other hand, conclusions of lesser probative value are possible. For example, if class characteristics only are present, the strongest statement that may be given about a suspect's glove is that it could have made the impression. Conversely, a suspected glove can be definitely eliminated and such a finding is, of itself, an important part of crime laboratory work. The difference between the positive assertion that it is the glove and a weaker statement that it is possible that it could be the glove rests upon the number of individual characteristics present and how common or unusual they are. Evaluation by the expert of the quality of the characteristics and the interpretation to be placed upon them is at present a subjective matter.

Individual characteristics are not always obvious. To the inexpert eye it may seem impossible that anyone would be able to do anything with an imprint which obviously appears to be of poor quality. The cases selected for this section are in this category and therefore are moderately difficult. They have been included because they illustrate the principle that the eye of the expert perceives details that the untrained person does not see readily. Physical trace evidence, which appears to be quite poor from an investigator's view, may have great probative value when an expert has an opportunity to study it. When the education of a police officer normally includes the study of a wide variety of cases such as those in this text, the possibility of exploiting the full potential of crime scene evidence will have been enhanced greatly.

5.3 Exercises 9, 10 (p 243)

5.4 Clothing Accessories

In the course of a robbery a valuable tie clasp was forcibly torn from the victim. This particular piece of jewelry was held in place by a pin inserted through the cloth of the tie and shirt, and secured by a spring clasp. In Fig. 5—12 the round object at the top left is the spring clasp. The pin is in the middle, while the square object on the right is the back of the decorative portion of the jewelry. Figure 5—13 is an enlargement (ca. 8X). At the top is the back of the decorative part of the jewelry, and at the bottom of the illustration is the head of the pin. (In an undamaged tie clasp these two parts would be joined together.) Determining whether an identity can be established between the two tie clasp pieces is the subject of Case Exercise 11.

5.4 Exercise 11 (p 244)

Fig. 5 — 12
Parts of tie clasp broken during robbery.

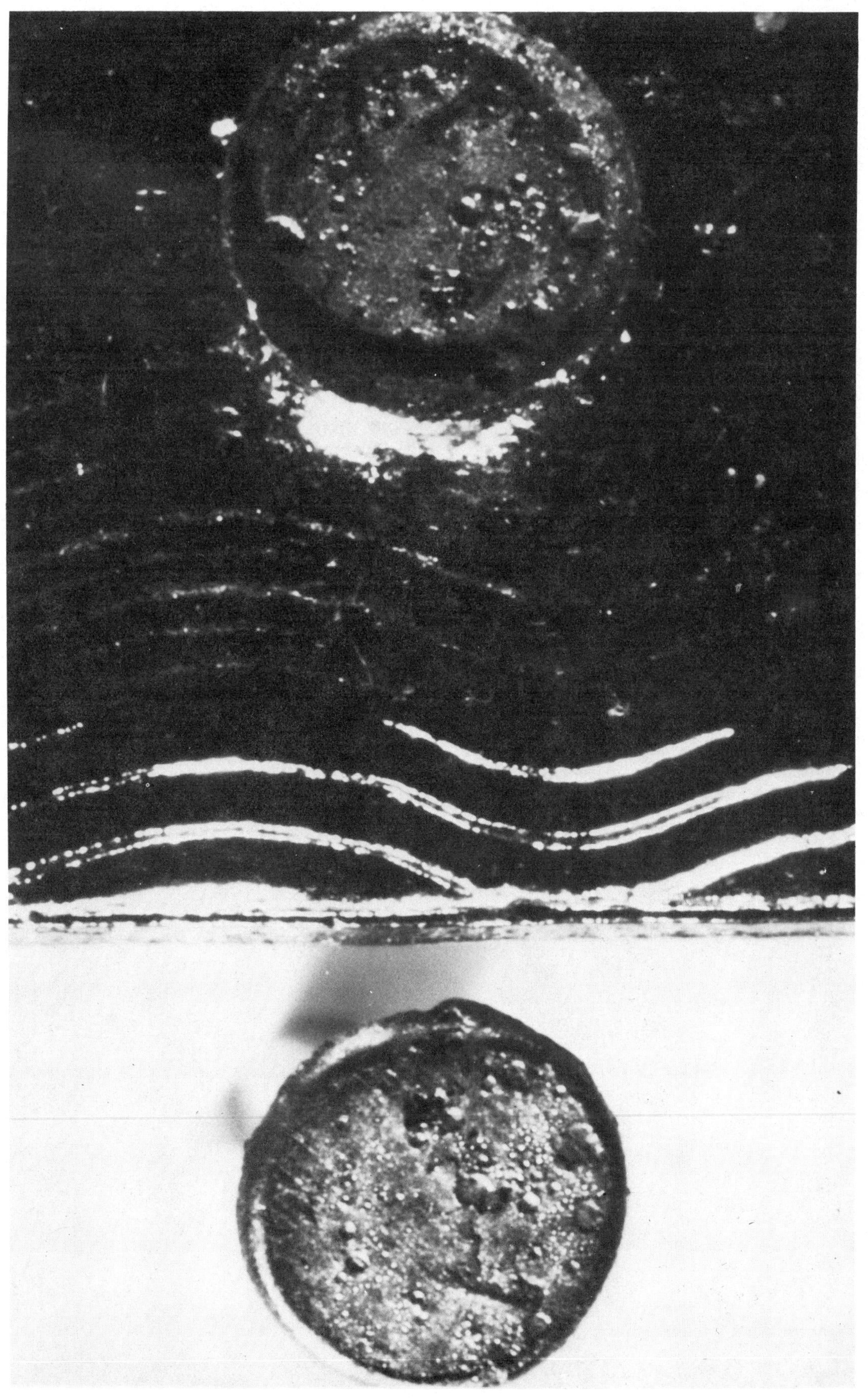

Fig. 5 — 13
Top: back of broken tie clasp found on suspect. Bottom: head of tie clasp remaining in victim's shirt. (ca. 8X).
(Courtesy, New Jersey State Police.)

References

Shoeprints

1. Zmuda, C.W. "Identification of Crepe Sole Shoes," *J. Crim. Law, Criminol., and Pol. Sci.* 44, 374-378 (1953). Speller, H.C. "The Identification of Crepe Rubber Sole Impressions," *The Pol. J.* (Brit.) 22, 269-274 (1949).
2. Zmuda, pp 377-378.
3. Speller, p 273.
4. Roncker, Robert J., training office, Police Academy, Cincinnati Police Department. Letter dated December 27, 1965.
5. Mapp v. Ohio, 367 U.S. 643.
6. Miranda v. Arizona, 384 U.S. 436.
7. Rochin v. California, 342 U.S. 165.
8. Schmerber v. California, 384 U.S. 757.

Cloth: Weave Pattern and Stitching

9. Kirk, P.L. *Crime Investigation.* New York: Interscience, 1953. Pp 116-125.
10. Ibid., pp 126-145.

Gloves

11. Bridges, B.C. *Practical Fingerprinting.* 2d ed. Revised by C.E. O'Hara. New York: Funk & Wagnalls, 1963. P 235.

Suggestions for Further Reading

Shoeprints

Abbot, J.R. *Footwear Evidence: The Examination, Identification, and Comparison of Footwear Impressions.* Edited by A.C. Germann. Springfield, Ill.: Thomas, 1964.

Davis, R.J. and Dehann, J.D. "A Survey of Men's Footwear," *For. Sci. Soc. J.* 17, 271-285 (1977).

Jobing, R.J. "Shoeprints: Quantum of Proof," *J. For. Sci.* 13, 223 (1968).

Lucock, L.J. "Identification from Footwear," *Med. Sci. Law* 4, 225-230 (1979).

Mansfield, E.R. "Footwear Impressions at Scenes of Crime," *The Pol. J.* (Brit.) 43, 93-96 (1970).

McCafferty, J.D. "The Shoe Fits," *The Pol. J.* (Brit.) 23, 125-139 (1955).

Owen F., "A Latent Heel Impression," *The Pol. J.* (Brit.) 27, 221-223 (1954).

Svensson, A., Wendel, O., and Fischer, B. *Techniques of Crime Scene Investigation.* 3rd ed. New York: Elsevier, 1981. Pp 188-206.

Cloth: Weave Pattern and Stitching

Johri, M.C. and Jatar, D.P. "Identification of Some Synthetic Fibers by Their Bifringence," *J. For Sci.* 3, 692-697 (1979).

Kirk, P.L. *Crime Investigation.* 2d ed. Edited by John I. Thornton. New York: Wiley, 1974. Pp 117-123.

Saferstein, R. *Criminalistics: An Introduction to Forensic Science.* Englewood Cliffs, N.J.: Prentice-Hall, 1977. Pp 234-238.

Gloves

Beltran, J.S. "Traces of Gloves," *Internat. Crim. Pol. Rev.* 7, 79 (1952).

Lambourne, G. "Glove Print Identification: A New Technique," *The Pol. J.* (Brit.) 48, 219-246 (1975).

Svensson, A., Wendel, O., and Fischer, B. *Techniques of Crime Scene Investigation.* 3rd ed. New York: Elsevier, 1981. Pp 78-82.

6

Instruments of Crime

A potential source of physical evidence exists when the criminal has utilized instruments that aid his efficiency or minimize the risk of his detection. In this light, an automobile may be viewed as a means of providing anonymity when the criminal attains distance from his usual haunts or as a means of hasty departure following the completion of a crime. When the transgression is committed indoors, a tool may be required to gain access or otherwise to execute the crime effectively. With other violations — robbery, assault, and homicide, for example — guns, knives, ice picks, and the like may be employed to threaten, intimidate, or wound the victim. The final opportunity to use an instrument in crime lies in any attempt made to deter detection: burying a body, concealing a weapon, or disposing of any fruit of the crime.

Consideration of instruments in this chapter involves an analysis of their functional value to the criminal and differs from the more conventional treatment which is based largely on characterization according to tool design or natural usage. Stated in another way, the present material is developed from the standpoint of the investigator while the traditional approach is based on the viewpoint of the criminalist in the crime laboratory.

Thus, instruments may be considered as

being used by criminals for the following purposes:

1. To furnish mobility.
2. To gain access to premises.
3. To execute the crime.
4. To provide a threat to someone.
5. To effect concealment of a body or other evidence.

6.1 Automobiles

The automobile has revolutionized almost all aspects of twentieth century living. For the criminal, a much broader area has become prey to his marauding. The local detective is not longer kept *au courant* through a departmental line-up. Surveillance of criminal activity has been made more difficult and if this technique is employed in an investigation, considerable allocation of personnel and equipment is required for an effective operation.

The necessity for the criminal's hasty departure from the locus of the crime and his willingness to violate traffic regulations, if necessary, occasionally result in some object or person being struck by the vehicle. Physical evidence is often available in the form of broken headlight lenses (cf. Fig. 7—11, p 128), ornaments (Fig. 6—1), and grillwork fragments (Figs. 6—2 and 6—3) following a collision or hit-and-run accident. At other times, tire tracks may serve to link the vehicle to the path along which the car was driven or to the place where it was parked.

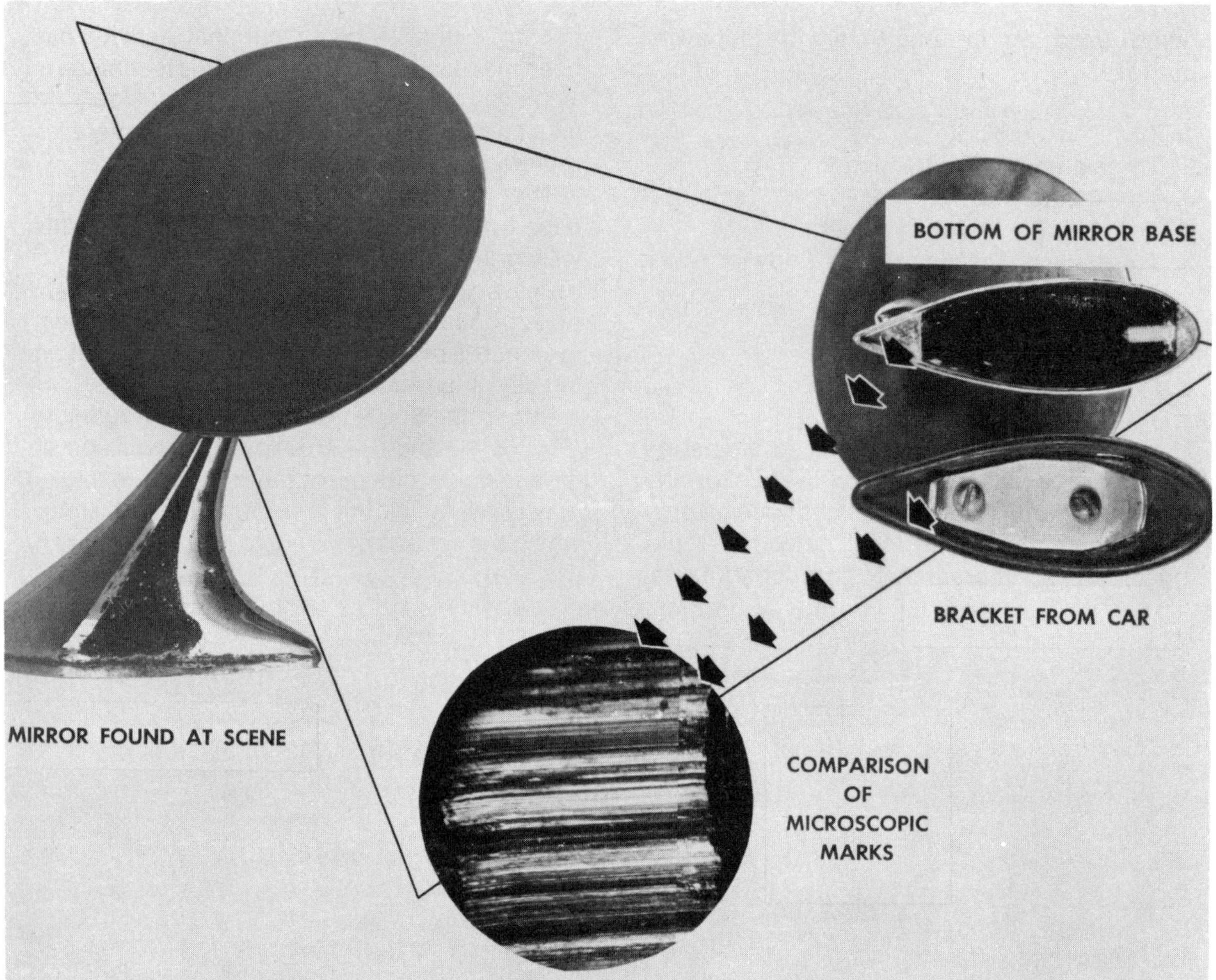

Fig. 6 — 1
An outside rear view mirror found at the scene of a Pennsylvania hit-and-run provided the link which refuted the suspect's alibi. Upon location of the suspect's car, officers found missing the rear view mirror normally attached to the bracket on the car's door. Claiming that the suspect had removed the mirror from the bracket a year prior to the accident, the suspect's attorney appeared at police headquarters with a mirror exactly like that found at the scene and stated that the second mirror was the one which had been on the bracket on the suspect's car.
FBI laboratory examination revealed marks inside the base of the suspected mirror which were produced as a result of forcible removal of the mirror from its mounting bracket. The mirror furnished by the suspect's attorney contained no such marks. These marks were identified as having been produced by the bracket found on the suspect's car. In addition, paint particles found in the victim's clothes were determined to be similar to the paint of the suspect's car.
(Courtesy, Federal Bureau of Investigation.)

Fig. 6 — 2
Damaged grillwork on automobile alleged to have fled from scene of collision.

Fig. 6 — 3
Photomacrograph (ca. 8X) showing physical match of piece of grillwork (bottom) with piece of metal found at crime scene (top).
(Courtesy, New York City Police Department.)

A. The Comparison of Tire Tracks and Tires

Tire tracks are retained in sand, clay, and ordinary dirt if the environmental conditions are suitable; however, wind can destroy a tire pattern in sand, and too much or too little water can make it impossible for an impression to be recorded in clay. Despite these limitations tire marks are found sufficiently often to warrant study by investigators, especially those whose jurisdictions include suburban and rural areas. The unconscious victim of an assault, the body in a homicide, and the stolen safe often are discarded unceremoniously in unused, open lots located on the outskirts of a city. Often these areas are unpaved and the possibility of a tire impression remaining should not be overlooked. As with footprints, a photograph must be made before a cast is attempted.[1] It is more often possible to compare the tire trace impression directly with the known impression made by rolling the suspected tire, covered with fingerprint ink, over a long sheet of wrapping paper.

6.1 Exercise 1 (p 288)

6.2 Jimmies, Axes, Hammers, and Metal Cutters

A considerable amount of crime is committed indoors. The closure may be breached in private homes and commercial buildings, while at other times entry to a locked desk, safe, garage, truck, or automobile is gained through force. Although almost any tool may be used to open a secured object, jimmies, axes, hammers, and metal cutters have been selected for more detailed study since they are most commonly employed for this purpose.

A. Jimmies

Whether it be a pry bar, tire iron, screwdriver, or other instrument, the term *jimmy* is used to describe the lever-like tool a criminal uses to break into a business establishment or locked object such as a safe. Because of the force required to open a secured object, the resulting visibly damaged area (Fig. 6 — 4) is likely to bear physical clues of some importance to the investigator (Fig. 6 — 5). In wood an area of compression should be observed at the point where force was applied in using the tool; in metal, scratches are retained as fresh marks in the otherwise uniformly colored surface. It is often but not always possible to associate in a unique manner the imprint which remains at the crime scene with the tool that made it. The actual object bearing the jimmy mark should be protected and safeguarded against tampering. At the start of the investigation the tool is seldom available, hence it is important to preserve the clue impression. This may be accomplished photographically, by casting, or both (Fig. 6 — 6). Furthermore, the type of tool that made the mark can often be determined with accuracy. The patrol force, as well as the investigator, should be informed to be on the lookout for such a tool. For a reasonable time thereafter, any arrest for burglary should include a search for similar instruments among the burglar's tools. When a suspected tool is discovered during the course of an investigation, a laboratory comparison may be made between it and the clue imprint (Fig. 6 — 7). The identity of the tool which left the crime scene impression is usually established by making a test impression in material similar to that bearing the questioned imprint.

A synopsis of the case in which Figs. 6 — 4 through 6 — 7 were obtained illustrates the application of these ideas in practice:

> In response to an audible burglary alarm, an officer discovered an attempted burglary of a pharmacy. It was determined that entry had not been effected although the aluminum window casing had been pried and the window broken.
>
> Although the window had been broken beyond all repair, the casing in which the best marks were impressed was still serviceable. The victim indicated that it was not his intention to replace the window casing; therefore, photographs of the marks were taken and a cast using Dow Corning RC900 Silicone Rubber was made.

Approximately one month later, an officer in response to an unknown disturbance call found that the co-owners of another pharmacy had subdued a would-be robber who had demanded narcotics. Nearby the vehicle of the culprit was found and impounded. In the vehicle (not in the trunk) were found a tire iron and screwdriver. These tools were submitted to the laboratory as possible burglary tools.

The tire iron tip was approximately the size of the marks in the window casing of the attempt burglary. To prepare exemplar material for comparison with the prepared casts, numerous marks were made with the tire iron on aluminum plate. The marks so made were then cast with Dow Corning RC900 Silicone Rubber. The suspect casts and the exemplar casts were examined together using the comparison microscope. Sufficient points of identification were recorded by the casting material to show that the tire iron was used in the attempted burglary.[2]

At other times the jimmy itself may be damaged or broken and the metal piece remaining behind may be useful in linking a tool found in someone's possession to the crime (Figs. 6 — 8 through 6 — 10). Paint specks or other potential evidence adhering to a suspected jimmy should be removed and preserved since such clue materials can serve as evidence in their own right. This must be done, of course, before the tool is used to prepare the test mark. This point needs to be emphasized. The tool should not be placed into the crime scene impression unwittingly and certainly not deliberately. There is seemingly a natural tendency for many police officers to make this error, thereby creating opportunity for a damaging line of questioning by an astute defense counsel starting with: "Officer, is it not possible that the insertion of the tool in the crime scene mold was responsible for the paint traces which were found on it?" Furthermore, counsel may argue that the laying of the tool into the crime scene mold was responsible for the presence of those imprint characteristics upon which the identity between tool and impression is based. These distracting and damaging arguments gratuitously handed to the defense can be avoided when police officers have a thorough understanding of the legal import of their unwitting behavior. The following description of a case involving jimmy marks found on a wooden door demonstrates one of the correct methods that is employed in tool mark identity cases.

A burglary in progress was interrupted by the arrival of a police officer. The culprit briefly managed to elude the officer who pursued him on foot. Shortly thereafter an individual was discovered nearby hiding behind the shrubbery of a residence. A large screwdriver was found in his possession. The place of entry was inspected upon returning to the burglarized premises. Figure 6—11 depicts the door that had been pried open. A jimmy mark is being pointed to by the hand of a police officer. The door was removed and brought to the laboratory and a cast of the impression, using Dow Corning Silicone Rubber, was made. Figure 6—12 is an enlarged photograph of that cast (ca. 9X). Establishing an identity by a careful examination of a tool mark on the door and a tool found on a suspect is the subject of Case Exercises 2 and 3, p 288.

Fig. 6 — 4
Point of entry in attempted burglary of a pharmacy.

Fig. 6 — 5
Enlargement of tool mark in aluminum window casing shown in Fig. 6 — 4.

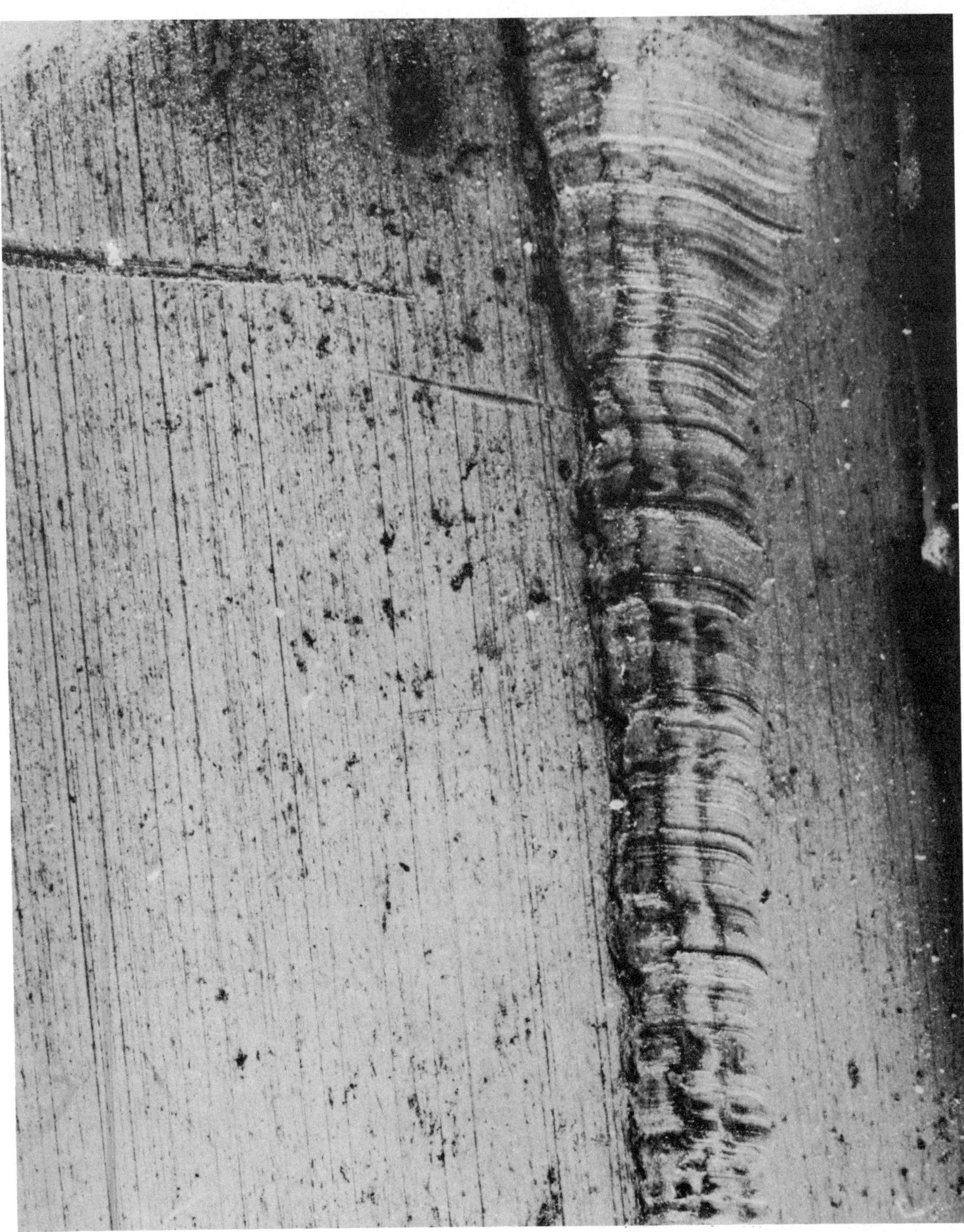

Fig. 6 — 6
Enlarged photograph of silicone rubber cast of tool mark.

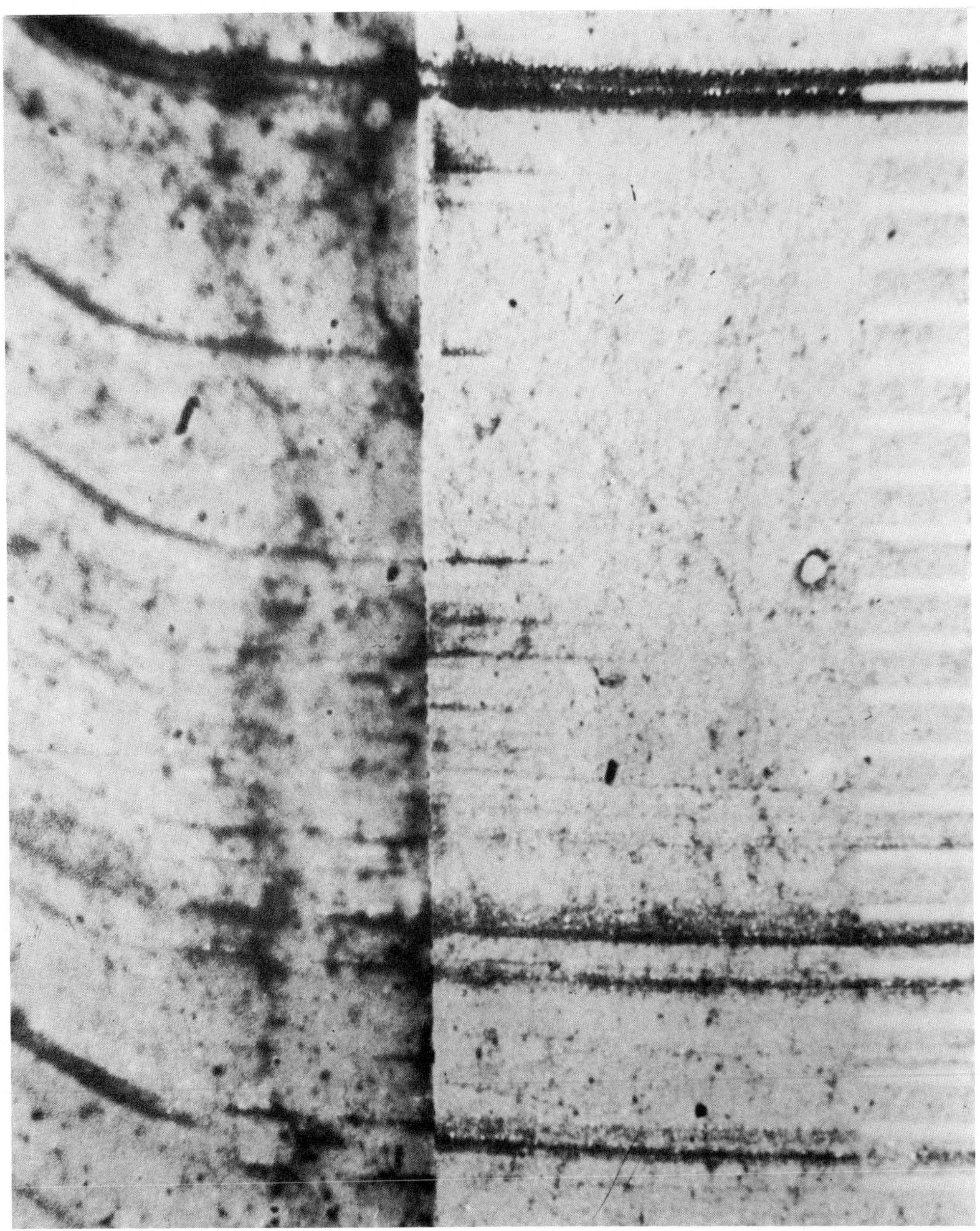

Fig. 6 — 7
Comparison microscope photograph: left, crime scene tool mark cast; right, test mark cast made using suspect's tool.
(Courtesy, Santa Ana Police Department, California.)

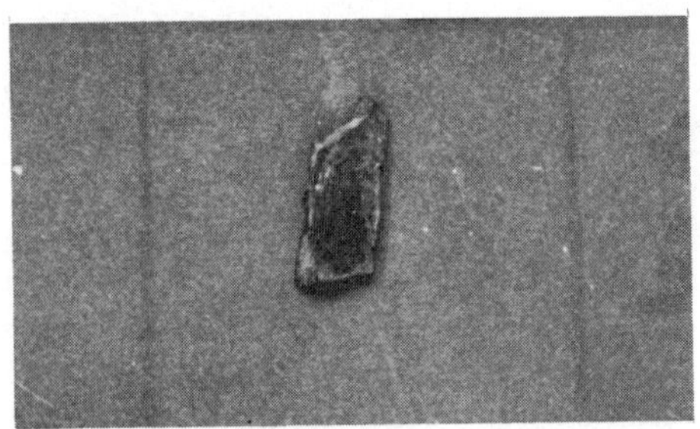

Fig. 6 — 8
Piece of metal found in door by lock in burglary case.

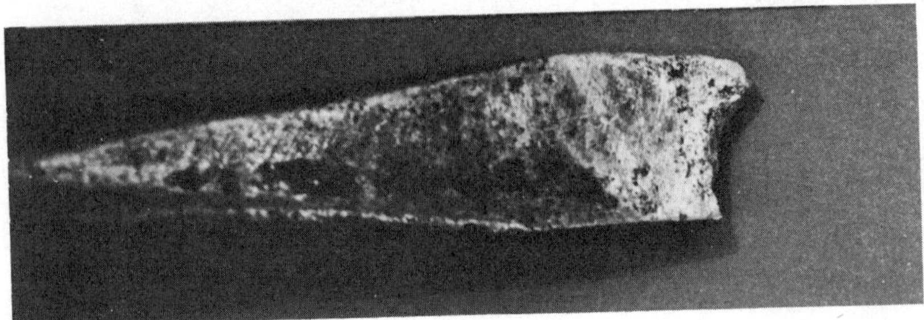

Fig. 6 — 9
Screwdriver found on suspect.

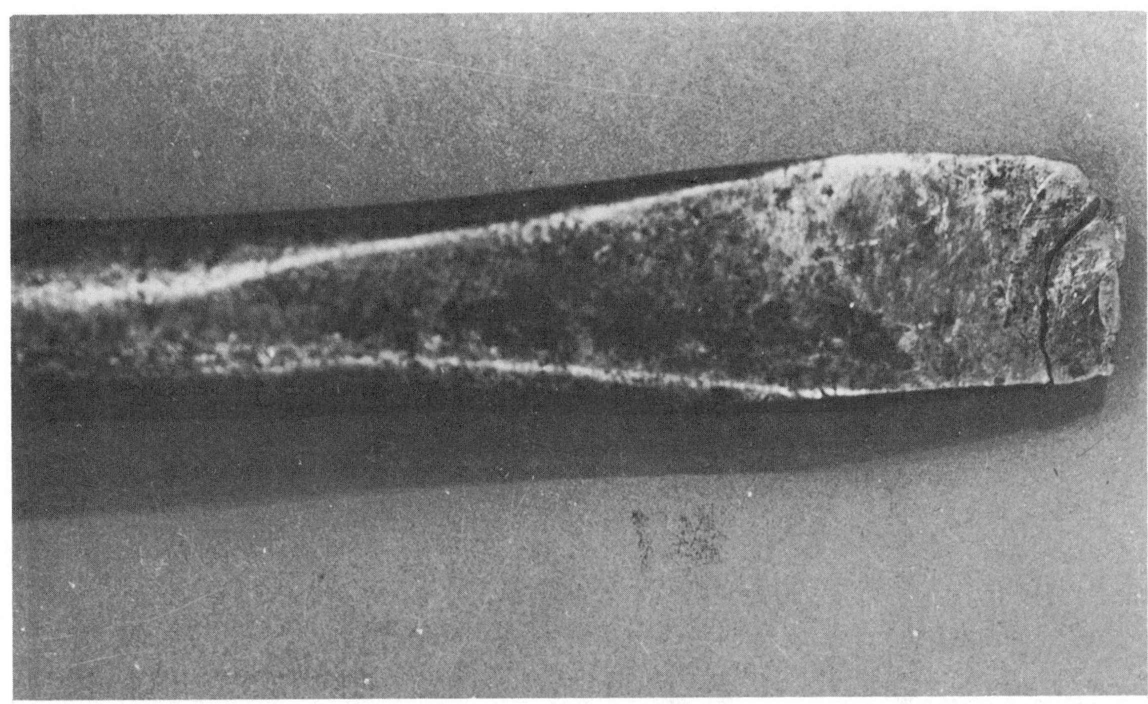

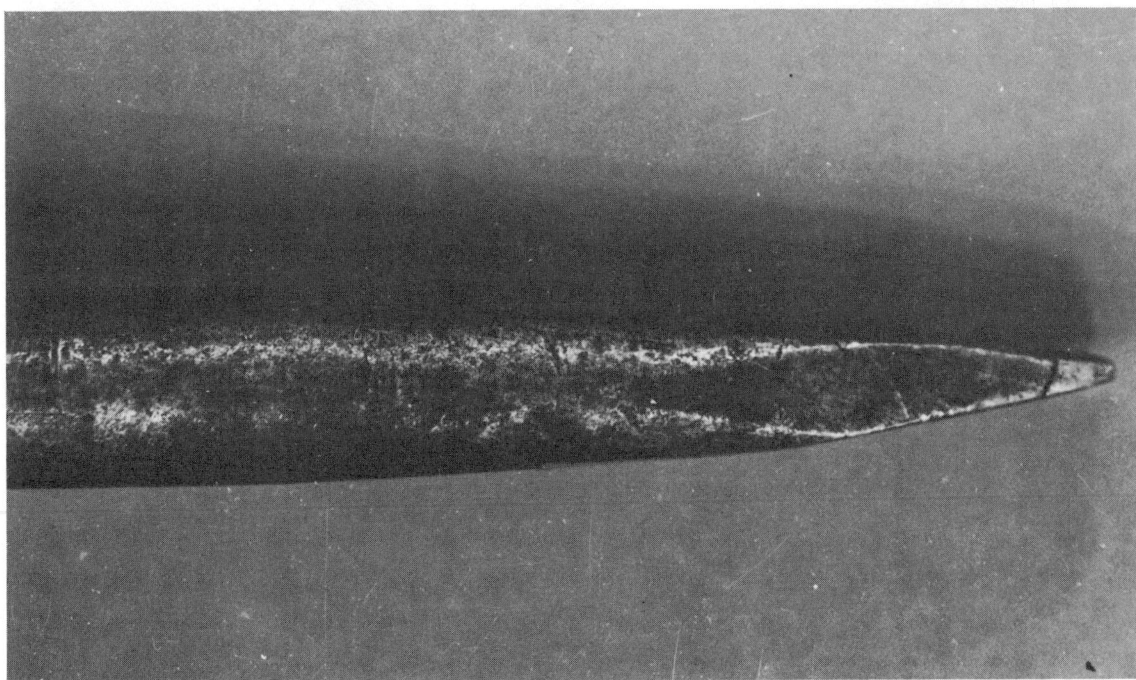

Fig. 6 — 10
Two enlarged views of the piece of metal inserted into tip of suspect's damaged screwdriver.
(Courtesy, Sheriff's Office, Kern County, California.)

Fig. 6 — 11
Door that had been pried open.

Fig. 6 — 12
Cast of tool mark on door (ca. 9X).
(Courtesy, Santa Ana Police Department, California.)

B. Axes

As an instrument of crime the ax runs the gamut from homicide, assault, and burglary to the cutting of tree limbs to construct a cover for hunting out of season. In homicide cases it is the function of the forensic pathologist to establish that a confiscated ax could have been the weapon. Because of the nature of the evidence in other crimes the laboratory is sometimes able to demonstrate conclusively that an individual ax was used to commit a particular offense.

The basis of this analysis is the constant reproducibility, at least over a short span of time and usage, of the nicks, dents, and other minute irregularities in the cutting edge of the ax. The object cut must be suitable for receiving and capable of retaining these cutting-edge characteristics. When the student completes Case Exercise 4 (p 289) it should become evident that the insulation or fire retarding material in some safes is capable of retaining the identifying characteristics of an ax. Wood, copper wire, and sheet lead are other clue materials which have been found bearing ax marks useful for identity.

In the case presented in Case Exercise 4, the top of a safe was cut through in order to obtain the contents. Figure 6 —13 is a photograph of the safe. After the exterior metal skin was penetrated, the fire resistant lining of the safe was chopped with an ax. If a series of similar crimes had been committed over the next several months, it may have been possible to correlate them and to establish that they were the work of one person or gang. Even though an ax was not recovered this could have been accomplished by comparing the marks of one job with those of the others. Sometimes the pooled data which result are sufficient to provide the investigator with information that may suggest a suspect or that may solve the case(s). This is an example of the recognition of modus operandi through the use of science.

If an ax is recovered it is sometimes possible to establish that it was the one that was used to cut through the safe lining. Of course, this assumes that the part of the insulation materials bearing the ax characteristics has been preserved without alteration. Unfortunately, few investigators take the trouble to preserve such evidence. This neglect is attributable partly to lack of training and in part to the relative ease with which a confession is obtained upon apprehension of the criminal. The subsequent "bargain justice" or "deal" that is often made in return for a guilty plea to a lesser crime obviates the necessity for a trial. So commonplace is this procedure that physical evidence is frequently ignored by detectives. Because of the Supreme Court constitutional strictures now placed upon confessions, disregarding available physical evidence is becoming increasingly damaging and failure to provide the necessary proof that science makes possible may inflict a fatal blow to a case.

The processing of the physical evidence in this case required no more equipment than a good "4x5" camera and a photographic enlarger. Figure 6 — 14 is a photograph of a piece of safe insulation material removed from the lining remaining in the safe depicted in Fig. 6 — 13. Notice the several sets of ax-cut marks that are visible. In Case Exercise 4 two of these sets will be studied in detail.

It is important for investigators to know that the cutting-edge characteristics of an ax are reproducible. This knowledge is significant because it embodies, with some modification, the basic principle upon which all tool mark identification is based. The two photographs for Case Exercise 4 are enlargements of two separate ax marks illustrated in Fig. 6—14.

In this case an ax was not submitted for comparison purposes. Had this occurred, it would have been necessary to use the ax to make test cuts or chop marks in safe lining material similar to that bearing the crime scene impression or in another suitable medium such as plasticine or sheet lead. This would have permitted a comparison of the questioned crime scene impression against the exemplar or known test impression made with the particular ax. In Case Exercise 4 one ax mark is to be matched against another; both were present on the same piece of crime scene safe insulation as shown in Fig. 6 — 14. In other words, this exercise is a bit unusual, for it does not represent a comparison of a known with an unknown; instead, the source of both marks is unknown, that is, the particular ax involved was never obtained for comparison purposes. The case is included because it is admirably suited to demonstrate the reproducibility of tool marks.

Conclusion

Safe insulation material may bear evidence of the tool used to cut through it. Such marks must be recognized and preserved for comparison against any tool which is obtained for this purpose during the course of an investigation.

Simple photographic equipment available in most police agencies is capable of recording this evidence and of demonstrating that a particular ax was used, and the person in whose possession it was found may be linked to the crime.

The reproducibility of tool mark characteristics has been studied. This is a basic concept in tool mark individualization. Figure 6 — 15 depicts another method of establishing tool mark identity.

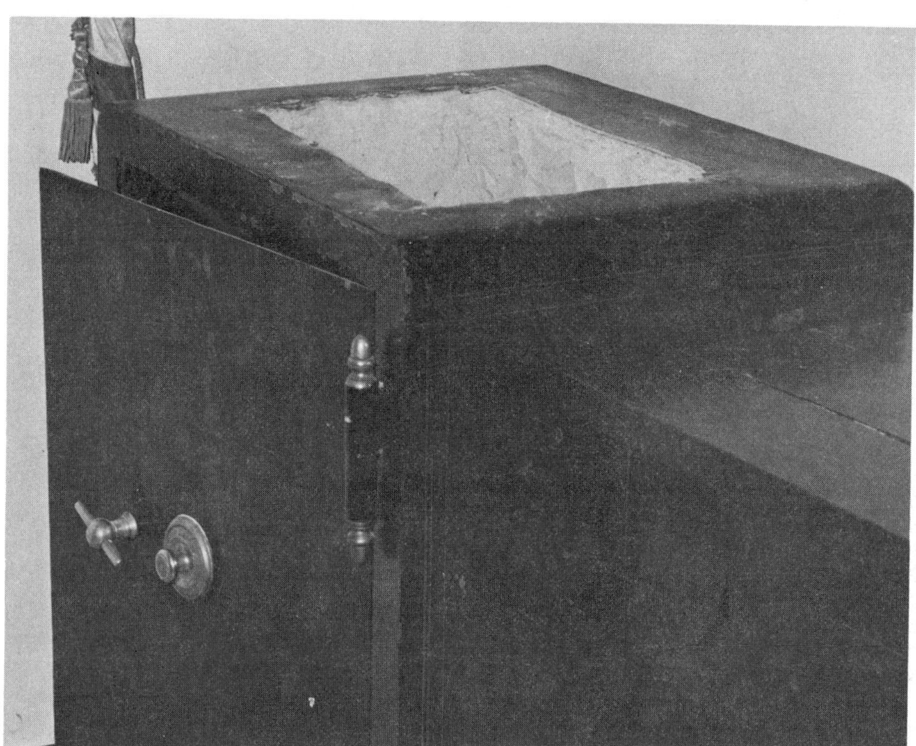

Fig. 6 — 13
Safe burglarized by a "chop job."

Fig. 6 — 14
Safe insulation material bearing several sets of chop marks.
(Courtesy, Dansville Police Department, New York.)

Fig. 6 — 15
Photomicrograph taken through comparison microscope. On the left is the scene evidence, heavy copper wire bearing an ax cut mark. On the right is a test cut mark made in sheet lead with a hatchet obtained from a suspect.
(Courtesy, Pittsburgh-Allegheny County Crime Laboratory, Office of District Attorney.)

C. Hammers

The most common criminal usage of hammers occurs when a dial is knocked off preparatory to "punching" a safe. (See Case Exercise 5, p 289.) Hammers also may be used to construct a ladder or other item necessary for the commission of a crime. A hammer's face quickly acquires scars and other evidence of improper use. Figure 6 — 16 depicts the face of a hammer showing evidence of hard work. Figure 6 — 17 shows an impression in wood left by striking with this hammer. If this were an actual case, an investigator would be confronted with the problem of preserving this impression for comparison purposes if a hammer is recovered during the course of the investigation. The following discussion is intended to cover the means of dealing with this problem and to indicate the value of the various methods that are available.

In general the means of comparing a tool with its impression are as follows:

1. Make a cast of the tool imprint (Fig. 6 — 18) and compare it directly with the tool in question (Fig. 6 — 16).
2. Compare the tool directly with the impression, i.e., compare Fig. 6 — 16 with Fig. 6 — 17.
3. Print the face of the tool — photographically reversed — and then compare it directly with the tool impression, i.e., compare Fig. 6—19 with Fig. 6 — 17.

The student should make no generalizations from the above study but should appreciate that there is no one best way to establish an identity. Ingenuity and a willingness to try all alternative methods are far more important than relying on "armchair science" or in blindly following the recommendations in a textbook.

Figure 6—20 depicts a method of comparison of hammer marks left on the face of a safe door with a suspected hammer.

Fig. 6 — 16
Face of hammer showing imperfections.

Fig. 6 — 17
Impression left in wood after being struck by hammer face shown in Fig. 6 — 16.

Fig. 6 — 18
Metal cast of impression shown in Fig. 6 — 17. Note loss of details.

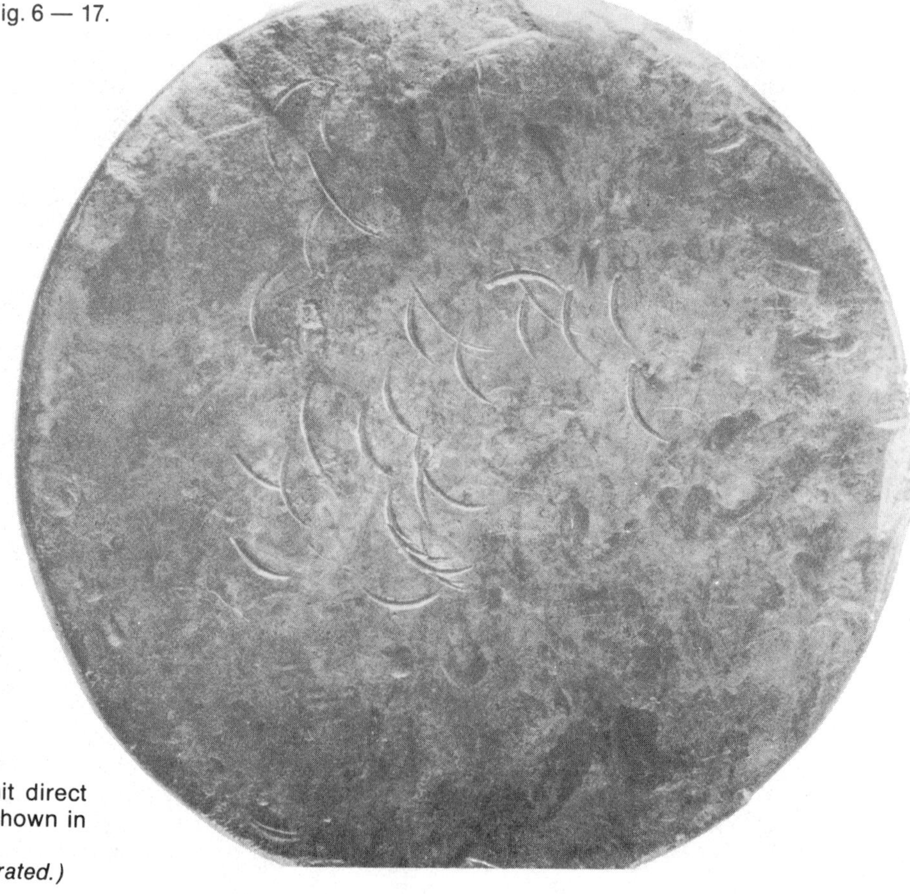

Fig. 6 — 19
Reverse printing of Fig. 6 — 16 to permit direct comparison of hammer face with imprint shown in Fig. 6 — 17.
(Courtesy, MacDonell Associates, Incorporated.)

Fig. 6 — 20
Photomicrograph comparison of questioned hammer marks on face of safe door and known hammer marks, made with the suspected hammer, in a safe burglary case.
(Courtesy, Federal Bureau of Investigation.)

D. Metal Cutters

The variety of instruments which are used to cut metal ranges from the cold chisel and hacksaw to the can opener. Four tools commonly employed by criminals, especially burglars, have been selected to illustrate how crime evidence generally is converted to associative evidence when the tool is discovered during the investigation.

Figure 6—21 is a photomicrograph comparing the edge of a piece of sheet metal cut from a safe to a test cut made with a pair of metal shears found in the possession of a suspect.

A padlock shackle which was clipped with a bolt and rod cutter is shown in Fig. 6 — 22. In Fig. 6—23 the severed shackle ends are shown fitted into the area of the cutter jaws which were damaged while shearing the hardened steel of the padlock. A normal three dimensional view, or better, a low-power stereomicroscopic examination is even more convincing. With the actual evidence, of course, this type of examination is possible although it is not difficult to perceive the relationship involved even in a two dimensional photograph.

Figure 6 — 24 illustrates a rather unusual tool comparison in that although the actual tool was never located, an identity was nevertheless established. A piece of pipe, with a chisel inserted into it for leverage, was found at the scene of a burglary. Subsequently, a piece of galvanized pipe was recovered from a suspect's automobile. Both pieces were quite different, *viz.*, in diameter and composition; however, both had ends which were cut with an ordinary rotary pipe cutter. The extremities of both pipes were examined under the comparison microscope.

Many investigators would assume that because the two pipes were of different diameter such a comparison would not be possible. The photomicrograph (Fig. 6 — 25) dispels this notion, and the case illustrates that clue materials should not be ruled out until they are thoroughly examined in the crime laboratory.

The case illustrations selected for this section will provide the reader with a realization that there is more to tool mark identification than the mere examination of jimmies and safe tools. The range of possibilities in tool mark investigations is, according to Meyers and Kivela, almost limitless:

> The availability of tool markings as evidence in criminal cases goes beyond the human imagination. Almost any type of crime can be solved through the recognition of tool mark evidence and the subsequent examination and identification in the laboratory.
>
> . . . important tool mark evidence may be overlooked by the criminal investigator if he is not cognizant of the wide applicability of this type of evidence.
>
> . . . By showing [criminal investigators] what can be done with tool marks and acquainting them with the unlimited possibilities in this work, more and more tool mark cases have come to the attention of the laboratory.[3]

6.2 Exercises 2, 3, 4, 5, 6 (pp 288-289)

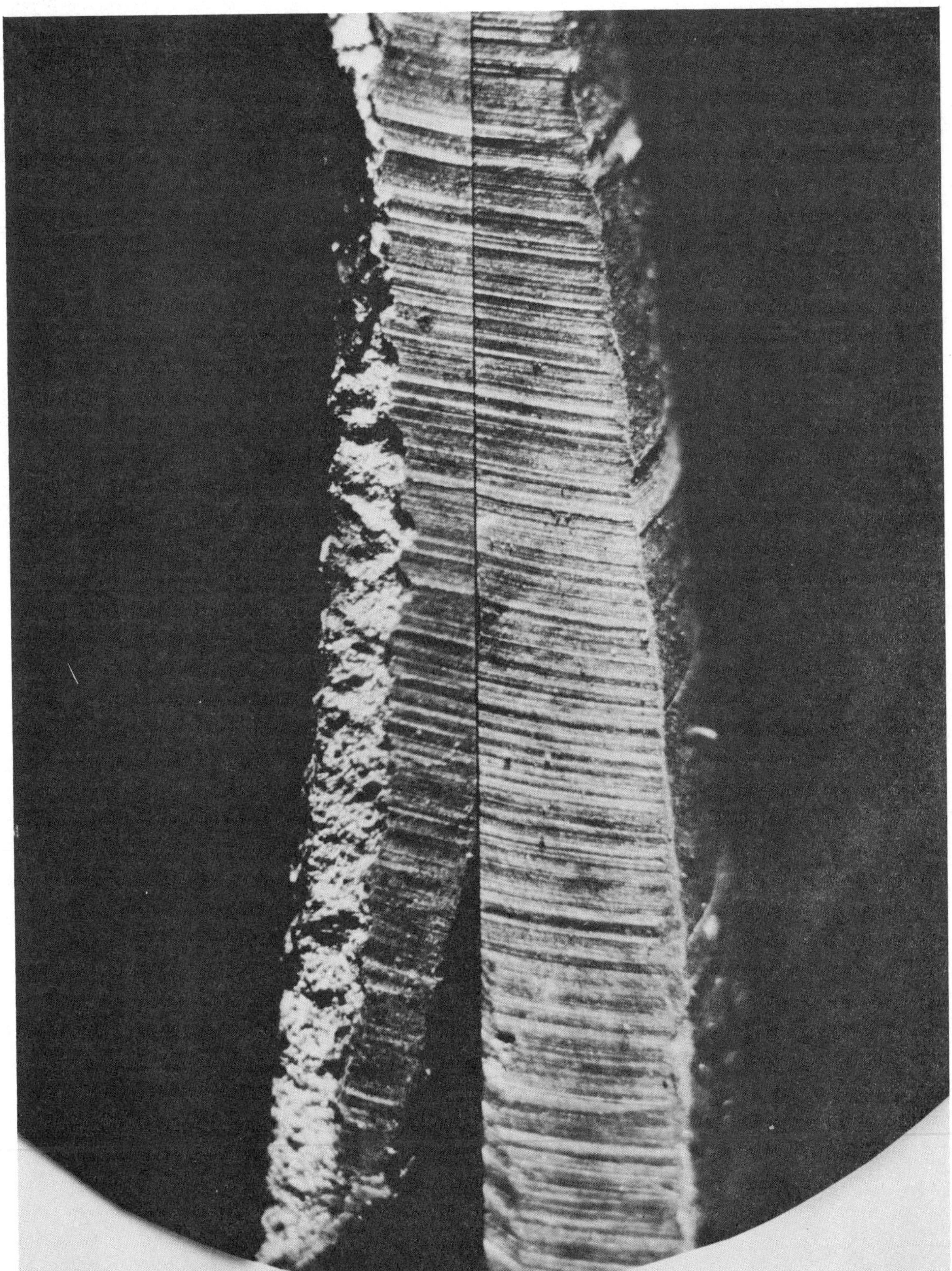

Fig. 6 — 21
Comparison photomicrograph. On the left is the edge of a sheet metal section cut from a safe. On the right is a test cut made with the suspect's metal shears.
(Courtesy, Pittsburgh-Allegheny County Crime Laboratory, Office of District Attorney.)

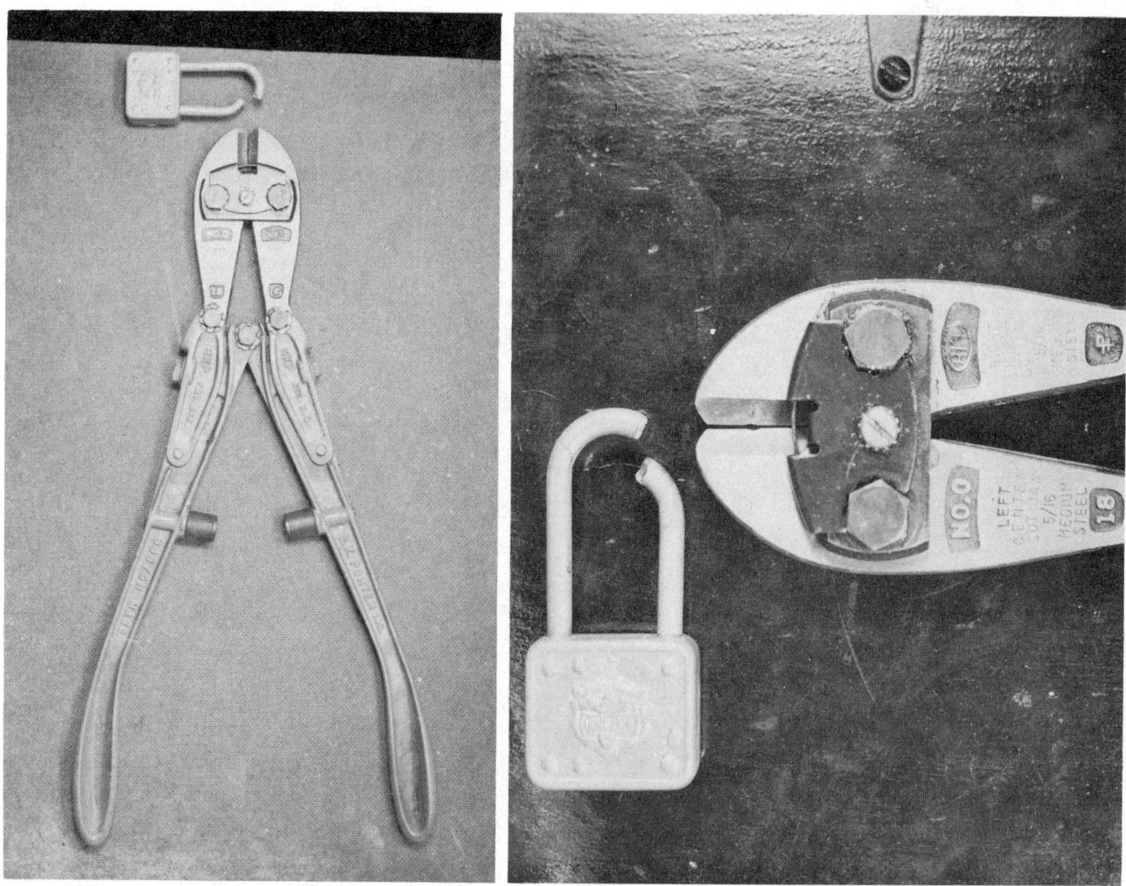

Fig. 6 — 22
Bolt cutter and cut padlock. Note damaged area (indentation) in cutter jaws.

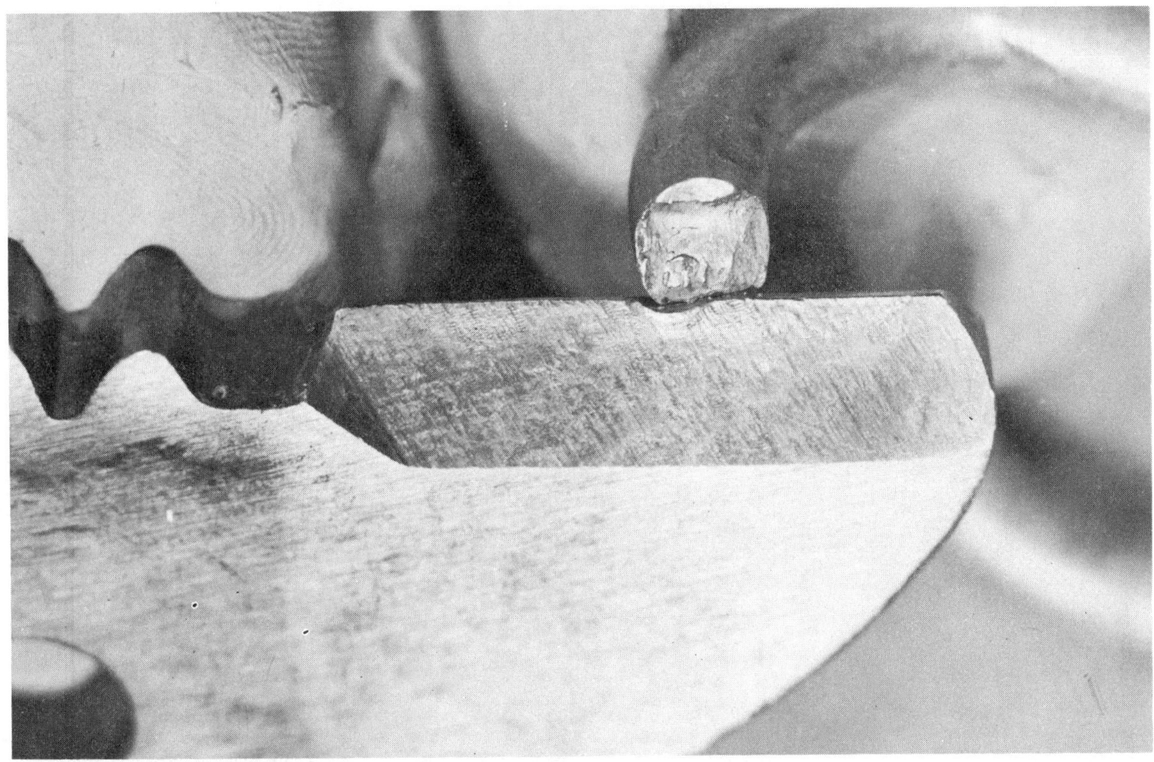

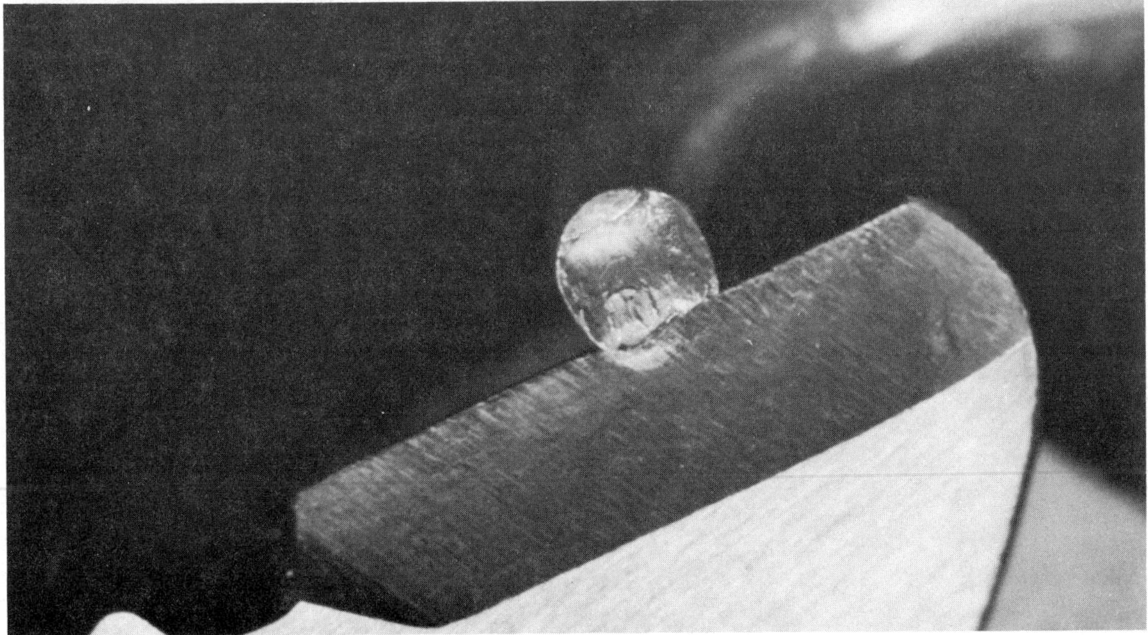

Fig. 6 — 23
Cut shackle ends fitted into damaged area of bolt cutter jaws.
(Courtesy, Toledo Police Department, Ohio.)

Fig. 6 — 24
Pipe on the left, with chisel inserted into one end, was found at crime scene. Galvanized pipe on the right was recovered from automobile of suspect.

Fig. 6 — 25
Comparison photomicrograph of two cut ends of different sized pipes. Lower half is contributed by crime scene evidence; top half was made using pipe found in suspect's automobile.
(Courtesy, Illinois Bureau of Criminal Identification and Investigation.)

6.3 Machinist Dies, Typefaces, and Metal Punches

The more elaborate the crime, the greater the preparation required for its successful execution. Forgery, auto thefts involving alterations of motor serial numbers, counterfeiting, and burglary are but a few examples that require some skill in the use of tools and instruments. When a crime of this nature is discovered, sufficient physical evidence may be available to link a suspect to the crime if the tools employed in its execution are found in his possession or in some area under his control.

A. Machinist Dies and Typefaces

Identifying serial numbers are placed on products by the manufacturers of automobiles, guns, typewriters, sewing machines, outboard motors, and so on. The owner may have a record of the serial number and when such property is stolen, the prospect of locating the culprit through the stolen property file is greater than if no serial number is available. When a gang systematically steals items such as automobiles, they often resort to altering the serial numbers to avoid risk of apprehension. Metal dies are used to make the changes; therefore, it is sometimes possible to demonstrate that a set of dies found in the possession of a gang was used to stamp the new numbers now present on the evidence. (See Case Exercise 7, p289.) Figure 6—26 is a photomacrograph (*v.i.*) of a suspected die seized in a case.

Die marks are also placed on articles by some governments as an official indication of genuineness or superior quality. In some countries the presence of this stamped impression attests that the tax or duty has been paid on the material in question. It is obvious that under these circumstances counterfeit dies will be used from time to time to defraud both the individual and the state. Nickolls provides an illustration of the unlawful use of a hallmark on a gold cigarette case.[4]

Typewriter individualization is a laboratory problem related to the identity of machinist dies. Without fully exploring this subject it may be said that imperfectly shaped letters serve in part to characterize typewritten material. Among other things, the wear and damage to the die or typeface characterize them from the criminalist's viewpoint.[5] One technique that renders visible details of the damage and wear is called *photomacrography*, a process in which the lens of the camera is used as though it were the objective lens of a microscope. The enlarged image has details which are clearer or more discernible than otherwise to the naked eye. Photomacrography is therefore a technique of considerable importance in crime laboratory operation. Figures 6 — 27, 6 — 28, and 6—29 are photomacrographs of typefaces "H," "O," and "g."

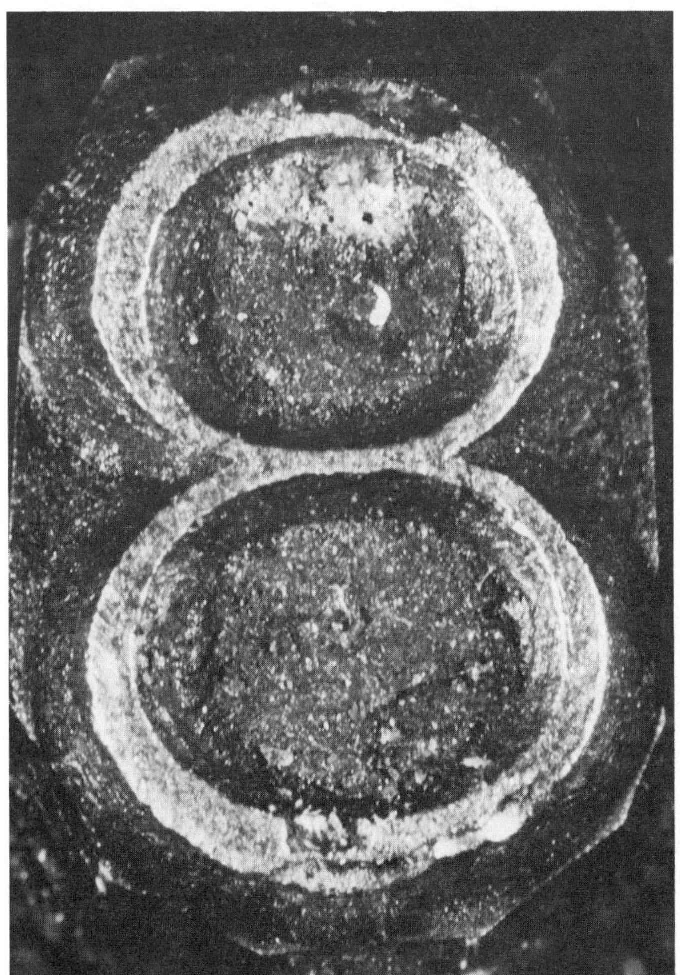

Fig 6—26
Photomacrograph (ca. 17X) of a suspected die (original size 3/16 inch). Note defects on face of die in the twelve and six o'clock positions that would serve to characterize any impression made with this die.
(Courtesy, New York City Police Department.)

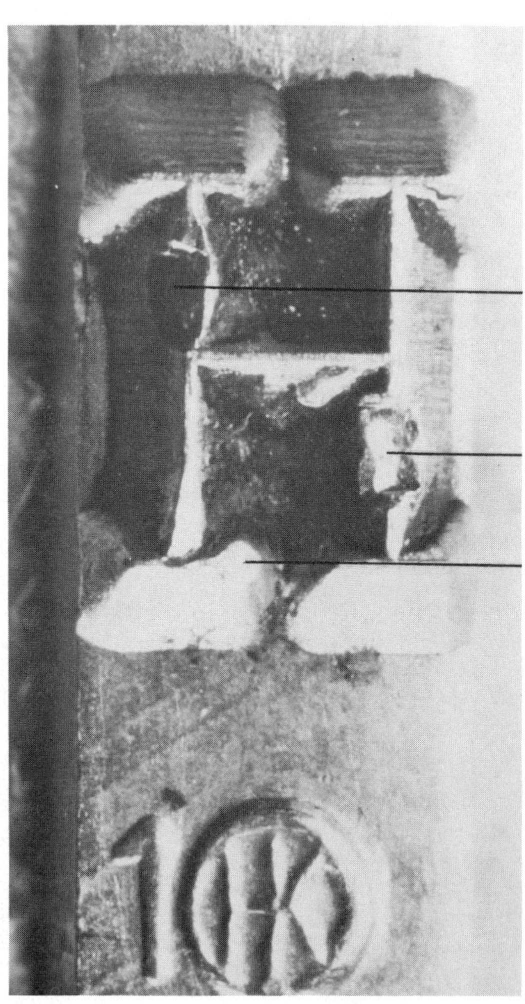

Fig. 6 — 27
Photomacrograph (ca. 15X) of a typeface of the letter "H" marked to indicate areas of damage or individual characteristics.

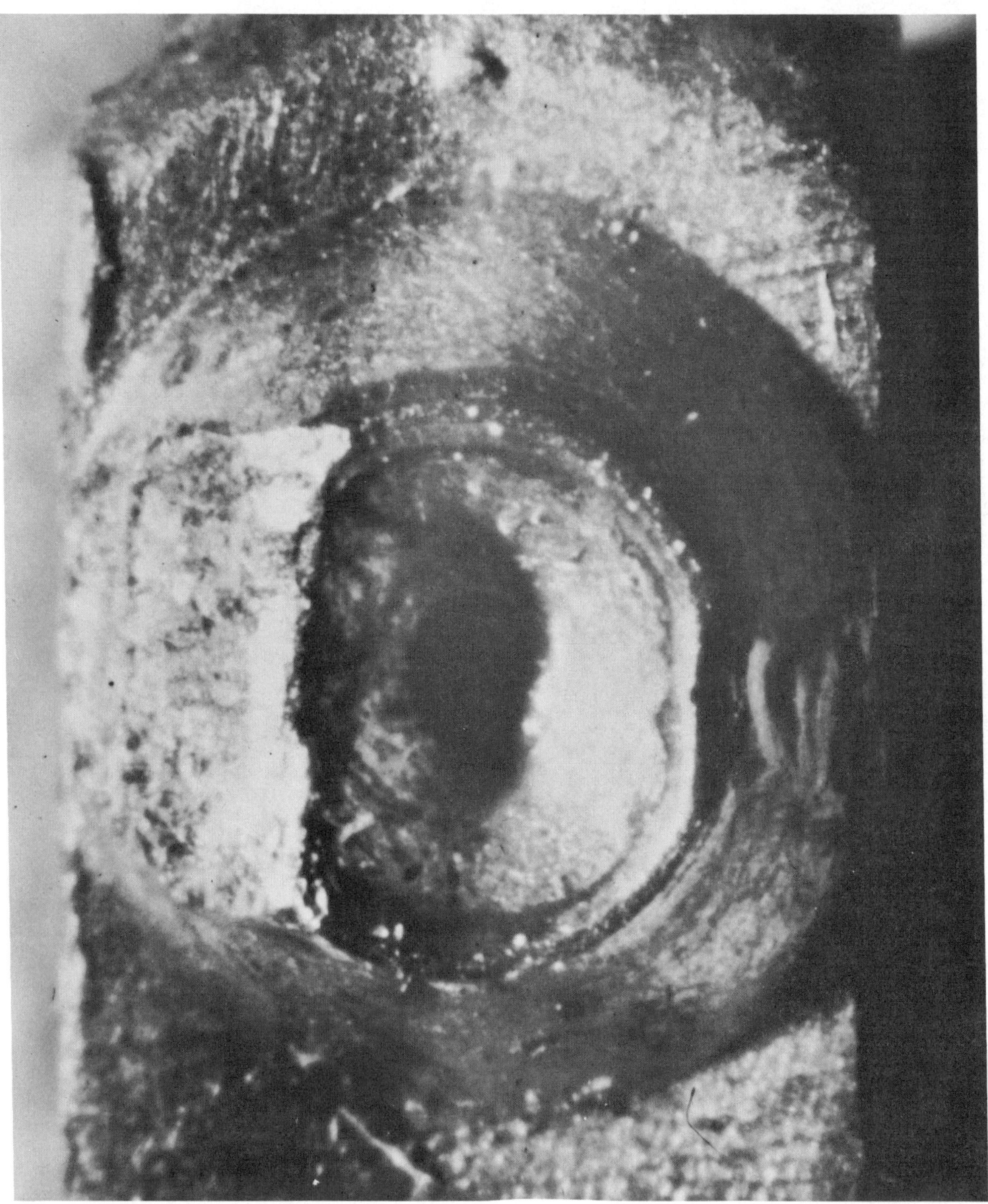

Fig. 6 — 28
Photomacrograph (ca. 30X) of a typeface of the letter "O." Characterizing defects are present but unmarked.

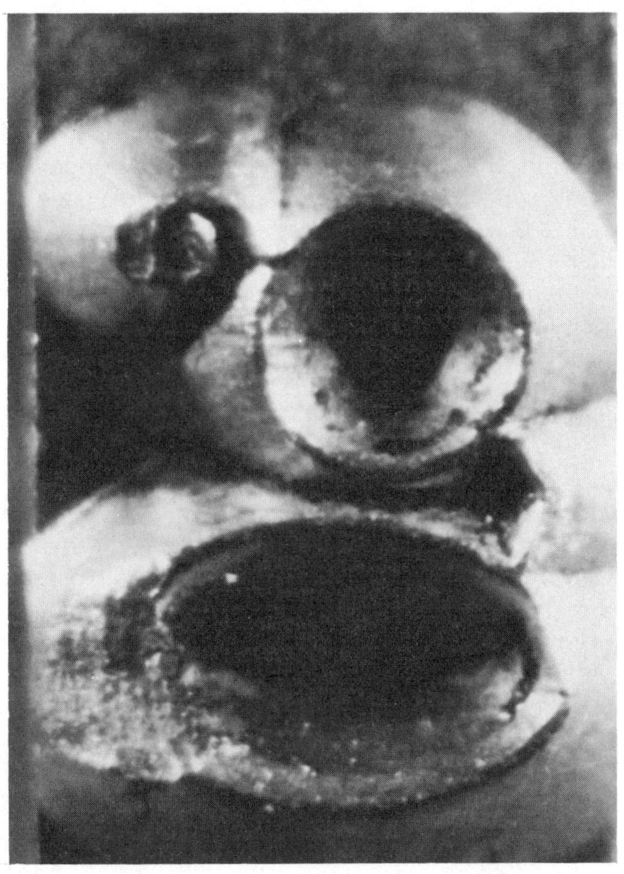

Fig. 6 — 29
Photomacrograph (ca. 20X) of a typeface of the letter "g." Characterizing defects are present but unmarked.

B. Metal Punches

Tool impressions in the form of compression marks are left by metal punches, stamping dies, and hammers. The latter two instruments are considered elsewhere in the text; this section will concern itself with two cases involving punches — one is a burglary and the other a larceny by counterfeit.

The first case involves the illegal entry of a shoe store and the subsequent opening of its safe, which was accomplished by knocking off the dial and punching out the spindle. In the course of this operation the metal punch slipped and struck the brass surrounding the spindle, leaving an impression of a section of the tip of the punch. Figure 6 — 30 shows an end-on view of the brass surrounding the spindle. Striated marks left by the punch are visible at the five to six o'clock position. The photograph has been printed in reverse to facilitate comparison later when a tool is submitted for this purpose. As a part of the laboratory investigation, a silicone rubber cast was made of the brass area containing the tool mark. This is shown in Fig. 6 — 31 where the tool's striations may be noted again in the lower middle portion of the photograph.

When a suspect was apprehended, a punch was discovered in his possession. It was photographed by directing the light perpendicular to the striations on its tip (Fig. 6 — 32). Figure 6—33 is an enlarged composite photograph of Fig. 6—32 upon which Fig. 6—30 (the punched brass impression) has been superimposed; in turn, the striations recorded in the photograph of the silicone cast have been cut out of Fig. 6 — 31 and superimposed on Fig. 6 — 30. The alignment of all three sets of striations is visible upon study of the composite picture.

The next case occurred in western Pennsylvania, where several self-operated laundries were plagued by a rash of thefts of silver coins from money-changing machines through the use of valueless quarter- and half-dollar-sized copper blanks (Fig. 6—34). The situation involved the crime laboratory when two suspects were apprehended in one of the establishments with 243 quarter- and 535 half-dollar-sized copper blanks in their possession and the confiscated blanks were submitted for examination.

Meanwhile, a teletype description of the modus operandi sent to neighboring police departments resulted in the receipt of additional blanks which had been used to victimize over seventeen laundries in other western and central Pennsylvania counties. An examination of the blanks submitted from all areas disclosed similarities in thickness, general appearance, and surface imprint marks.

Subsequent investigation revealed that the source of the blanks was a reputable machine shop. An examination of the stamping dies in the shop disclosed the origin of the imprints noted on the blanks. The operation of the stamping process involves an upper assembly that rides down upon a spring loaded lower assembly. The blank stock and the stripper of the lower assembly are forced down while the unyielding punch forces a punched blank up into the die and against the knockout which then removes the blank when the upper assembly is raised again for another cycle. Figures 6 — 35, 6 — 36 further illustrate the origin of the die imprints on the blanks. Figure 6—37 is a photograph taken with the comparison microscope of the matching of the striated marks present on the blanks in the area of the die imprint.

Inasmuch as the counterfeit blanks were produced in separate production runs, the depth of the impressed marks varied from a deep, obvious design to those which were barely visible and not suitable for a comparison purpose. Those blanks that did not bear suitable impressed marks were identified by the shear marks on the thin edge of the blanks which were caused by irregularities on the inner edge of the stamping dies (Fig. 6—38).

6.3 Exercises 7, 8 (p 289)

Fig. 6 — 30
End view of brass surrounding spindle of punched safe.

Fig. 6 — 31
Silicone rubber cast of area of brass shown in Fig. 6 — 30 bearing striated marks left by the punch or tool.

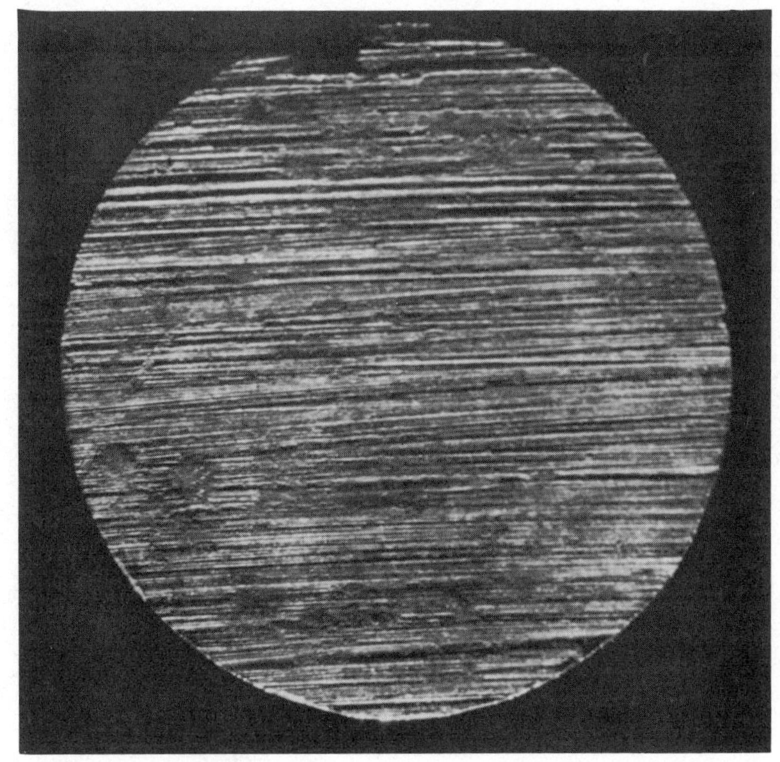

Fig. 6 — 32
Suspected punch photographed by oblique illumination to highlight striated marks on its tip or "working end."

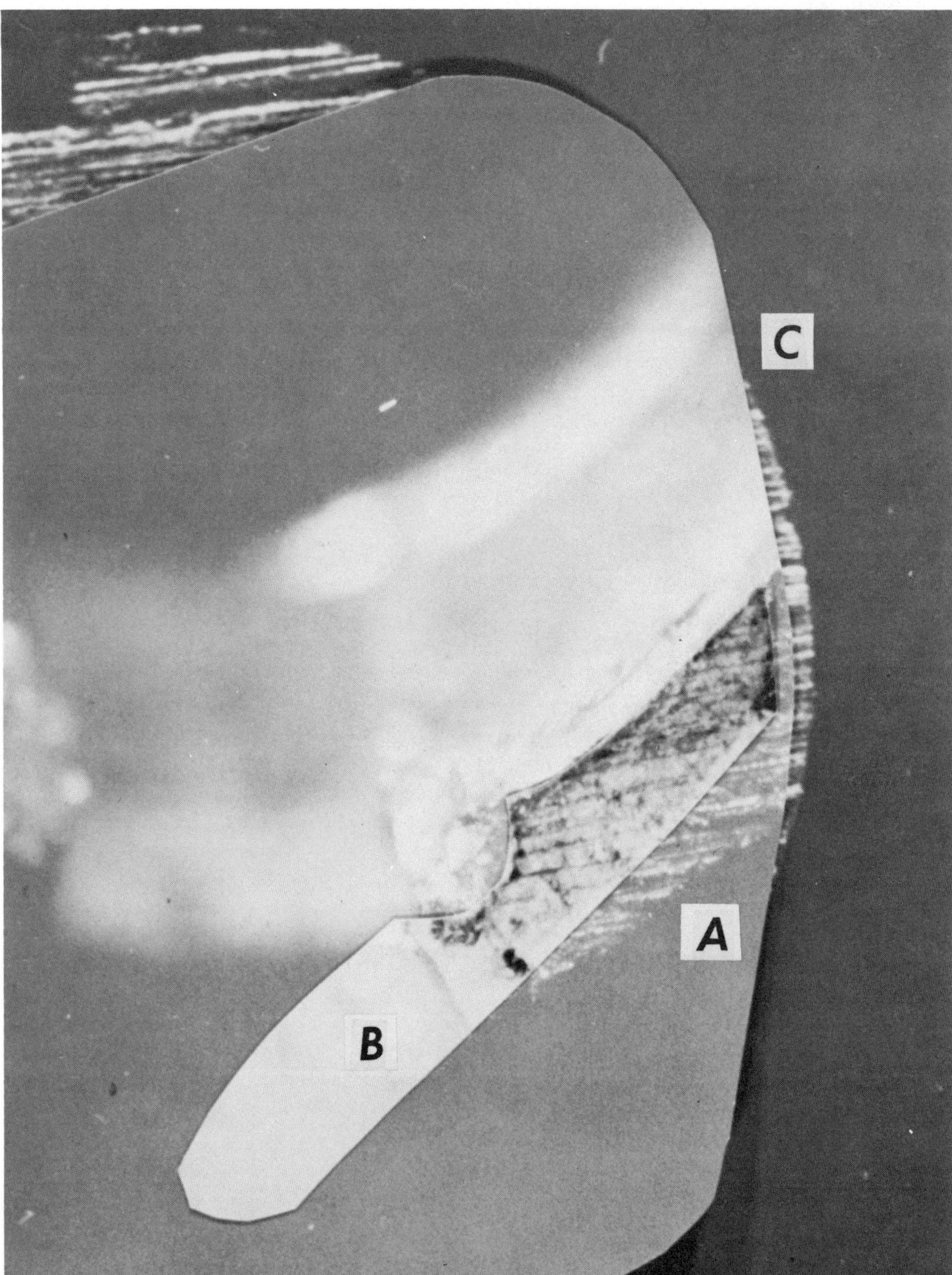

Fig. 6 — 33
Enlarged composite photograph prepared by superimposing portions of the first two figures on Fig. 6 — 32:

A. Cutout portion of Fig. 6 — 30
B. Cutout portion of Fig. 6 — 31
C. Portion of Fig. 6 — 32

(Courtesy, Illinois Bureau of Criminal Identification and Investigation.)

Fig. 6 — 34
Photomacrograph of stamped quarter-size blank used to defraud coin change machine. Note die mark in the two to four o'clock position.

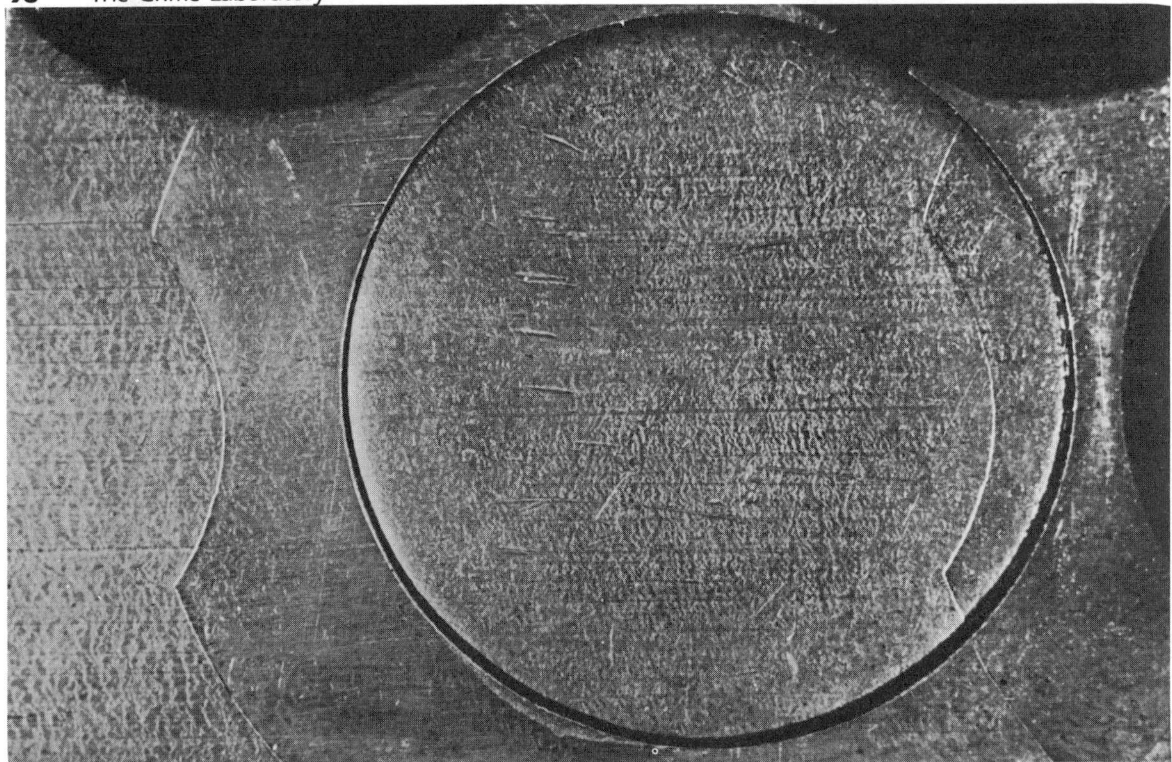

Fig. 6 — 35
Photomacrograph of stamped quarter blank replaced in stock to illustrate position (and origin — cf. Fig. 6 — 36) of die mark.

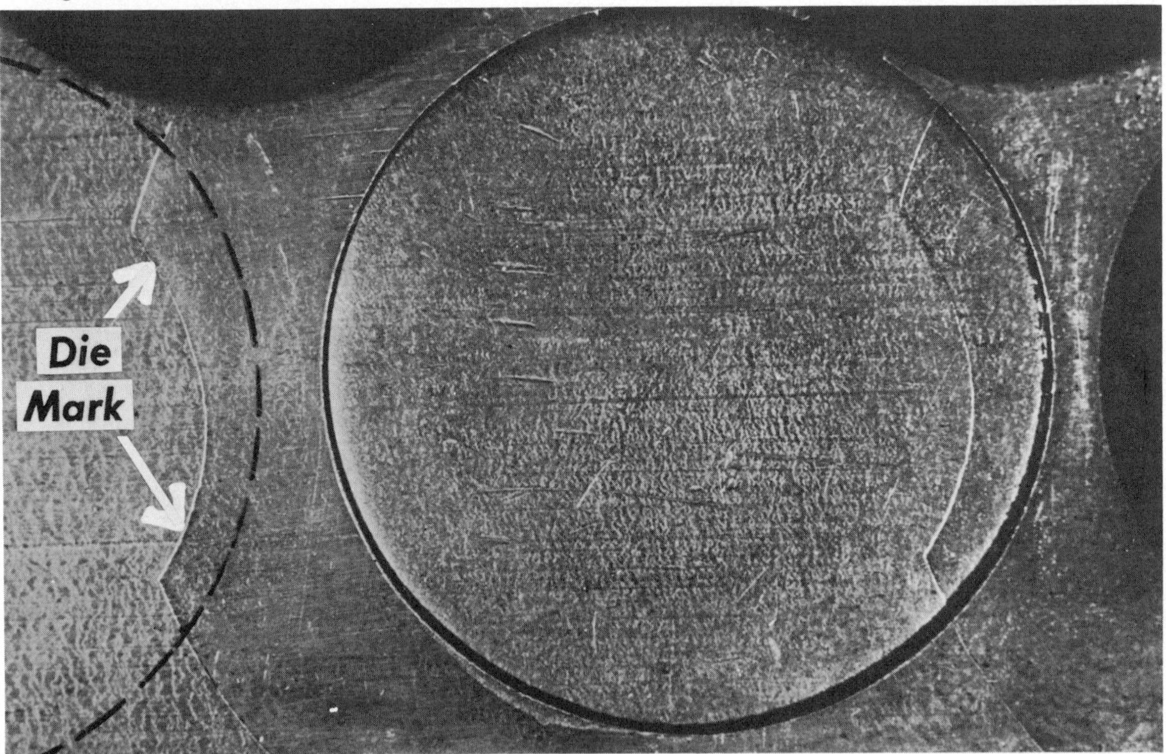

Fig. 6 — 36
Die mark on quarter-size blank is received when the blank to its right is stamped. The dotted ink line on the left side of the stock outlines partially the next blank and its die mark after (and if) it is punched.

Striated marks (cf. Fig. 6 — 37), although not visible under the conditions of illumination used to make this photograph, are left along the edge of the depressed die mark.

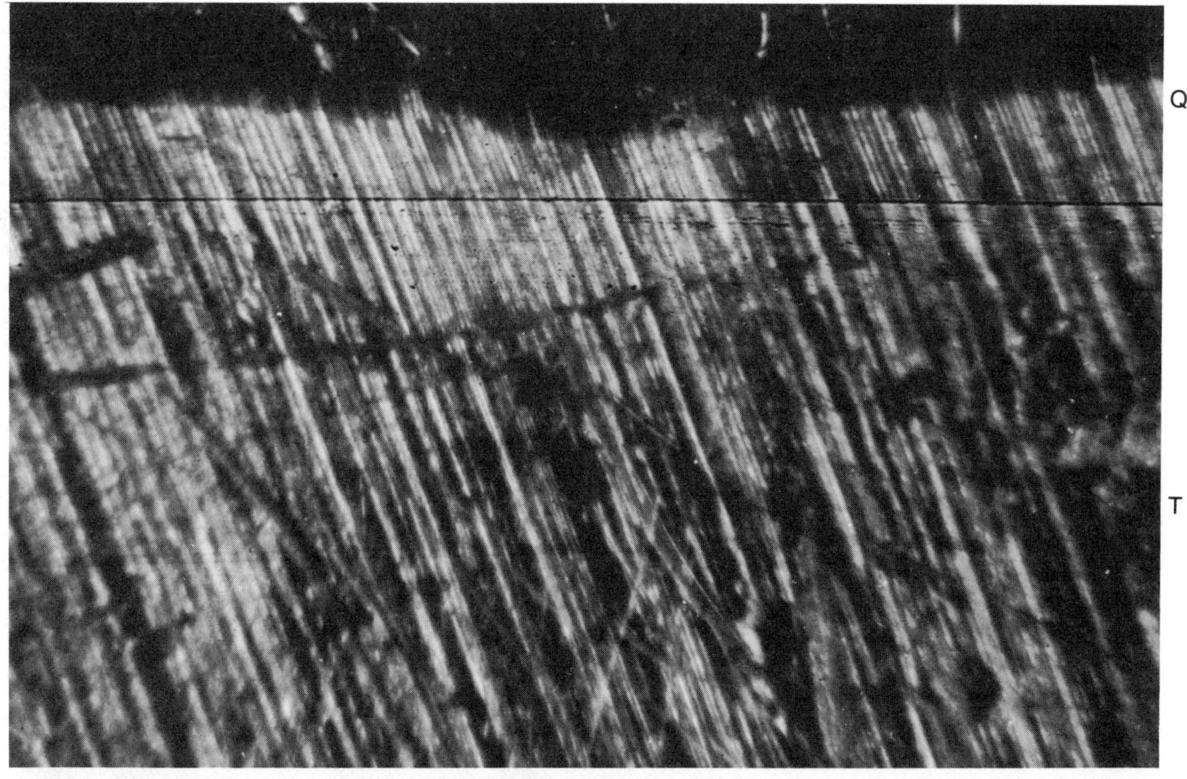

Fig. 6 — 37
Match of striated marks present on face of known test blank (T) and base of counterfeit blank (Q) found in defrauded coin changer.

Fig. 6 — 38
Comparison microscope photograph of shear marks on edge of test blank (T) and edge of counterfeit blank (Q) found in defrauded coin changer.
(Courtesy, Pittsburgh-Allegheny County Crime Laboratory, Office of District Attorney.)

6.4 Weapons

Valuables are surrendered under compulsion induced by some form of intimidation. Guns, knives, clubs, and similar weapons are employed in crime because of their universal recognition and effectiveness as a menace to the intended victim's safety. Notes used in kidnaping or bank robbery serve to remind the victim of a latent or future threat if compliance with the criminal demand is not forthcoming. Rape is yet another crime in which intimidation is often important to its execution.

In crimes where more than implied threat is used, physical evidence (a fired bullet or cartridge case) may be recovered at the scene, or a weapon is sometimes discarded along the path of flight taken by the criminal. Identification and thorough search of the escape route is required to recover a weapon or other physical evidence that may have been discarded.

The use of these clue materials in the development of associative evidence is studied in this chapter.

A. Firearms

Defense attorneys are relying more and more frequently on the opinions of expert physical evidence consultants to check the work of the state's expert in cases involving firearms. Undoubtedly, this reliance will become entrenched as attorneys become better informed of the availability of these experts and realize the extent of expertise brought to the task of establishing an identity between a suspect's firearm and the cartridge found at a crime scene.

In urban areas, revolvers and pistols are favorite weapons employed in the commission of numerous felonies — homicide, robbery, assault, and malicious mischief being some of the more serious. In comparison, rifles and shotguns are more likely to be used in a rural area. Regardless of the type of firearm, when it is discharged, physical evidence in the form of a bullet, cartridge case or shell, and occasionally a gunshot pattern, may be available to the investigator.

1. Bullets

Although there are many technical questions that arise in connection with the use of a firearm,* a major query is: "Can the gun found in the possession of the defendant be linked with the bullet (or cartridge case) found at the scene of the crime?" There are several ways in which an answer can be provided. A test bullet is fired through the suspected firearm with great care so that no damage occurs to the bullet. The crime scene and test fired bullets are then compared under the comparison microscope. (See Case Exercise 9, p 289.)

Figure 6 — 39 is a photograph of a match between the bullet that was found on the stretcher used to carry Gov. John B. Connally of Texas into Parkland Memorial Hospital in Dallas, Texas, and a test bullet fired by the FBI through Lee Harvey Oswald's (Mannlicher-Carcano) rifle.

Crime scene bullets quite often are recovered in a mutilated condition. For example, the fragmented bullet depicted in Fig. 6 — 40 passed through a plate glass window and the body of the victim before it was finally stopped by a stainless steel sink. Even though it was badly damaged, an identity was readily established (Fig. 6 — 41). Bullets without any damage have been recovered in other cases (Fig. 6 — 42).

*For example: "At what distance was the victim shot?" "Can you determine from an examination of a person's hand or cheek whether he fired a gun?" "Could the gun have been discharged accidentally?" "What kind of gun fired the bullet?"

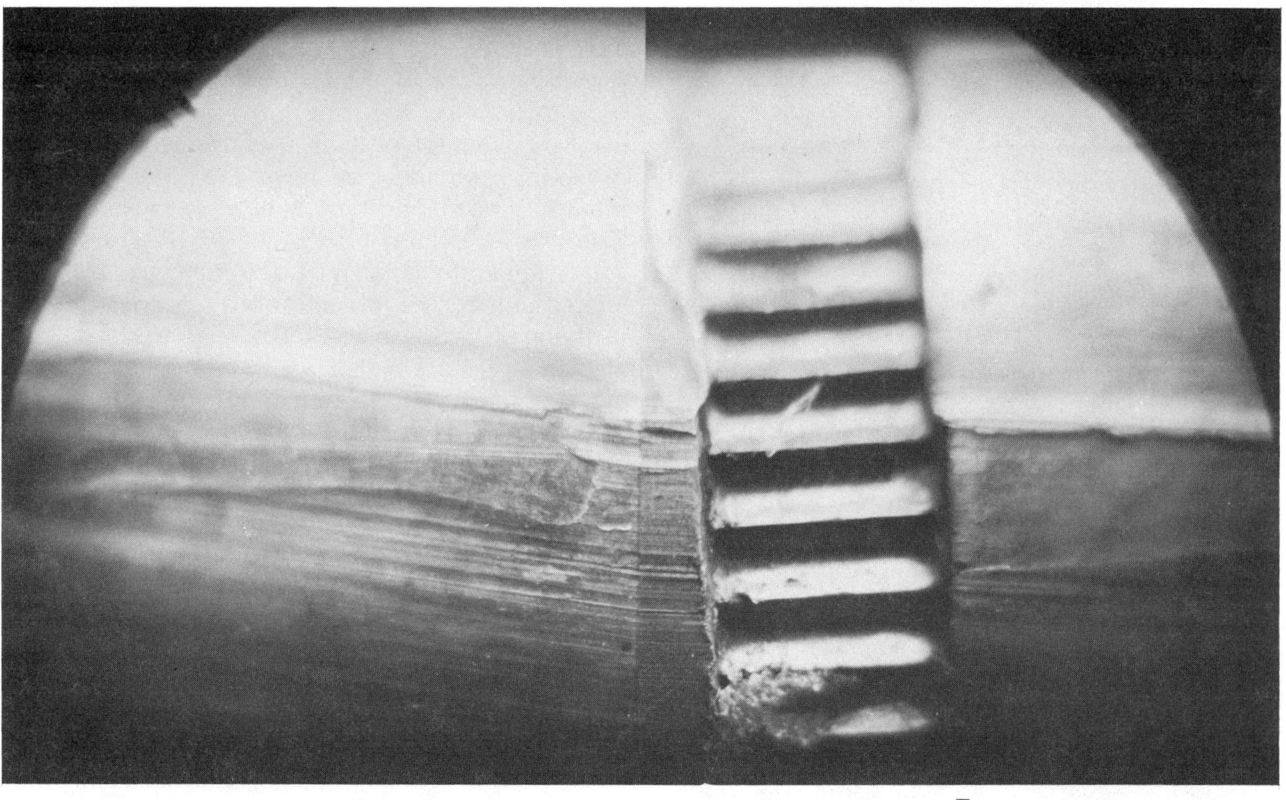

Fig. 6 — 39
Comparison microscope photograph of stretcher bullet (Q) and the test bullet (T) fired through Oswald rifle in Kennedy assassination.
(Courtesy, Joseph D. Nicol.)

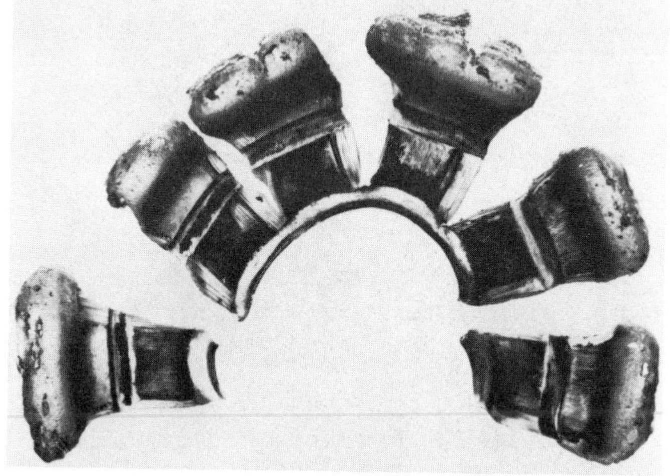

Fig. 6 — 40
Fragmented crime scene bullet.

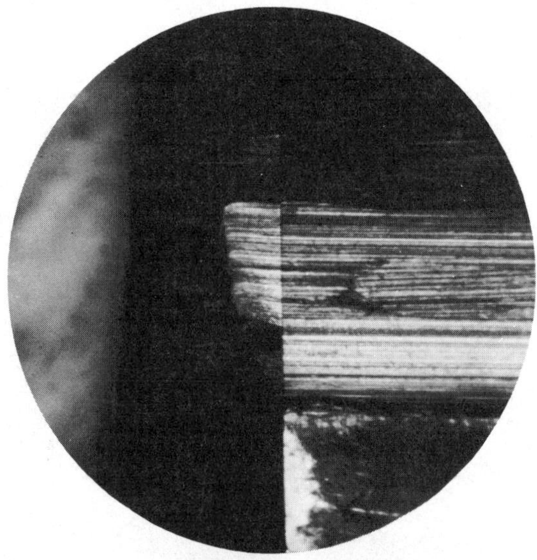

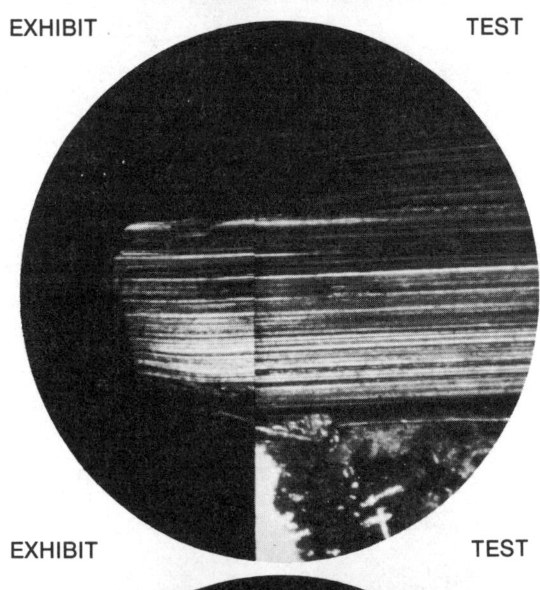

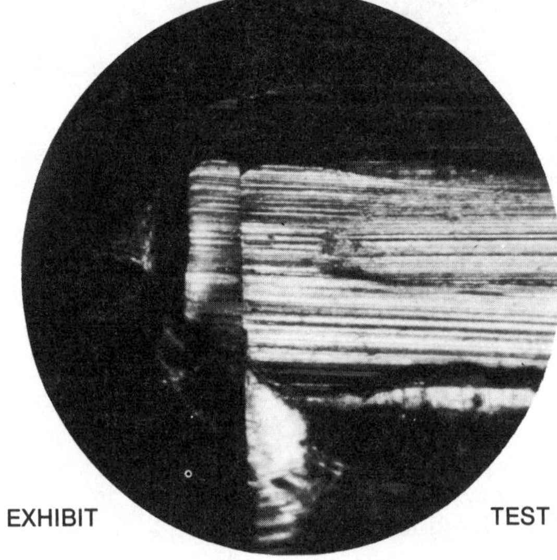

2. Cartridge Cases

A cartridge case can be linked to the gun that fired it in more than one way. One method involves a comparison of photomacrographs of the firing pin impressions on the primers of the questioned and test bullets. (See Case Exercise 10, p 289)

Individual characteristics of a firing pin are impressed onto the primer for two reasons: (a) the firing pin is driven with force into the primer after the trigger is pulled, and (6) the primer is pressed hard against the firing pin by the explosive reaction of heated powder in the cartridge, causing surface irregularities in the pin to be impressed onto the primer metal. The second reason also accounts for the impression and retention of the breech face marks of a rifle or hand gun on the head of a cartridge fired in the weapon. (See Case Exercise 11, pp 289-290.)

The second method involves a comparison of photomacrographs of breech marks on the cartridge heads. Figure 6—43 depicts an identity between two cartridge heads based on breech face marks. An interesting set of marks on a cartridge head is shown in Figs. 6 — 44, 6—45, and 6—46. They represent different areas of the head of one of the spent rifle shells found at the book depository in Dallas following the assassination of President Kennedy. The marks appear to be randomly located around the rim of the shell which suggests that the same mechanical operation had taken place three times. One possible explanation offered is that the marks are the result of chambering and withdrawal of the cartridge in some practice or dry firing operation. Figure 6—47 illustrates the common origin of all three marks.

Fig. 6 — 41
Comparison photomicrographs of three areas of fragmented exhibit bullet (Fig. 6 — 40) matched against a test bullet fired through a suspected weapon.

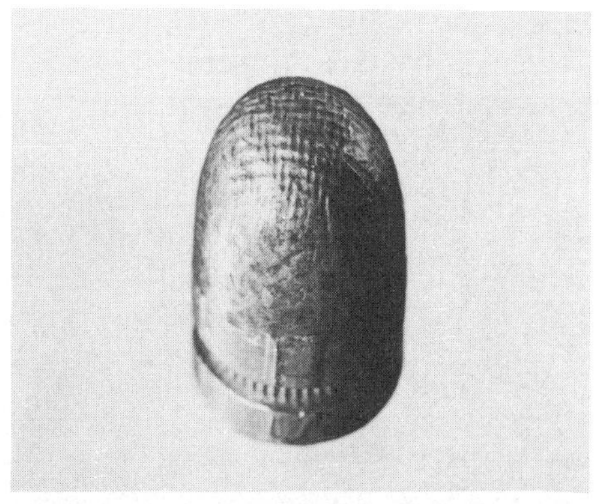

Fig. 6 — 42
Crime scene bullet recovered with an imprint on its nose of the texture of the jacket through which it passed.

Fig. 6 — 43
Comparison microscope photograph showing a match between two cartridge heads. Dividing line between test and crime scene bullet runs horizontally through middle of illustration.
(Courtesy, Attorney-General Laboratory, Ontario, Canada.)

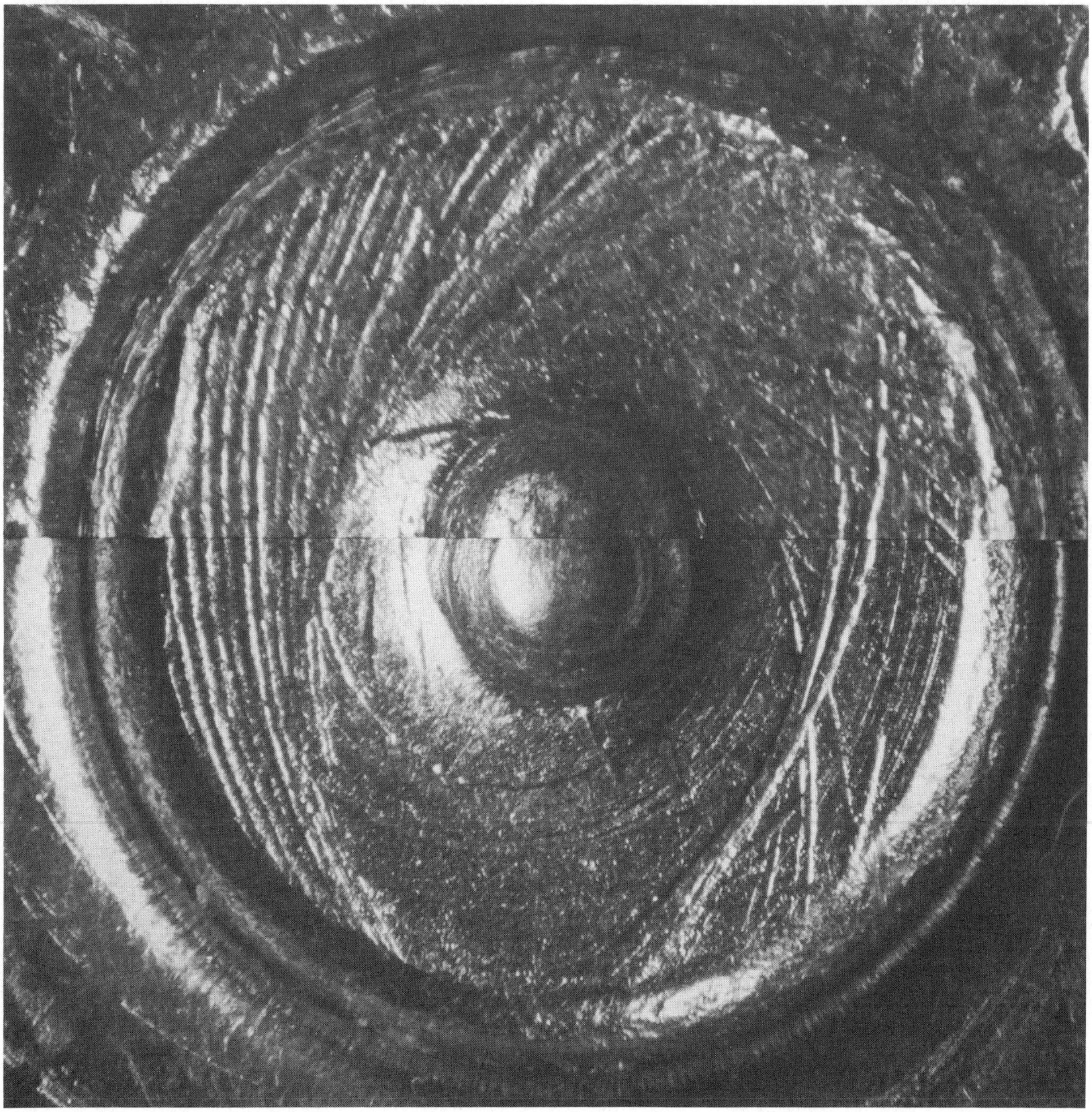

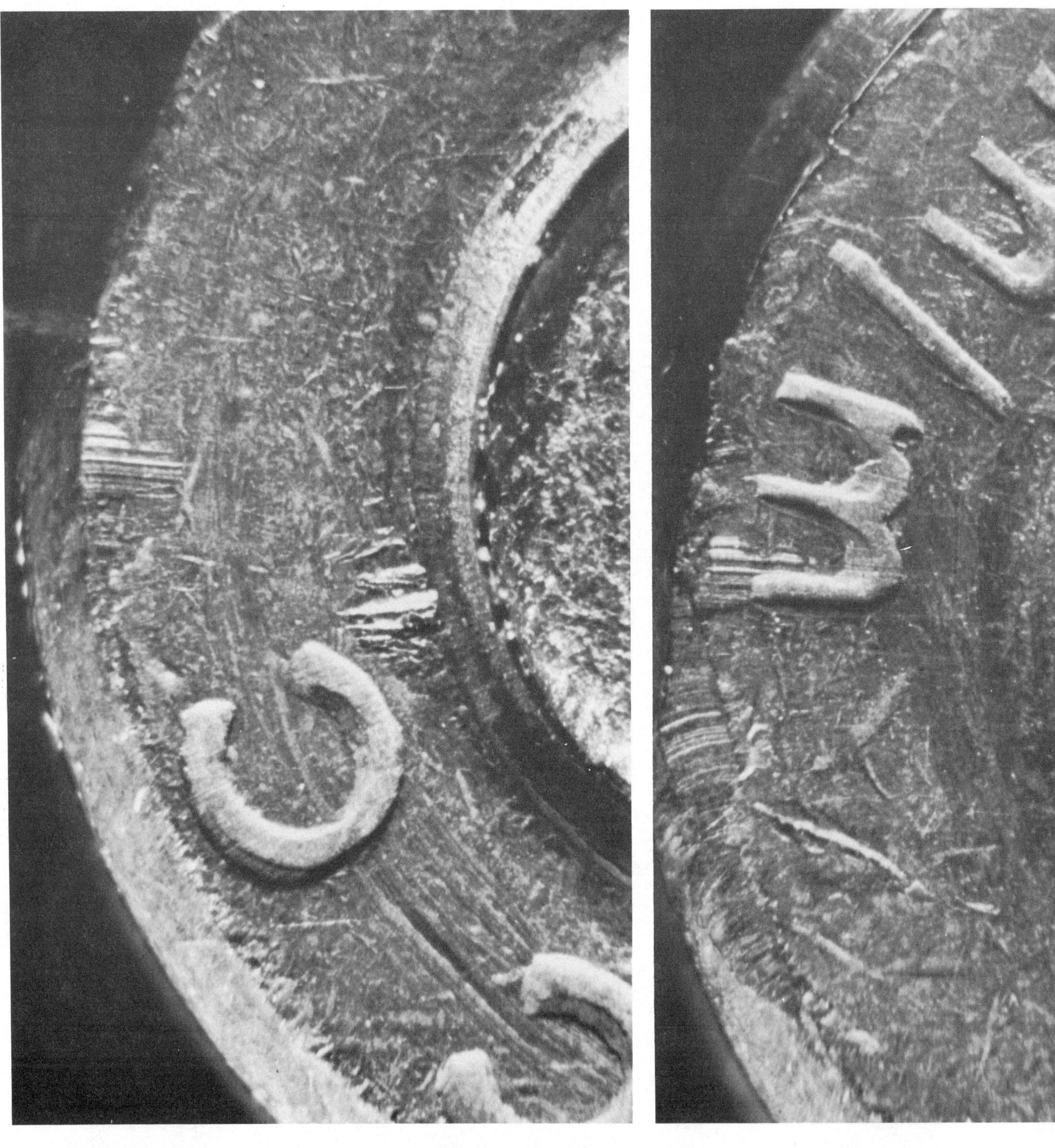

Fig 6 — 44
Mark on rifle shell head.

Fig. 6 — 45
Mark on rifle shell head.

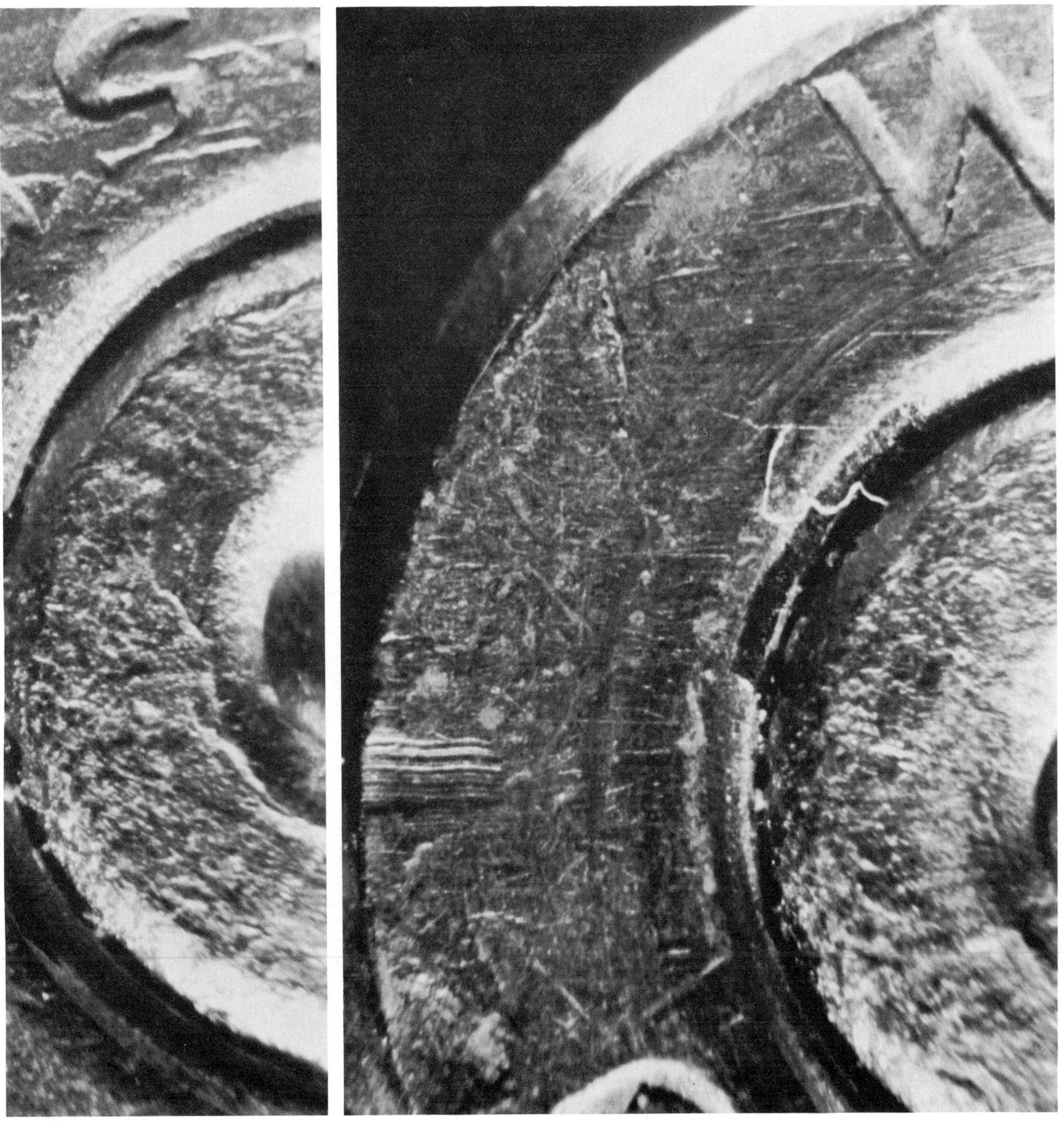

Fig. 6 — 46
Mark repeated in three locations on head of rifle shell found at book depository following assassination of President Kennedy.

Fig. 6 — 47
Composite photograph prepared using the three preceding figures to demonstrate the match relationship between the three marks on the rim of the shell.
(Courtesy, Joseph D. Nicol.)

3. Powder Patterns

An important aspect of firearms work is the question of the determination of the distance at which a gun was fired, especially if it was discharged at close range. The distribution of burnt and unburnt powder granules and the size of the powder residue pattern provide a basis for estimation of the distance involved.

Dark clothing presents some difficulty for the examination of the pattern unless special techniques are employed. Figure 6—48 illustrates how the necessary details can be made visible by a variety of techniques.

Figure 6—49 is another illustration of powder patten details being masked by the design and color of a fabric. The shirt in this figure is the subject of Case Exercise 12 (p 290).

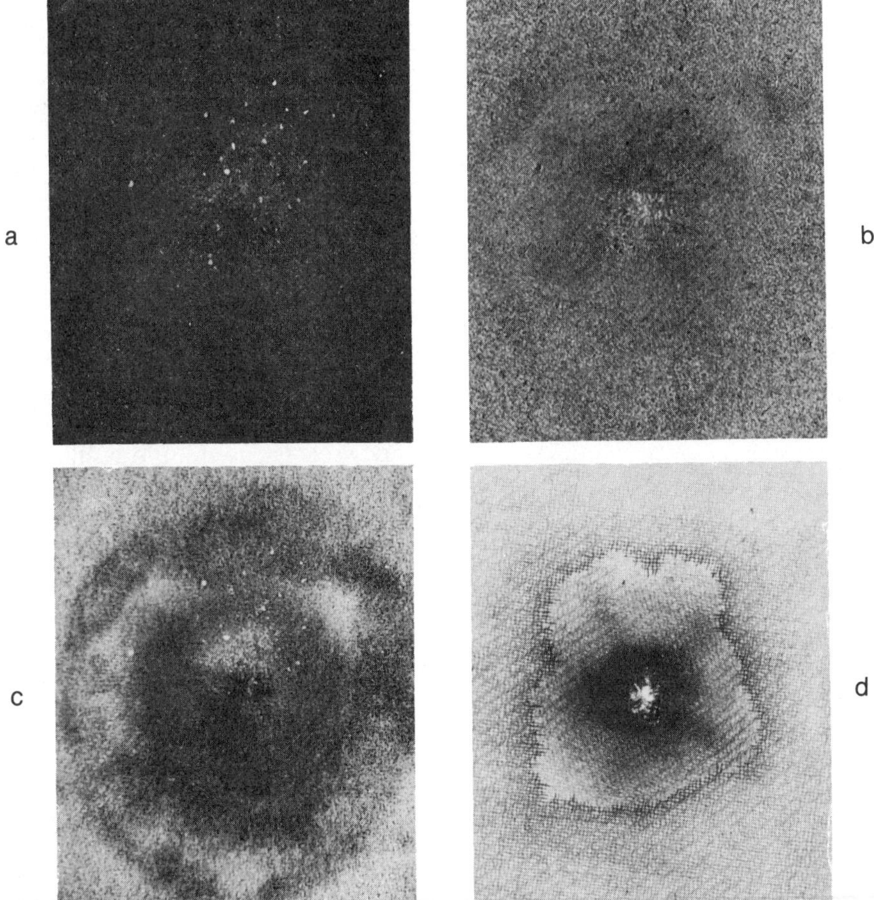

Fig. 6 — 48
Gunshot through sailor's dark middy blouse.

a. This is the view as seen by the unaided eye. The burnt powder particles are revealed only because of the reflected illumination and are not normally visible.
b. Contrast and details have been somewhat improved by using process orthofilm, making a transparency of this negative on commercial type film, and printing the transparency.
c. Contrast and details have been considerably improved by using infrared film (Wratten 87 filter).
d. Additional detail may be obtained by means of soft X-rays. This is a print of the radiograph. (Technical details: Type M. Eastman Kodak film, 12 Kv peak, 50 ma, 20 inch focus-film distance, 5 second exposure.)

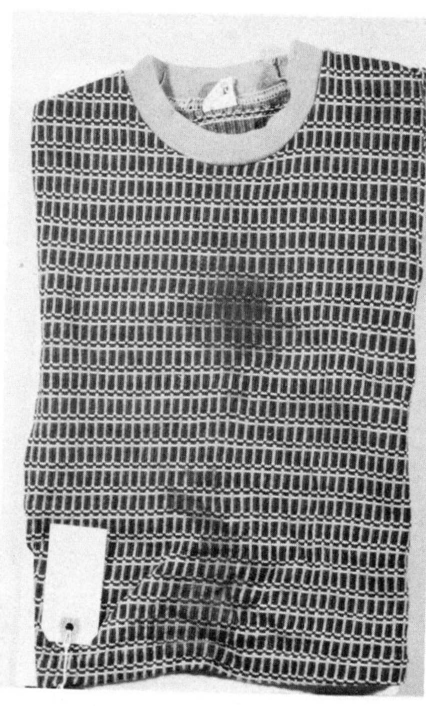

Fig. 6 — 49
Shirt bearing powder pattern.
(Courtesy, Minnesota State Bureau of Criminal Apprehension.)

B. Knives

Whether it be the pocket or kitchen variety, the knife is a threatening instrument which is readily available and easily concealed and therefore of great utility for the commission of crime. Indoors the carving knife is very often used for assault and in extreme cases, homicide. Generally, the forensic pathologist is requested to determine whether a specific instrument was the one that was employed in the homicide. It is seldom possible to show conclusively that a specific carving knife was the particular one involved in the case, even when blood remains on the knife. On the other hand, the hunting or pocket knife used to fashion a wooden bludgeon or to cut bush or tree limbs often has minor nicks and dents in its cutting edge. These imperfections are imparted to and retained by the wood in the form of slight gouge marks similar to the striations impressed on a bullet by the barrel of a gun. They constitute the individual characteristics upon which an identity between knife and wood cutting is established. The early literature of criminalistics recounts some cases, which are now classics, of knife cutting evidence.[6]

Wood, of course, is not the only material capable of retaining knife edge characteristics; for example, hose and tubing of suitable plasticity also can hold the engraving of a knife edge used to sever the hose. (See Case Exercise 13, p 290.)

A double possibility may exist for linking the criminal to the evidence in a crime involving severed tubing. The most obvious opportunity is presented when a knife is obtained from a suspect. Less evident but equally effective is an examination of the end of the tubing or hose that may be in the possession of the suspect. In either case the end located at the crime scene is the questioned evidence to be compared with the known test evidence from either source suggested above.

Cut hose or tubing can be linked in other ways. Random surface marks as well as gripping device marks can establish an identity between two severed pieces. In Fig. 6 — 50 the ends of catheter tubing involved in an abortion were linked through a study of the contour angle of the cut and, in addition, by the alignment of printed matter present on the surface. In another case in which the hands of a homicide victim were tied, the ends of plastic clothesline were matched. Figure 6—51 shows tangled clothesline found in a suspect's home. Figure 6 — 52 shows one end of a piece of the line in Fig. 6—51 (labeled "Known") in juxtaposition to an end of the line used to bind the victim's hands (labeled "Ques.?"). Figure 6 — 53 is a photomacrograph illustrating more clearly the end match of Fig. 6—52.

6.4 Exercises 9, 10, 11, 12, 13 (pp 289-290)

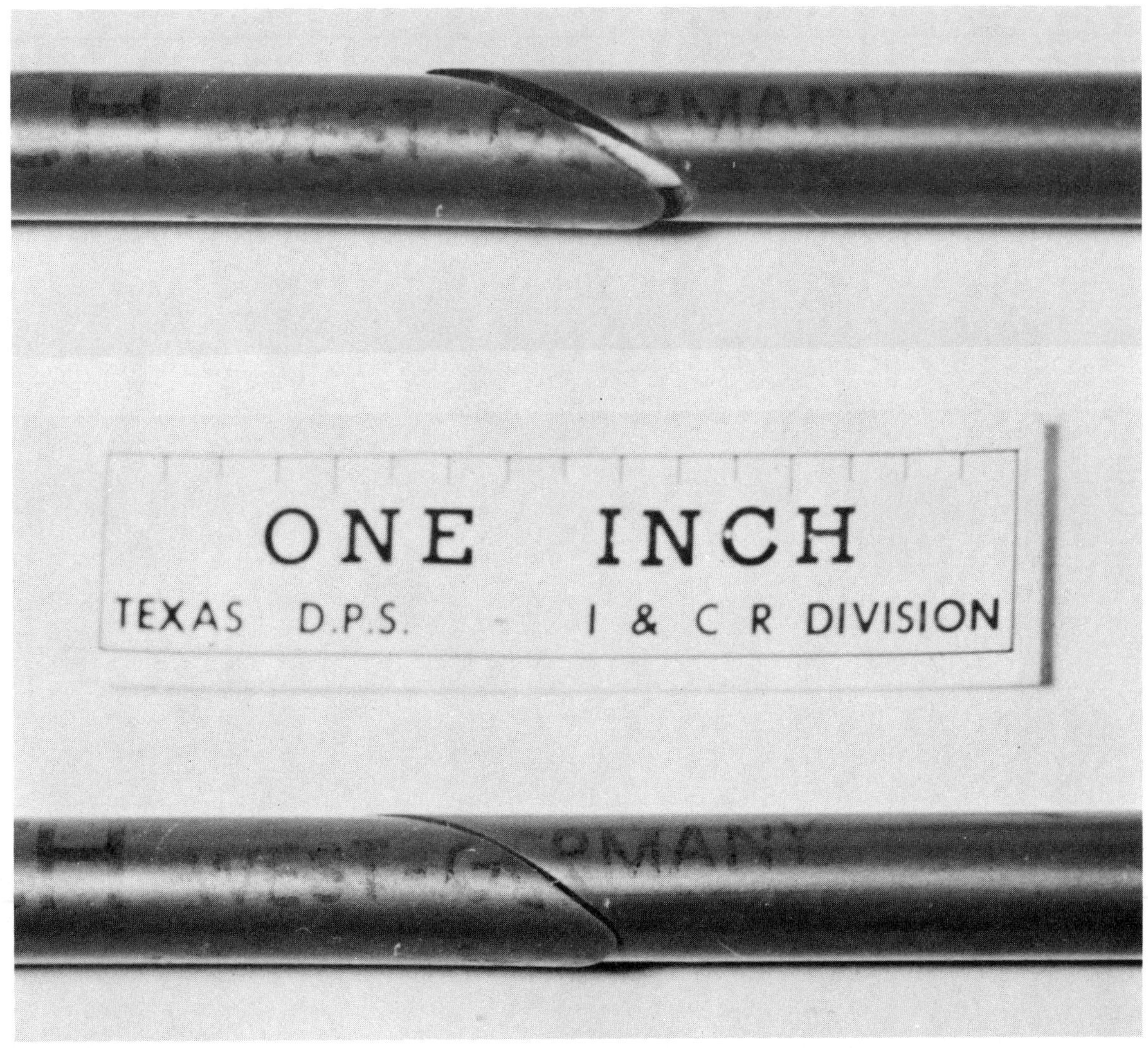

Fig. 6 — 50
Two ends of catheter. End on the left side was discovered in abortionist's office; end on the right side was found with the victim.
(Courtesy, Texas Department of Public Safety.)

Fig. 6 — 51
Tangled mass of clothesline found in suspect's home.

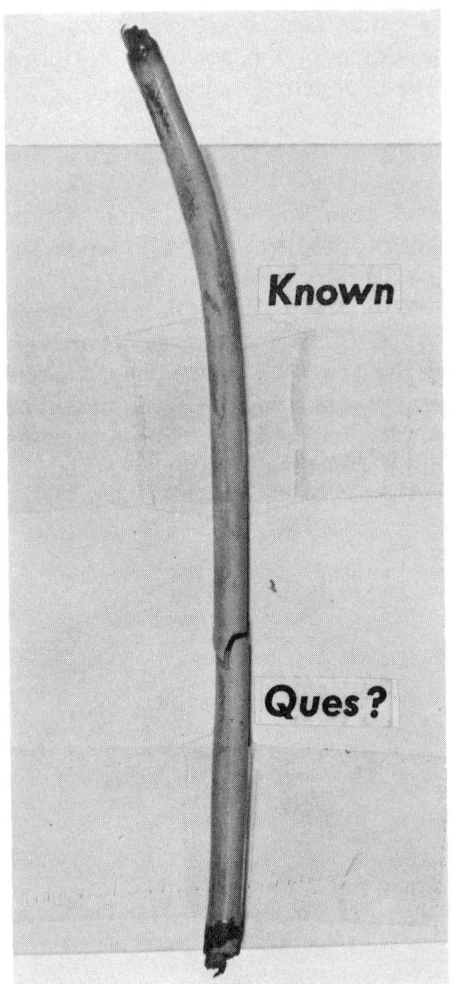

Fig. 6 — 52
Clothesline ends from crime scene and suspect's home placed in juxtaposition.

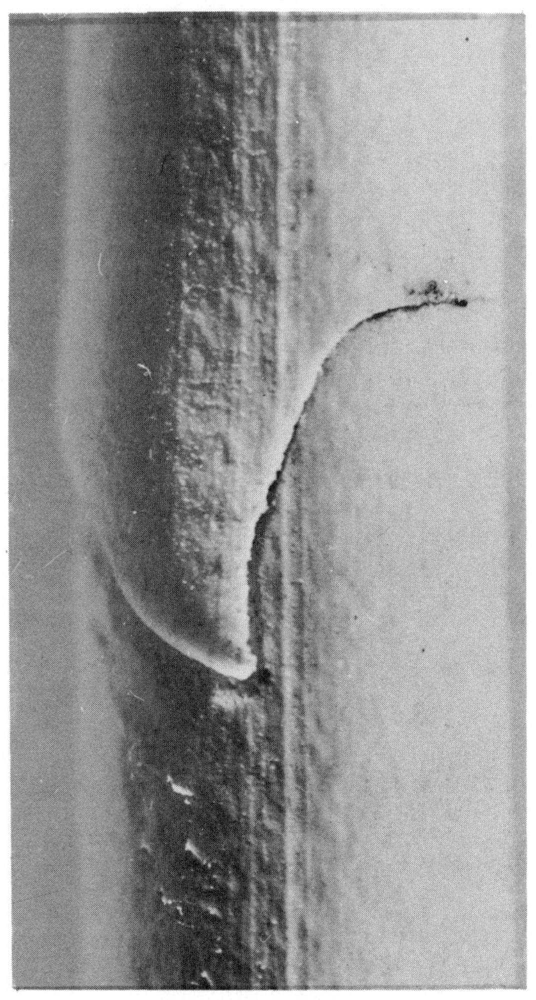

Fig. 6 — 53
Photomacrograph of end match shown in Fig. 6—52. *(Courtesy, Pittsburgh-Allegheny County Crime Laboratory, Office of District Attorney.)*

6.5 Shovels

Some crimes are planned with considerable care while others are executed in a most haphazard fashion. There are times when circumstances evolve during the commission of the crime which dictate that the weapon, proceeds, or body of the victim be hidden in order to reduce the risk of apprehension. Thus it is not uncommon for a criminal to discard in flight the gun or other weapon as well as the fruit of the crime. Homicide victims are secreted in trunks of automobiles, their bodies weighted and thrown into water, or the corpse may be buried in an obscure, generally inaccessible grave. Discovery of the burial place of the body presents a chance for the recognition and development of associative evidence.

Case Exercise 14 centers on a case in which a shallow grave was hastily prepared in an attempt to conceal the body of a state policeman who had been kidnaped and murdered.[7] Some of the soil near the grave appeared to bear large, visible marks of the instrument used in digging a hole to bury the uniform equipment of the trooper. A small clod of hardened clay was taken from the excavation. Figure 6—54 is a photographic enlargement of the earthen clod on which the marks of the digging implement were recorded. Figure 6—55 is a photograph of a shovel located in the trunk of a suspect's car. This shovel was used to dig in the soil near the plot used in burying the trooper's equipment. The striated marks recorded in the soil were photographed and are shown enlarged in Fig. 14B of Case Exercise 14.

6.5 Exercise 14 (p 290)

Fig. 6 — 54
Soil near burial plot dug with shovel (Fig. 6 — 55).

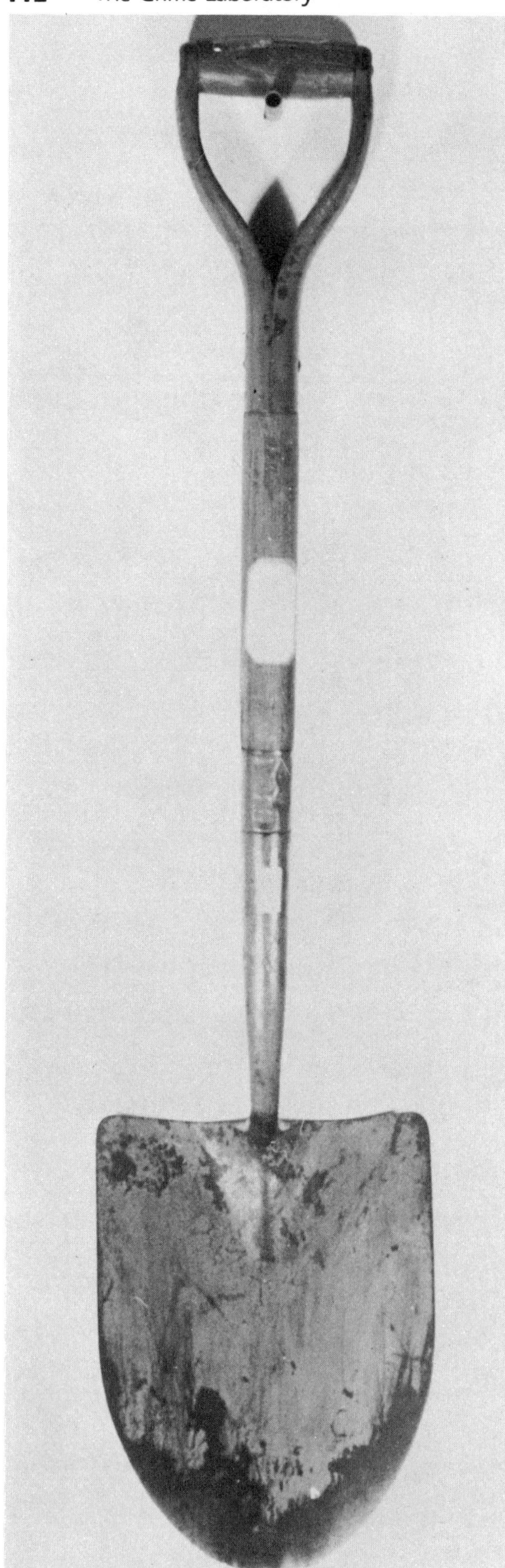

Fig. 6 — 55
Suspected shovel.
(Courtesy, Michigan State Police.)

References

The Comparison of Tire Tracks and Tires

1. Chavigny, M. "Tracks of Vehicles," *Am. J. Pol. Sci.* 1, 156-77 (1930).
   Kirk, P.L. *Crime Investigation*. New York: Inter-Science, 1953. Pp 306-10.
   Nickolls, L.C. *The Scientific Investigation of Crime*. London: Butterworth, 1956. Pp 136-49.
   O'Hara, C.E., and Osterburg, J.W. *An Introducton to Criminalistics*. Bloomington, Ind.: Indiana University Press, 1972. Pp 114-118.
   Svensson, A., Wendel, O., and Fischer, B. *Techniques of Crime Scene Investigation*. 3d ed. New York: Elsevier, 1981. Pp 370-371.

Jimmies

2. Kearns, J.A. Criminologist, Santa Ana, California. Letter dated May 22, 1965.

Metal Cutters

3. Meyers, C.R., and Kivela, E.W. "Interesting Applications of Tool Mark Identification," *J. For. Sci.* 6, 316-20 (1961).

Machinist Dies and Type Fonts

4. Nickolls, L.C. *The Scientific Investigation of Crime*. London: Butterworth, 1956. Pp 125-26.
5. Harrison, Wilson R. *Suspect Documents: Their Scientific Examination*. London: Sweet & Maxwell Ltd., 1958. Pp 257-59.
   Hilton, Ordway. *Scientific Examination of Questioned Documents*. Chicago: Callaghan, 1956. Pp 184-87.
   Kirk, P.L. *Crime Investigation*. New York: Interscience, 1953. Pp 467-68.
   Osborn, Albert S. *Questioned Documents*. 2d ed. Albany, N.Y.: Boyd Printing Co., 1929. Pp 589, 595-96.

Knives

6. May, L.S. "The Identification of Knives, Tools, and Instruments: A Positive Science," *Am. J. Pol. Sci.* 1, 246-59 (1930).
   Mathews, J.H. "The Murder of Blackie Atkins," *Am. J. Pol. Sci.* III, 7-13 (1932).

Shovels

7. Myers, C.R., and Kivela, E.W. "Interesting Applications of Tool Mark Identification," *J. For. Sci.* 6, 316-20 (1961). P 317, Case 3.

Suggestions for Further Reading

Tiremarks

Grogan, R.J. and Watson, T.R. "Tyre Punctures — How, Why and Where," *For. Sci. Soc. J.* 14, 165-176 (1974).

Hamilton, D. "Traces of Footwear, Tyres and Tools, etc. in Criminal Investigation," *The Pol. J.* (Brit.) 22, 42-49 (1949).

Vandiver, J.V. "Tire Marks," *Law and Order* 25(7), 16-23 (July 1977).

Jimmies

Burd, D.Q., and Kirk, P.L. "Tool Marks: Factors Involved in their Comparison and Use as Evidence," *J. Crim. Law, Criminol. and Pol. Sci.* 32, 679-86 (1942).

_____, "Tool Mark Comparisons in Criminal Investigation," *J. Crim. Law, Criminol. and Pol. Sci.* 39, 379-91 (1948).

Nickolls, L.C. *The Scientific Investigation of Crime*. London: Butterworth, 1956. Pp 110-17.

Walls, H.J. *Forensic Science*. 2d ed. New York: Praeger, 1974. Pp 19-21.

Axes

Biasotti, A.A. "A Comparison of Hatchet Cuts on Wire," *J. Crim. Law, Criminol. and Pol. Sci.* 47, 497-499 (1956).

Burd, D.Q., and Greene, R.S. "Tool Mark Comparisons in Criminal Investigations," *J. Crim. Law, Criminol. and Pol. Sci.* 39, 379-91 (1948-49). P 391.

Metzger, O., Hasslacher, F., and Frankle, P. "Identification of Marks Made on Trees," *Am. J. Pol. Sci.* 1, 358-65 (1930).

Tool Marks

Andahl, R.O. "The Examination of Saw Marks," *For. Sci. Soc. J.* 18, 31-46 (1978).

Biasotti, A.A., "The Principles of Evidence Evaluation as Applied to Firearms and Tool Mark Identification," *J. For. Sci.* 9, 428-33 (1964).

Bonte, W. "Tool Marks in Bones and Cartilage," *J. For. Sci.* 20, 315-323 (1975).

Burd, D.Q., and Gilmore, A.E. "Individual and Class Characteristics of Tools," *J. For. Sci.* 15, 115-126 (1975).

Butcher, S.F. and Pugh, P.D. "A Study of Marks Made by Bolt Cutters," *For. Sci. Soc.* 15, 115-126 (1975).

Cunliffe, F., and Piazza, P.D. *Criminalistics and Scientific Investigation*. Englewood Cliffs, N.J.: Prentice-Hall, 1980. Pp 254-263.

Davis, J.E. *An Introduction to Tool Marks, Firearms, and Striagraph*. Springfield, Ill.: Thomas, 1958. Pp 7-67.

Flynn, E.M. "Tool Mark Identification," *J. For. Sci.* 2, 95-106 (1957).

Scott, J.D. *Investigative Methods*. Reston, Va.: Reston, 1978. Pp 209-231.

Vandiver, J.V. "Identification and Use of Tool Mark Evidence," *Law and Order* 24(7), 77-91 (1976).

Firearms

Burrard, G. *The Identification of Firearms and Forensic Ballistics*. 1st American ed. New York: Barnes, 1962. Pp 103-137.

Davis, J.E. *An Introduction to Tool Marks, Firearms and Striagraph*. Springfield, Ill.: Thomas, 1958. Pp 68-148.

Gunther, J.D., and Gunther, C.O. *The Identification of Firearms*. New York: Wiley, 1935.

Hatcher, J.S. *Textbook of Firearms Investigation, Identification and Evidence*. Plantersville, S.C.: Small Arms Technical, 1935. Pp 265-74.

_____, Jury, F. and Weller, J. *Textbook of Firearms Identification*. Harrisburg, Pa.: Stackpole, 1957.

Kirk, P.L. *Crime Investigation*. 2d ed. Edited by John I. Thornton. New York: Wiley, 1974. Pp 379-409.

Krcma, V. *Identification and Registration of Firearms*. Springfield, Ill.: Thomas, 1971.

Mathews, J.H. *Firearms Identification*. Springfield, Ill.: Thomas, 1972.

Sinha, J.K., Mehrotra, V.K., and Kumar, L.A. "Direct Breech Face Comparison," *J. Pol. Sci. and Admin.* 4, 261-273 (1976).

7

Miscellaneous Traces

The preceding chapters permitted the categorization of clue materials according to three common sources: persons, wearing apparel, and instruments involved in the commission of crime. The present chapter departs from this logic and shifts its view to that of matching visually, at low-order magnification, some physical characteristic of the clue material. In criminalistics this method for the development of associative evidence is termed *physical match*. Two of the more common clue materials, paint chips and glass fragments, have been singled out for special consideration.

7.1 Physical Matches

Physical match quite often involves placing two objects in juxtaposition so that it is fairly obvious from the examination of the contours that both pieces were originally one. The matching of two ends that were broken, torn, or cut in an irregular fashion represents the simplest form of physical matching. Fortunately, in many cases crime scene evidence is available to the trained and imaginative investigator for this purpose. Through photography, the relationship of crime clue material to evidence that is found on or in the possession of the suspect is often self-evident.[1] Well-made photographic enlargements permit the jury to see for itself the intimate association existing between both edges or ends of evidence. Several cases serve to demonstrate this.

Figure 7—1 depicts a metal pipe fitting which a burglar cut in two in order to steal a water pump. In addition to the alignment of the slight curve in the cut, note how the teethmarks of a wrench also are aligned near the top and bottom of the middle section of both halves of the metal coupling. It is self-evident that these two pieces of pipe were originally one.

The physical match shown in Fig. 7—2 speaks for itself. One part of a ripped female's undergarment was found near where the victim was thrown from a car; the other part was in a suspect's car.

The insertion of a wrinkled piece of newspaper into a page of the newspaper from which it was torn (Fig. 7—3) is a graphic illustration of a physical match. The torn scrap was used to wrap a packet of narcotics and the larger piece of newsprint was located in a suspect's home.

Figure 7—4 shows the restoration of a broken knife blade. Merely placing the crime scene evidence in juxtaposition to the evidence found on a suspect was sufficient; not only do the two edges match, but the marks and scars acquired through usage were also aligned.

Two pieces of plastic electrical insulating tape are depicted in Fig. 7—5. One end was wrapped around a hammer located at the crime scene; the other end was obtained from a chisel located in the trunk of a suspect's automobile. The common origin of both is perhaps less evident than in the preceding figure. However, the examiner (or the jurors) can handle and inspect the actual evidence and the physical match can be more easily observed in this manner than from a photograph.

7.1 Exercises 1, 2, 3 (pp 347-348)

Fig. 7 — 1
Metal pipe fitting reassembled after being cut in the theft of a water pump. The lower piece was found at the burglary scene; the upper piece was found attached to an unconnected pump located in the home of a suspect.
(Courtesy, New York State Police.)

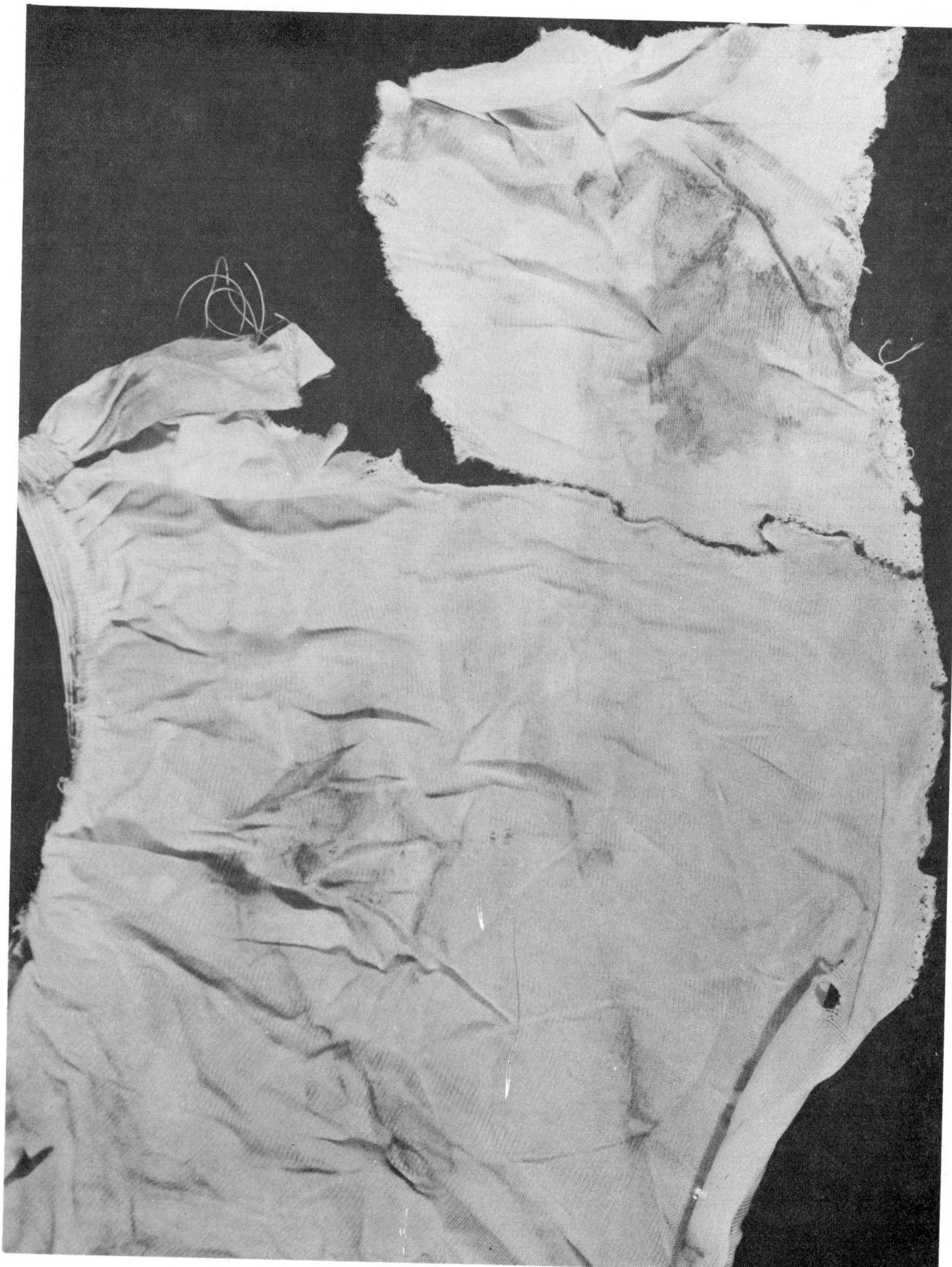

Fig. 7 — 2
Restoration of torn female undergarment. The large piece remained on the body of the victim; the smaller piece was found in a suspect's car.
(Courtesy, Laboratories for Scientific Criminal Investigation, University of Rhode Island.)

Maniac 'Hitler' Kills at School

(Story in Col. 3)

L. A. POLICE 'BATTLE' ANTI-SHAH PLANE

Eisenhower: 'I'm Not a Puppeteer'

By MARVIN L. ARROWSMITH and WALTER R. MEARS
Associated Press Writers

GETTYSBURG, Pa., June 11—Former President Dwight D. Eisenhower wants a wide open Republican national convention to stir the party's and the nation's interest—and insists he is no candidate's partisan or foe.

Eisenhower told the Asso-

City Council

LOS ANGELES EVENING AND SUNDAY

HERALD EXAMINER

LARGEST EVENING CIRCULATION IN AMERICA

VOL. XCIV 10 CENTS THURSDAY, JUNE 11, 1964 NO. 77

8 STAR LATEST SPORTS
Complete N. Y. Stocks

'Copter Wins 'Dog-Fight' Over UCLA

COMMENCEMENT

DISTURBANCE

Fig. 7 — 3
Wrinkled piece of newspaper used to wrap a packet of narcotics inserted into torn page of a newspaper found in a suspect's house.
(Courtesy, Los Angeles County Sheriff's Department.)

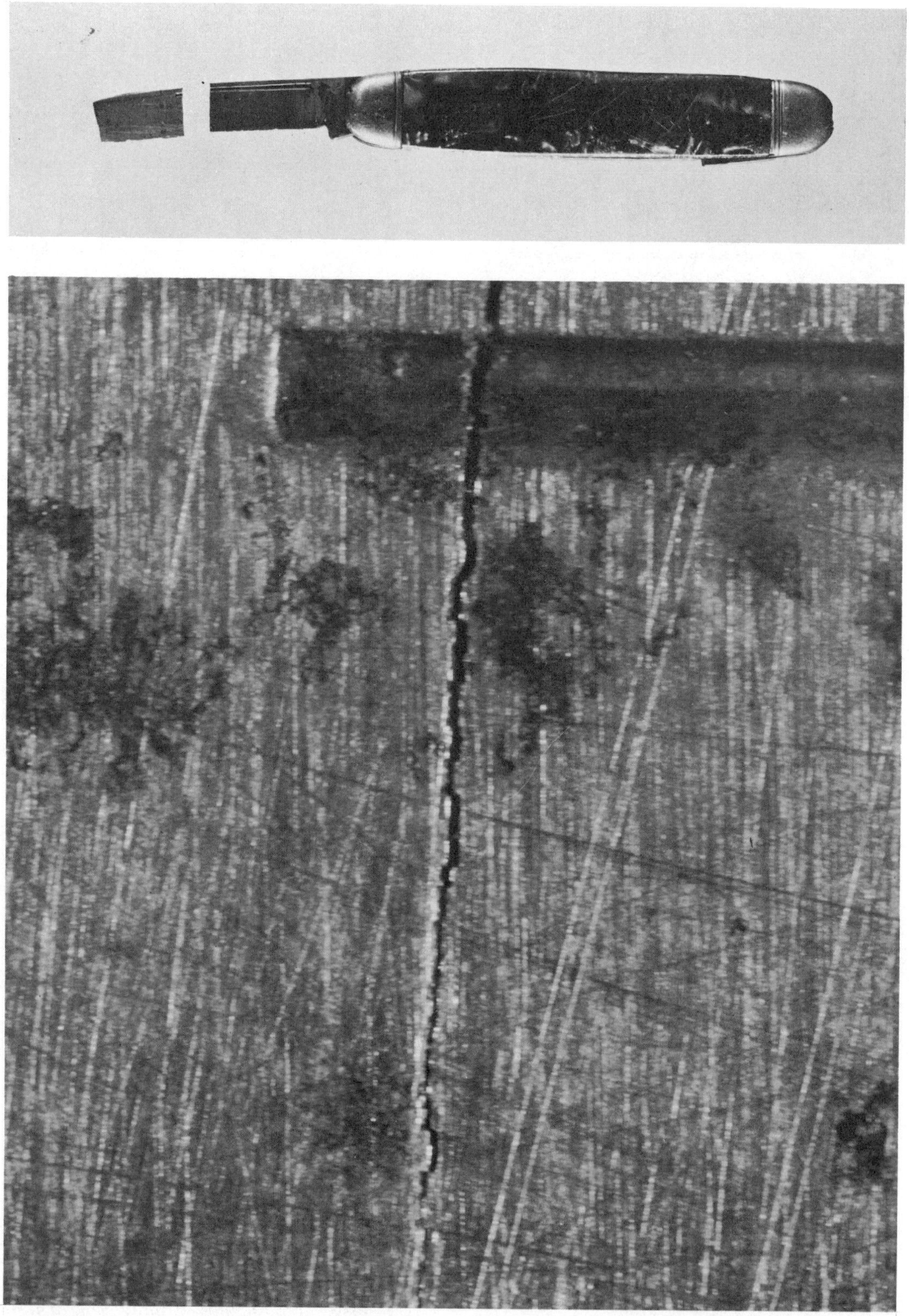

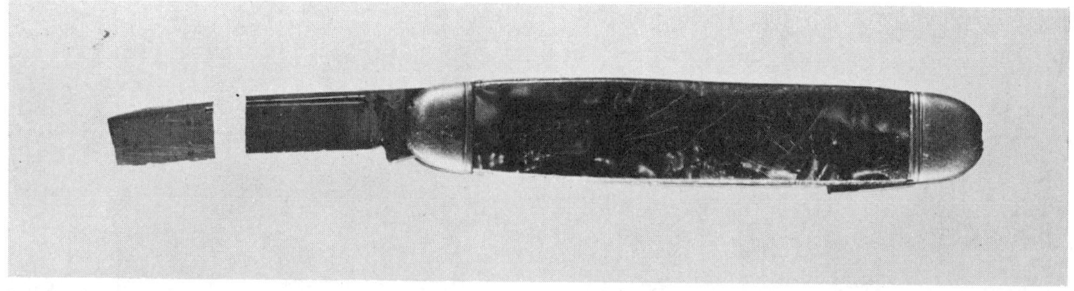

Fig. 7 — 4
Top: Knife with broken blade taken from suspect. Small piece of blade on the left was found at scene of attempted burglary. Bottom: Photomacrograph showing both edges of broken knife blade in juxtaposition. Note that in addition to the fit of the indentations on the edges, there are scratch marks running across the restored blade which are also in perfect alignment.
(Courtesy, New York City Police Department.)

Fig. 7 — 5
Plastic electrical insulating tape. Piece on left was found on a hammer left at the scene of a crime. Piece on the right was removed from a chisel found in the trunk of the defendant's automobile. *(Courtesy, San Bernardino County Sheriff's Office, California.)*

7.2 Paint Chips

Paint is such a commonplace substance that it is not surprising that it often appears as a clue material. It is most frequently found as chips in hit-and-run automobile accident cases and on jimmies used in burglaries; sometimes paint chips are found in the trouser cuffs of the pants worn by a burglar.

Figure 7 — 6 is a photomicrograph of the edge of a paint chip and is composed of twenty-two layers of paint. They are more readily visible in color than in a black and white reproduction. A side by side comparison for similarities of a crime scene paint chip with one of known origin is a somewhat common laboratory examination. If a sufficient number of layers, each differing in color and thickness, are present they individualize a paint chip; however, many objects have had but two or three coats of paint and the layers on these are probably too few to serve as characterizing details. Confronted with this situation many investigators immediately request a chemical analysis of the paint chip. There are numerable cases in which an object was brought to the crime laboratory for such analysis. In some of these the investigator had overlooked some other important aspect of paint chips as evidentiary material. For example, Fig. 7—7 shows two paint chips which had been coated previously with a varnish. The checking or cracking of the varnish permitted a positive comparison to be made, i.e., an identity established. Another possibility is that of fitting (in jigsaw puzzle fashion) the paint fragment into an area from which paint has flaked off.[2] At the scene of a hit-and-run accident, paint chips should be carefully collected and preserved against damage to their edges. If a vehicle is suspected of having been involved in the accident it may be possible to demonstrate its presence at the scene by inserting a fragment of paint into a damaged area of the vehicle where some paint has been chipped off.

If pieces of dirt or mud, rather than paint, are found in the road debris of the accident it may be possible to find corresponding cavities in the dirt remaining under a fender of a suspected car.[3] This is an example of the extension of an idea applicable to other types of evidence besides the clue material under consideration. The reader should strive constantly to recognize such possibilities.

A. Paint Chip Casts

A well-made cast of an impression records all of the topographic features of the imprint. For example, if some paint chips off when force is applied in the use of a jimmy, the outline of the craters in the paint will appear as slightly raised mounds in the cast. If a jimmy is recovered with any paint chips intact on its surface it may be possible to insert a chip vicariously into the mold of the cast by a comparison of photographs of the evidence or by using the comparison microscope. This procedure is illustrated in the following example.

Figure 7—8 is a silicone cast of a tool impression in a doorjamb. An outline of a paint crater is visible as a protuberance in the jimmy mark. Figure 7—9 is a photograph of a screwdriver on which a paint chip is clearly visible. Figure 7—10 is a photomicrograph of the paint chip and the embossed area of the cast. The points of comparison have been marked.

7.2 Exercise 4 (p 348)

Fig. 7 — 6
Paint chip taken from a door in a housebreaking case. In color, twenty-two layers of paint are visible in the photomicrograph.
(Courtesy, Federal Bureau of Investigation.)

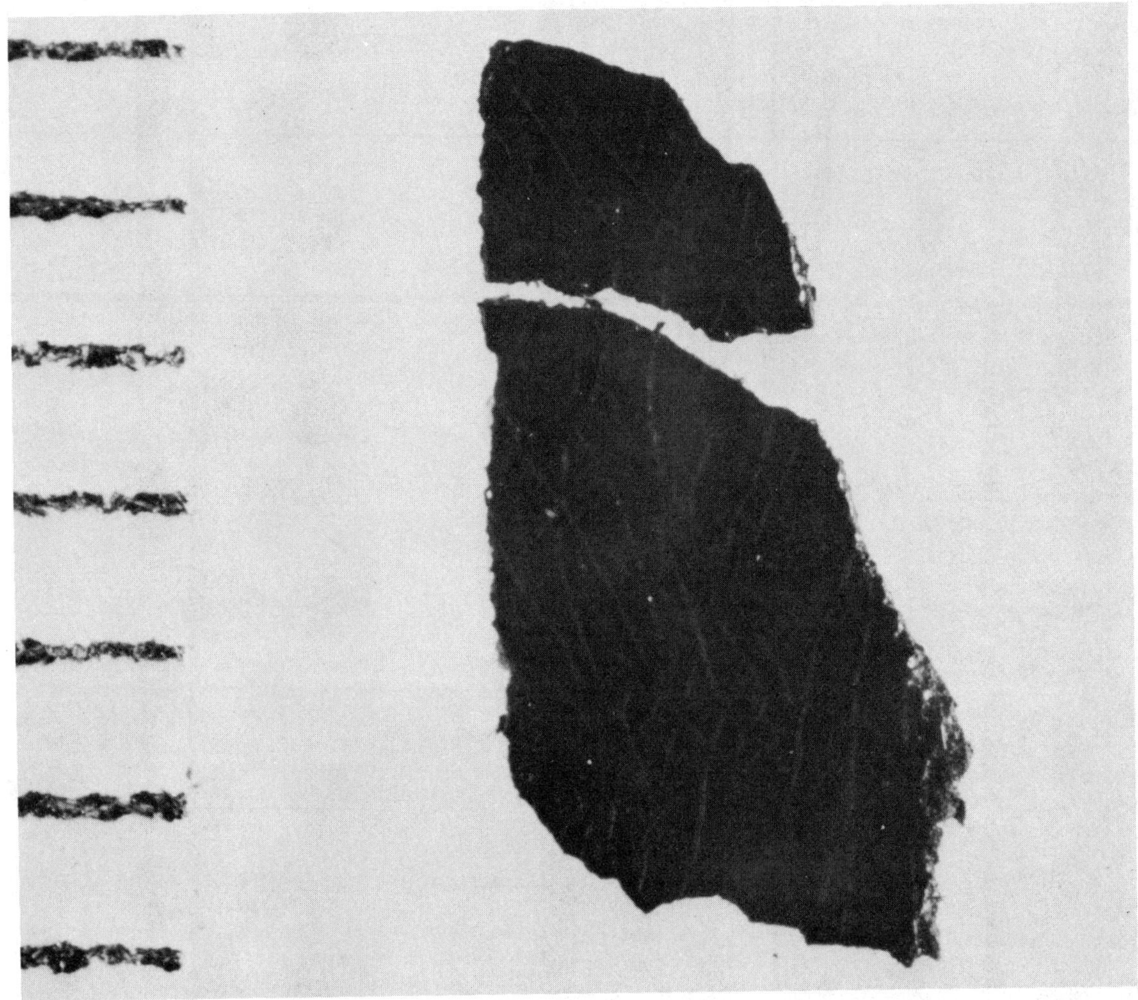

Fig. 7 — 7
Two varnished paint chips. The upper chip was recovered from the trunk compartment of a suspect's automobile. The lower chip was obtained from the outer surface of a burglarized safe. The checking of the varnish coat allowed a positive comparison to be made.
(Courtesy, Pittsburgh-Allegheny County Crime Laboratory, Office of District Attorney.)

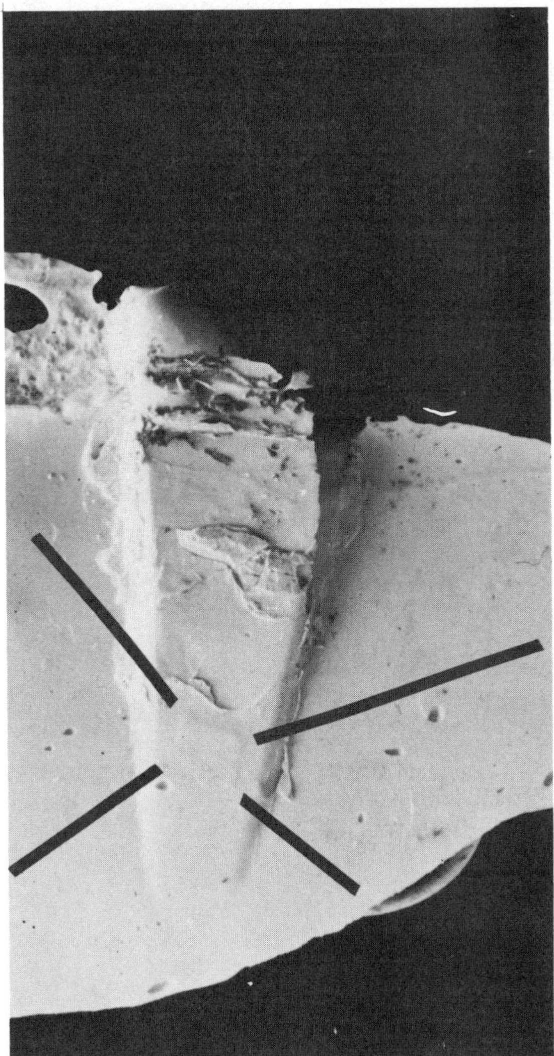

Fig. 7 — 8
Silicone cast of a tool impression in a doorjamb. The outline of a missing paint chip is indicated.

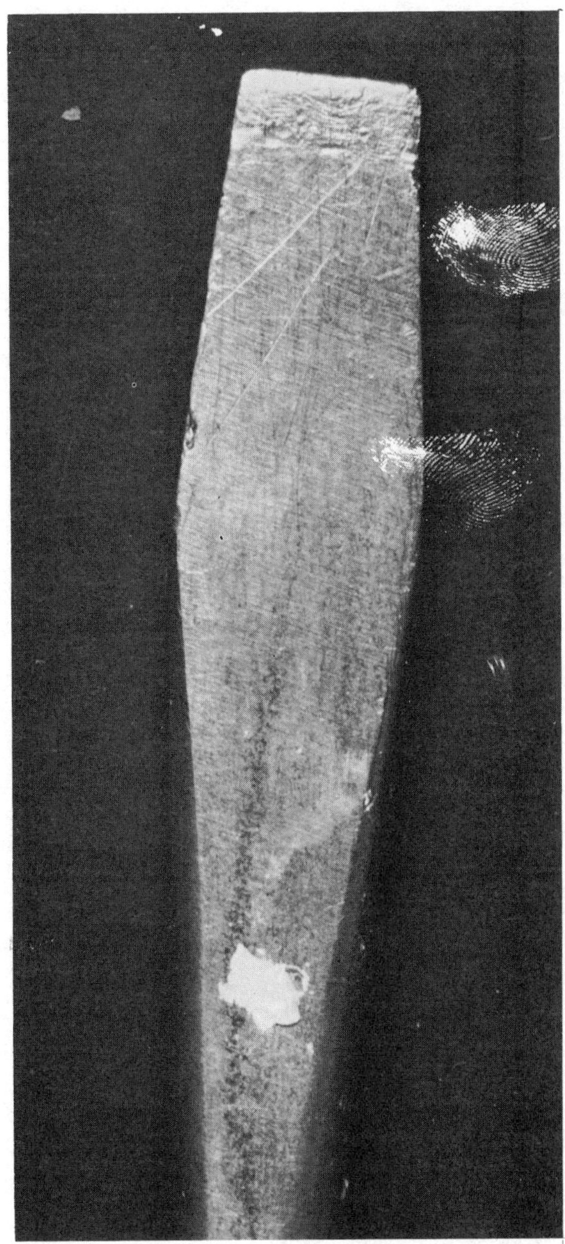

Fig. 7 — 9
Screwdriver obtained from a suspect. Note paint chip on the surface of the tool.

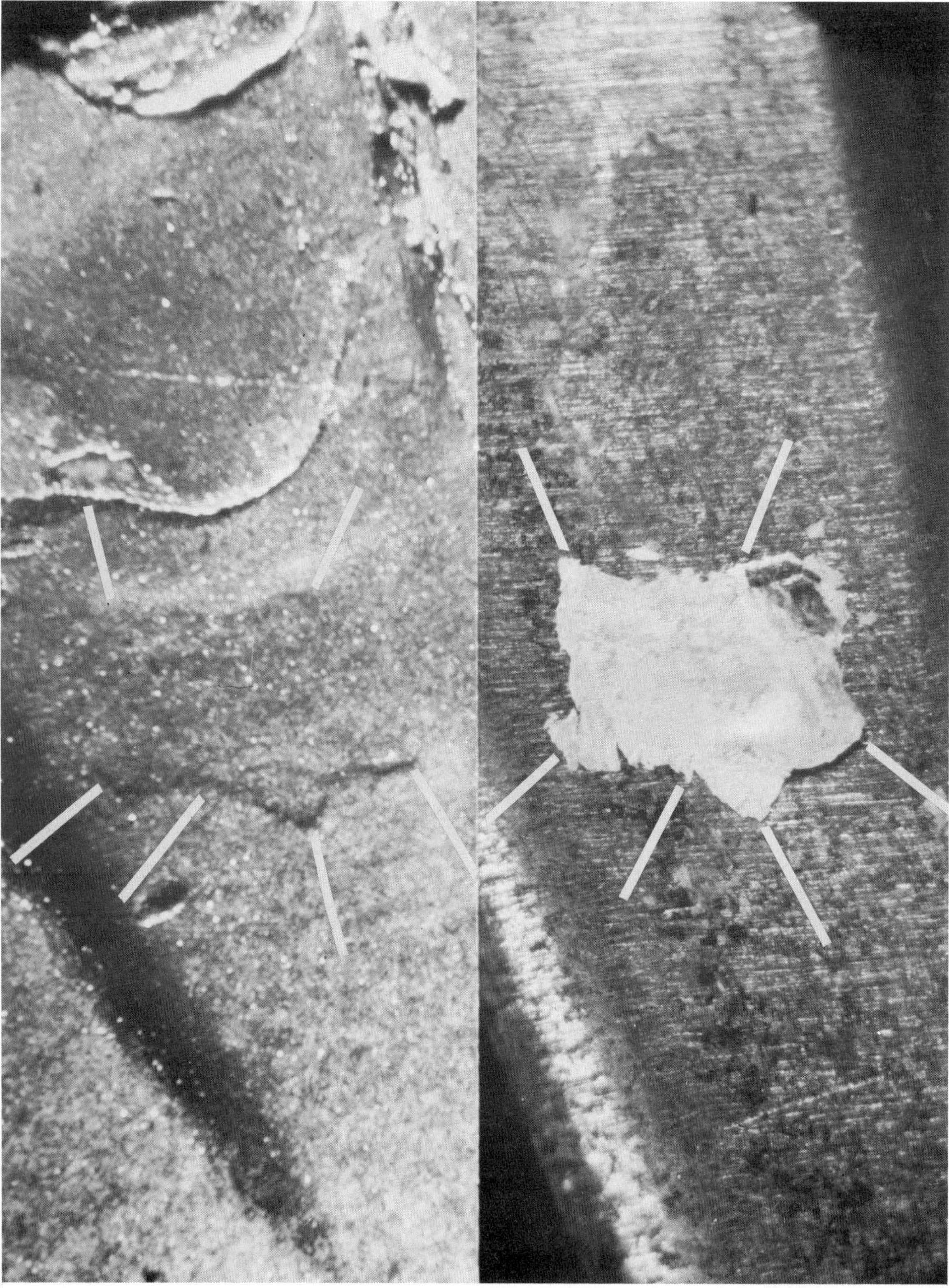

Fig. 7 — 10
A photomicrograph of the paint chip (Fig. 7 — 9) is shown on the right while the embossed area of the cast is visible in the left half of the photograph. The points of similarity are marked to show the shape and size.
(Courtesy, San Francisco Police Department.)

7.3 Broken Glass

Glass is a common clue material. It is well known to crime investigators that a broken headlight lens can be reconstructed as though the fragments are part of a jigsaw puzzle.[4] Figure 7—11 is a photograph of a large glass fragment that remained in the broken headlight of a car and four smaller fragments found at the scene of an accident. The alignment of the fluting in the lens design together with the three dimensional fit of the broken edges is an excellent example of a physical match.

Glass evidence in the form of a cracked window is often found in burglary cases, homicides, and in automobile larcenies. In a few of these cases the investigator may have reason to question the validity of a complainant's story. The detective's doubts may readily be resolved if it could be determined from which direction the force came that broke the window. Investigative experience records many cases in which a glass pane was deliberately broken to create an appearance of illegal entry or to suggest that a shot was fired into the house or vehicle. The knowledgeable detective is aware of the possibility of simulation intended to mislead. The crime laboratory can determine the direction from which the force came that caused the glass to break.

Figure 7—12 depicts the scene of a homicide, a kitchen with one of its windows broken. The death involved a young boy who suddenly slumped forward while eating lunch in this kitchen. He had been shot through the chest. The adults in the apartment, as well as the other children with whom he was eating, all stated that the bullet came through the kitchen window and suggested that it was probably fired by a sniper. After considerable investigative effort, but with no success in developing any other evidence of sniper activity, the detectives asked that the break in the window be examined to determine if the bullet had, in fact, come from the outside. Figure 7—13 is an exterior view of the kitchen wall and windows. Figure 7—14 is a photograph of the broken window removed from its frame and Fig. 7—15 is similar except that one piece of glass has been removed for further study. An examination of the edges of this broken piece for rib marks (Fig. 7—16) provides the basis for determination of the direction of the force that broke the window.[5] The outside and inside of the window, of course, are known from simple inspection at the crime scene. Relating these facts permits an answer to be given to the question propounded. In the case used as the illustration, the force was shown to have come from the inside. This fact changed the complexion of the investigation, and shortly thereafter admissions were obtained from the adult occupants of the apartment that the shot was fired within the room.

In addition to studying glass fragments for the investigative purposes described above, it is often possible to predict the original source of a glass fragment and the probable usage of the glass by analyzing the chemical composition and measuring the physical properties of the fragment. At times such information may be valuable as an investigative lead.[6]

7.3 Exercise 5 (p 348)

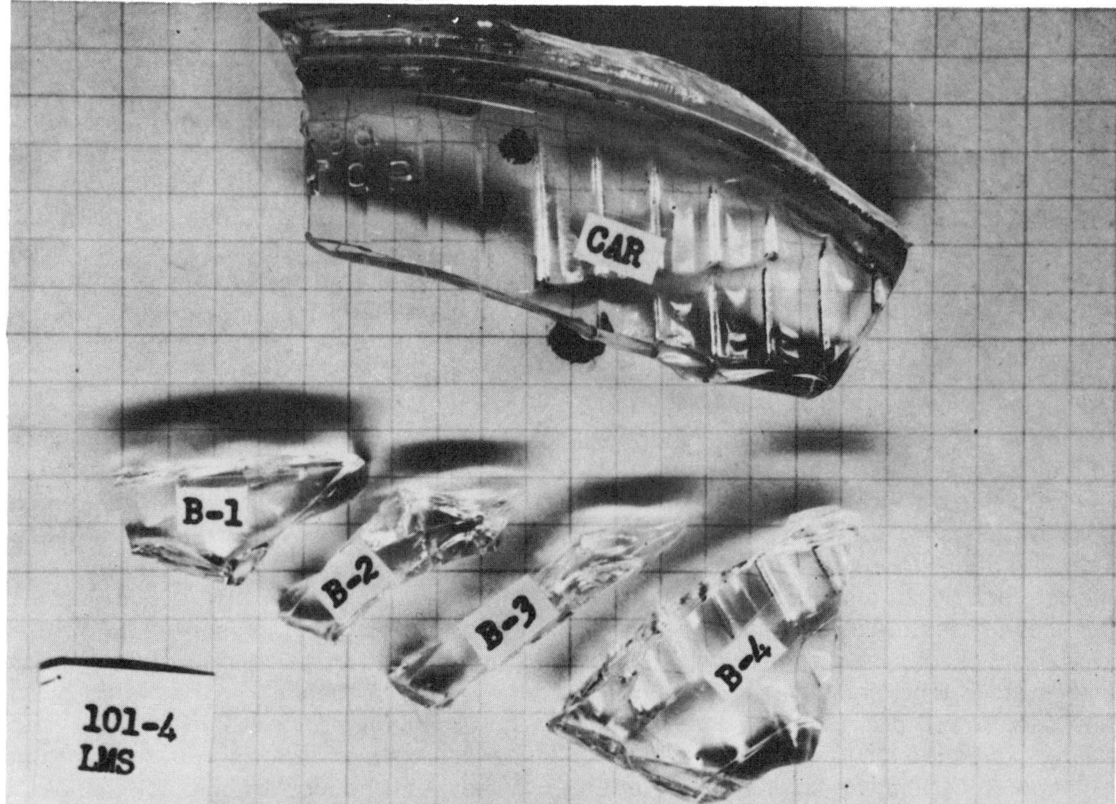

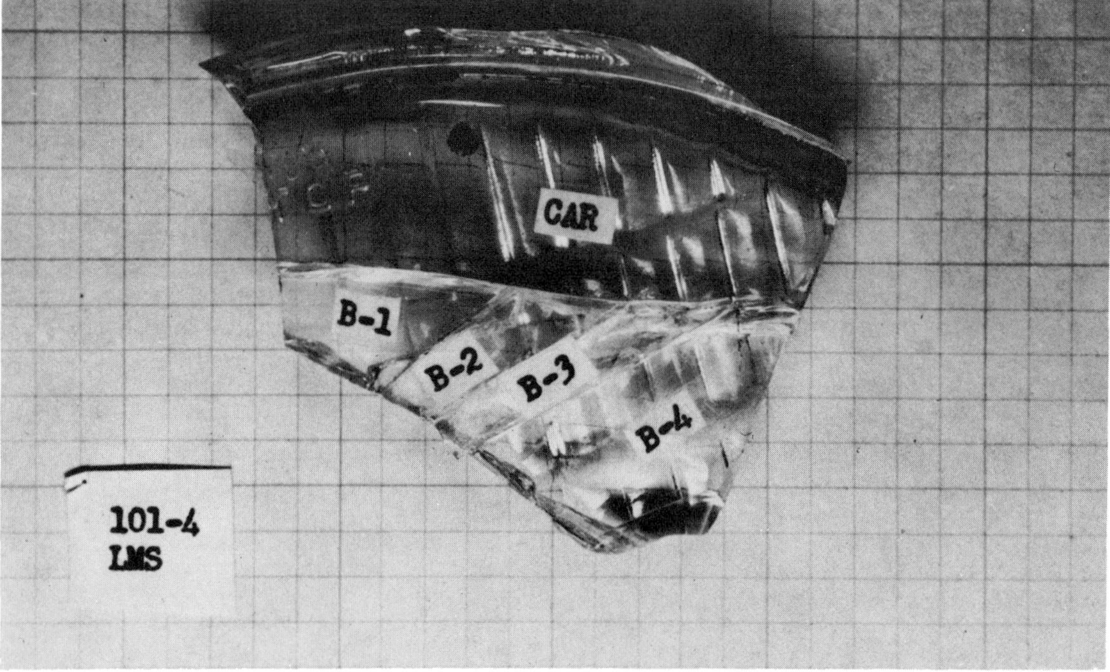

Fig. 7 — 11
Small glass fragments in hit-and-run case. In the upper portion the fragments are separated but ready for reassembly; in the lower portion the lens fragments have been pieced together.
(Courtesy, Columbus Police Department, Ohio.)

Fig. 7 — 12
Homicide scene. Note broken left window.

Fig. 7 — 13
Exterior view of kitchen windows shown in Fig. 7—12.

Fig. 7 — 14
Sash of broken window (seen in Fig. 7—12) removed from its frame. Gummed labels were used to hold cracked window in place.

Fig. 7 — 15
Same window as seen in Fig. 7—14 except one piece of glass has been removed for examination of its radial and spiral cracks.

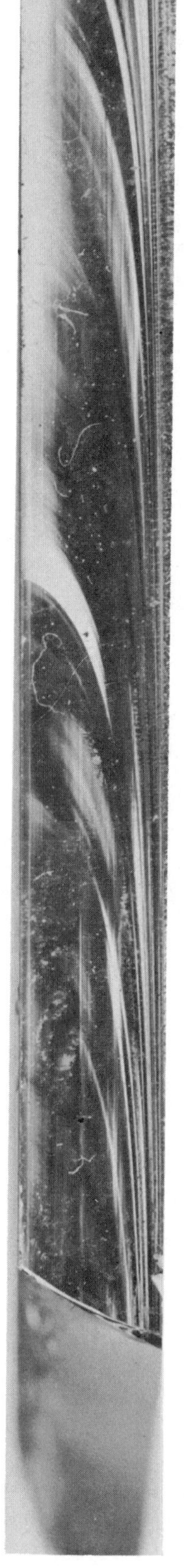

Fig. 7 — 16
A photomacrograph of the edge of a radial crack of the piece of glass mentioned in Fig. 7—15. Rib marks are clearly visible. They indicate to an expert that the direction of force came from the right. In removing the glass, the outside of the window was placed facing the left; thus, the window was broken from the inside.
(Courtesy, New York City Police Department.)

References

Physical Matches

1. Svensson, A., and Wendel, O. *Techniques of Crime Scene Investigation*. 2d rev. American ed. Edited by Joseph D. Nicol. New York: Elsevier, 1965. Pp 114-15 (Figs. 55-57), 163 (Fig. 75), 165 (Fig. 76), 177 (Fig. 82), 198 (Fig. 100).

Paint Chips

2. Davis, John E. *An Introduction to Tool Marks, Firearms and the Striagraph*. Springfield, Ill.: Thomas, 1958. Pp 22-25.
3. O'Hara, C.E., and Osterburg, J.W. *An Introduction to Criminalistics*. Bloomington, Ind.: Indiana University Press, 1972. P 290.

Broken Glass

4. Tryhorn, F.G. "The Examination of Glass," *J. Crim. Law, Criminol. and Pol. Sci.* 30, 404-19 (1939).
5. O'Hara and Osterburg, p 242.
6. MacDonell, H.L. "Identification of Glass Fragments," *J. For. Sci.* 9(2), 244-54 (1964).

Suggestions for Further Reading

Physical Matches

Kirk, P.L. *Crime Investigation*. 2d ed. Edited by John I. Thornton. New York: Wiley, 1974. Pp 138, 360-378.

Nickolls, L.C. *The Scientific Investigation of Crime*. London: Butterworth, 1965. Pp 38-44.

Walls, H.J. *Forensic Science*. 2d ed. New York: Prager, 1974. Pp 13-21.

Paint Chips

Cunliffe, F. and Piazza, P.B. *Criminalistics and Scientific Investigation*. Englewood Cliffs, N.J.: Prentice-Hall, 1980. Pp 130-132.

Kirk, pp 245-247.

Linde, H.G. and Stone, R.P. "Application of the Rosin Test to Paint Analysis," *J. For. Sci.* 3, 650-655 (1979).

Nickolls, pp 73-74.

Broken Glass

Fong, W., Flohr, M., and Roche, G.W. "Identification of Parking and Turn Signal Lenses," *J. Crim. Law, Criminol. and Pol. Sci.* 51(1), 99-119 (1960).

Kirk, pp 261-272.

Rhodes, E.F. and Thornton, J.D. "The Interpretation of Impact Fractures in Glassy Polymers," *J. For. Sci.* 20, 274-282 (1975).

Svensson, A., Wendel, O., and Fischer, B. *Techniques of Crime Scene Investigation*. 3d ed. New York: Elsevier, 1981. Pp 147-152.

8

Trace Evidence Sources

The evidence considered in the preceding chapters consisted almost exclusively of traces left at the crime scene. It should be obvious that evidence removed from the scene may also serve to link the criminal to it. It is a moot question whether more associative evidence is developed through traces left at the scene or whether more arises out of evidence taken from it deliberately or accidentally by the criminal. The significant point to be recognized is that it is the interaction of criminal, victim, and the crime scene environment that provides the potential clue material which a knowledgeable investigator transforms into associative evidence through the medium of the crime laboratory.

8.1 Traces Taken from the Scene

A common type of evidence acquired from the scene is the fruit of the crime as in burglary and robbery cases. Of course, the stolen property must be uniquely identifiable; thus, serial numbers on automobiles and, if recorded, on watches, guns, television sets, money, and so on are useful in meeting this requirement. It is more common, however, for the crime laboratory to be asked to examine traces obtained inadvertently by the criminal. For example, the hair of the victim and fibers from his clothing can be transferred to the criminal if the two have been in close contact. The debris that accumulates in trouser cuffs has also been the source of valuable evidence. One method of recovering clue materials from clothing is to use a vacuum cleaner modified to permit recovery of any trace evidence that might be present. Thus, glass fragments, wood splinters, safe lining particles, paint chips, and metal fragments are among the most common types of clue materials found on a criminal's clothing. In cases where the victim was cut or wounded some blood may spurt or wipe off on the assailant.

A few actual cases will serve to illustrate further some typical physical evidence acquired accidentally in the commission of a crime. For example, Fig. 8 — 1 is a photograph of a section of a heavy wire screen intended to serve as a protective device by the owner of a burglarized shop. It was apparent from an examination of the crime scene that the burglar had to squeeze through the confined space and that his clothing would likely bear an imprint of the wire mesh. Figure 8 — 2 is a photograph of a shirt recovered from a suspect in the case. The probative value of this evidence depends upon the criminalist's conclusions concerning his examination of this potential associative evidence. Another example of physical evidence picked up inadvertently in a burglary (of a picture-frame factory) is illustrated in Figs. 8—3 through 8—6. In Fig. 8—7 a comparison is shown of metal debris discovered in a burglar's trouser cuff with metal fragments found at the point of entry into the building.

Fig. 8 — 1
Pattern of wire screen installed as a protection against burglary.

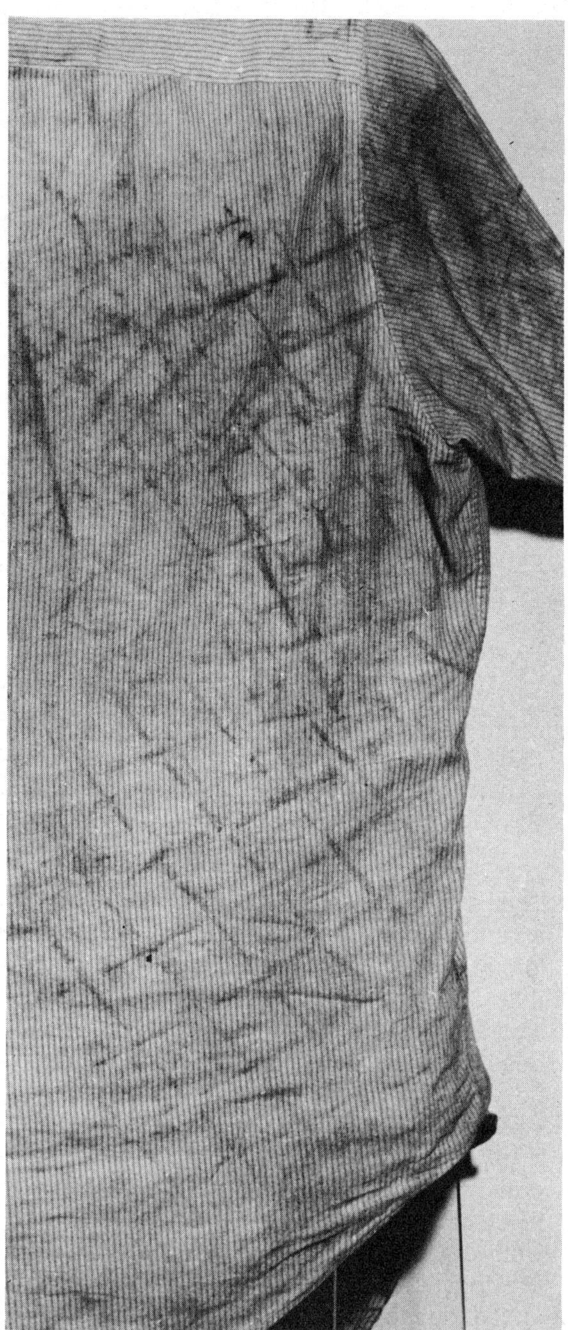

Fig. 8 — 2
An imprint found on a shirt owned by a suspect. *(Courtesy, Columbus Police Department, Ohio.)*

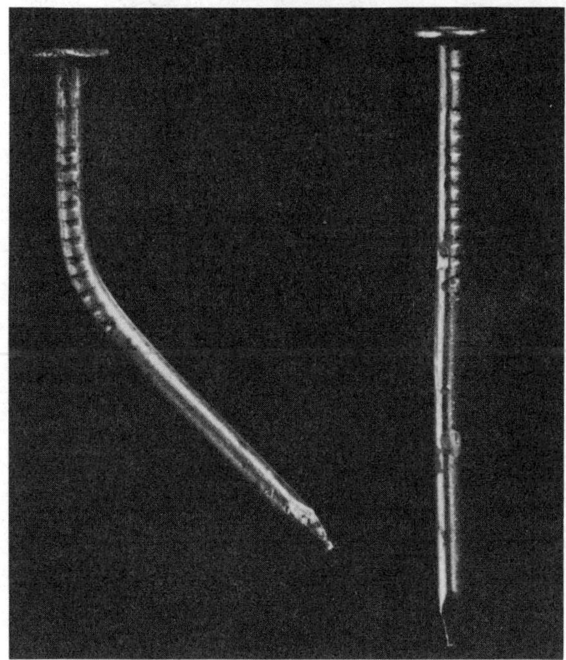

Fig. 8 — 3
Nail embedded in the instep of the sole of a shoe (ca. 3X).

Fig. 8 — 4
Two nails: left side shows nail in its entirety after removal from instep; right side is a comparison (known) nail obtained from burglarized factory (ca. 3X).

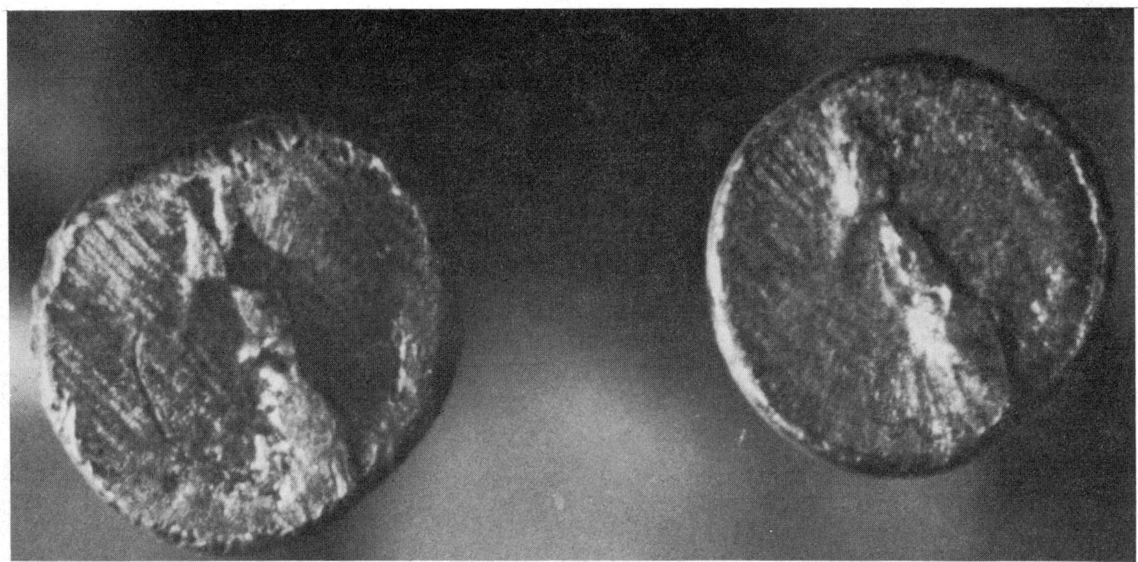

Fig. 8 — 5
Photomacrograph (ca. 18X) of the heads of the same nails (Fig. 8 — 4) showing the characteristic shapes and markings resulting from the "upset process" in the die used.

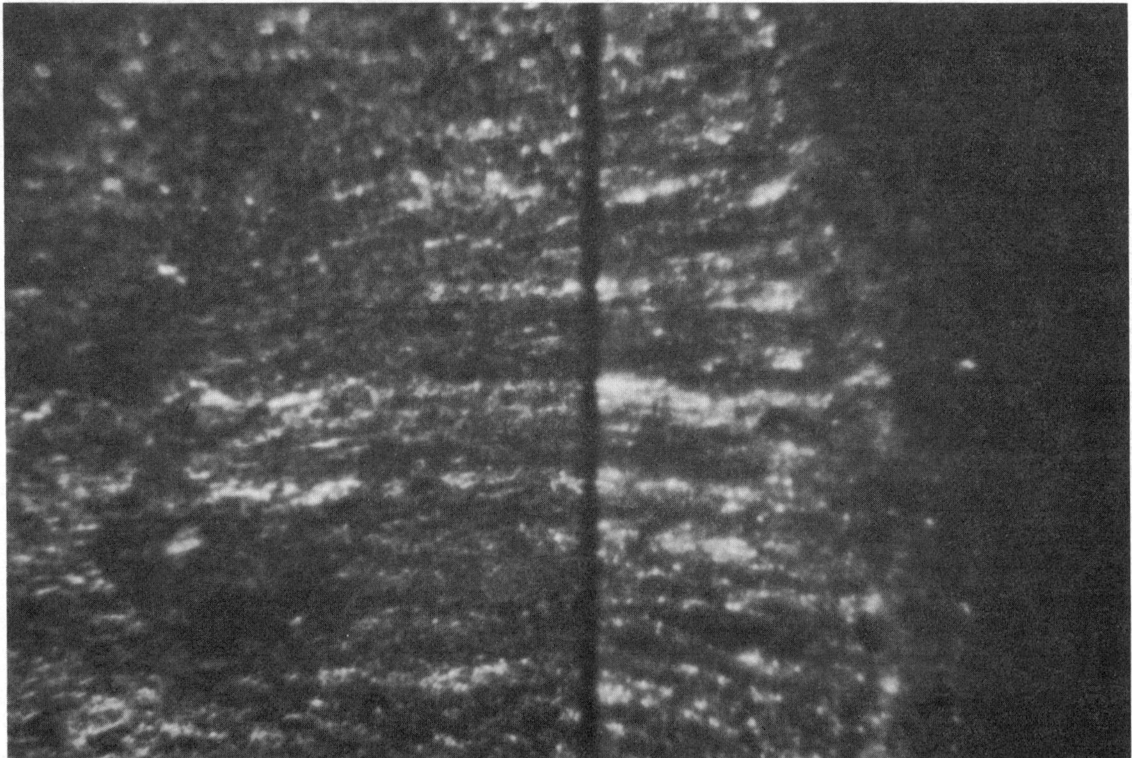

Fig. 8 — 6
Photomicrograph (ca. 100X) showing the comparison between die markings on the evidence nail head and the known nail head.
(Courtesy, Michigan State Police.)

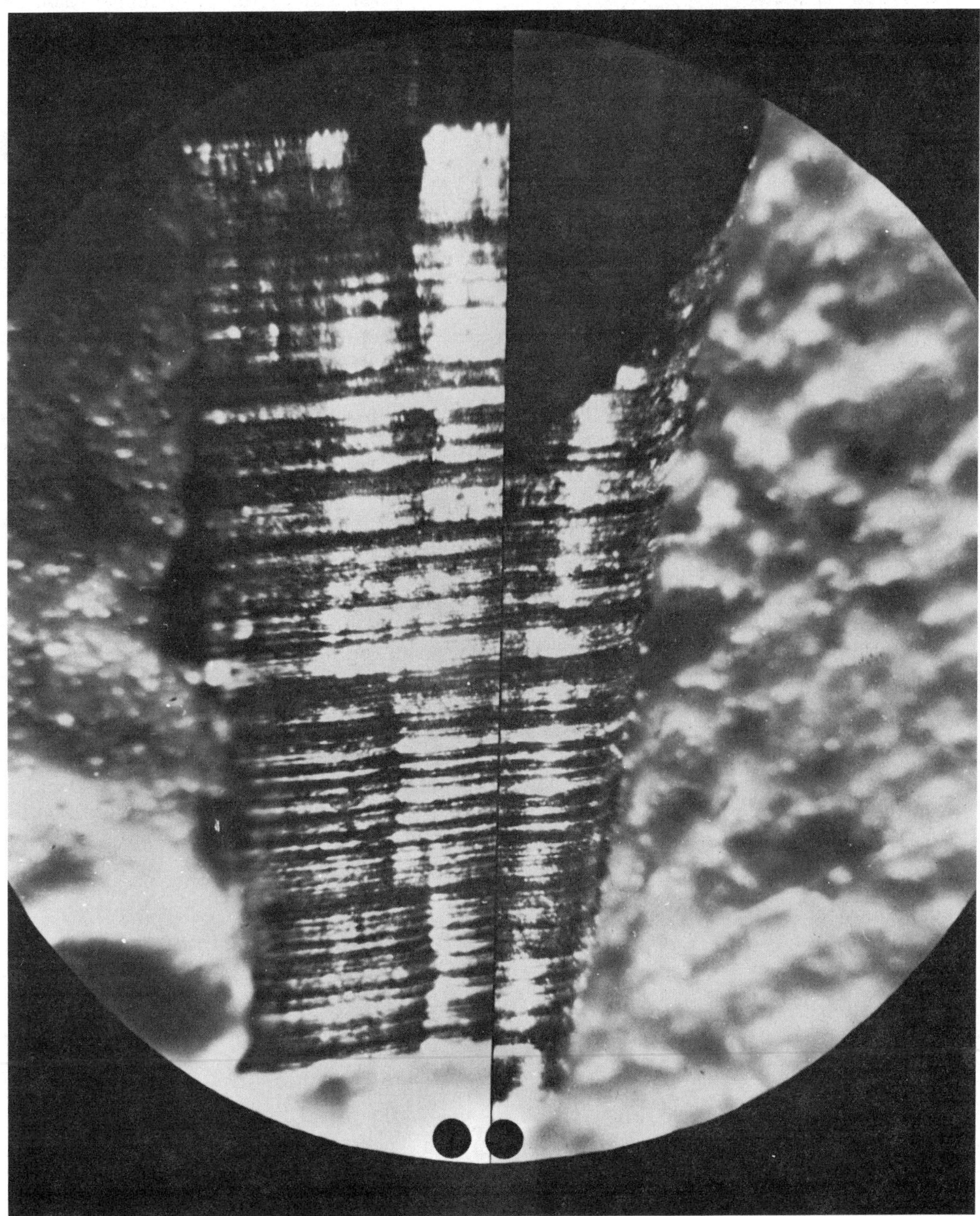

Fig. 8 — 7
Comparison of metal fragments. Piece on left is a brass metal turning obtained from lock at crime scene. The right half of the photograph shows drill marks on a piece of brass turning found in a suspect's trouser cuff.
(Courtesy, Pittsburgh-Allegheny County Laboratory, Office of District Attorney.)

A. Wood Traces

Nature never duplicates. Grains of sand or tree leaves may appear identical to the uncritical eye but even a cursory examination will soon reveal significant differences. Fingerprints are perhaps the best known example of this disparity. Identical twins originating from the same fertilized ovum and thus having the same genetic inheritance are not really identical.

Another example of nature's failure to reproduce itself precisely is found in the annual growth rings of two trees of the same species, planted side by side, the manifestation of which is most commonly observed as the grain design or growth pattern in wood. Occasionally, wood emerges as a clue material in a criminal investigation.[1] Perhaps the most familiar example of this is the now famous wooden ladder employed by Bruno Richard Hauptmann in the kidnaping of the Lindbergh baby.[2] In this case a wood identification expert of the United States Forest Service, Arthur Kohler, demonstrated that the annual growth rings in "rail 16" of the kidnap ladder were identical in number, curvature, and variation in width when compared with the annual growth rings in a floorboard (from which a piece had been sawed) in Hauptmann's attic.

Another example of a physical match involving wood is shown in Figs. 8 — 8 and 8 — 9. The most significant aspect of this case is the comment made by the investigator involved. He informed his instructor in a community college course in criminalistics that he probably would not have considered the small sticks to be of evidential value nor have submitted them for examination had he not had the background of this course which he took voluntarily and on his own initiative. This frank remark supports the belief of this author that there is considerable physical evidence available that is not utilized at present. Certainly great improvement in this respect can be anticipated when the information in texts such as this is made a part of the education of every police officer during recruit training.

B. Burglarized Article Traces

While trace evidence taken from the crime scene by the criminal is generally acquired inadvertently, some is taken deliberately. In one case a large searchlight was among the articles missing from a marine equipment factory that had been burglarized. Subsequently several suspects were apprehended and a searchlight answering the description of the stolen item was recovered. There were no identifying marks or serial numbers on any of the items taken. However, it was learned by the investigator that the electrical wiring and terminals in the searchlight had been installed at the burglarized factory. A special type of pliers was used to crimp the electrical terminals in place. Possible tool marks on the shaft of the light terminals were noted. This case is the subject of Case Exercise 2.

8.1 Exercises 1, 2 (pp 371-372)

Fig. 8 — 8
Evidence obtained following theft of a coin change device that was bolted to the floorboards in an all-night laundry. The three smaller fragments were discovered in the vehicle of a suspect. The two large boards were then obtained by the investigator from the laundry.
(Courtesy, Painted Post Police Department, New York)

Fig. 8 — 9
Two of the small fragments shown in juxtaposition with the larger boards. There are several physical matches to be noted in addition to the grain of the wood: paint on the ends of the boards, irregularity of the cracks, and scuff marks just above the painted ends.
(Courtesy, New York State Police and the Painted Post Police Department, New York.)

8.2 Mutual Transfer Evidence

Trace evidence is not necessarily left exclusively at the crime scene or taken exclusively from it; sometimes it may simultaneously be both acquired from and left at the scene during the commission of a crime. When this occurs there is a respective transfer of clue materials and the traces involved are referred to as *mutual transfer evidence*.

One of the most common situations involving mutual transfer evidence occurs when an automobile strikes another object.[3] When a person is struck, some trace of his clothing, skin, hair, or blood may be transferred to the vehicle; and paint, grease, or an outline of an ornament or other part of the vehicle may be left on the victim or his clothing.

8.2 Exercise 3 (p 372)

References

Wood Traces

1. Kukachka, B.F. "Wood Identification: Limitations and Potentialities," *J. For. Sci.* 6, 98-102 (1961).
2. Kohler, A. "Technique Used In Tracing The Lindbergh Kidnaping Ladder," *J. Crim. Law, Criminol. and Pol. Sci.* 27, 712-24 (1937).

   Radin, E.D. *12 Against Crime*. New York: Putnam, 1950. Pp 169-88.

Mutual Transfer Evidence

3. Muehlberger, C.W. "The Investigation of Deaths Due to Highway Accidents," in LeMoyne Snyder, *Homicide Investigation*. Springfield, Ill.: Thomas, 1944.

Suggestions for Further Reading

Cassidy, F.H. "Examination of Tool Marks from Sequentially Manufactured Tongue-and-Groove Pliers," *J. For. Sci.* 25, 796-809 (1980).

Watson, D.J. "The Identification of Consecutively Manufactured Crimping Die," *Assn. Firearms and Tool Mark Examiners J.* 10(3), 19-21 (Sept. 1978).

Part 3

Laboratory Work: General Considerations

9

Laboratory Reports-Report Writing

In working out the case exercises in Part 4 the student may be required to write laboratory reports summarizing his or her findings. Similarly, in crime laboratories scientific evidence examiners must prepare an account of their activities in a case. This chapter, then, provides the basic guidelines for writing standard laboratory reports.

Two model reports, one in general form and the other on a particular exercise, are given in this chapter. The student may use them as guides for writing his or her report after each exercise has been completed. The suggested style most nearly resembles a typical crime laboratory report. The reasons for using this format are twofold: (a) the student will better appreciate the problems the laboratory examiner encounters in writing a report, recognizing that it may be subpoenaed and must be able to withstand critical scrutiny during cross-examination; and (b) the student, as a potential investigator, will be able to evaluate better the thoroughness and significance of any laboratory examination made of evidence which he or she may one day submit to a laboratory.

For some exercises, an instructor may find it more suitable to request the student to compose a more traditional college-course style laboratory report comparable to those used in the natural and biological sciences. In this case, a student writes a report on the work of each laboratory exercise. The report should be concise but complete. The following should be included:

1. Title of the exercise and date performed.
2. General purpose of the exercise.
3. Any information about the method used for the examination that is not covered by the directions. Any useful experiences in performing the work.
4. Enumeration and tabulation of the data in a meaningful way.
5. Evaluation and interpretation of the data.

Whatever form the report may take, it should be completed as soon as possible after the exercise has been performed.

Laboratory Report Format
(A Generalized Illustration)

Date:

FROM: Name (including any official title)
TO: Name (or position — as Commanding Officer, etc.)
SUBJECT: IN CAPITALS RE: Lab Case No. —/yr.

1. The facts concerning the evidence. (Who delivered it; when and where it was received; what it consisted of—including type container, seals, markings; what type of laboratory examination was requested.)
2. What was done to the evidence in the laboratory. (More than one paragraph may be required to describe the work and examinations made in the laboratory. As many paragraphs as are necessary are used for doing this. Each paragraph is numbered consecutively.
3. Statement of conclusions, if any. Sometimes the work described in paragraph 2

and any following paragraphs obviates the necessity for this paragraph.

4. Disposition of the evidence.

(Your signature)

Laboratory Report for Exercise 1

(Sample)

October 3, 1981

FROM: John A. Smith, Student Laboratory Course P 451

TO: Professor James W. Osterburg, Department of Criminal Justice

SUBJECT: CREPE-SOLE PRINT EXAMINATION RE: Lab Case No. 789/81

1. On September 26, 1981 at 2:30 PM, in laboratory rm. 7, Professor James W. Osterburg submitted to this examiner two reproductions of photographs of two crepe-sole shoe impressions. One reproduction was alleged to be that of a crime scene impression and was labeled Fig. 1A. The other, labeled Fig. 1B, was alleged to be that of an impression made with the left shoe of Richard Roe, 456 Avenue X, Chicago, Ill. It was requested that these reproductions be examined in order to determine if both were made by the same shoe. Laboratory number 789/81 was assigned to this case.
2. A visual inspection of the two figures was made and twelve points of similarity were observed. In each figure the corresponding points of identity were marked and numbered from 1 through 12.
3. As a result of this examination, it is the opinion of the writer that the alleged crime scene impression (Fig. 1A) and the known test impression (Fig. 1B) were both made by the same crepe-sole shoe.
4. The marked figures will be retained in the laboratory files pending trial or other disposition of the case.

[SIGNED] *John A. Smith*

10

FBI Suggestions for Handling of Physical Evidence

The following is a reprint of a Federal Bureau of Investigation pamphlet, *Scientific Aids in Criminal Investigations: Suggestions for Handling of Physical Evidence—Identification, Preservation, Wrapping and Packing, Transmittal.* This material contains specific details covering various types of physical evidence that are helpful in implementing the handling and transmission of evidence to a laboratory. These explicit recommendations are particularly useful when evidence must be sent through the mail or by United Parcel Service or Air Express. It is helpful to read this section in the light of the general principles discussed in Chapter 2.

Proper Sealing of Evidence

The method shown below permits access to the invoice letter without breaking the inner seal. This allows the person entitled to receive the evidence to receive it in a sealed condition just as it was packed by the sender.

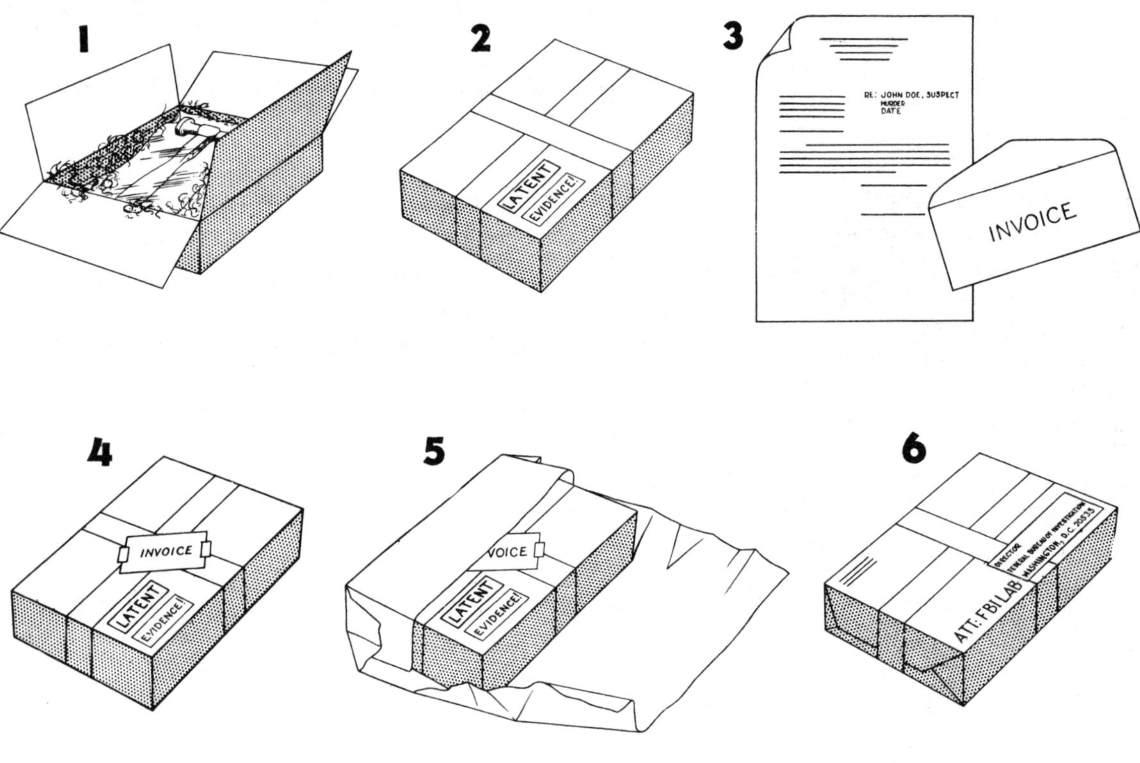

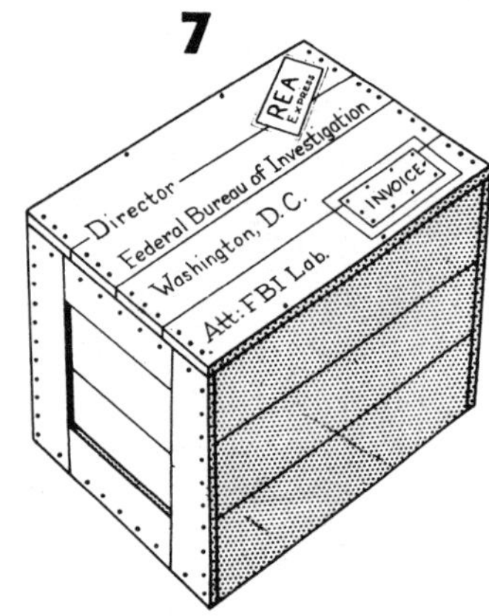

1. Pack bulk evidence securely in box.
2. *Seal* box and mark as evidence. Mark "Latent" if necessary.
3. Place copy of transmittal letter in envelope and mark "Invoice."
4. Stick envelope to *outside* of sealed box.
5. Wrap sealed box in outside wrapper and *seal* with gummed paper.
6. Address to Director
Federal Bureau of Investigation
Washington, D.C. 20535
and mark "Attention FBI Laboratory."
7. If packing box is wooden—tack invoice envelope to top under a clear plastic cover.

Chart to be Used in Submitting Evidence to the FBI Laboratory*

SPECIMEN	IDENTIFICATION	AMOUNT DESIRED STANDARD	AMOUNT DESIRED EVIDENCE	PRESERVATION	WRAPPING AND PACKING	TRANSMITTAL	MISCELLANEOUS
Abrasives, including carborundum, emery, sand, etc.	On outside of container. Type of material. Date obtained. Name or initials.	Not less than one ounce	All	None	Use containers, such as ice-cream box, pillbox, or plastic vial. Seal to prevent any loss.	Registered mail or RR or air express	Avoid use of envelopes.
Acids	Same as above	One pint	All to one pint	None	Plastic or all-glass bottle. Tape in stopper. Pack in sawdust, glass, or rock wool. Use bakelite- or paraffin-lined bottle for hydrofluoric acid.	RR express only	Label acids, glass, corrosive.
Adhesive type	Same as above	Recovered roll	All	None	Place on waxed paper or cellophane.	Registered mail	Do not cut, wad, or distort.
Alkalies— caustic soda, potash, ammonia, etc.	Same as above	One pint liquid One pound solid	All to one pint All to one pound	None	Plastic or glass bottle with rubber stopper held with adhesive tape.	RR express only	Label alkali, glass, corrosive.
Ammunition	Same as above	Two		None	Pack in cotton, soft paper, or cloth in small container. Place in wooden box.	RR express only	If standard make, usually not necessary to send. Explosive label.
Anonymous letters, extortion letters, bank robbery notes	Initial and date each document unless legal aspects or good judgment dictate otherwise.		All	Do not handle with bare hands.	Place in proper enclosure envelope and seal with "Evidence" tape or transparent cellophane tape. Flap side of envelope should show (1) wording "Enclosure(s) to Bureau from (name of submitting office)," (2) title of case, (3) brief description of contents and (4) file number, if known. Staple to original letter of transmittal.	Registered mail	Advise if evidence should be treated for latent fingerprints.
Blasting caps	On outside of container. Type of material, date obtained, and name or initials.		All	Should not be forwarded until advised to do so by the Laboratory. Packing instructions will be given at that time.			
Blood: 1. Liquid Known samples	Use adhesive tape on outside of test tube. Name of donor, date taken, doctor's name, name or initials of submitting Agent or officer.	1/6 ounce (5cc) collected in sterile test tube	All	Sterile tube only. NO PRESERVATIVE. NO REFRIGERANT.	Wrap in cotton, soft paper. Place in mailing tube or suitably strong mailing carton.	Airmail, special delivery, registered	Submit immediately. Don't hold awaiting additional items for comparison.

* This chart is not intended to be all-inclusive. If evidence to be submitted is not found herein, consult the specimen list for an item most similar in nature and submit accordingly.

SPECIMEN	IDENTIFICATION	AMOUNT DESIRED STANDARD	AMOUNT DESIRED EVIDENCE	PRESERVATION	WRAPPING AND PACKING	TRANSMITTAL	MISCELLANEOUS
2. Drowning cases	Same as above	Two specimens: one from each side of heart		Same as above	Same as above	Airmail, special delivery, registered	Same as above
3. Small quantities: a. Liquid Questioned samples	Same as above as applicable		All to 1/6 ounce (5cc)	Allow to dry thoroughly on nonporous surface.	Same as above	Airmail, special delivery, registered	Collect by using eye-dropper or clean spoon, transfer to non-porous surface. Allow to dry and submit in pillbox.
b. Dry stains Not on fabrics	On outside of pillbox or plastic vials. Type of specimen, date secured, name or initials.		As much as possible	Keep dry.	Seal to prevent leakage.	Registered mail	
4. Stained clothing, fabric, etc.	Use tag or mark directly on clothes. Type of specimens, date secured, name or initials.		As found	If wet when found, dry by hanging. USE NO HEAT TO DRY. No preservative.	Each article wrapped separately and identified on outside of package. Place in strong box packed to prevent shifting of contents.	Registered mail or air or RR express	
Bullets (not cartridges)	Initials on base		All found	None	Place in cotton or soft paper. Place in pill, match or powder box. Pack to prevent shifting during transit.	Registered mail	
Cartridges	Initials on outside of case near bullet end	Two		None	Same as above	RR express only	
Cartridge cases (shells)	Initials preferably on inside near open end or on outside near open end.		All	None	Same as above	Registered mail	
Charred or burned paper	On outside of container indicate fragile nature of evidence, date obtained, name or initials.		All	None	Pack in rigid container between layers of cotton.	Registered mail	Added moisture, with atomizer or otherwise not recommended
Checks (fraudulent)	See anonymous letters.		All	None	See anonymous letters.	Registered mail	Advise what parts questioned or known. Furnish physical description of subject.

Check protector, rubber stamp and dater stamp sets, known standards Note: Send actual device when possible.	Place name or initials, date, name of make and model, etc., on sample impressions.	Obtain several copies in full word-for-word order of each questioned check-writer impression. If unable to forward rubber stamps, prepare numerous samples with different degrees of pressure.		None	See anonymous letters or bulky evidence wrapping instructions.	Registered mail	Do not disturb inking mechanisms on printing devices.
Clothing	Mark directly on garment or use string tag. Type of evidence, name or initials, date.		All	None	Each article individually wrapped with identification written on outside of package. Place in strong container.	Registered mail or RR or air express	Leave clothing whole. Do not cut out stains. If wet, hang in room to dry before packing.
Codes, ciphers, and foreign language material	As anonymous letters		All	None	As anonymous letters	As anonymous letters	Furnish all background and technical information pertinent to examination
Drugs: 1. Liquids	Affix label to bottle in which found including name or initials and date.		All to one pint	None	If bottle has no stopper, transfer to glass-stoppered bottle and seal with adhesive tape.	Registered mail or RR or air express	Mark "Fragile." Determine alleged normal use of drug and if prescription, check with druggist to determine supposed ingredients.
2. Powders, pills, and solids	On outside of pillbox. Name or initials and date		All to 1/4 pound	None	Seal to prevent any loss by use of tape.	Registered mail or RR or air express	
Dynamite and other explosives	Consult the FBI Laboratory and follow their telephonic or telegraphic instructions.						
Fibers	On outside of sealed container or on object to which fibers are adhering.	Entire garment or other cloth item	All	None	Folded paper or pillbox. Seal edges and openings with tape.	Registered mail	Do not place loose in envelope.
Firearms	Attach string tag. Name of weapons, caliber, serial number, date found, name or initials. Serial number in notes.		All	Keep from rusting.	Wrap in paper and identify contents of package. Place in cardboard box or wooden box. Label "Firearms, For Official Law Enforcement Agency, Official Shipment."	Registered mail or RR or air express	Unload all weapons before shipping.

SPECIMEN	IDENTIFICATION	AMOUNT DESIRED STANDARD	AMOUNT DESIRED EVIDENCE	PRESERVATION	WRAPPING AND PACKING	TRANSMITTAL	MISCELLANEOUS
Fuse, safety	Attach string tag or gummed paper label, name or initials, and date	One foot	All	None	Place in manila envelope, box, or suitable container.	Registered mail or RR or air express	
Gasoline	On outside of all-metal container, label with type of material, name or initials, and date.	One quart	All to one gallon	Fireproof container	Metal container packed in wooden box.	RR express only	
Glass fragments	Adhesive tape on each piece. Name or initials and date on tape. Separate questioned and known.		All	Avoid chipping.	Wrap each piece separately in cotton. Pack in strong box to prevent shifting and breakage. Identify contents.	Registered mail or RR or air express	Mark "Fragile."
Glass particles	Name or initials, date on outside of sealed container.	3" piece of broken item	All	None	Place in pillbox, plastic or glass vial; seal and protect against breakage.	Registered mail	Do not use envelopes.
Gunpowder tests: 1. Paraffin	On outside of container. Type of material, date, and name or initials.		All	Containers must be free of any nitrate-containing substance. Keep cool.	Wrap in waxed paper or place in sandwich bags. Lay on cotton in a substantial box. Place in a larger box packed with absorbent material.	Registered mail	Use "Fragile" label. Keep cool.
2. On cloth	Attach string tag or mark directly. Type of material, date, and name or initials.		All	None	Place fabric flat between layers of paper and then wrap, so that no residue will be transferred or lost.	Registered mail	Avoid shaking.
Hair	On outside of container. Type of material, date, and name or initials.	Dozen or more full length hairs from different parts of head and/or body	All	None	Folded paper or pillbox. Seal edges and openings with tape.	Registered mail	Do not place loose in envelope.
Handwriting and hand printing, known standards	Name or initials, date, from whom obtained, and voluntary statement should be included in appropriate place.	See footnote.*		None	See anonymous letters.	Registered mail	
Matches	On outside of container. Type of material, date, and name or initials.	One to two books of paper. One full box of wood.	All	Keep away from fire.	Metal container and packed in larger package to prevent shifting. Matches in box or metal container packed to prevent friction between matches.	RR express or registered mail	"Keep away from fire" label

* Duplicate the original writing conditions as to text, speed, slant, size of paper, size of writing, type of writing instruments, etc. Do not allow suspect to see questioned writing. Give no instructions as to spelling, punctuation, etc. Remove each sample from sight as soon as completed. Suspect should fill out blank check forms in cases (FD-352). In hand printing cases, both upper- (capital) and lower-case (small) samples should be obtained. In forgery cases, obtain sample signatures of the person whose name is forged. Have writer prepare some specimens with hand not normally used. Obtain undictated handwriting when feasible.

Medicines (See drugs)							
Metal	Same as above	One pound	All to one pound	Keep from rusting.	Use paper boxes or containers. Seal and use strong paper or wooden box.	Registered mail or RR or air express	Melt number, heat treatment, and other specifications of foundry if available.
Oil	Same as above	One quart together with specifications	All to one quart	Keep away from fire	Metal container with tight screw top. Pack in strong box using excelsior or similar material.	RR express only	DO NOT USE DIRT OR SAND FOR PACKING MATERIAL.
Obliterated, eradicated, or indented writing	See anonymous letters.		All	None	See anonymous letters.	Registered mail	Advise whether bleaching or staining methods may be used. Avoid folding.
Organs of body	On outside of container. Victim's name, date of death, date of autopsy, name of doctor, name or initials.		All to one pound	None to evidence. Dry ice in package not touching glass jars.	Plastic or all-glass containers (glass jar with glass top)	RR or air express	"Fragile" label. Keep cool. Metal top containers must not be used. Send autopsy report.
Paint:							
1. Liquid	On outside of container. Type of material, origin if known, date, name or initials.	Original unopened container up to 1 gallon if possible	All to 1/4 pint	None	Friction-top paint can or large-mouth, screw-top jars. If glass, pack to prevent breakage. Use heavy corrugated paper or wooden box.	Registered mail or RR or air express	
2. Solid (paint chips or scrapings)	Same as above	At least 1/2 sq. inch of solid, with all layers represented	All. If on small object send object.	Wrap so as to protect smear.	If small amount, round pill-box or small glass vial with screw top. Seal to prevent leakage. Envelopes not satisfactory.	Registered mail or RR or air express	Do not pack in cotton. Avoid contact with adhesive materials.
Plaster casts of tire treads and shoe prints	On back before plaster hardens. Location, date, and name or initials.	Send in shoes and tires of suspects. Photographs and sample impressions are usually not suitable for comparison.	All shoe prints; entire circumference of tires.	Allow casts to cure (dry) before wrapping.	Wrap in paper and cover with suitable packing material. Do not wrap in unventilated plastic bags.	Registered mail or RR or air	Use "Fragile" label. Mix approximately four pounds of plaster to quart of water.
Powder patterns (See gunpowder tests.)							
Rope, twine, and cordage	On tag or container. Type of material, date, name or initials.	One yard	All		Wrap securely.	Registered mail	

SPECIMEN	IDENTIFICATION	AMOUNT DESIRED STANDARD	AMOUNT DESIRED EVIDENCE	PRESERVATION	WRAPPING AND PACKING	TRANSMITTAL	MISCELLANEOUS
Safe insulation or soil	On outside of container. Type of material, date, name or initials.	1/2 pound	All to one pound		Use containers, such as ice-cream box, pillbox, or plastic vial. Seal to prevent any loss.	Registered mail or RR or air express	Avoid use of glass containers and envelopes.
Shoe print lifts (impressions on hard surfaces)	On lifting tape or paper attached to tape. Name or initials and date.	Photograph before making lift of dust impression.	All	None	Prints in dust are easily damaged. Fasten print or lift to bottom of a box so that nothing will rub against it.	Registered mail	Always rope off crime scene area until shoe prints or tire treads are located and preserved.
Tools	On tools or use string tag. Type of tool, identifying number, date, name or initials.		All		Wrap each tool in paper. Use strong cardboard or wooden box with tools packed to prevent shifting.	Registered mail or RR or air express	
Toolmarks	On object or on tag attached to or on opposite end from where toolmarks appear. Name or initials and date.	Send in the tool. If impractical make several impressions on similar material as evidence using entire marking area of tool.	All	Cover ends bearing toolmarks with soft paper and wrap with strong paper to protect ends.	After marks have been protected, wrap in strong wrapping paper, place in strong box, and pack to prevent shifting.	Registered mail or RR or air express	
Typewriting, known standards	Place name or initials, date, serial number, name of make and model, etc., on specimens.	Obtain at least one copy in full word-for-word order of questioned typewriting. Also include partial copies in light, medium, and heavy degrees of touch. Also carbon paper samples of every character on the keyboard.		None	See anonymous letters.	Registered mail	Examine ribbon for evidence of questioned message thereon. For carbon paper samples either remove ribbon or place in stencil position.
Urine or water	On outside of container. Type of material, name of subject, date taken, name or initials.	Preferably all urine voided over a period of 24 hours	All	None. Use any clean bottle with leakproof stopper.	Bottle surrounded with absorbent material to prevent breakage. Strong cardboard or wooden box.	Registered mail	
Wire (See also toolmarks.)	On label or tag. Type of material, date, name or initials.	Three feet (Do not kink.)	All (Do not kink.)		Wrap securely.	Registered mail	Do not kink wire.
Wood	Same as above	One foot	All		Wrap securely.	Registered mail	

NOTES

The work of science is to substitute facts for appearances, and demonstrations for impressions.

John Ruskin, Stones of Venice, III, 1853

Part 4

Case Exercises

Introduction

A major function of the crime laboratory is to link the crime scene and criminal through physical evidence. The term *associative evidence* is used to describe this aspect of criminalistics. Associative evidence lends itself readily to courtroom presentation through photographs, which can demonstrate to a jury the factual evidence and grounds upon which the connection between crime scene and criminal is based.

There are many ways in which crime scene evidence may be considered. From an investigative viewpoint, as well as for convenience, it is logical to categorize physical clues as shown in Table I.

TABLE I

Categories of Physical Clues

Source	*Examples*
Criminal's body	Fingerprints, blood, hair, semen
Wearing apparel	Shoe impressions, glove marks, fibers
Instruments employed in the commission of the crime	Tool marks, bullets, and cartridge cases
Miscellaneous	Paint chips, broken glass, and trouser cuff debris

As the reader works through the case exercises presented in this section, he or she will observe that the evidence is generally brought to the crime scene by the criminal. While this is the more common circumstance, evidence taken from the scene of the crime can be equally effective in tying scene and criminal together. The last exercise to be performed provides a few examples of the latter. In any event, associative evidence is the result of a successful comparison between a crime scene clue and similar clue material found on the person or in the possession of a suspect.

Comparison Characteristics and Their Significance

There are two types of characteristics or details which are useful in the comparison of two objects. *Class characteristics* are the more obvious, gross features distinguishable in an object. In fingerprints they are the patterns that form a loop, whorl, or arch. In firearms the features involved are the caliber of the barrel and the number and direction of twist of the lands in the barrel. With evidence involving impressions such as those left by shoes, tires, and some tools, the general dimensions, design, and contour of the imprint constitute the class characteristics. For fabrics, the type of fiber, weave pattern, and thread count comprise the class characteristics.

The visual comparison of two objects for class characteristics may be rather simple yet quite important because it serves as a screening technique that determines whether further examination is necessary. When two objects do not agree in their class characteristics they are clearly of different origin. Any further comparison is unnecessary if the goal of the examination is an inference of identity in origin. Class differences therefore are conclusive. When the evidence survives this screening test the examination is extended and individual characteristics (*v.i.*) are sought in each object. It is through the comparison of these characteristics that an inference becomes possible concerning the likelihood of a common source for the crime scene evidence and the known, reference specimen.

In Chapter 3 the concept of *individual, characterizing details* was developed. The minutiae of detail in the ridge formation on digital skin were used to illustrate the basis of fingerprint identity. The fine scratch marks, called *striations*, imparted to a bullet by a gun barrel, constitute the individual details that characterize a firearm. A general appreciation of the origin of individual characteristics should be of some assistance in their recognition when they are present in less familiar types of physical evidence. Individual characteristics are attributable to several sources:

1. Natural phenomena — as in the details present in the skin ridges of a finger, the topographical irregularities in crepe-rubber sole pattern, or the reamer marks in a gun barrel.
2. Minor damage through abuse — as in attempting to use a tool that is inadequate for the job. For example, employing a ball peen hammer where a sledge hammer would have been necessary to accomplish the task.
3. More serious damage through misuse — as in using an instrument carelessly or for a job for which it was never intended. For example, repeated striking of one typewriter key on another to the point of battering the design of the letter, or employing an ax to cut through the metal skin of a safe.
4. Uneven or accidental wear — as an automobile tire on an improperly aligned wheel or the worn places on the sole and heel of a shoe.

The recognition of and distinction between class and individual characteristics is not always obvious or simple and sometimes is quite subtle. For example, is the damaged serif on the typeface the result of normal wear through normal typewriter usage, or has its damage been hastened through misuse as indicated above in category 3. If the former is the reason, the damage to the typeface represents a class characteristic; if the latter is true, the damage represents an individual characteristic. A clear-cut decision may not always be possible, for as with all science there is a gray area that poses difficulty. Specialized education and experience are the foundations upon which the solution of questions of this kind is based. Table II illustrates the difference between a class and an individual characteristic. It is important to note that individual characteristics vary with the nature of the evidence.

Careful study of this book should impart some understanding concerning class and individual characteristics. The importance of this understanding lies in the fact that the essence of the problem of the recognition and preservation of much physical evidence is an informed awareness of the presence of class and individual characteristics in crime scene evidence. The case exercises are intended to provide a clear and more than superficial understanding of the significance of these characteristics for the transformation of potential evidence into associative evidence with investigation and probative value.

When the basis for the laboratory examination of such evidence is grasped by crime scene officers through performance of the case exercises, recognition of potential clue material will be more frequent and its preservation, based on scientific understanding, will be accomplished with discernment and confidence.

Basic Procedure For Case Exercises

The essential part of the physical evidence in a case may often be presented in the form of two photographs. One is of the crime scene evidence and the other is of the comparison sample whose source and identity are known.

This question is almost invariably posed: "Is there a common explanation or origin for the subjects recorded in the two photographs?" Or as a concrete example, the question asked is: "Was the fingerprint in blood on the glass win-

TABLE II

Class and Individual Characteristics in Various Types of Evidence

Type of Evidence	*Characteristics*		
	CLASS	**INDIVIDUAL**	
	Example	*Example*	*Visual Appearance*
Fingerprints	arches loops whorls	ridge ending, bifurcation short ridge, enclosure dot, bridge, spur, trifurcation	see p *15*
Bullets and cartridges	caliber number of lands and grooves direction of twist of rifling	scratch marks or striations in the lands and grooves	see Figs. 6 — 39, 6 — 43
Handwriting	hand printing cursive writing	any deviation from the any model letters of the *system used to teach handwriting, i.e., peculiarities of letter formation*	for *R* *for g*
Shoe impressions	heel design sole design manufacturer's name	gouges, cuts, and other marks acquired accidentally through wear	see Figs. 5 — 6 - 5 — 9
Tool impressions	hammer screwdriver jimmy metal cutters	nicks, dents, broken edges, and other damage from misuse or abuse	see Figs. 6 — 9, 6 — 16, 6 — 22

dow made by the same finger that made one of the inked impressions on this fingerprint record card?" If the answer to this question is "yes," then the criminal has been linked to the crime scene.

In each case exercise two photographs generally are presented for examination by the student. They have been reproduced in an enlarged form so that visual inspection is sufficient for their comparison. Occasionally additional photographs may be used to increase understanding of the issue involved.

The first step in each exercise is to determine if the class characteristics in the crime scene and comparison photographs are similar and if there are any obvious or subtle discrepancies. If no differences are observed, attention is focused upon locating in each photograph those minute details which constitute the various individual characteristics. As an individual characteristic is observed, it is marked and given the same number in each photograph. This process is continued until no further individual details can be found. At this juncture the question arises as to how the details which were noted may be evaluated and interpreted in terms of associative evidence.

Interpretation of Comparison Details

When the class characteristics are similar in both objects or photographs, and the individual characteristics have been noted, three conclusions are possible depending upon the number, relative position, and degree of unusualness of the individual characteristics:

1. The evidence details recorded in both photographs arise from the same source; that is, they have a common origin. There are many, but not unusual, individual characteristics present in both photographs. If one or more unusual characteristics are present in a fingerprint (such as trifurcation, or a spur, or both) fewer of the more common characteristics (such as a ridge ending) are required. The relative position of each comparable characteristic must be the same in each object or photograph.
2. The evidence details recorded in both photographs could have a common origin. (There are several individual characteristics, none of which is particularly unusual, present in both photographs.)
3. No explanation such as a common source or origin is possible for the evidence depicted in both photographs. (There are no, or at best only a few, individual characteristics present in both photographs.)

The evaluation of the details permitting conclusions (1 or 2) is still a subjective rather than an objective matter in many areas of criminalistics.[1] Education, experience, and knowledge of the literature provide the basis for expert opinion. It might be useful at this point to examine how the legal mind views the process of inference. Wigmore has elucidated the problem in such a manner as to satisfy both legal and scientific considerations when he stated:

> The process of inference . . . operates by *comparing common marks*, found to exist in the two hypothetically separate objects of thought, with reference to the possibility of their being really the same.
>
> 1. It follows that its force depends on the *necessariness of the association between the mark and a single object.* Where a certain circumstance, feature, or mark, may commonly be found associated with a large number of objects, the presence of that feature or mark in two supposed objects is little indication of their identity. . . . But where the objects possessing the mark are only one or a few, and the mark is found in two supposed instances, the chances of the two being different are "nil" or are proportionately small.
>
> 2. . . . The evidencing feature is usually a *group of circumstances*, which as a whole constitute a feature capable of being associated with a single object. Rarely can one circumstance alone be so inherently peculiar to a single object. It is by adding circumstance to circumstance that we obtain a composite feature or mark which as a whole cannot be supposed to be associated with more than a single object.
>
> The process of constructing an inference . . . thus consists usually in *adding together a number of circumstances* each of which by itself might be a feature of many objects, but *all of which together can most probably, in experience, coexist in a single object only.* Each additional circumstance reduces the chances of there being more than one object so associated.[2]

Case Selection and Order

In the cases selected for use in this book, the essence of the exercise is the recognition of the significant details and an evaluation of their import. In the first few exercises the problems of recognition and interpretation will be quite simple. As the student works through the book, one or both problems will increase in difficulty. When the study of the text is completed, the problems of the recognition and preservation of evidence should have new meaning for the serious student.

A certain logic provided the basis for grouping the case material into chapters; however, the difficulty experienced in working through each exercise for the first time is totally unrelated to the demands of that logic.

Therefore, the order of exercises listed on pp 167-168 is suggested to permit study of the easier cases first. As the student works through the cases in the order suggested he or she will probably find the exercises progressively more difficult. Upon completion of all of the exercises the student should review them in the sequence of the chapters. The student should find that the book may now be studied more readily as a traditional text than on first reading.

References

1. Osterburg, J.W. "An Inquiry into the Nature of Proof," *J. For. Sci.* 9, 413-27 (1964).
   Biasotti, A.A. "The Principles of Evidence Evaluation as Applied to Firearms and Tool Mark Identification," *J. For. Sci.* 9, 428-33 (1964).
   Kirk, P.L., and Kingston, C.R. "Evidence Evaluation and Problems in General Criminalistics," *J. For. Sci.* 9, 434-44 (1964).
   Conrad, E.C. "The Expert and Legal Certainty," *J. For. Sci.* 9, 445-55 (1964).
2. Wigmore, John H. *The Science of Judicial Proof*. 3rd ed., rev. and enl. Boston, Mass.: Little, Brown, 1937. Pp 258-59.

Case Exercises

The cases in this section are to be performed one at a time, and in the order presented in the list below. *They are not to be performed by chapter order.* This order of performance permits the student to progress from the least difficult cases to the most difficult by degrees. The appropriate chapter and section material should be read before any attempt is made to study the case evidence.

There are a limited number of cases for which solutions, as developed by experts in the field, are provided. (These cases are marked by an * next to the case exercise number.) These solutions have been included in this text to indicate the amount of expertise necessary in the professional demands of criminal investigation. They have also been included to help guide the student in analyzing his or her approach to some of the more difficult cases presented. When the student has completed examination of these cases, marked the photographs, and written the report, he or she should turn to the page where the case solution is presented.

For those who might be tempted to examine the marked case material in the Appendix before they study the evidence as presented in this section, an admonition is necessary. The value of the first reading of the text is considerably enhanced by following the procedure recommended here. The student who finds onerous the slight self-discipline necessary to follow this prescription will find it more difficult to measure up to the greater and very real demands of a life in law enforcement.

Order of Performance	*Chapter and Section*	*Case Exercise*
1. Introductory Exercise A		p 168
2. Introductory Exercise B†		p 168
3. Crepe Sole Print	Ch. 5, §5.1	Ex. 1, p 242
4. Latent Fingerprints	Ch. 4, §4.1	Ex. 1, p 173
5. Heelprint†	Ch. 5, §5.1	Ex. 7, p 243
6. Firing Pin Impression	Ch. 6, §6.4	Ex. 10, p 289
7. Crimping Plier Tool Mark†	Ch. 8, §8.1	Ex. 2, pp 371-372
8. Tire Sand Impression	Ch. 6, §6.1	Ex. 1, p 288
9. Die	Ch. 6, §6.3	Ex. 7, p 289
10. Jimmy Mark in Wood†	Ch. 6, §6.2	Ex. 2, p 288
11. Heelprint in Sand	Ch. 5, §5.1	Ex. 4, p 242
12. Inked Fingerprints	Ch. 4, §4.1	Ex. 2, p 173
13. Paint Chip Match	Ch. 7, §7.2	Ex. 4, p 348
14. Ax Chop Marks	Ch. 6, §6.2	Ex. 4, p 289
15. Heelprint Comparison	Ch. 5, §5.1	Ex. 5, p 243
16. Bullet Comparison	Ch. 6, §6.4	Ex. 9, p 289
17. Kidnap Note Characteristics	Ch. 4, §4.5	Ex. 8, p 174

Order of Performance	*Chapter and Section*	*Case Exercise*
18. Palmprint Comparison	Ch. 4, §4.2	Ex. 4, p 173
19. Shovel Marks	Ch. 6, §6.5	Ex. 14, p 290
20. Earprint Comparison	Ch. 4, §4.6	Ex. 11, p 175
21. Sneaker Print	Ch. 5, §5.1	Ex. 2, p 242
22. Partial Fingerprints†	Ch. 4, §4.1	Ex. 3, p 173
23. Partial Palmprints†	Ch. 4, §4.2	Ex. 5, p 173
24. Lipstick Impressions†	Ch. 4, §4.9	Ex. 14, p 175
25. Powder Residue	Ch. 6, §6.4	Ex. 12, p 290
26. Headlamp Rims†	Ch. 7, §7.1	Ex. 2, p 348
27. Sneaker Print†	Ch. 5, §5.1	Ex. 3, p 242
28. Questioned Handwriting (Cursive)†	Ch. 4, §4.5	Ex. 10, p 175
29. Breech Face Marks†	Ch. 6, §6.4	Ex. 11, pp 289-290
30. Jimmy	Ch. 6, §6.2	Ex. 3, p 288
31. Metal Cutters — Copper Wire	Ch. 6, §6.2	Ex. 6, p 289
32. Wiper Blade Spot Weld	Ch. 7, §7.1	Ex. 1, p 347
33. Tie Clasp†	Ch. 5, §5.4	Ex. 11, p 244
34. Accoustic Patterns†	Ch. 4, §4.8	Ex. 13, p 175
35. Poor Heelprint	Ch. 5, §5.1	Ex. 6, p 243
36. Glove Impression†	Ch. 5, §5.3	Ex. 10, pp 243-244
37. Broken Glass Strain Marks	Ch. 7, §7.3	Ex. 5, p 348
38. Bra Strap	Ch. 5, §5.2	Ex. 8, p 243
39. Mattress Stain — Sheet Stain	Ch. 7, §7.1	Ex. 3, p 348
40. Questioned Printing†	Ch. 4, §4.5	Ex. 9, pp 174-175
41. Glove Impression	Ch. 5, §5.3	Ex. 9, p 243
42. Hose Knife Cut	Ch. 6, §6.4	Ex. 13, p 290
43. Teethmark Comparison	Ch. 4, §4.4	Ex. 7, p 174
44. Bloody Footprint	Ch. 4, §4.3	Ex. 6, pp 173-174
45. Armprint Impression†	Ch. 4, §4.7	Ex. 12, p 175
46. Hammer Impression	Ch. 6, §6.2	Ex. 5, p 289
47. Wood Grain — Auto Hood	Ch. 8, §8.1	Ex. 1, p 371
48. Punchmark†	Ch. 6, §6.3	Ex. 8, p 289
49. Coat — Auto Lens	Ch. 8, §8.2	Ex. 3, p 372

†New to this edition.

Introductory Exercise A*

In the illustration for this exercise, both drawings appear to have the same class characteristics. These drawings should be removed from the book and studied closely to determine if they are identical, or if there are individual differences in each, indicating nonidentity. The student should mark any discrepancies in the drawings with a straight horizontal line leading from the point where a difference is noted to the right or left margin of the paper. When you are satisfied that you have found all of the dissimilarities, refer to the Appendix for the solution to the exercise.

* *Case solution, p 394.*

Introductory Exercise B*

What Are Your Powers Of Observation?

Try this test of your visual acuity. First, read the sentence in the box.

FINISHED FILES ARE THE RE-SULT OF YEARS OF SCIENTIF-IC STUDY COMBINED WITH THE EXPERIENCE OF YEARS.

Next, count the number of "F"s in that sentence. Count them *only once*. Record your finding and refer to the Appendix for the correct answer.

* *Case solution, p 394.*

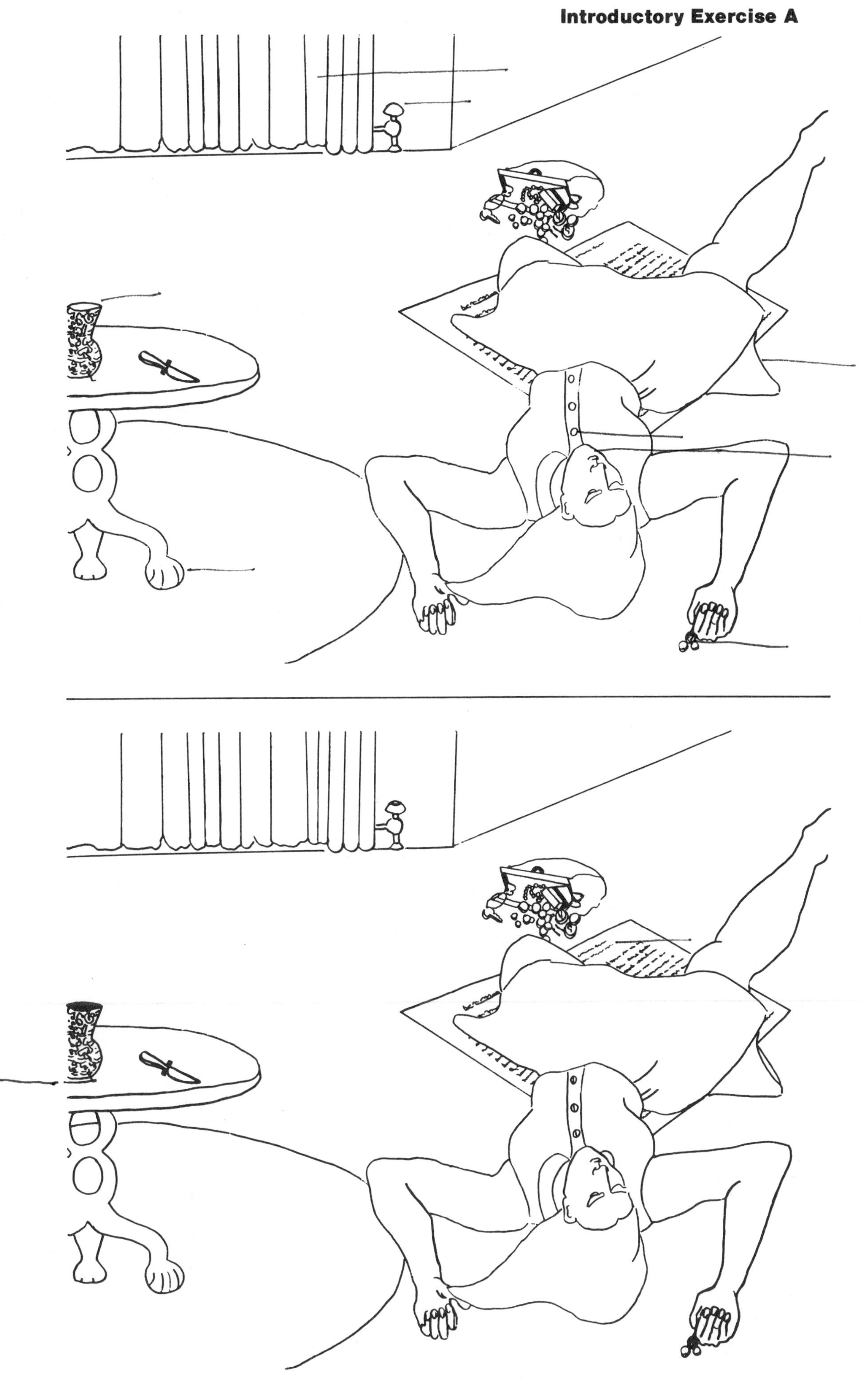

Traces of the Person Case Exercises

4.1 Fingerprints

Exercise 1: Latent Fingerprints
Fig. 1A — Latent fingerprint
Fig. 1B — Inked fingerprint

Exercise 2: Inked Fingerprints
Fig. 2A — Inked fingerprint
Fig. 2B — Inked fingerprint

Exercise 3: Partial Fingerprints
Fig. 3A — Partial fingerprint of limited size
Fig. 3B — Inked fingerprint

4.2 Palmprints

Exercise 4: Palmprint Comparison
Fig. 4A — Partial latent palmprint
Fig. 4B — Portion of inked palmprint

Exercise 5: Partial Palmprints
Fig. 5A — Partial palmprint of limited area
Fig. 5B — Partial palmprint of limited area

4.3 Bare Footprints

Exercise 6: Bloody Footprint
Fig. 6A — Bloody imprint of ulcerated sole
Fig. 6B — Inked impression of bare foot

4.4 Teethmarks

Exercise 7: Teethmark Comparison
Fig. 7A — Teethmarks in pencil
Fig. 7B — Comparison standard

4.5 Handwriting

Exercise 8: Kidnap note characteristics
Fig. 8A — Ransom note in Weinberger case

4.1 Fingerprints

Exercise 1: Latent Fingerprints

Figure 1A is an enlargement of a partial latent fingerprint developed at the scene of a homicide. Figure 1B is an enlargement of an inked impression of a suspect's finger. The question to be resolved is whether the same finger made both impressions. The discussion of fingerprint characteristics (pp 14-15, Chapter 3) should be referred to by the reader. Subsequently, the student should mark the photographs for individual characteristics after comparing Figs. 1A and 1B side by side.

*Exercise 2: Inked Fingerprints**

The reader is referred to the Introduction for this section, where it will be noted that the present exercise is twelfth in order of performance. Exercise 1 for Chapter 4 involved a comparison between a partial latent impression and an inked impression. This exercise involves the comparison of two inked impressions taken at two different times for the purpose of recording an arrest. The prints (Figs. 2A and 2B) should be examined side by side. The discussion of "Comparison Characteristics and Their Significance" (pp 161-162) might profitably be reviewed at this point.

* *Case solution, p 397.*

Exercise 3: Partial Fingerprints

Figure 3A is a partial fingerprint pattern developed on the trigger of a gun. Figure 3B is the right index finger of a suspect. Can the print on the trigger prove or disprove that the suspect handled the weapon?

4.2 Palmprints

Exercise 4: Palmprint Comparison

Figure 4A is an enlarged photograph of a partial, latent palmprint developed on the side of the roof of a taxicab. Prior to being garroted with an apron string, the cabdriver apparently became suspicious of the intentions of his passengers. As a precaution, he wrote on the back of his trip card the nicknames they used in addressing each other. The driver's concern was no doubt attributable to the common knowledge at that time among taxicab drivers that they were being preyed upon by a group of young people. A search of youthful gang files for companions who used the nicknames produced a limited set of suspects. Further investigation suggested two in particular as the most likely culprits. They denied involvement when first questioned, but when an examination proved one of their palmprints compared favorably with the palmprint shown in Fig. 4A, they changed their statements and each accused the other of the actual garroting. Figure 4B is an enlarged image of the palmprint of one of the two suspects.

Examine the two figures side by side. Students generally take a little time to become oriented to the pattern. The points of identity become apparent after the first point is located.

Exercise 5: Partial Palmprints

Figures 5A and 5B are enlargements of palmprints of limited size in the region of the delta formation. Do they have a common origin?

4.3 Bare Footprints

Exercise 6: Bloody Footprint

Figure 6A is an imprint in blood found on the floor of a kitchen. Through study it became apparent that the imprint was left by a person who had an ulcerated sole. The crime was committed by using a dah (a Burmese sword) to assault a man who was sleeping on the wooden floor. One of the suspects who emerged as a result of other aspects of the investigation was found to have pitted, open sores on the soles of both feet. Figure 6B is an inked impression of one of these soles. This exercise is a bit difficult and it requires, at first, a little patience to ascertain the individual characteristics. Examine both figures with great care. It is important to note that the points of identity may vary somewhat in shape and size since the recording media, blood and printer's ink, may reproduce pitted marks differently.

Important lessons may be learned from this exercise: an impression which seems fragmentary and indistinct should nevertheless be preserved; and crime scene evidence occurs in many varieties, some of which will be new to the investigator. The full potential of such clue material will be realized only when the education of criminal investigators includes academic study and is not dependent almost solely upon apprentice training.

4.4 Teethmarks

Exercise 7: Teethmark Comparison

Figure 7A is an enlarged reproduction of one section of the surface of the pencil recovered from the rear floor of the suspect's automobile. Figure 7B is the comparison standard, an enlargement of a portion of a pencil which the bookkeeper had clenched between her teeth in her usual manner.

The basis of bite pattern identity depends upon the observation that the relative position of the teeth, their size, normal wear, irregularities, injuries, and loss, as well as bite pressure, are manifest dental differences among individuals. Both figures should be examined side by side for evidence of individual characteristics. The angles at which the pencils were photographed varied somewhat, owing to the shape of the pencils; however, the configuration and morphology of the individual characteristics remain the same although their size may vary from one photograph to the other.

4.5 Handwriting

*Exercise 8: Kidnap Note Characteristics**

The purpose of this experiment is to examine the same kidnap note that was presented in Chapter 4 (Fig. 4—6) for those writing characteristics which seem significant after one has had an opportunity to study the note (Fig. 8A). To a surprising extent, our normal acquaintance with writing permits even the untutored to recognize unusual characteristics in unfamiliar writing. However, if several of the suggested readings are perused in advance they will be helpful in working through the exercise. In addition, they will also offer the reader a greater understanding of the potential of document examination in criminal investigation.

Your examination of the ransom note should not be confined to the formation of the letters in the words. Punctuation, for example, may prove to be of some value. There are other characteristics that should be noted.

Assume that the person who wrote this document is willing to cooperate with the investigator when he learns he is a suspect in this case. What precautions would you take and what would you do to obtain a comparison specimen of the suspect's handwriting? Treat these issues in your report.

* *Case solution, p 400.*

*Exercise 9: Questioned Printing**

A robber, using the same modus operandi (M.O.), had been quite successful over a three month period. His target was clothing stores. He robbed only on Thursday nights at closing time and generally tied his victim in the backroom or basement to a building support pole or other fixed object. A newspaper was employed to conceal his weapon while entering the store. When he had managed to maneuver the sales clerk to the rear of the premises he flashed the weapon to indicate his intention. In one case, owing to some distraction while tying up his victim, he inadvertently left the newspaper behind.

The investigator, instead of merely having the external pages examined for fingerprints, studied this potential evidence in its entirety. He noted with interest that the crossword puzzle had been completed. Shortly thereafter one of the victims, a store clerk, walking to a restaurant on his lunch hour, observed an individual who appeared to be the robber. He summoned the police who arrested the suspect. Figure 9A is the newspaper puzzle discovered at the crime scene. Figure 9B is a crossword puzzle completed by the suspect. Examine both exhibits to determine whether or not they were printed by the same person.

* Case solution, pp 403-405.

*Exercise 10: Questioned Handwriting (Cursive)**

In comparison of questioned handwriting it is most desirable to dictate to the suspect and have him or her write the message several times without ever having seen the original. Misspellings, peculiarities of punctuation, and so on may show up in the request standards if the original writer is among the suspects. By obtaining several dictated specimens of writing, the investigator usually will be able to discern any attempt at disguise. The dictated specimens should all appear alike, without obvious changes occurring. By collecting each dictated specimen when it is completed, and by delaying for several minutes dictation for the next specimen, the investigator is likely to spot a suspect who is unable to replicate the exact changes as introduced in preceding specimens. If this phenomenon is observed, it in itself is an investigative clue that must be followed up. In some cases, merely pointing out to the suspect that the camouflage attempt has been noted is sufficient to provoke a confession.

Figure 10A is a short threatening note. Figures 10B through 10G are specimen writings obtained by dictation from several suspects. Is the writer of Fig. 10A among the suspects?

* Case solution, pp 405-406.

4.6 Earprints

Exercise 11: Earprint Comparison

Figure 11A is a photograph of an ear imprint left on a safe just to the left of the dial. Figures 11B through 11F are earprints of five suspects. Examine Fig. 11A with the known earprints and determine if an identity exists between it and any of the suspects' ears.

4.7 Skin Patterns

Exercise 12: Armprint Impression

Figure 12A is a further enlargement of a section of Fig. 4 — 9 (p37), Chapter 4. Figure 12B is a corresponding enlargement of a portion of an inked impression of an area of skin below the elbow on an inner forearm of the suspect. Examine Figs. 12A and 12B to determine if an identity exists.

4.8 Voiceprints

*Exercise 13: Accoustic Patterns**

Figure 13A is a sound spectrum or an accoustic pattern of an unknown speaker. Accoustic patterns of four different speakers' voices are found in Figs. 13B and 13C. Is the unknown speaker among these patterns? Although unnecessary for this exercise, since pattern recognition is sufficient to determine an answer, it is nevertheless helpful to know that the horizontal axis represents time, the vertical axis measures sound frequency, and the loudness of the sound (volume or relative intensity) is depicted by the degree of darkness in each area of the voice pattern.

* Case solution, p 406.

4.9 Lip Impressions

Exercise 14: Lipstick Impressions

Figures 14A and 14B are photographs of two lipstick impressions, one found on the rear of an envelope, the other at the point where a letter is usually signed. Examine Figs. 14A and 14B to determine if the impressions were made by the same person.

Figures 14C through 14F are exemplars obtained from four potential suspects, former lovers of a man who received a threatening letter. Can an identity be established between any exemplar and the questioned impressions (Figs. 14A, 14B)?

Fig. 1A
Enlargement of a developed crime scene latent print.

Fig. 1B
Enlargement of an inked impression of a suspect's finger.
(Courtesy, St. Paul Police Department, Minnesota.)

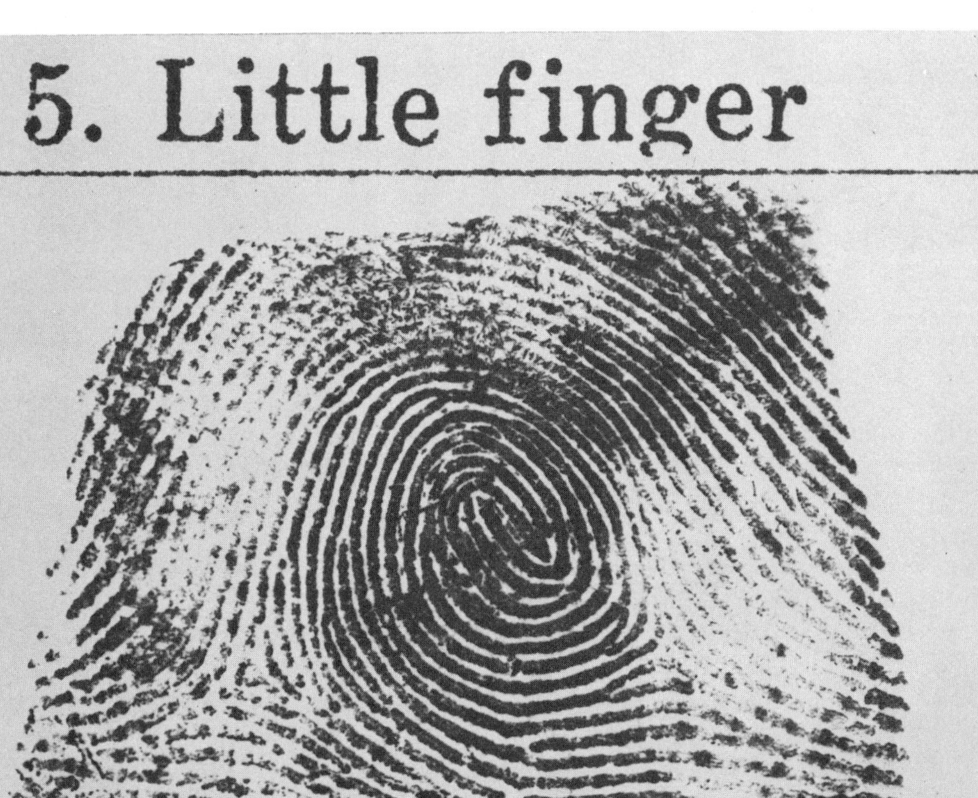

Fig. 2A
Inked fingerprint taken for record purposes.

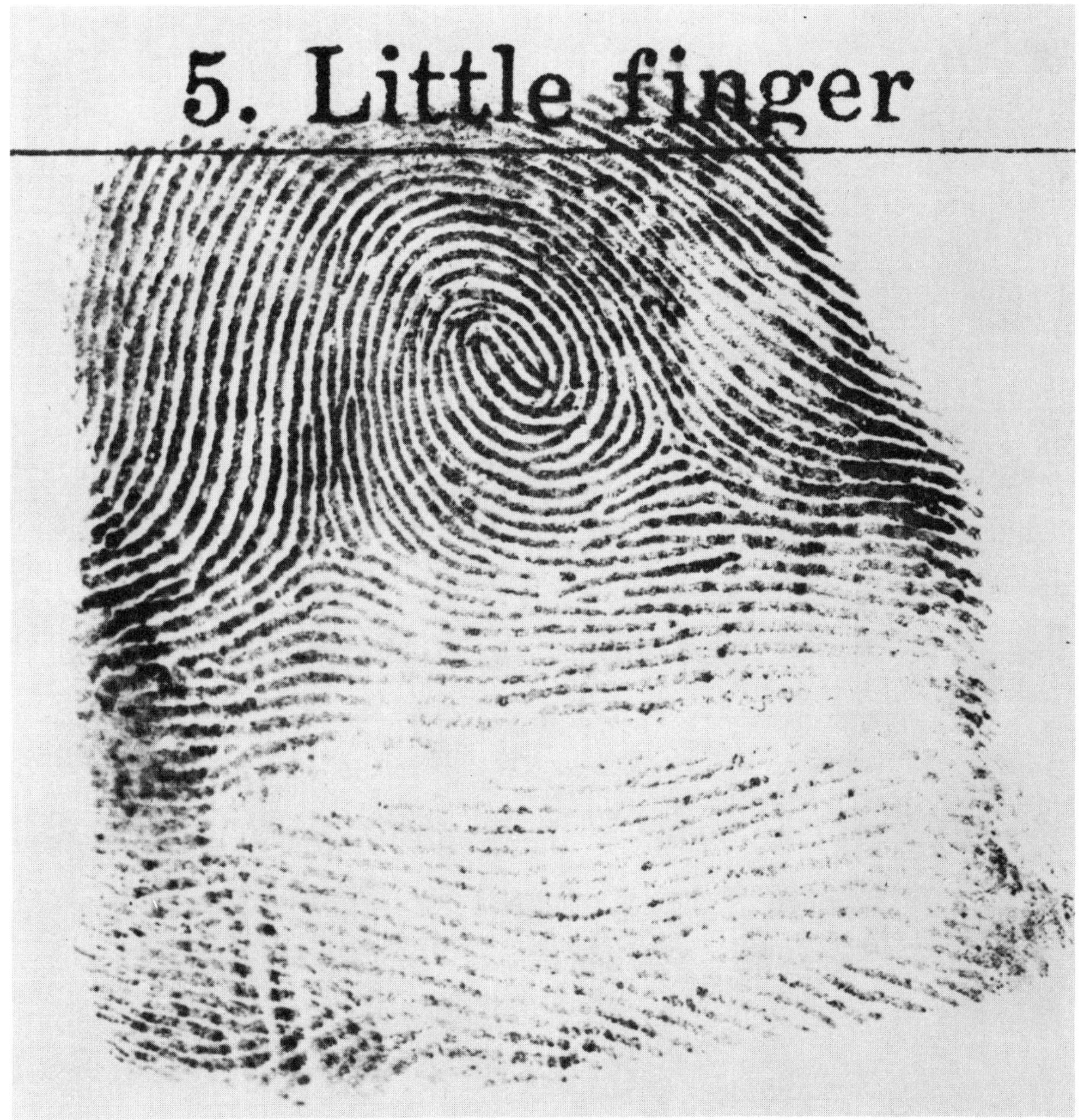

Fig. 2B
Inked fingerprint taken for record purposes. *(Courtesy, State Bureau of Investigation, Department of Justice, Raleigh, North Carolina.)*

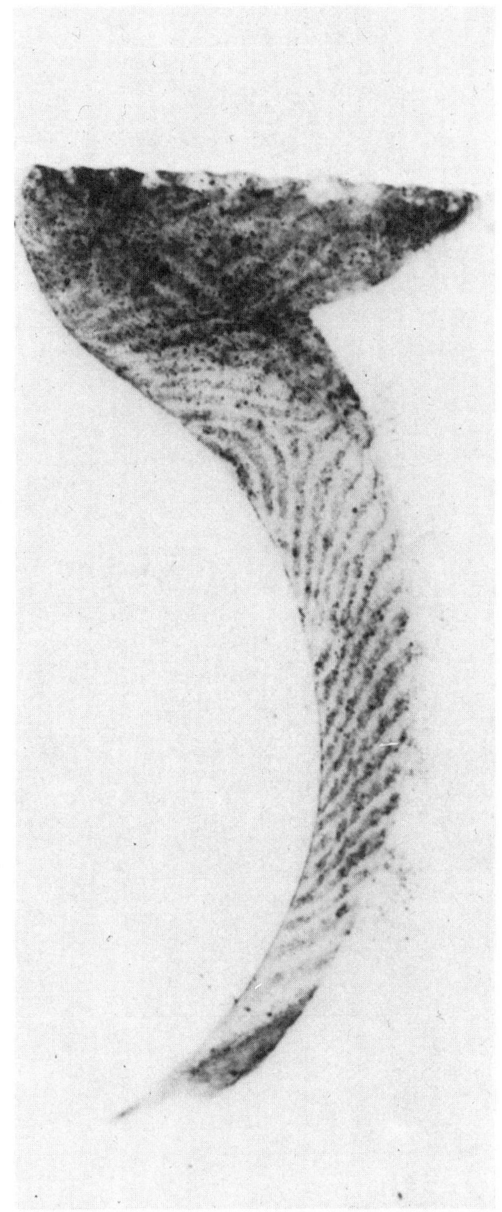

Fig. 3A
Partial fingerprint of limited size.

Fig. 3B
Inked fingerprint.
(Courtesy, Highland Park Police Department, Illinois.)

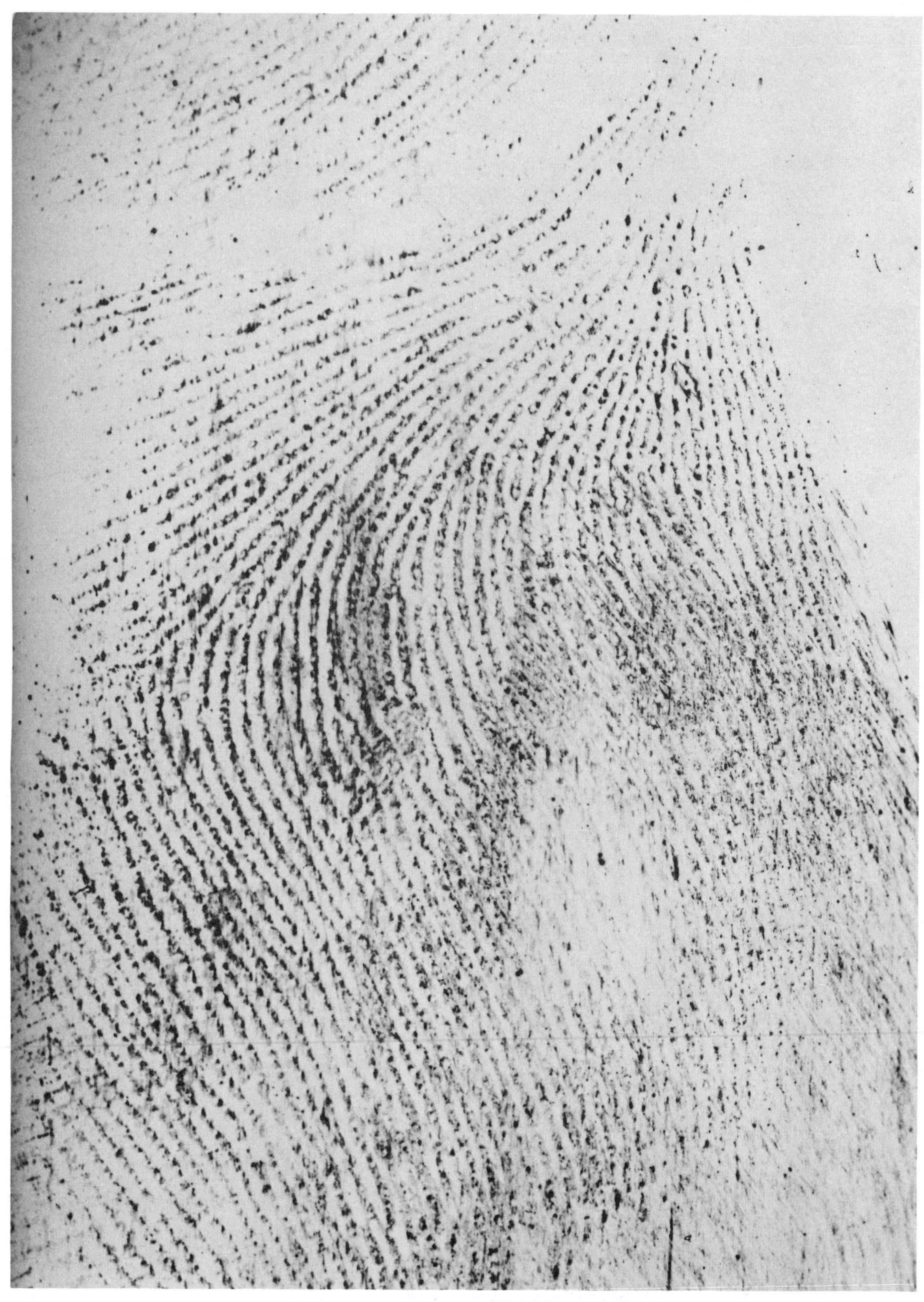

Fig. 4A
An enlarged, developed partial latent crime scene palmprint.

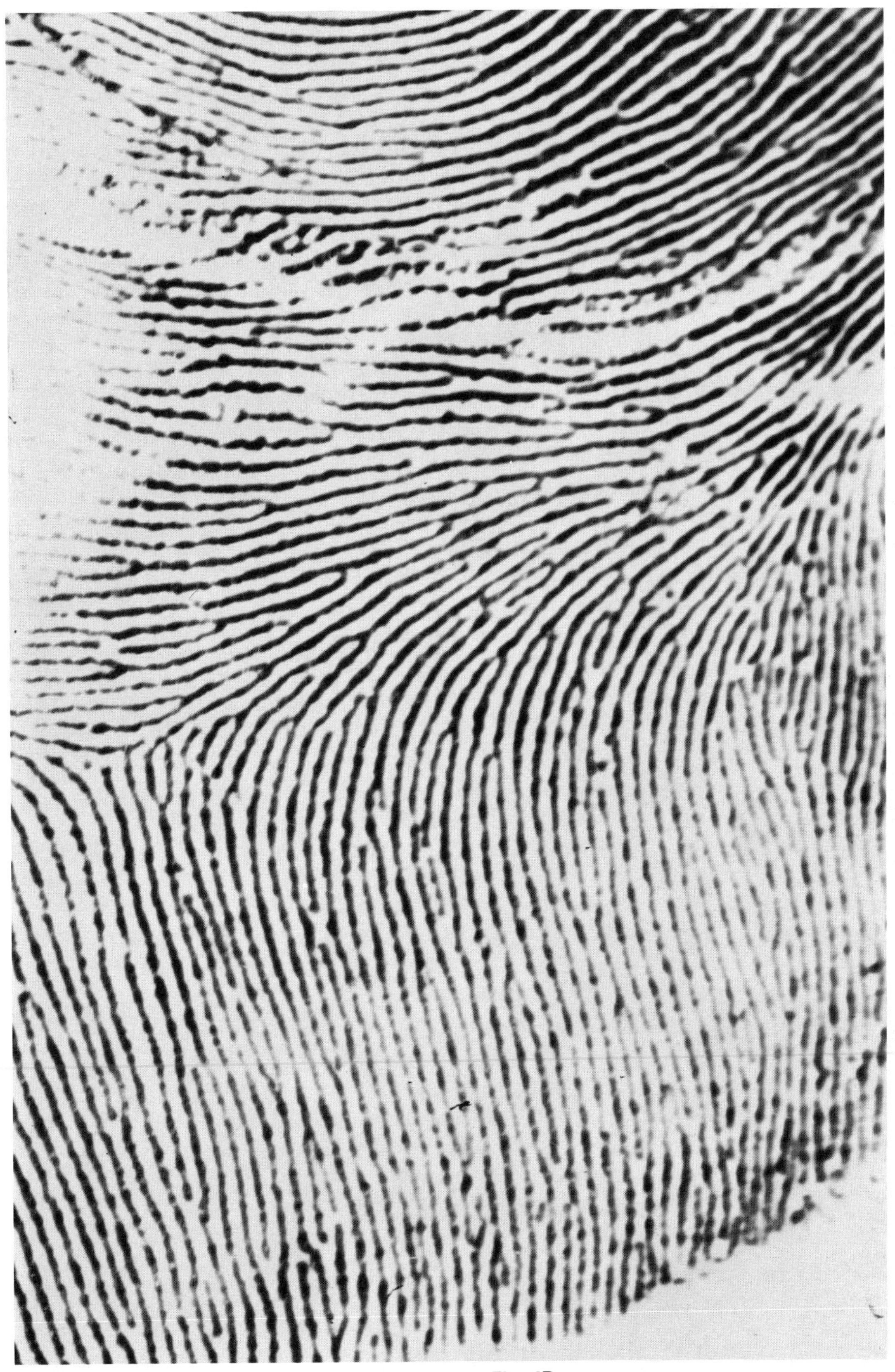

Fig. 4B
An enlarged portion of an inked palmprint.
(Courtesy, New York City Police Department.)

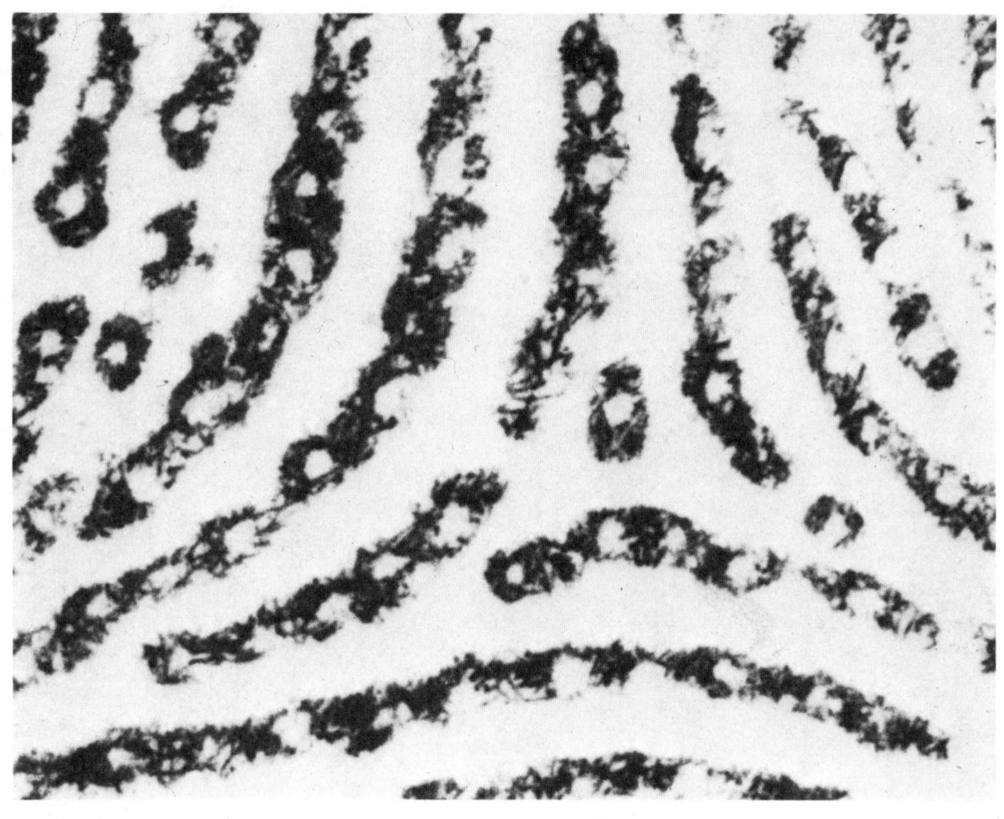

Fig. 5A
Partial palmprint of limited area (enlarged).

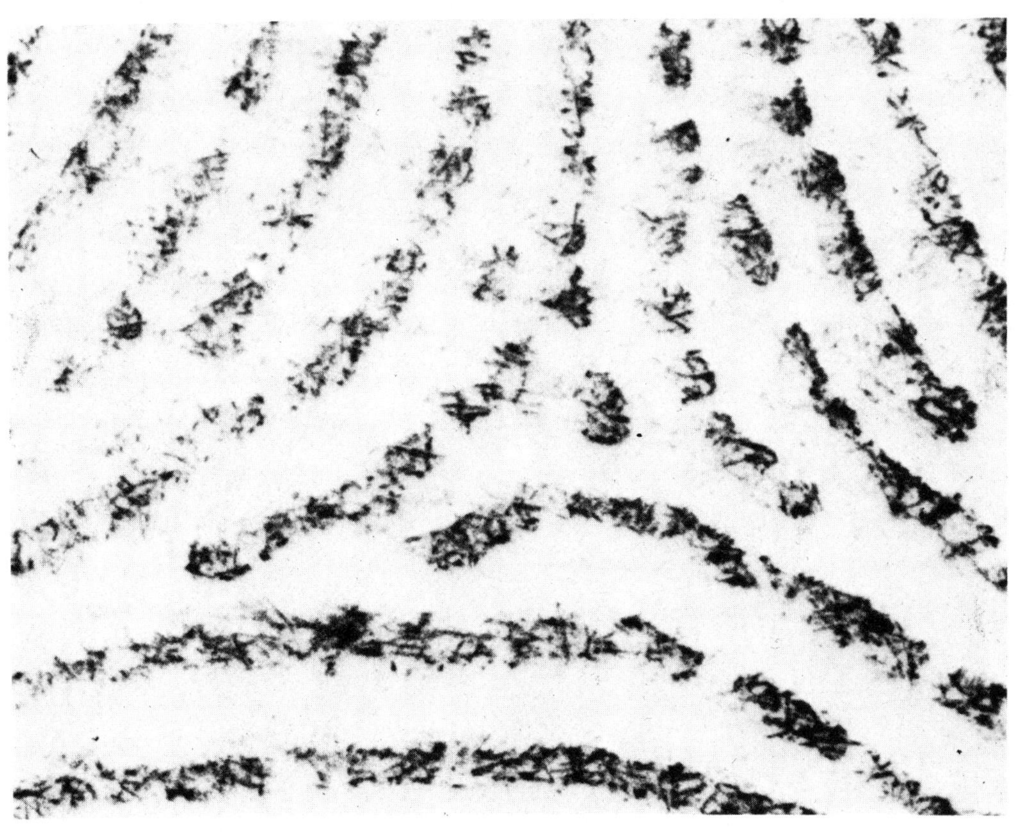

Fig. 5B
Partial palmprint of limited area.
(Courtesy, Robert D. Olsen.)

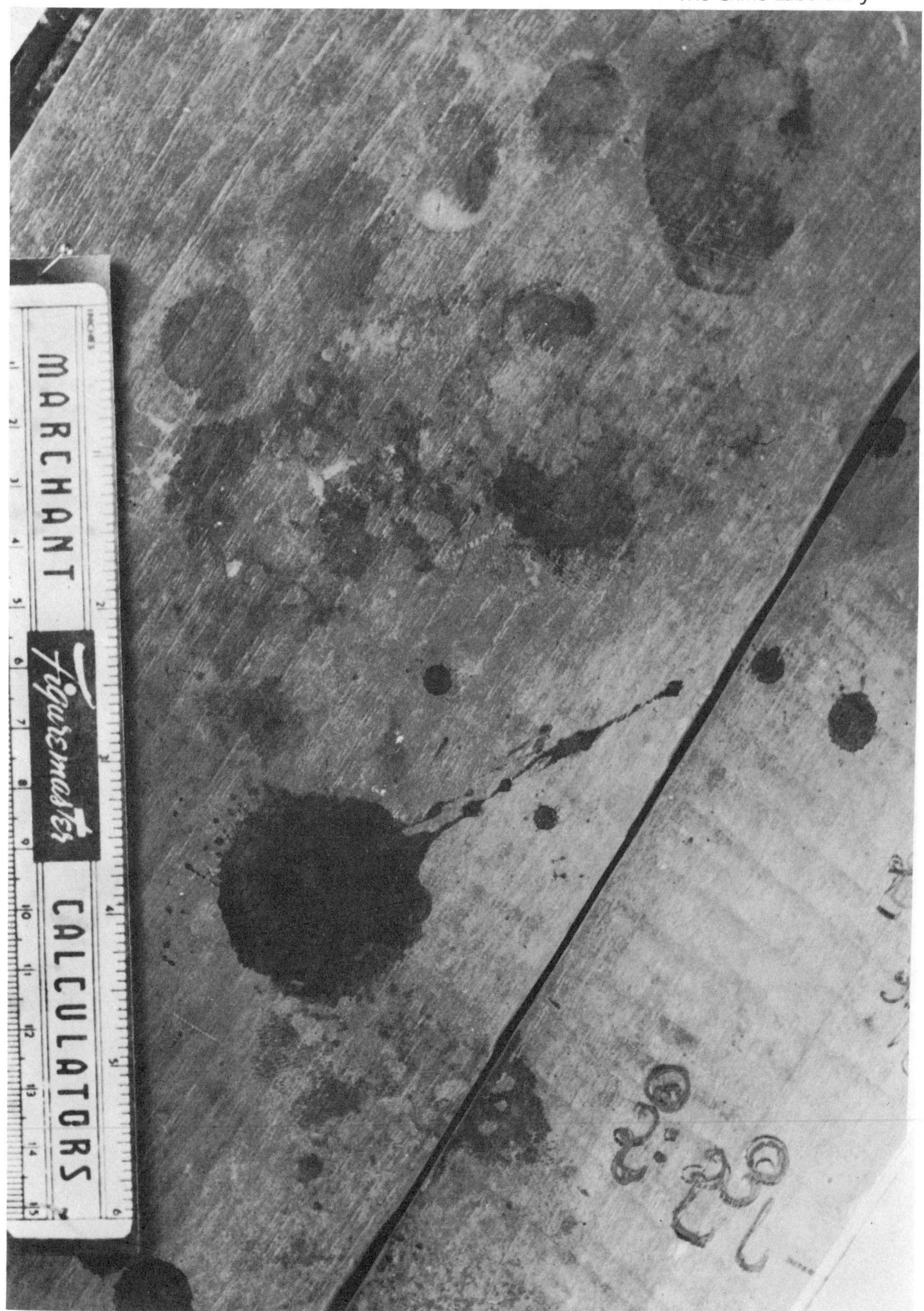

Fig. 6A
A bloody imprint on a wooden floor of an ulcerated sole.

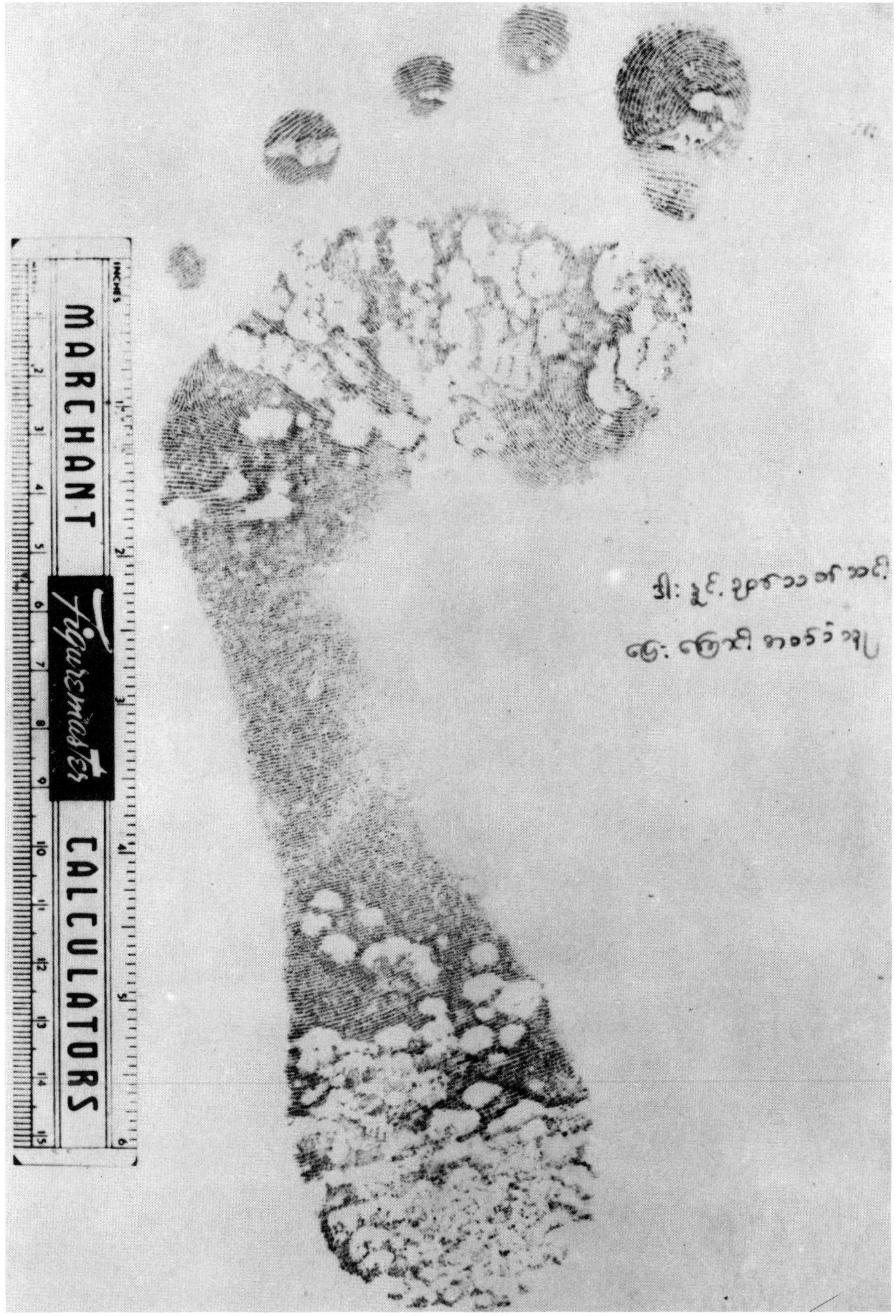

Fig. 6B
An inked impression of a suspect's bare foot.
(Courtesy, Burma Police—CID, Insein.)

Fig. 7A
An enlarged area of pencil surface showing teethmarks. Pencil was recovered from the rear floor of a suspect's automobile.

Fig. 7B
Comparison standard provided by victim after pencil was clenched between teeth in usual manner. (Enlarged to same size as Fig. 7A.)
(Courtesy, Laboratories for Scientific Criminal Investigation, University of Rhode Island.)

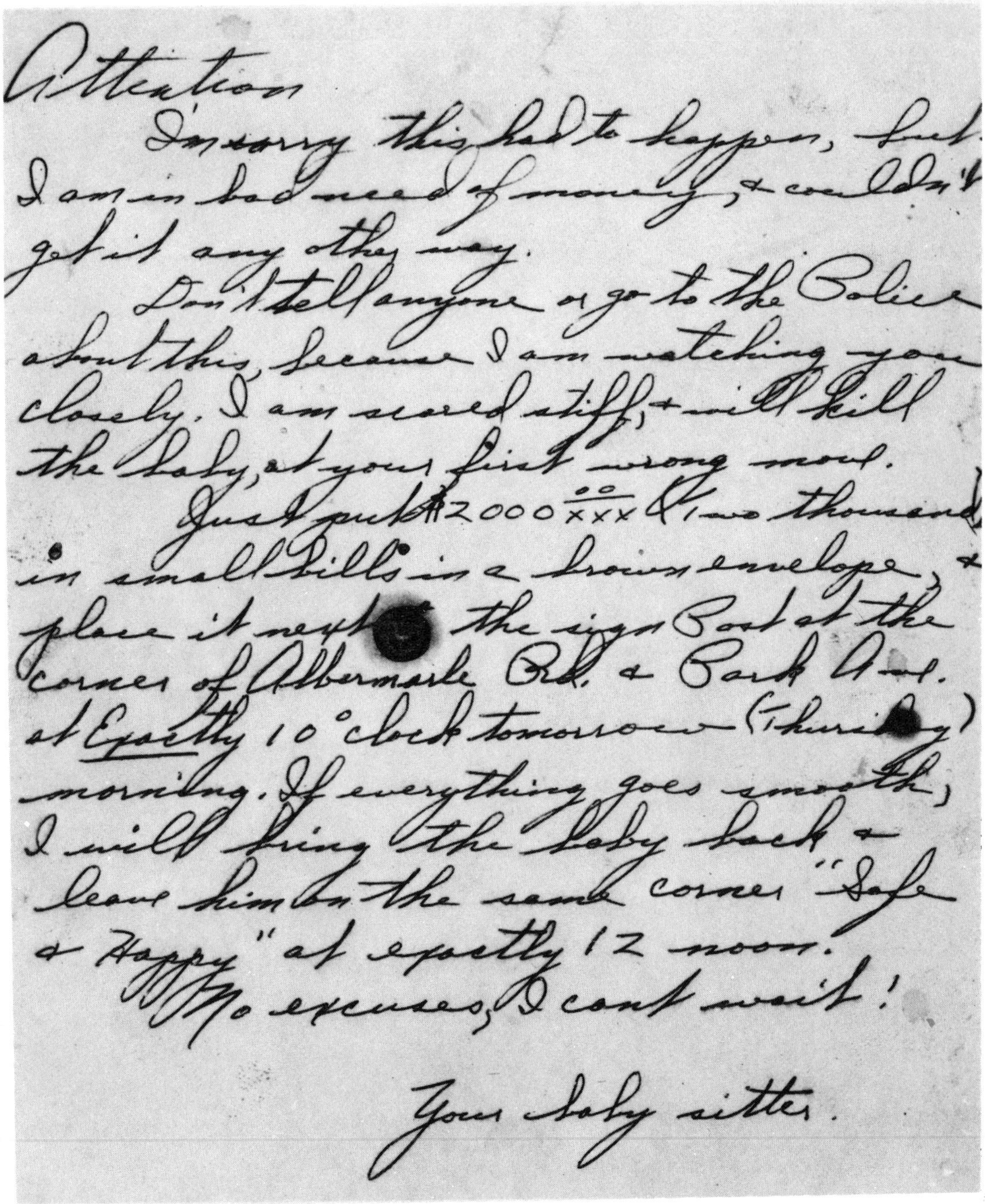

Attention

I'm sorry this had to happen, but I am in bad need of money, & couldn't get it any other way.

Don't tell anyone or go to the Police about this, because I am watching you closely. I am scared stiff, & will kill the baby, at your first wrong move.

Just put $2000 00/xxx (two thousand) in small bills in a brown envelope, & place it next to the sign Post at the corner of Albermarle Rd. & Park Ave. at Exactly 10 o'clock tomorrow (Thursday) morning. If everything goes smooth, I will bring the baby back & leave him on the same corner "Safe & Happy" at exactly 12 noon.

No excuses, I cant wait!

Your baby sitter.

Fig. 8A
Original ransom note in Weinberger kidnapping case.
(Courtesy, Federal Bureau of Investigation.)

Fig. 9A
Questioned printing – newspaper crossword puzzle.

Fig. 9B
Crossword puzzle completed by suspect.
(Courtesy, Columbus Police Department, Ohio.)

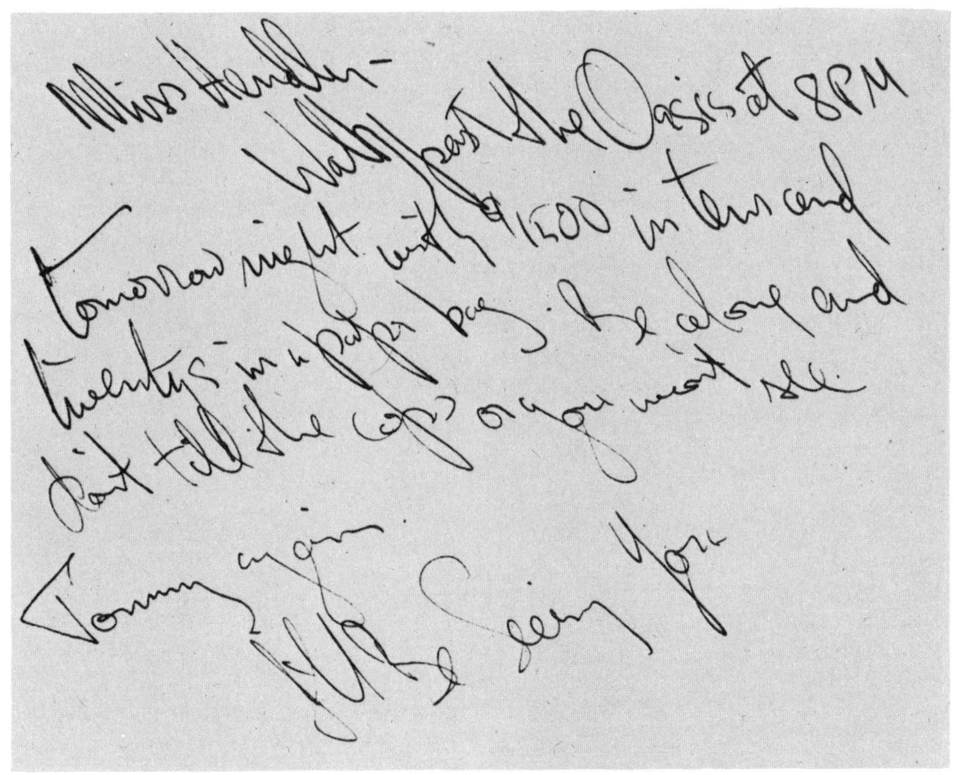

Miss Hendley—
Walk past the Oasis at 8PM
tomorrow night with $1500 in tens and
twentys in a paper bag. Be along and
don't tell the cops or you won't see
Tommy again.
Be Seeing You

Fig. 10A
Questioned handwriting.

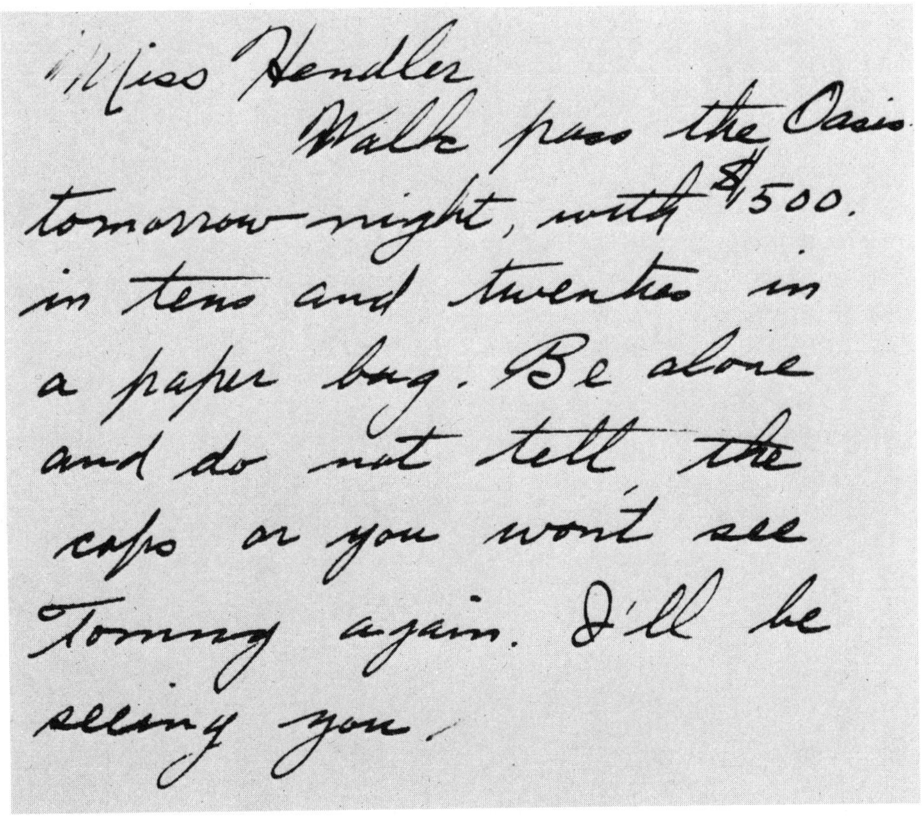

Miss Hendler
Walk pass the Oasis
tomorrow night, with $1500.
in tens and twenties in
a paper bag. Be alone
and do not tell the
cops or you won't see
Tommy again. I'll be
seeing you.

Fig. 10B
Suspect 1.

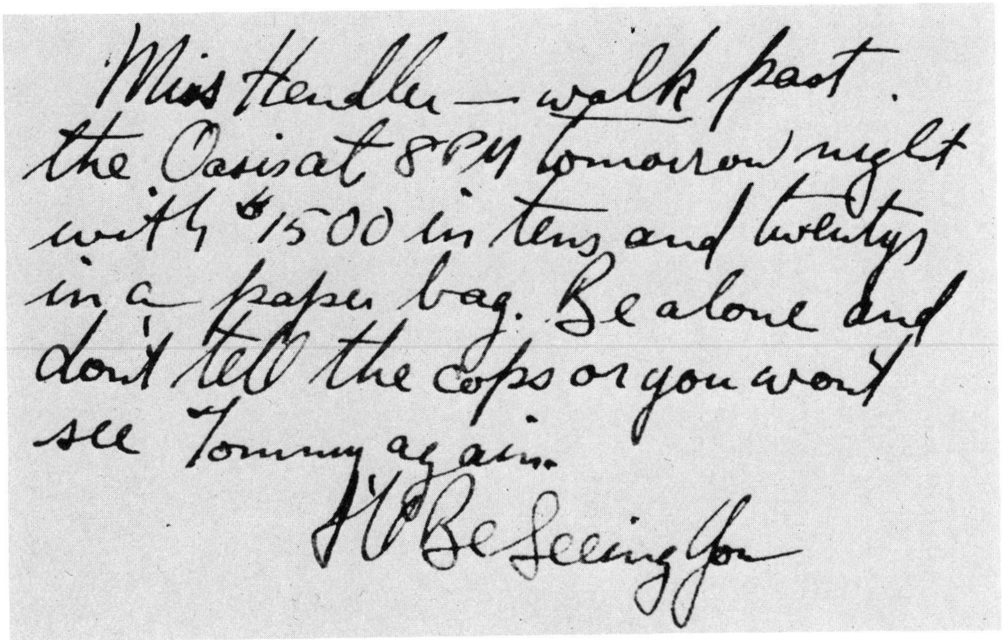

Miss Hendler — walk past
the Oasis at 8PM tomorrow night
with $1500 in tens and twentys
in a paper bag. Be alone and
don't tell the cops or you won't
see Tommy again.
I'll Be Seeing You

Fig. 10C
Suspect 2.

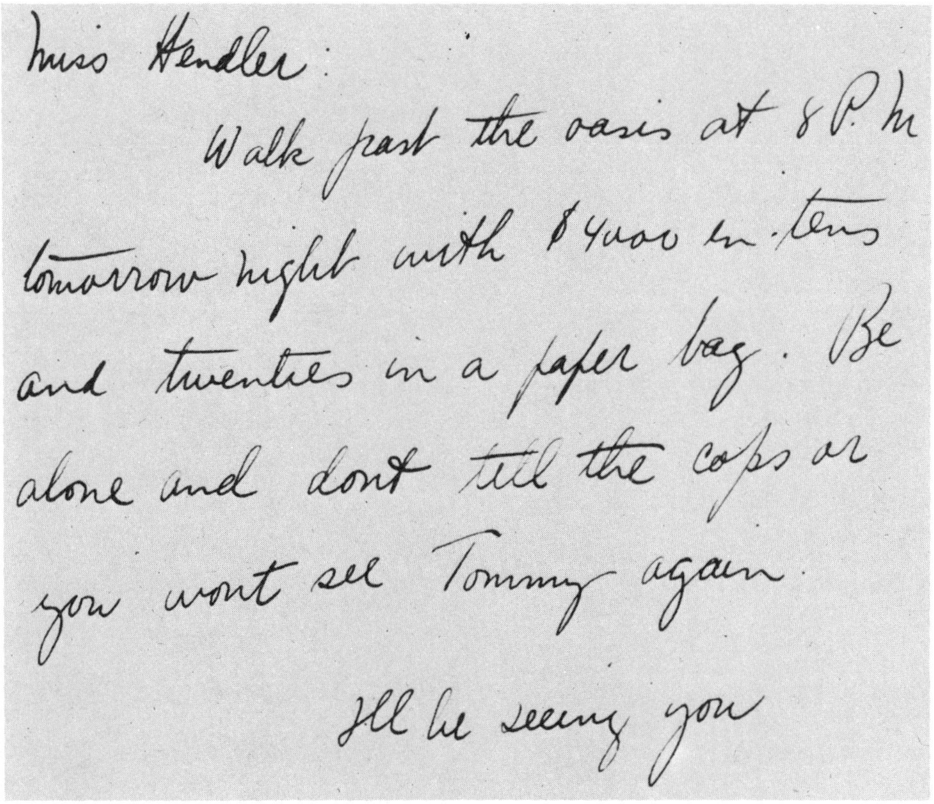

Miss Hendler:
Walk past the oasis at 8 P. M
tomorrow night with $4000 in tens
and twenties in a paper bag. Be
alone and dont tell the cops or
you wont see Tommy again.
Ill be seeing you

Fig. 10D
Suspect 3.

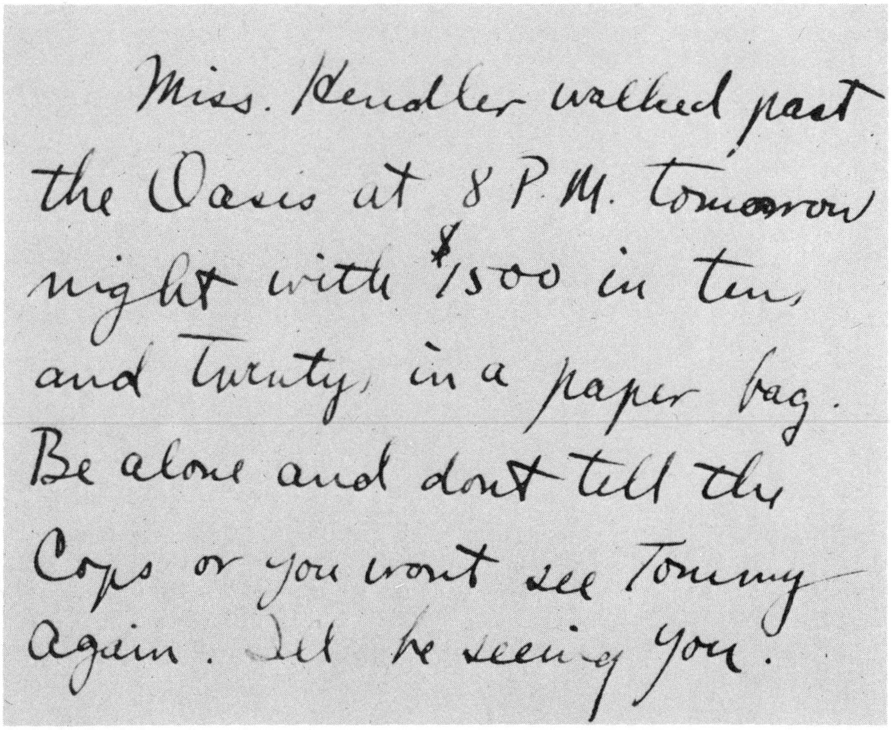

Miss. Hendler walked past
the Oasis at 8 P.M. tomorrow
night with $1500 in tens,
and Twenty, in a paper bag.
Be alone and dont tell the
Cops or you wont see Tommy
again. Ill be seeing you.

Fig. 10E
Suspect 4.

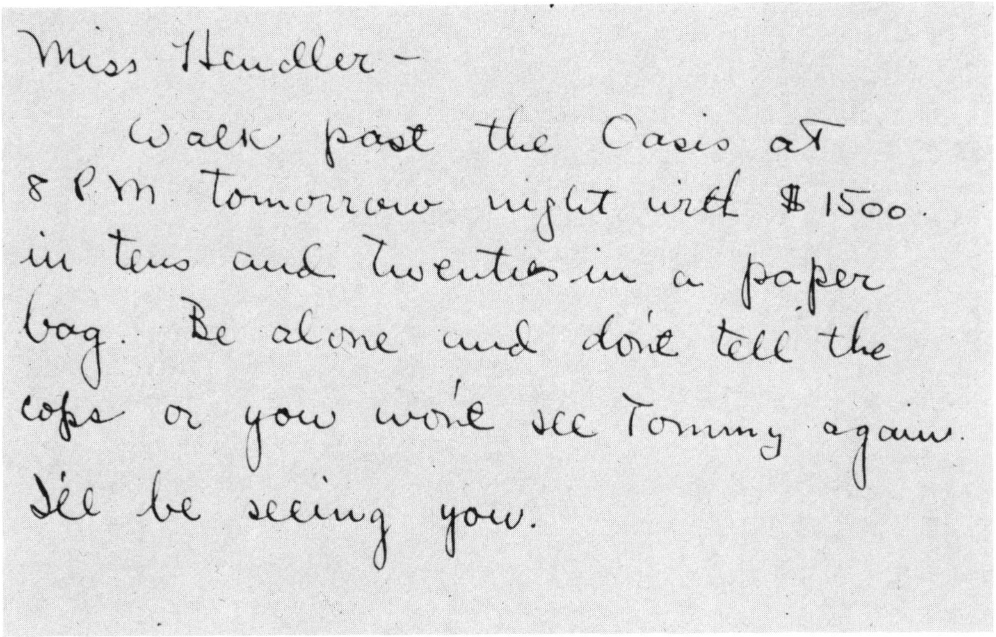

Miss Hendler –
Walk past the Oasis at
8 P.M. Tomorrow night with $1500.
in tens and twenties in a paper
bag. Be alone and don't tell the
cops or you won't see Tommy again.
I'll be seeing you.

Fig. 10F
Suspect 5.

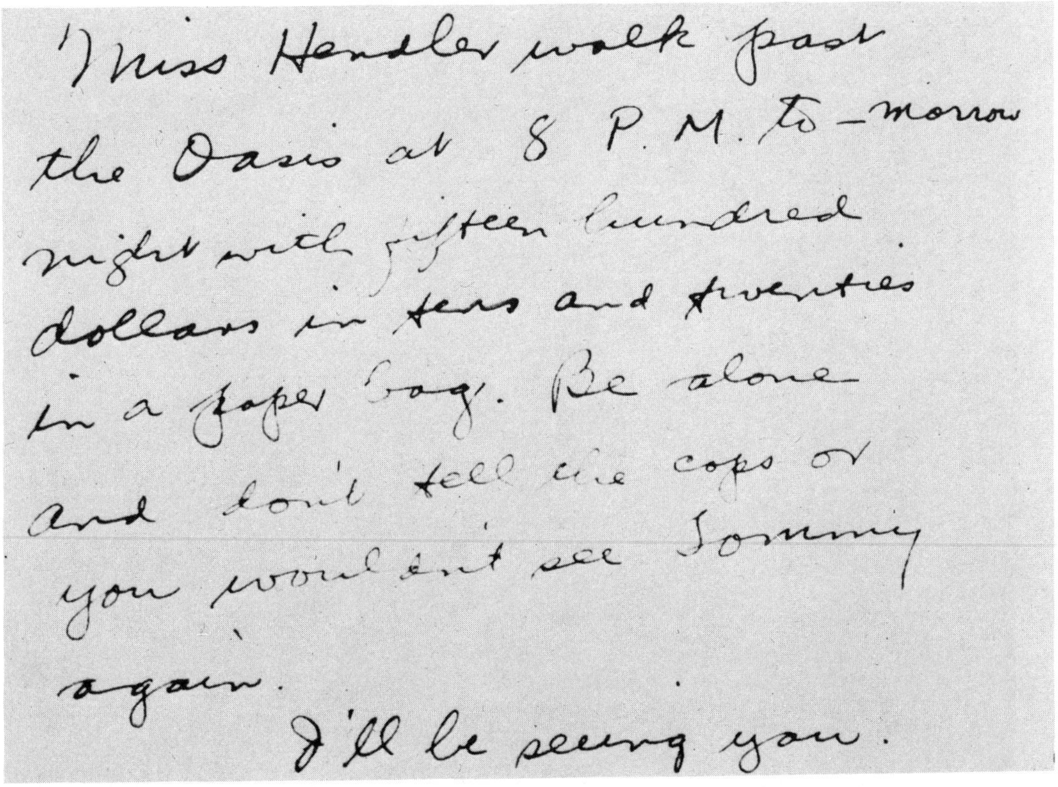

Miss Hendler walk past
the Oasis at 8 P.M. to-morrow
night with fifteen hundred
dollars in tens and twenties
in a paper bag. Be alone
and don't tell the cops or
you wouldn't see Tommy
again.
I'll be seeing you.

Fig. 10G
(Courtesy, Edward Palmer.)

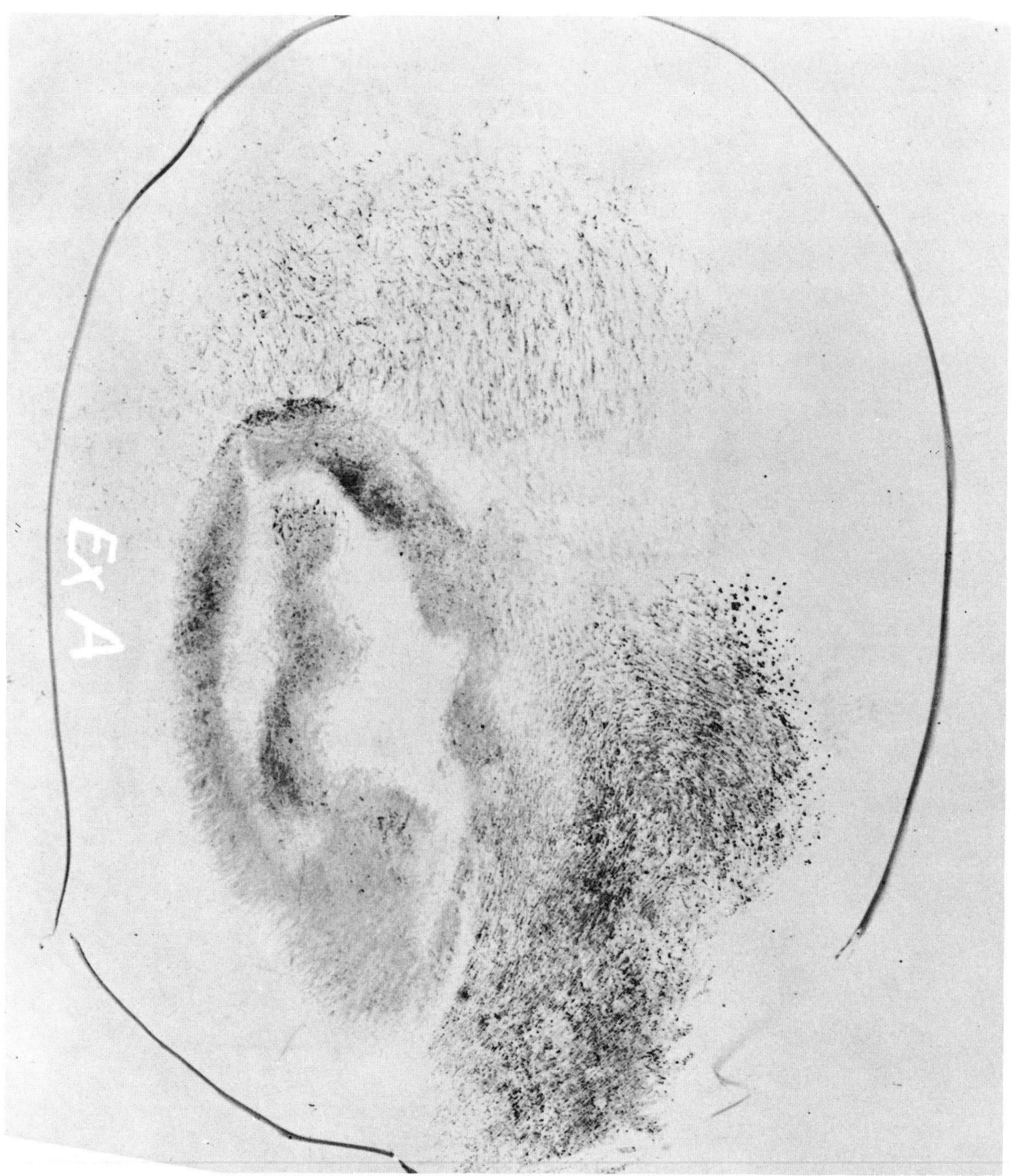

Fig. 11A
Ear imprint developed from a safe at a crime scene.

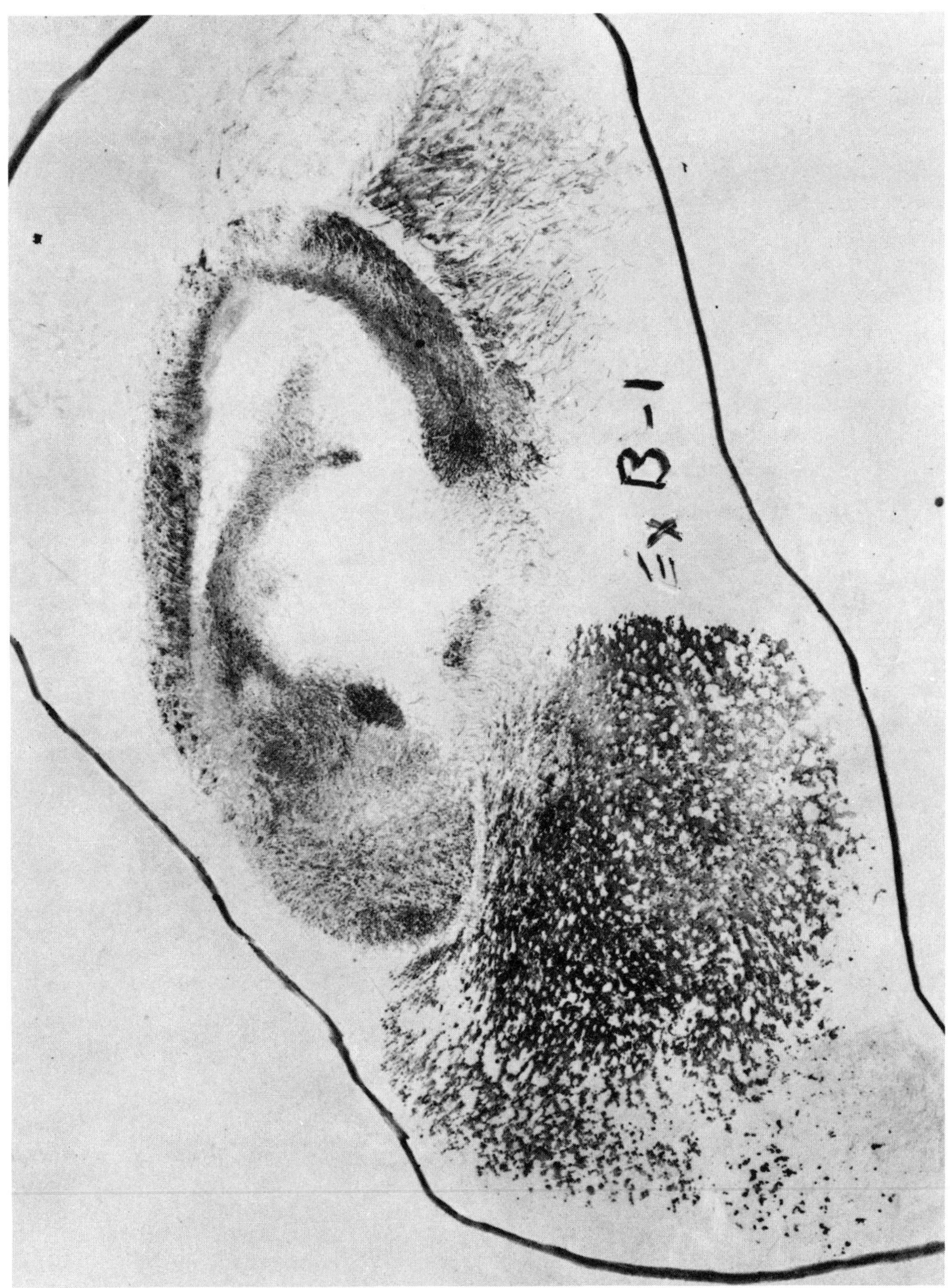

Fig. 11B
Suspect 1.

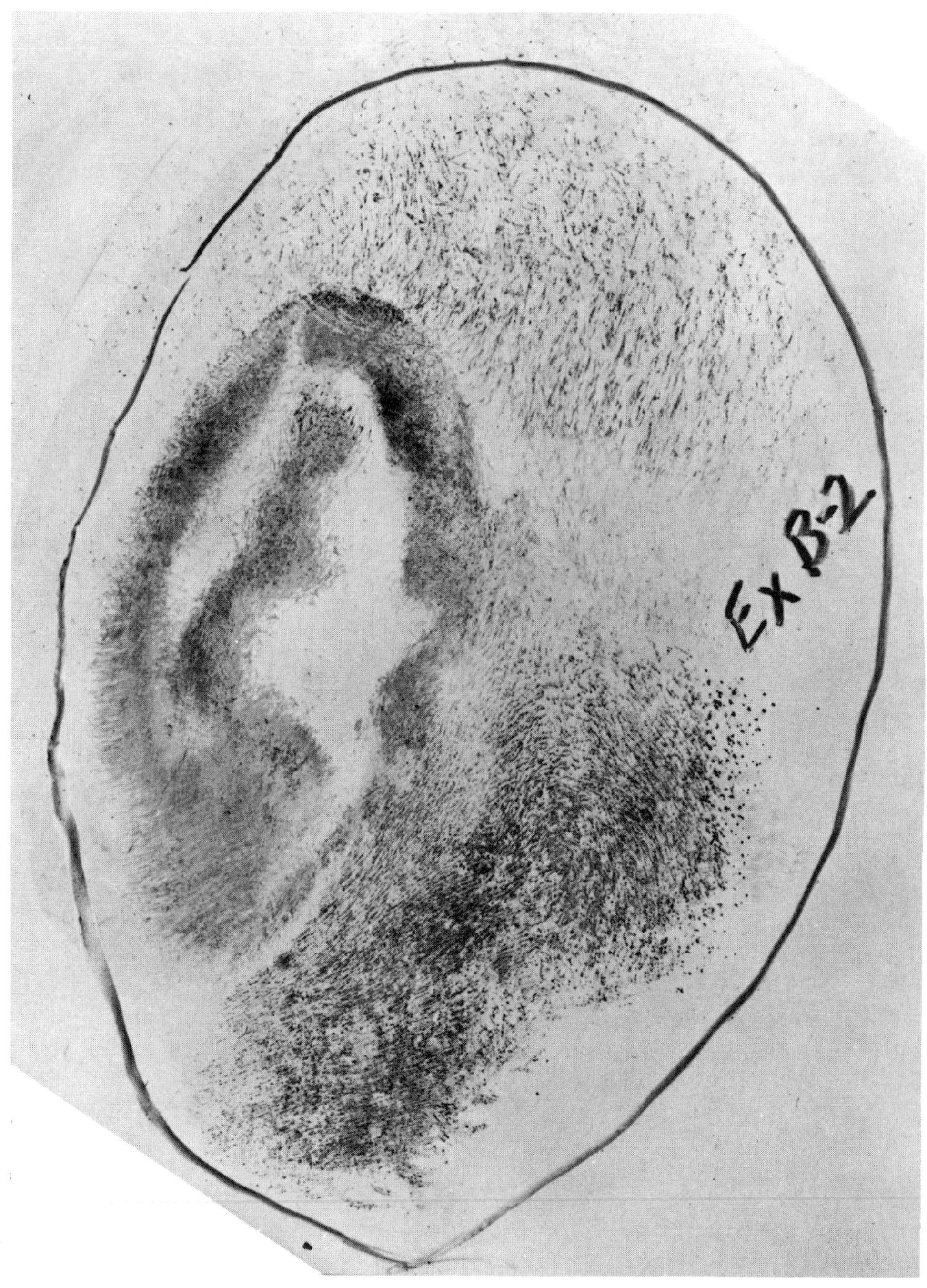

Fig. 11C
Suspect 2.

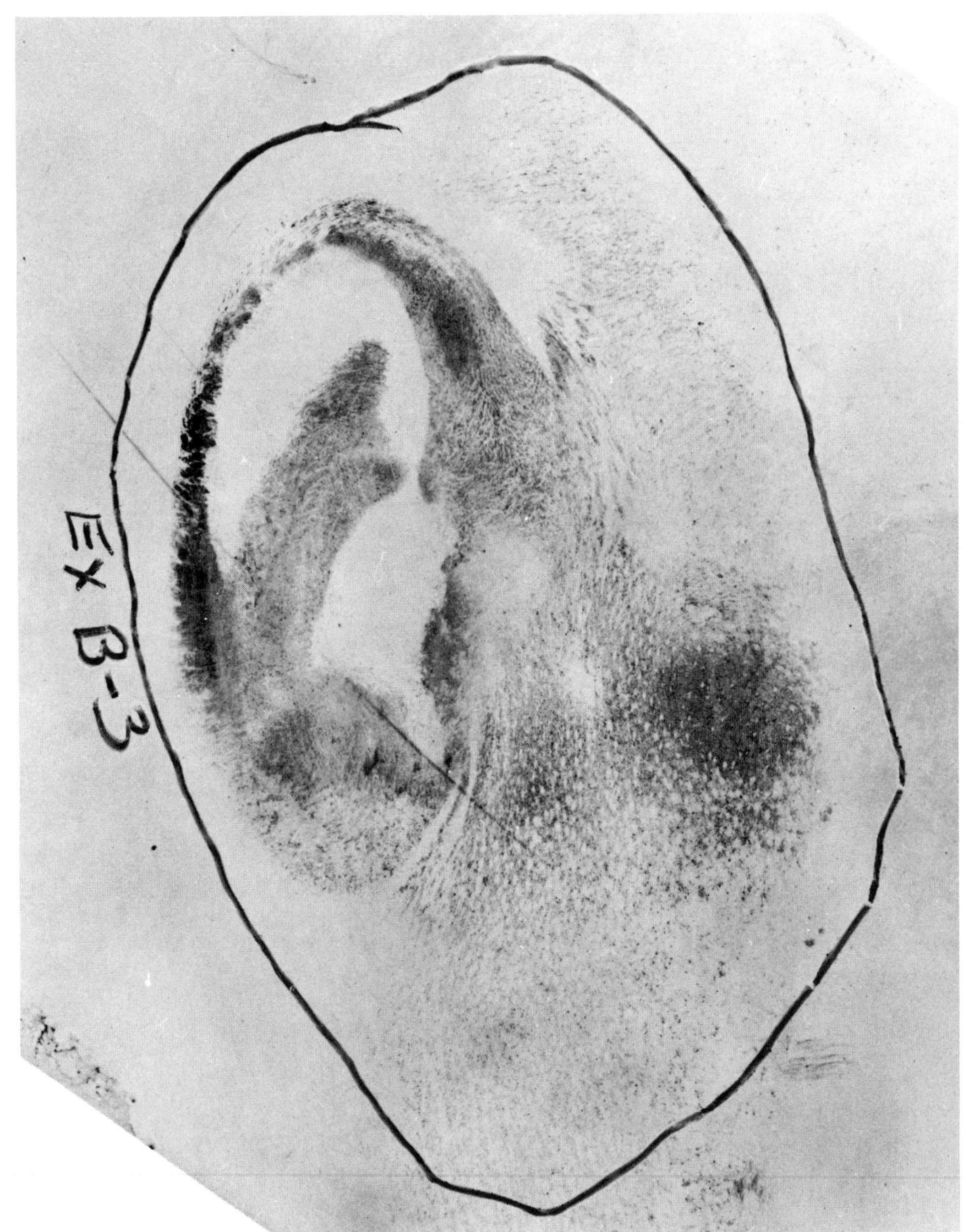

Fig. 11D
Suspect 3.

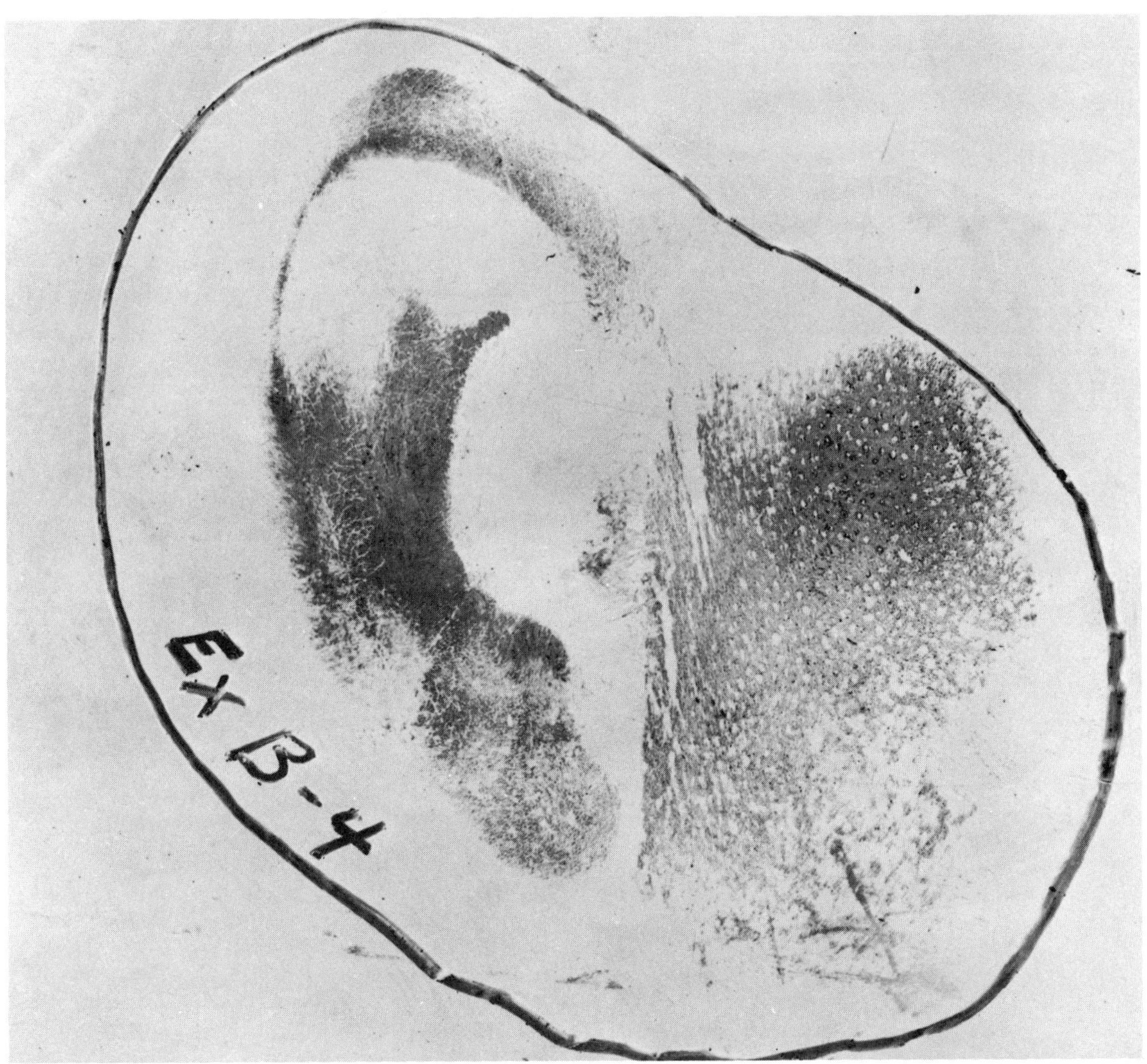

Fig. 11E
Suspect 4.

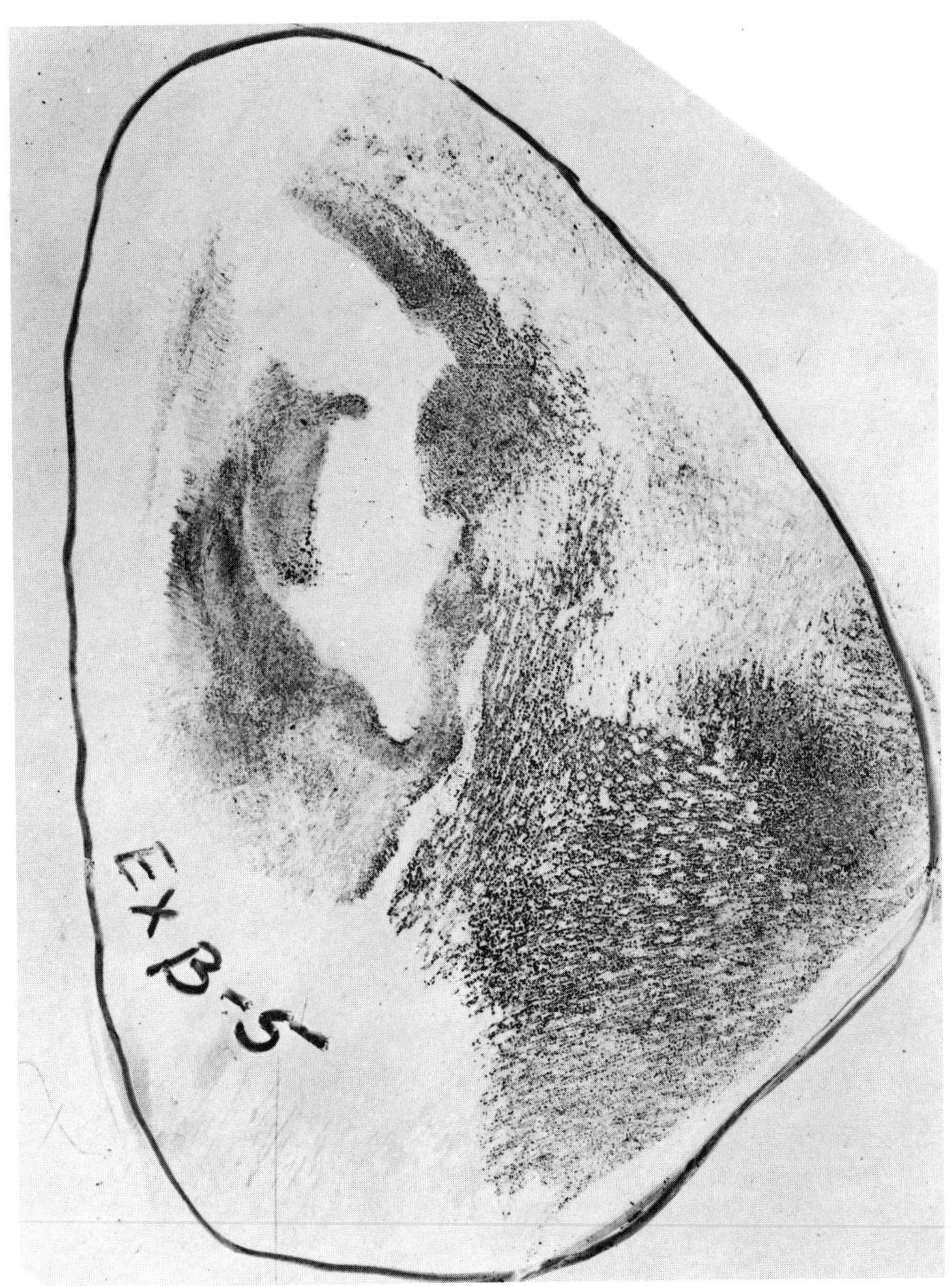

Fig. 11F
Suspect 5.
(Courtesy, U.S. Army Criminal Investigation Laboratory, Ft. Gordon, Georgia.)

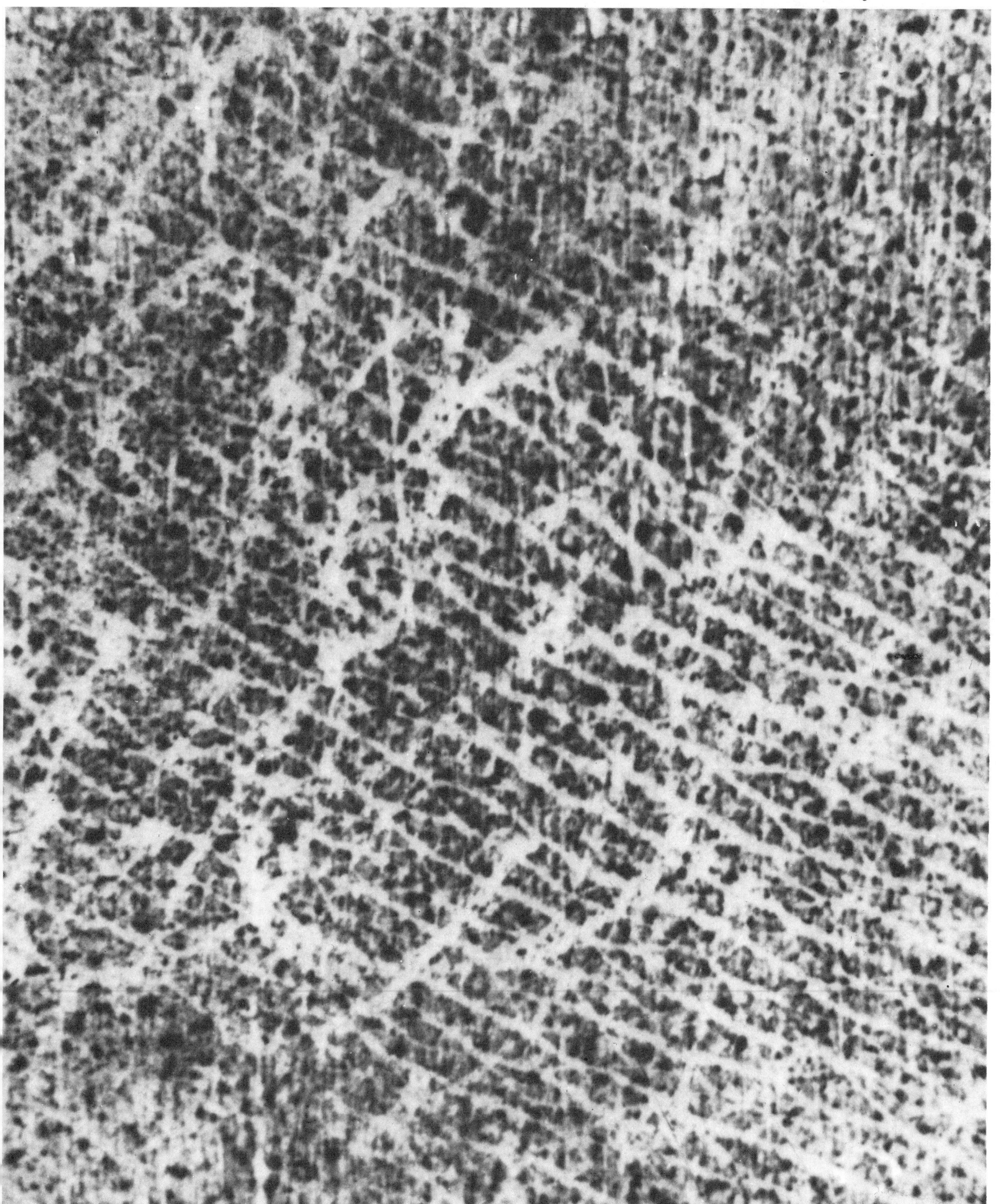

Fig. 12A
Section of crime scene armprint (enlarged).

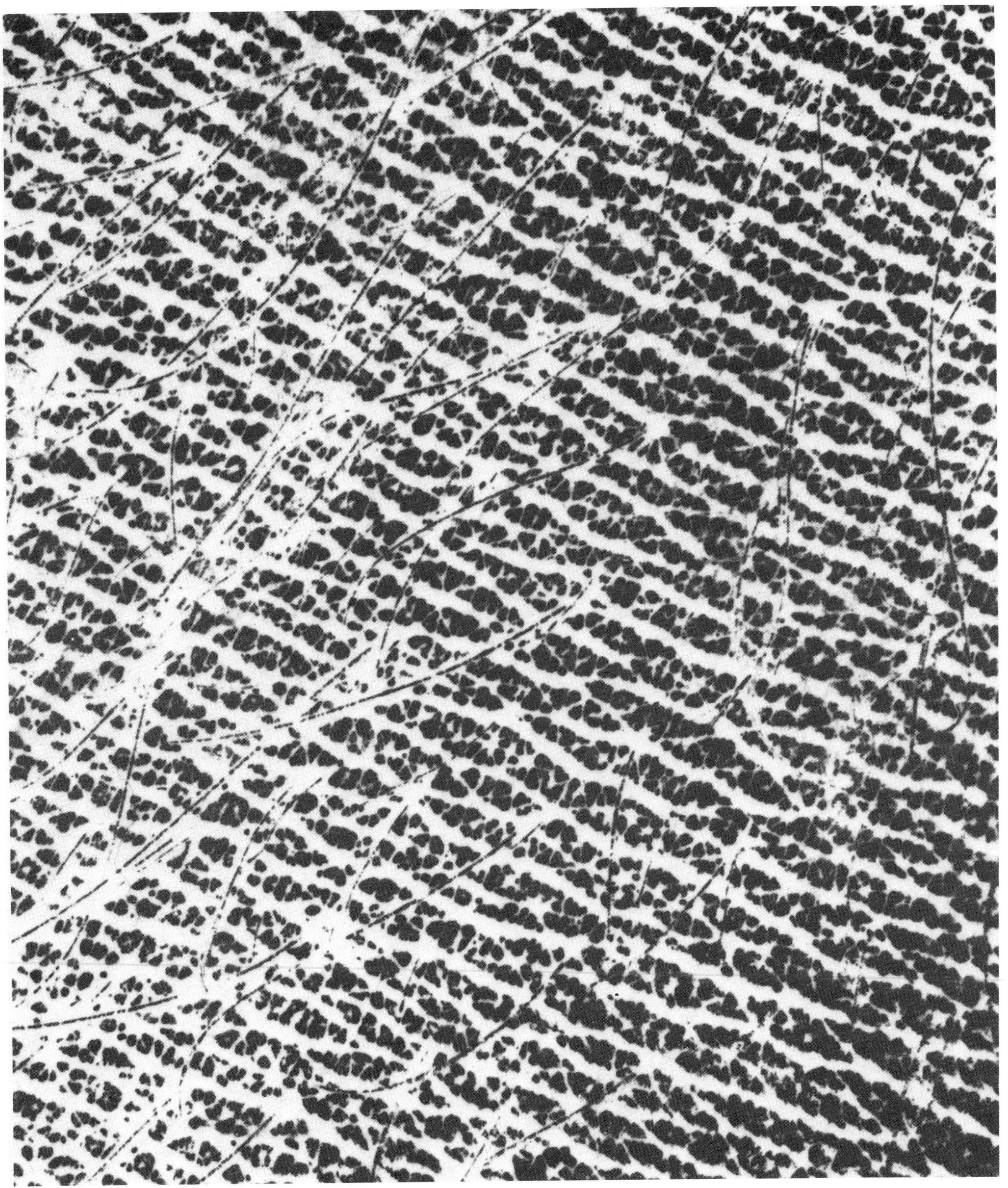

Fig. 12B
Portion of suspect's armprint (enlarged to same size as Fig. 12A).
(Courtesy, Sheriff's Department, Contra Costa County, California.)

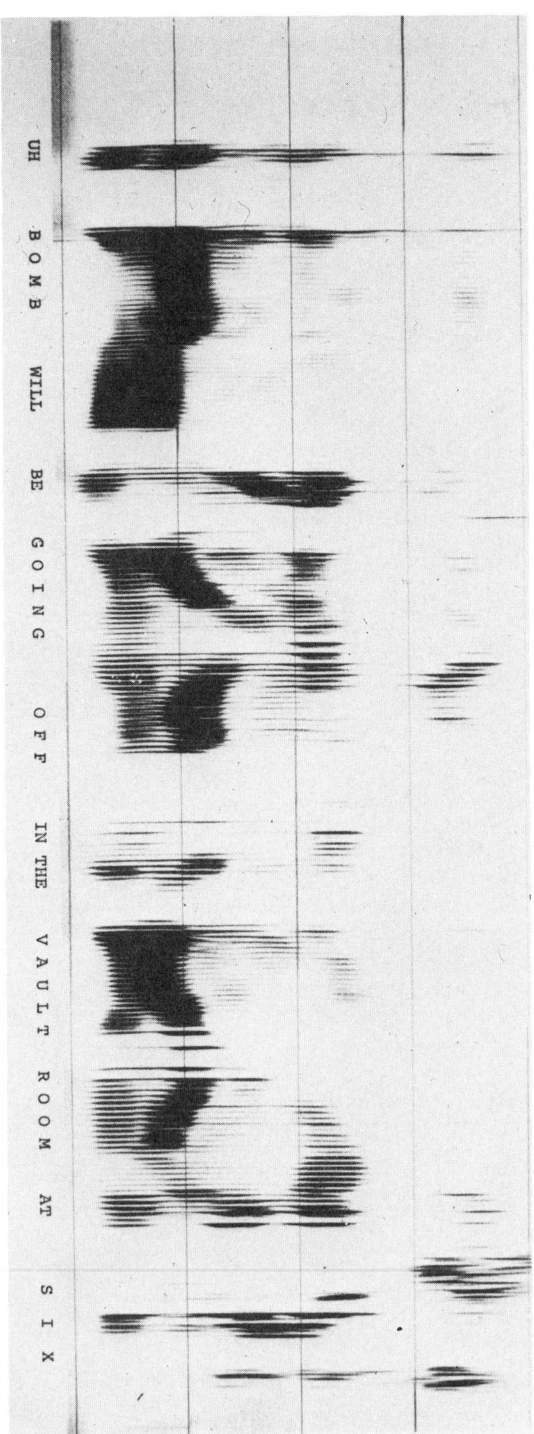

Fig. 13A
Sound spectrum of unknown voice.

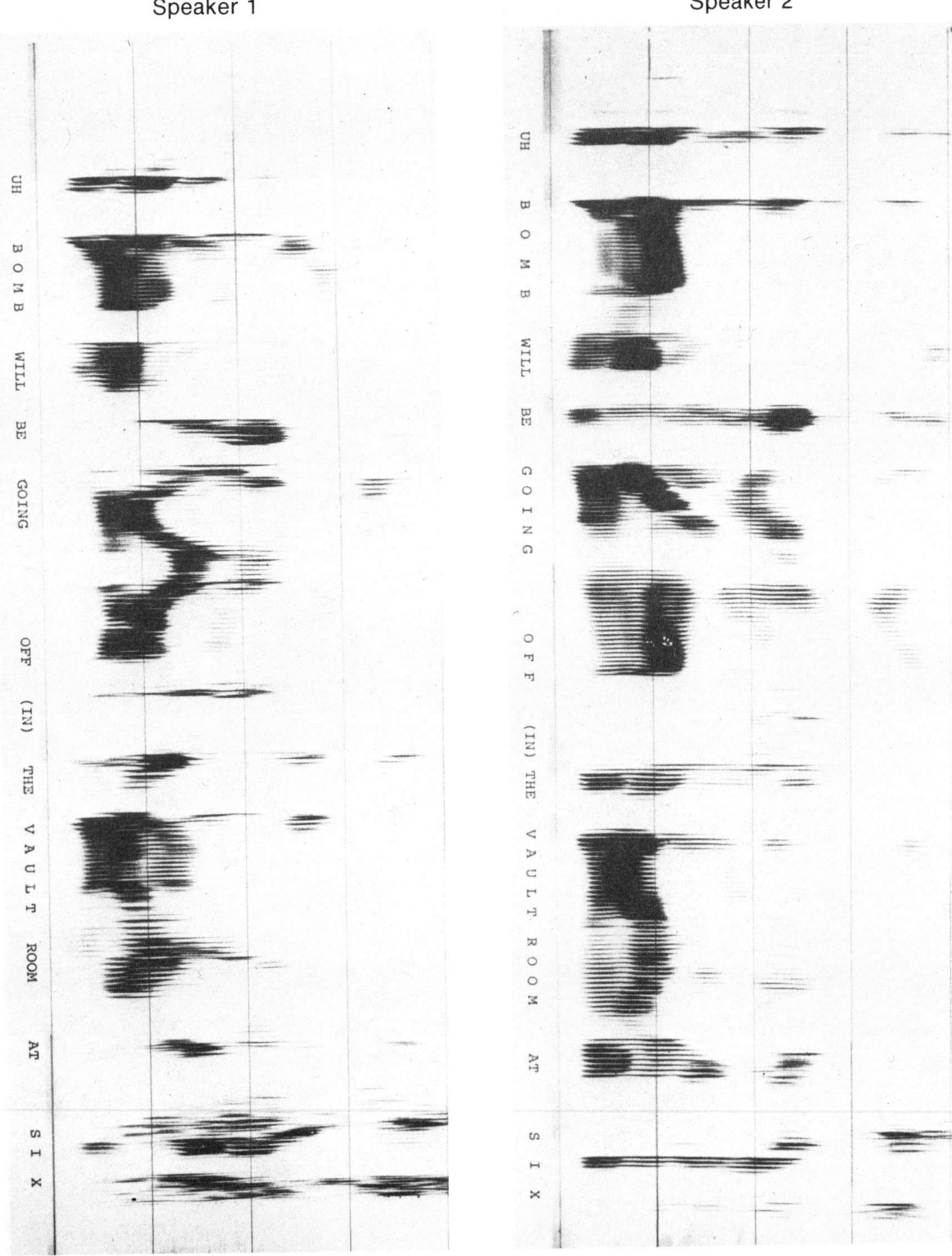

Fig. 13B
Speakers 1 and 2.

Speaker 3

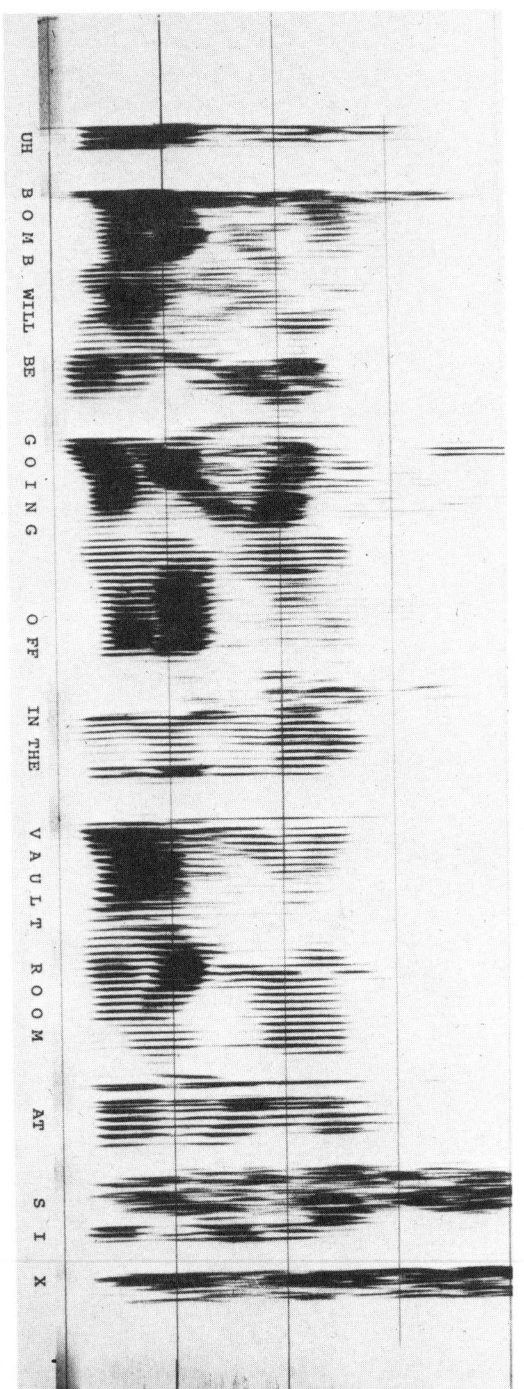

Speaker 4

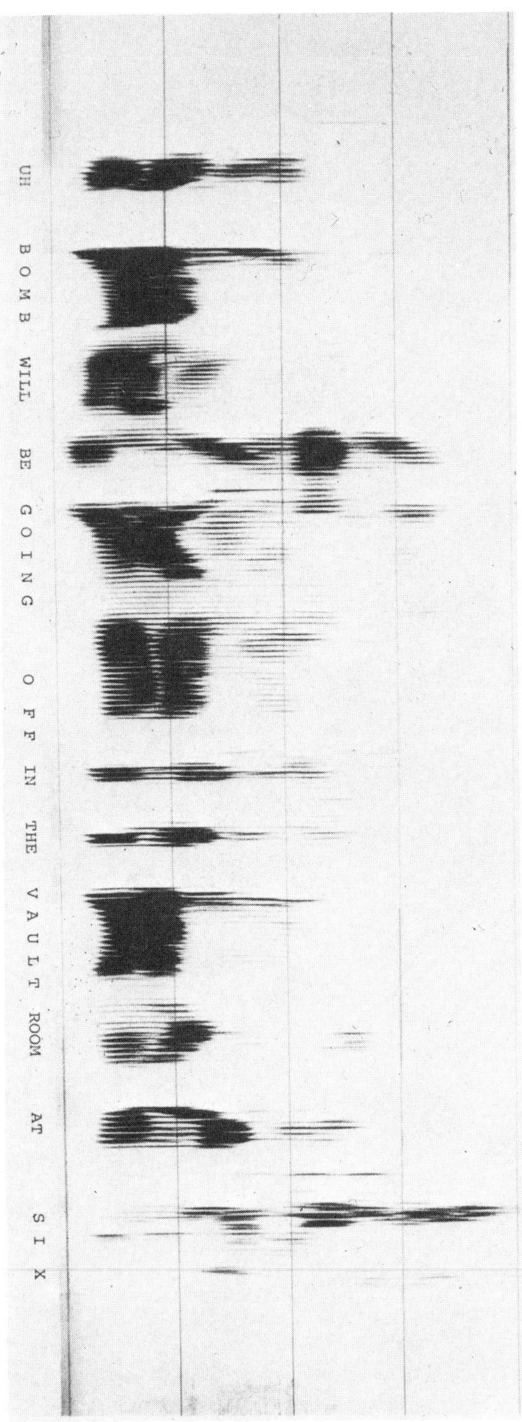

Fig. 13C
Speakers 3 and 4.
(Courtesy, Michigan State Police.)

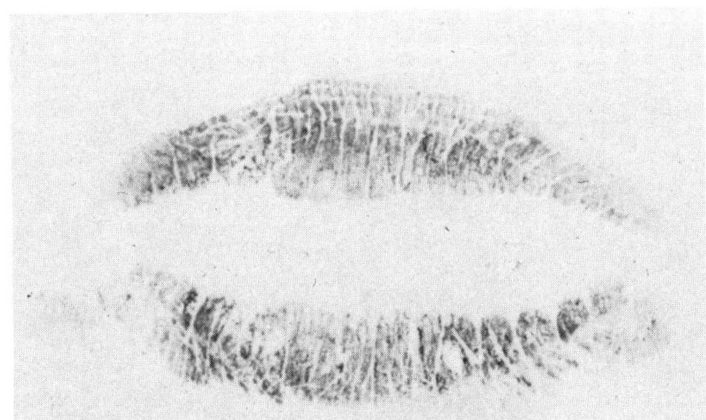

Fig. 14A
Lipstick impression on back of envelope.

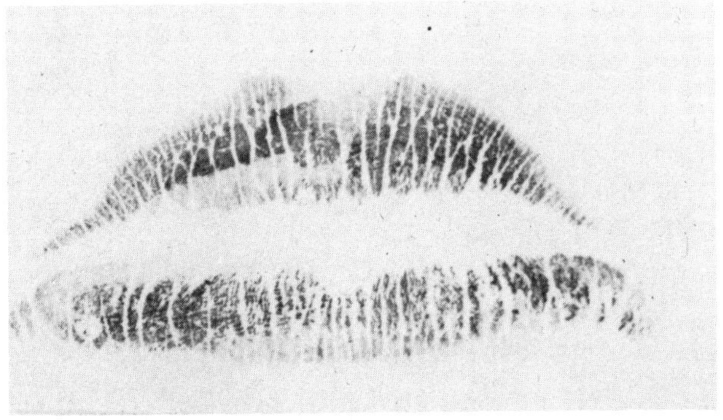

Fig. 14B
Lipstick impression on letter.

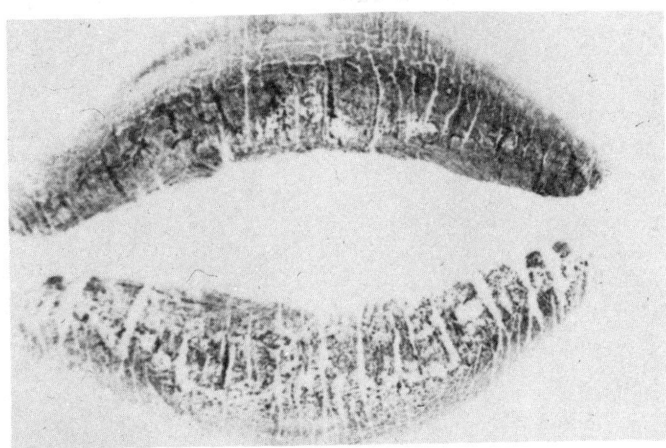

Fig. 14C
Suspect 1.

Fig. 14D
Suspect 2.

Fig. 14E
Suspect 3.

Fig. 14F
Suspect 4.
(Courtesy, New York City Police Department.)

Wearing Apparel Traces Case Exercises

5.1 Shoeprints
Exercise 1: Crepe Sole Print
Fig. 1A — Crepe sole impression
Fig. 1B — Known impression
Exercise 2: Sneaker Print
Fig. 2A — Crime scene sneaker impression
Fig. 2B — Impression of suspect's sneaker
Exercise 3: Sneaker Print
Fig. 3A — Crime scene sneaker impression
Fig. 3B — Impression of suspect's sneaker
Exercise 4: Heelprint in Sand
Fig. 4A — Crime scene heelmark in sand
Fig. 4B — Suspect's heel
Exercise 5: Heelprint Comparison
Fig. 5A — Crime scene heel imprint
Fig. 5B — Test impression of suspect's heel
Exercise 6: Poor Heelprint
Fig. 6A — Indistinct partial heelprint
Fig. 6B — Clear impression of suspect's heel
Exercise 7: Heelprint
Fig. 7A — Crime scene heelprint
Fig. 7B — Suspect's heel impression

5.2 Cloth: Weave Pattern and Stitching
Exercise 8: Bra Strap
Fig. 8A — End of cloth garrote
Fig. 8B — Portion of torn brassiere
Fig. 8C — Section of purchased brassiere

5.3 Gloves
Exercise 9: Glove Impression
Fig. 9A — Latent glove impression
Fig. 9B — Test glove impression
Exercise 10: Glove Impression
Fig. 10A — Partial latent glove impression
Fig. 10B — Test impression of leather glove

5.4 Clothing Accessories

Exercise 11: Tie Clasp

Fig. 11A — Top: back of broken tie clasp found on suspect
Bottom: head of tie clasp remaining in victim's shirt

5.1 Shoeprints

*Exercise 1: Crepe Sole Print**

Remove Figs. 1A and 1B. Examine each impression for points of comparison. When a similar point in each photograph is located, mark them with a common number. After a dozen or so characteristics have been found, prepare a report (see Part 3) describing the work performed and the conclusions reached. Refer to pp 408-409 to locate the exhibit prepared for court use by the expert who worked on the case.

If the performance of this exercise was unsuccessful, the inadequate observation should be compared and reconciled with the expert's report. The basis for future progress and personal development through the use of this text depends upon understanding of the lack of success.

* *Case solution, pp 407-409.*

Exercise 2: Sneaker Print

Figure 2A is an impression of a sneaker found on the floor near a burglarized safe. Apparently, some of the pulverized, fire-retardant lining adhered to the burglar's sneaker and was deposited as an impression on a clean area of the floor. Figure 2B is an inked impression of a sneaker owned by a suspect in the case.

Examine both figures side by side. Note any design irregularities, especially in the small inner squares of the sole pattern, that are present in both impressions in the same relative locations. Notice that the questioned imprint is white-on-black whereas the comparison imprint is black-on-white. This may create difficulty for some people in making their comparison. Of course, it is possible to convert the dust imprint into a black-on-white by photographic reversal.

Exercise 3: Sneaker Print

Figure 3A is an imprint of a sneaker that was photographed at a crime scene. Figure 3B is an inked impression taken of a suspect's sneaker. Compare the two to determine if an identity exists.

*Exercise 4: Heelprint in Sand**

Figure 4A is an impression of a heelmark in dirt. Since evidence of this kind is more likely to be encountered in rural areas than in cities, it is especially important that the police in small towns and county sheriffs be equipped to deal effectively with such trace evidence.

It is imperative that an imprint be photographed before it is disturbed in any fashion. In some cases, the questioned impression may be compared directly with a heel suspected of having left the imprint at the scene. Figure 4B is a photograph of a heel found on a suspect's shoe. The question raised is whether the crime scene imprint (Fig. 4A) was made by this particular heel. It is also possible to preserve an impression in soil by making a cast of it.

Examine Figs. 4A and 4B side by side for points of identity. Mark each point as it is discovered and compare the same area in the other photograph for a similar point. Refer to the section of the Introduction to Part 4 entitled: "Interpretation of Comparison Details" (pp 163-164). Write a report after giving serious thought to the evaluation of points of comparison already noted.

* *Case solution, pp 410-411.*

Exercise 5: Heelprint Comparison

The case material in this exercise was selected partly because it illustrates the natural variations described in Chapter 5, pp 48-49, Figs. 5 — 6 through 5 — 9, and partly because it bridges in difficulty the exercises that precede and follow it. Note that the crime scene imprint (Fig. 5A) is larger in area than the test impression (Fig. 5B). Other differences in appearance are also obvious and to be expected. Examine the two figures side by side in the usual manner.

Exercise 6: Poor Heelprint

This exercise is an examination requiring acuteness and may take some time to complete. As points of comparison are noted in Figs. 6A and 6B, mark them in the usual manner. Can an identity be established or not?

Exercise 7: Heelprint

Figure 7A is a reproduction of an impression left at the scene of a safe burglary. Figure 7B was made from an inked impression of the heel on a suspect's shoe. Note that by making a photographic transparency of the negative and printing it, the black ink has been changed to white. This facilitates comparison with the questioned (crime scene) print which was created by the dust of the safe insulation that was picked up by the rubber heel.

5.2 Cloth: Weave Pattern and Stitching

*Exercise 8: Bra Strap**

A fetus was found abandoned after having been strangled with a short piece of a heavy ribbonlike material. The investigation centered upon a young woman who soon confessed to strangling her newly born child. She stated that she had taken a slip from her dresser, ripped a strap from it, and garroted the infant; but a search of the dresser and room failed to disclose the torn slip. However, during this hunt another undergarment, a brassiere, was discovered with one of its shoulder supports missing. The investigator was immediately anxious to learn if the garrote was originally part of this brassiere. Figure 8A is a photograph of one end of the death instrument. Figure 8B is a photograph of the brassiere found in the suspect's room, showing the area where a strap would normally be attached. Figure 8C is a photograph of a similar brassiere especially purchased to illustrate how a brassiere strap is sewn to the body of the garment. An examination of stitching in several hundred brassieres by a criminalist disclosed that this is a machine-operator variable and that this aspect of the garment differs from one to another.

Examine Figs. 8A and 8B for the purpose of writing a report that will serve to satisfy the investigator's anxiety.

* *Case solution, pp 412-413.*

5.3 Gloves

Exercise 9: Glove Impression

Figure 9A is an enlargement (8X) of a latent glove impression developed in the process of making an examination of a crime scene for fingerprints. Figure 9B is a similar enlargement of a test impression made with a glove found in the possession of a suspect. These figures are to be studied carefully in order to determine if there are any possible points of comparison.

Exercise 10: Glove Impression

Figure 10A is an enlargement of one of a few partial glove impressions located at a crime scene. Figure 10B is a similar enlargement of a test pattern of the right index finger of a black leather glove found in the possession of a suspect. Can an identity be established?

5.4 Clothing Accessories

Exercise 11: Tie Clasp

The decorative portion of a tie clasp broken during a robbery, shown at the top of Fig. 11A, was found in possession of a suspect. The head of the pin shown at the bottom of Fig. 11A was removed from the shirt of the victim. Can an identity be established between the two parts?

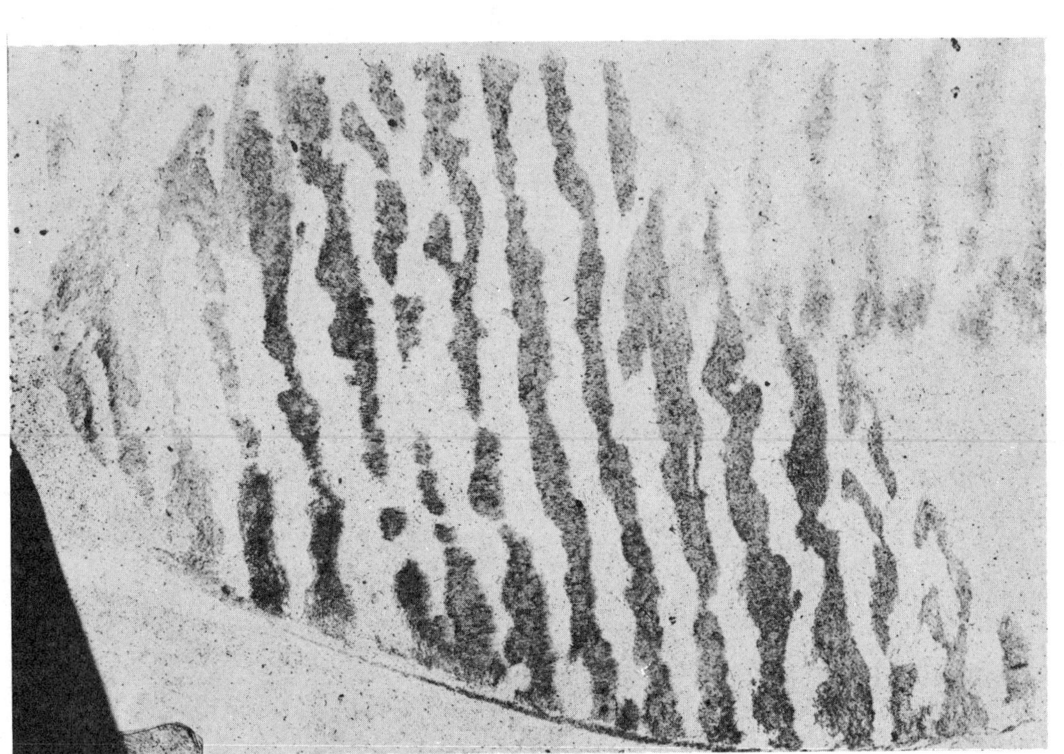

Fig. 1A
Crepe sole impression left by a burglar on a recently painted chair.

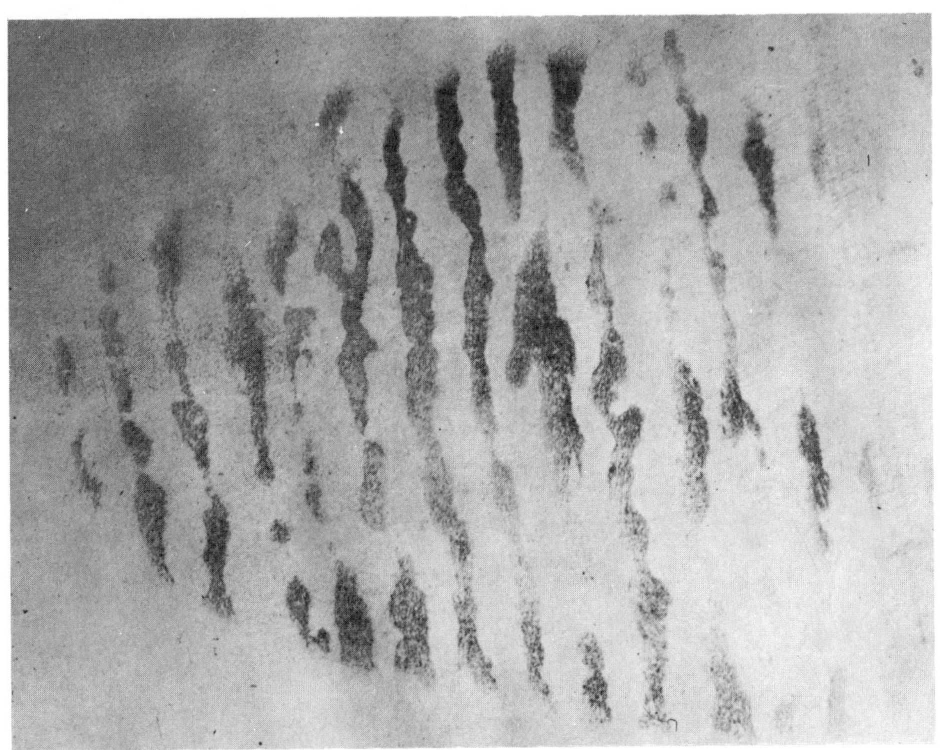

Fig. 1B
Known impression made by a detective using suspect's shoes.
(Courtesy, New York City Police Department.)

Fig. 2A
Impression of a sneaker found near scene of a safe burglary.

Fig. 2B
Inked impression of a sneaker owned by a suspect. *(Courtesy, Minnesota State Bureau of Criminal Apprehension.)*

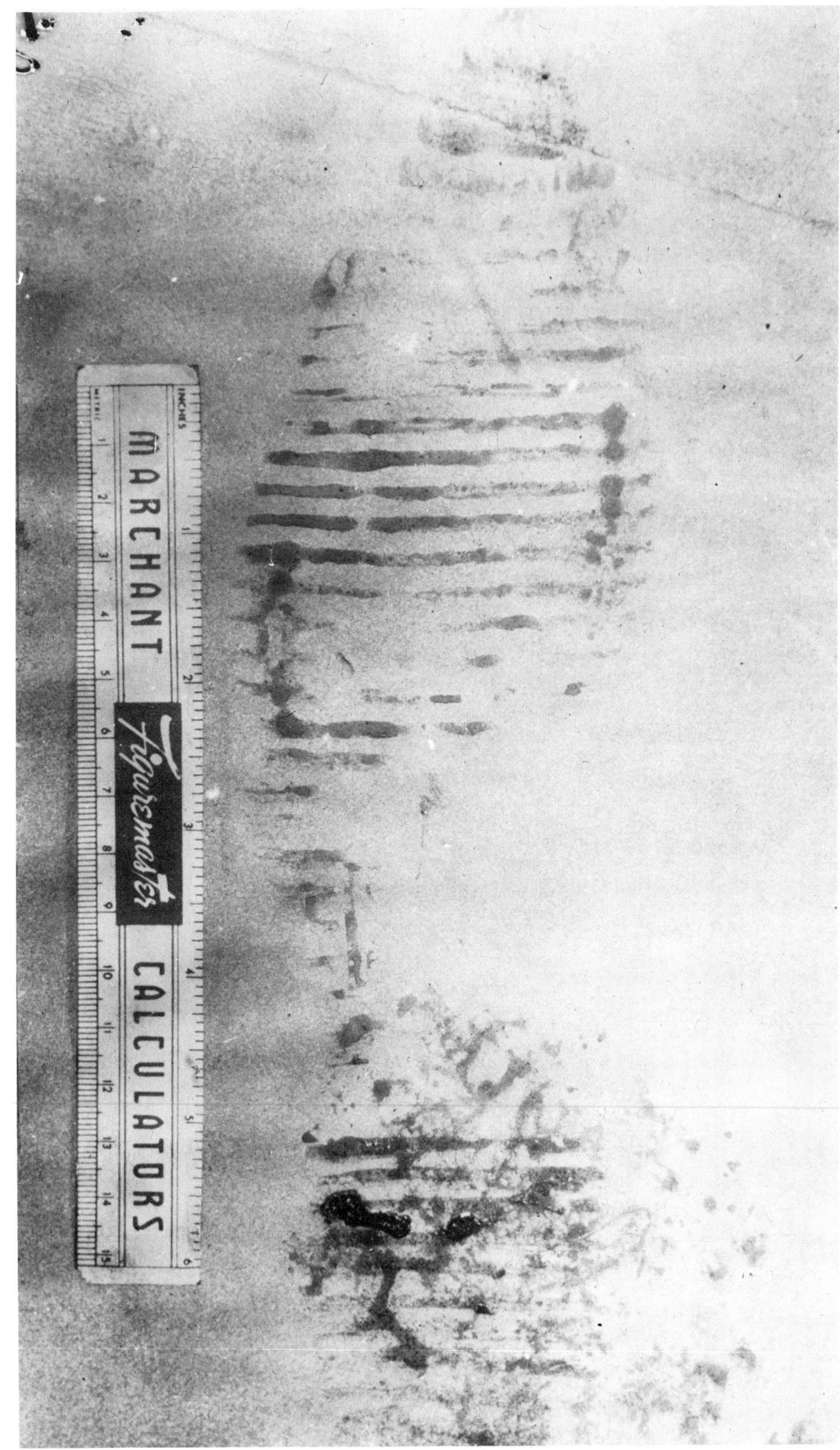

Fig. 3A
Crime scene sneaker impression.

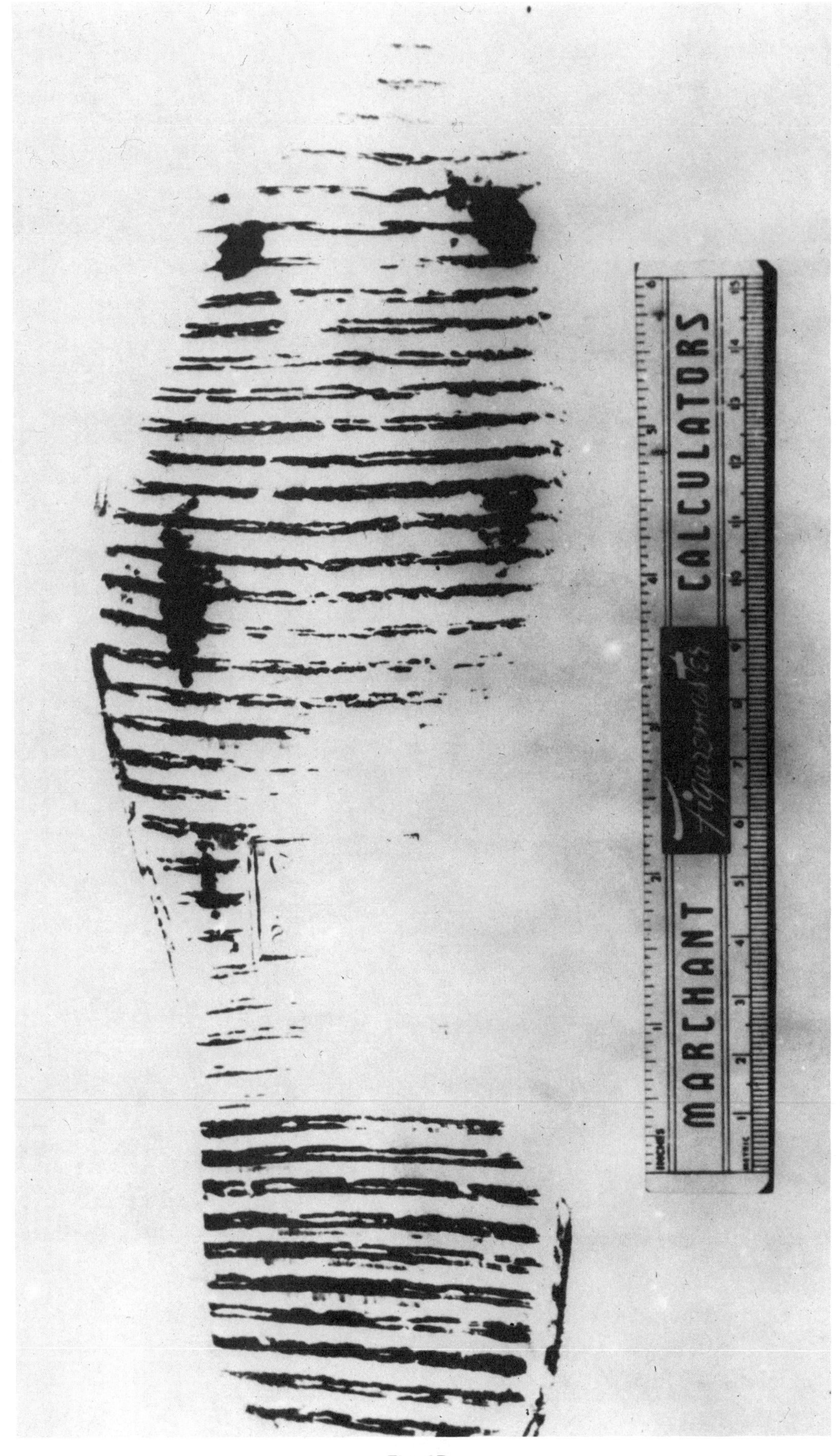

Fig. 3B
Impression of suspect's sneaker.
(Courtesy, Burma National Police.)

Fig. 4A
Impression of heelmark in sand at crime scene.

Fig. 4B
Heel found on shoe of a suspect in case.
(Courtesy, Sheriff's Office, Kern County, California.)

Fig. 5A
A crime scene heel imprint.

Fig. 5B
Test impression made with heel of a suspect's shoe. *(Courtesy, Los Angeles Police Department.)*

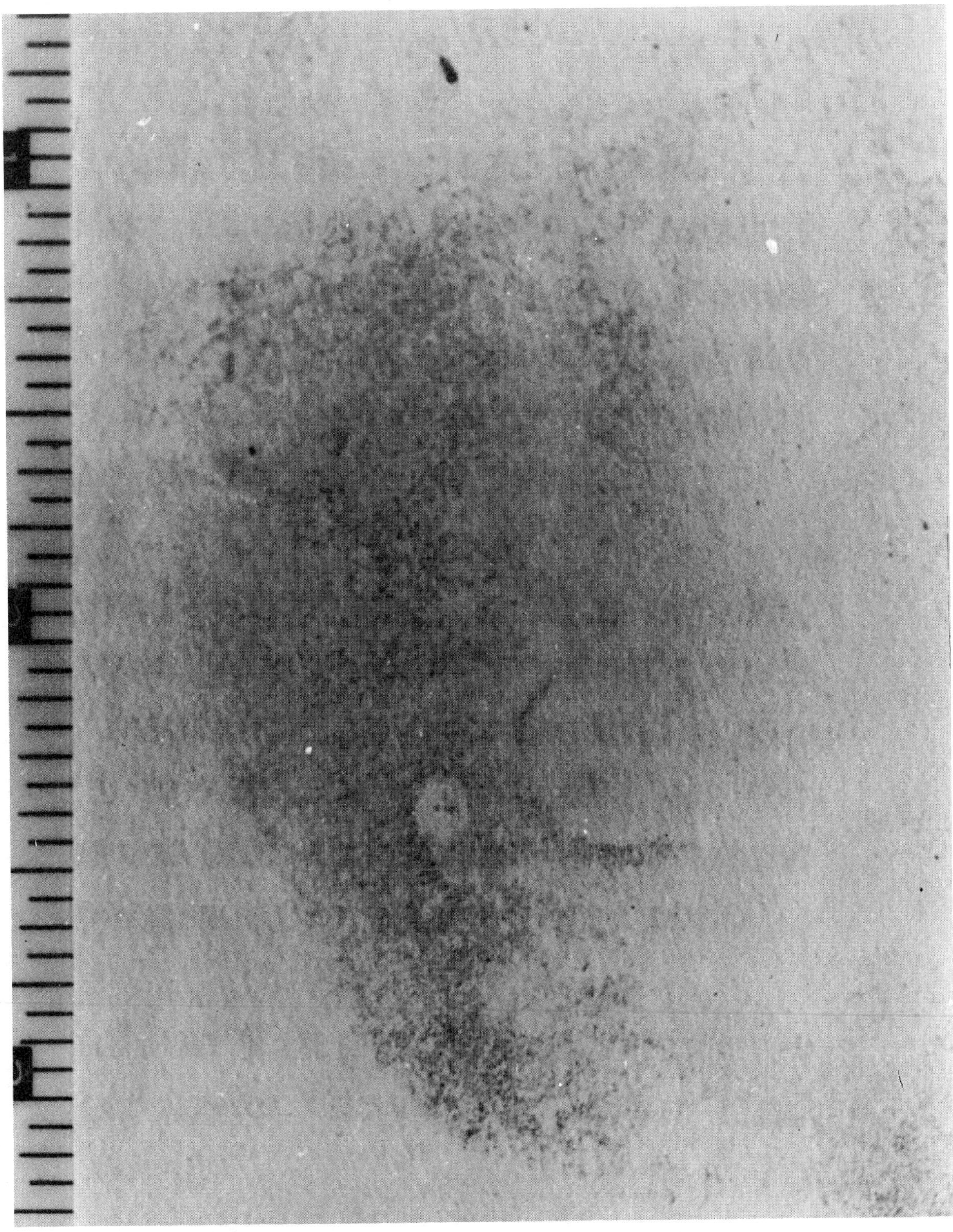

Fig. 6A
An indistinct and partial heelprint.

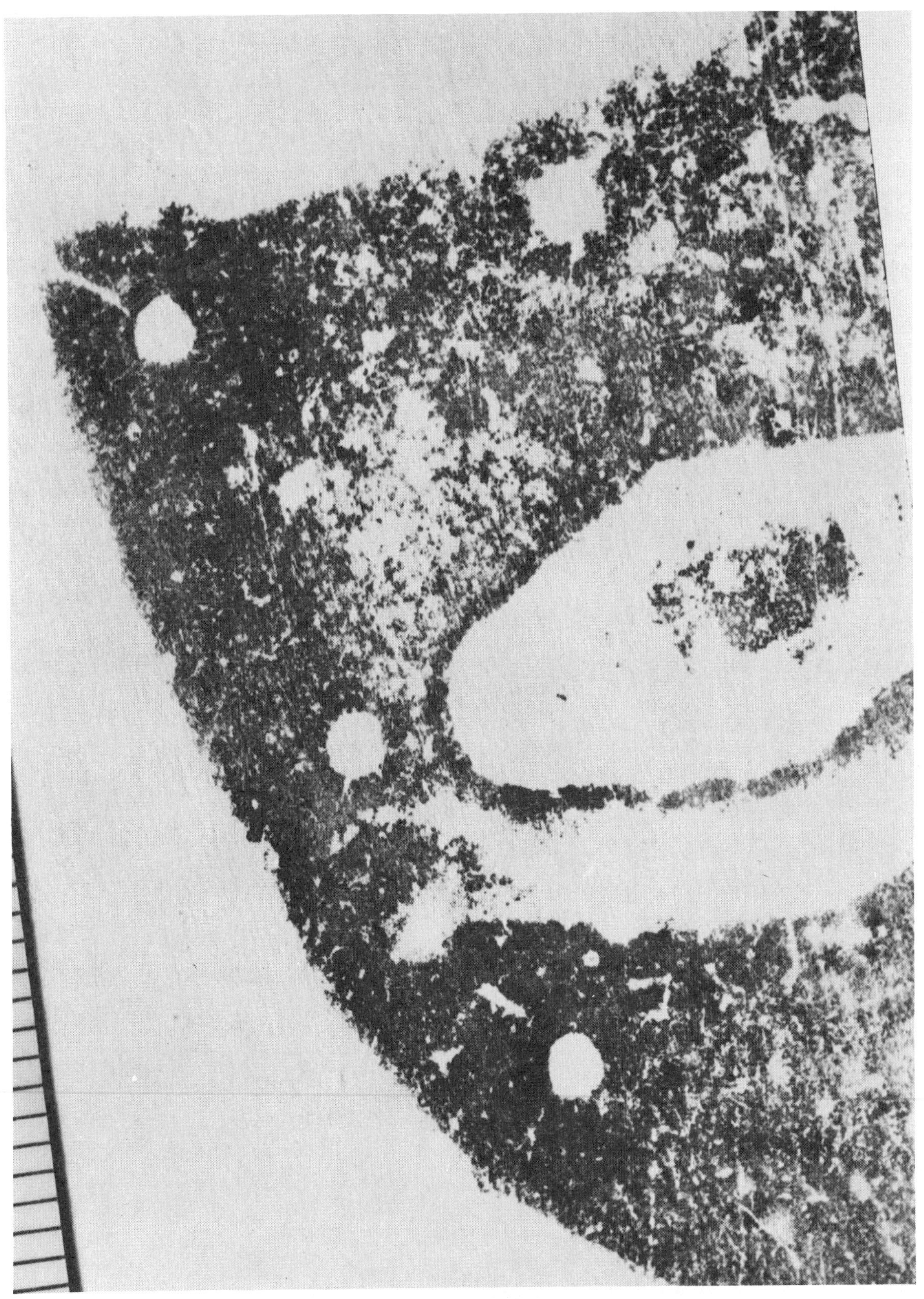

Fig. 6B
Clear impression made of a suspect's heel for comparison purposes.
(Courtesy, Michigan State Police.)

Fig. 7A
A crime scene heelprint.

Fig. 7B
Heel impression of a suspect in case.
(Courtesy, St. Paul Police Department, Minnesota.)

Fig. 8A
A photomacrograph of one end of cloth garrote.

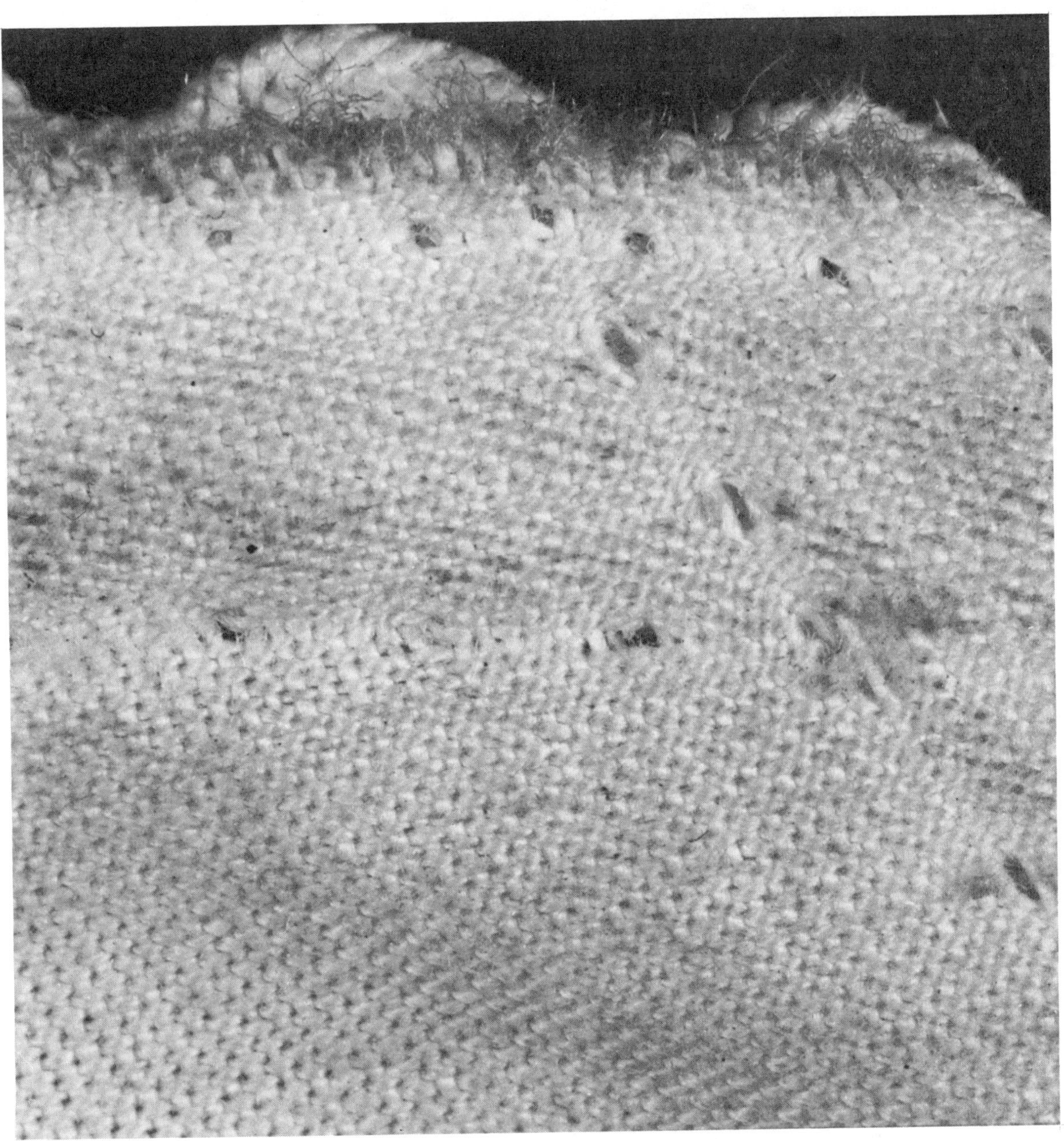

Fig. 8B
A photomacrograph of a portion of a torn brassiere.

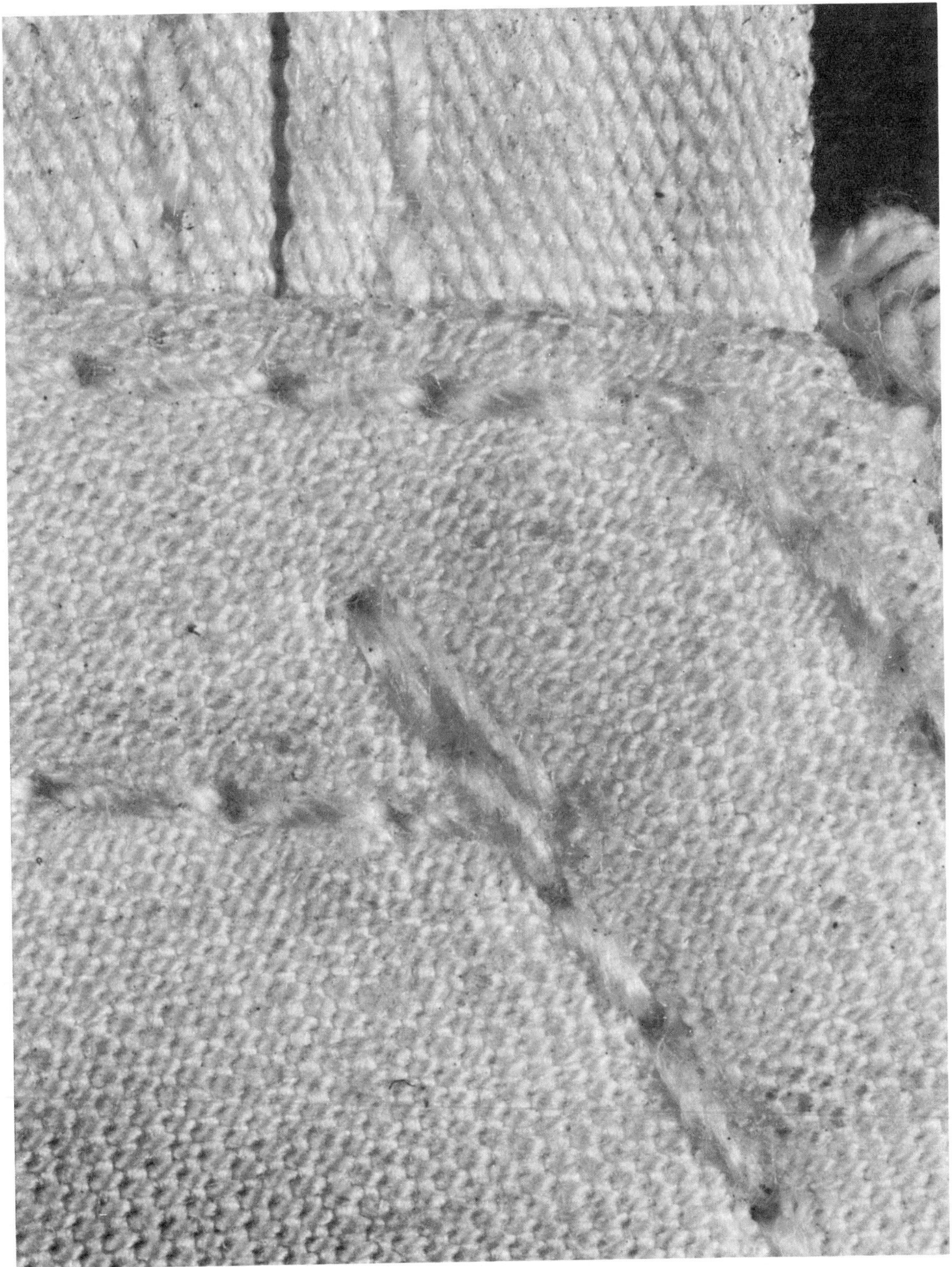

Fig. 8C
A photomacrograph of section of a specially purchased brassiere to show how a shoulder strap is sewn to the body of the garment.
(Courtesy, Indiana State Police.)

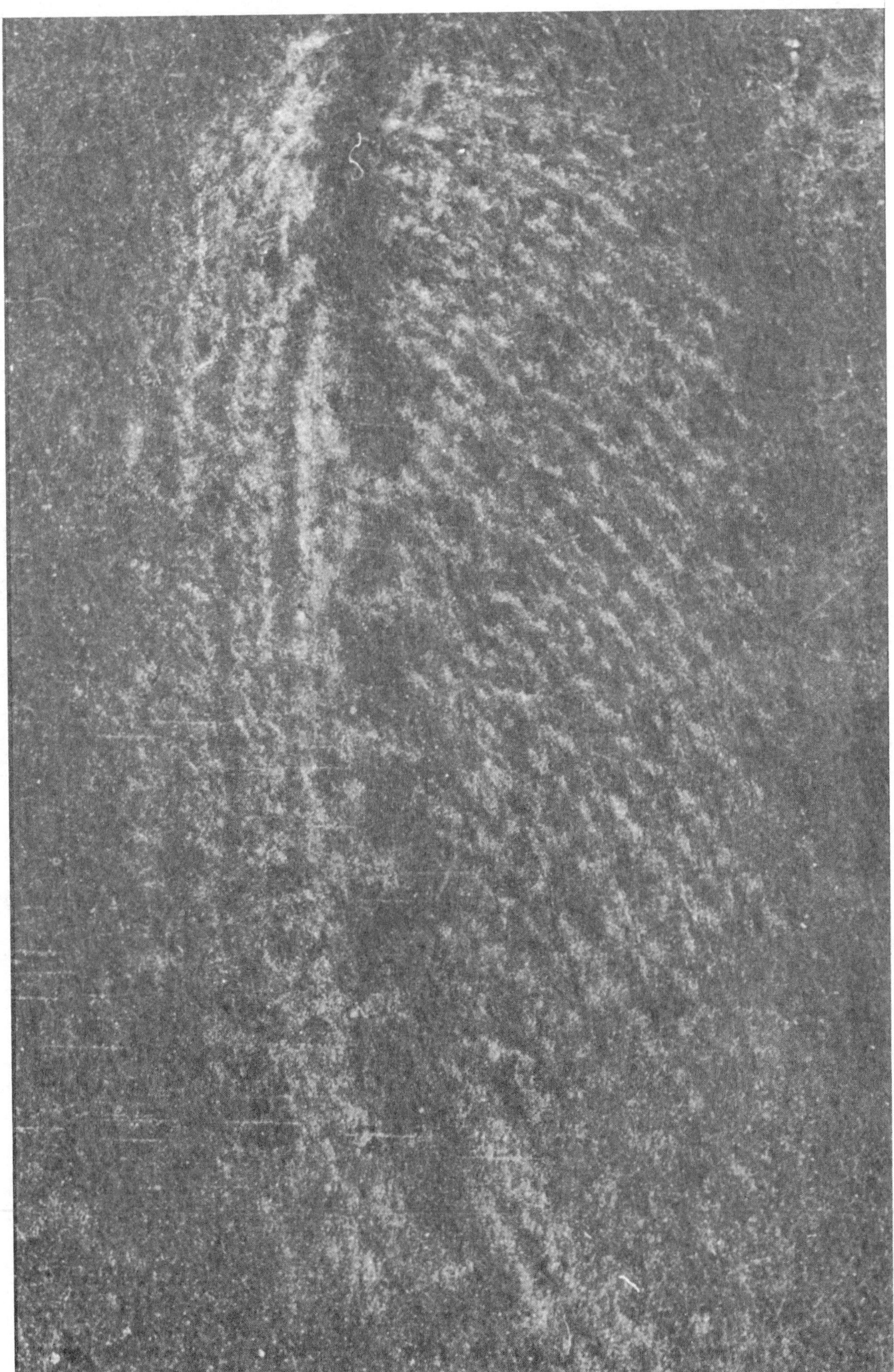

Fig. 9A
Latent glove impression (enlarged 8X) developed during examination of crime scene for fingerprints.

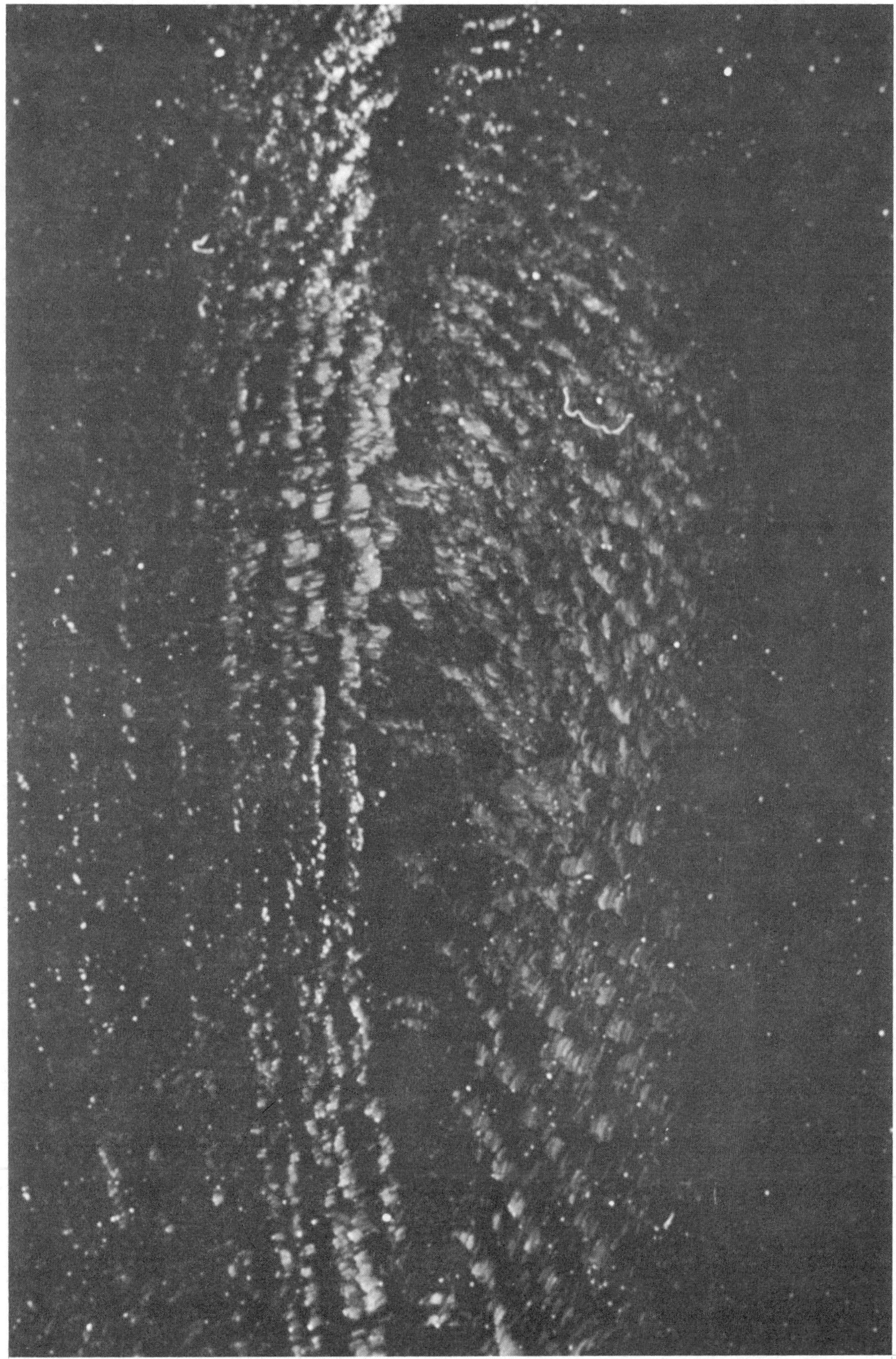

Fig. 9B
Test impression (8X) made with glove found in possession of suspect.
(Courtesy, Michigan State Police.)

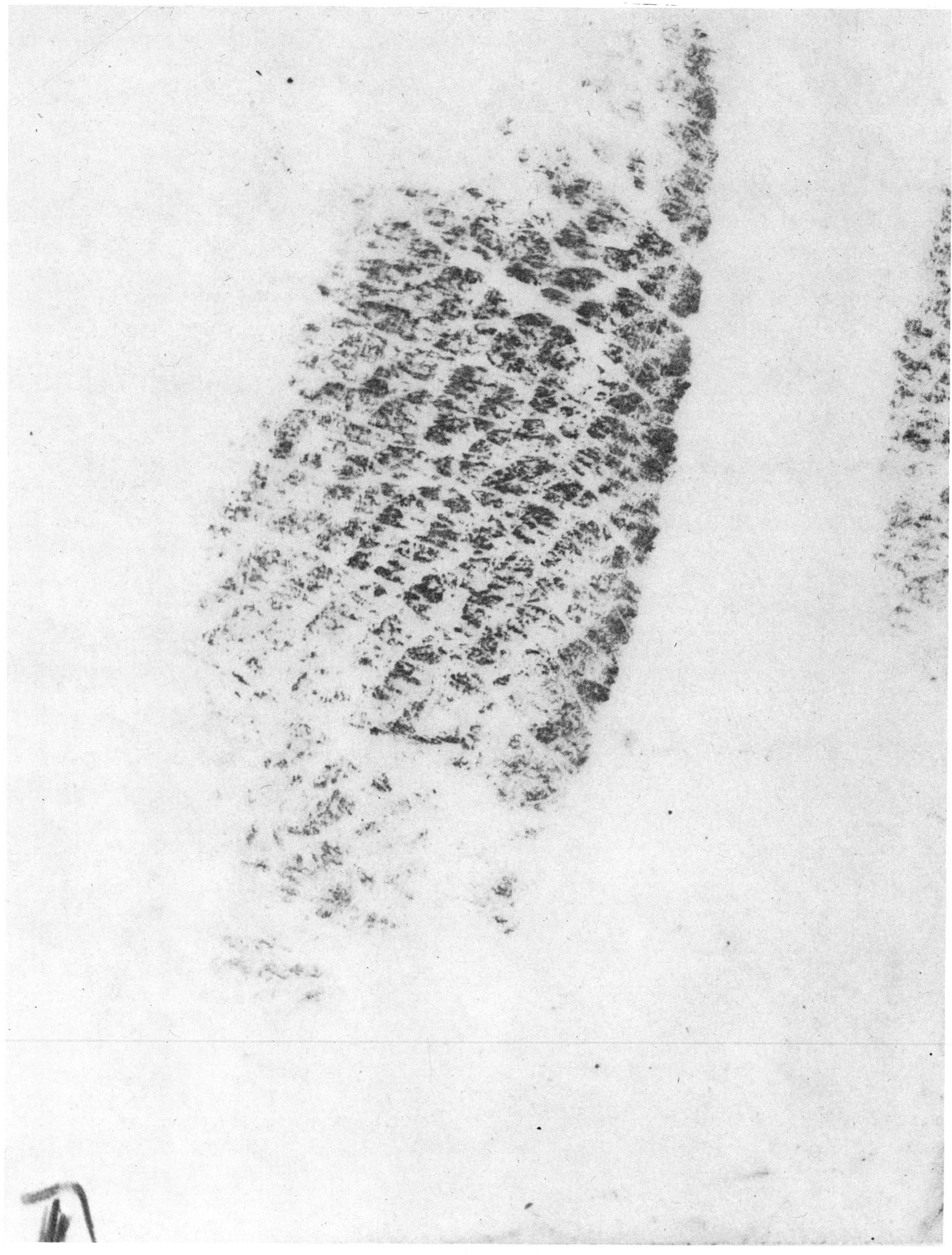

Fig. 10A
Partial latent glove impression.

Fig. 10B
Test impression of leather glove (enlarged).
(Courtesy, San Francisco Police.)

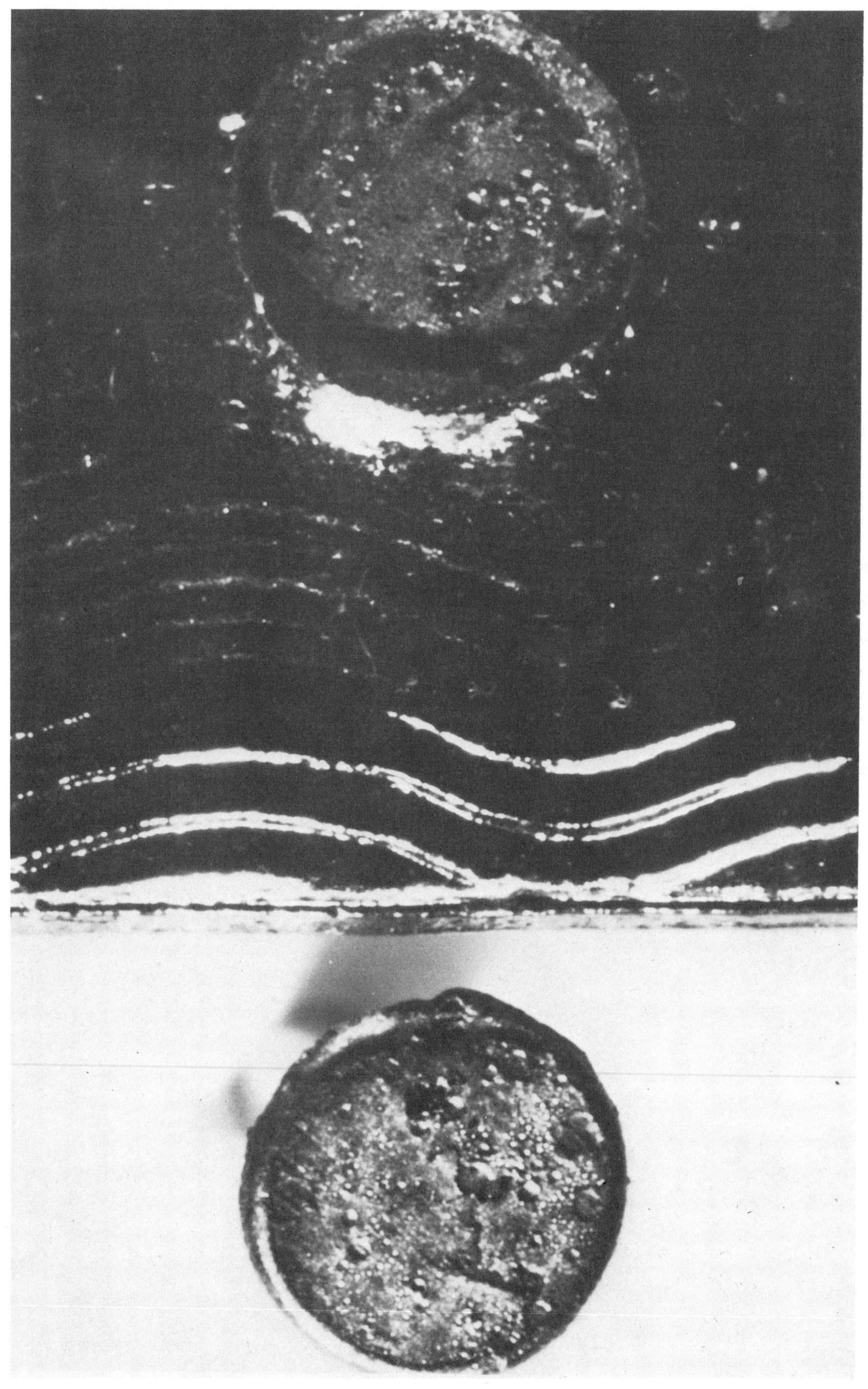

Fig. 11A
Top: back of broken tie clasp found on suspect.
Bottom: head of tie clasp remaining in victim's shirt.
(Courtesy, New Jersey State Police.)

Instruments of Crimes Case Exercises

6.1 Automobiles
Exercise 1: Tire Sand Impression
Fig. 1A — Tire impression left in sand
Fig. 1B — An inked impression of suspected tire

6.2 Jimmies, Axes, Hammers, and Metal Cutters
Exercise 2: Jimmy Mark in Wood
Fig. 2A — Jimmy impression on edge of door
Fig. 2B — Suspected tool

Exercise 3: Jimmy
Fig. 3A — Door that was pried open
Fig. 3B — Cast of jimmy mark on door
Fig. 3C — Tip of suspect's tool

Exercise 4: Ax Chop Marks
Fig. 4A — Top of safe opened by "chop job"
Fig. 4B — Safe insulation material bearing "chop marks"
Fig. 4C — Enlarged portion of Fig. 4B
Fig. 4D — Enlarged portion of another area of Fig. 4B

Exercise 5: Hammer Impression
Fig. 5A — Portion of safe dial face bearing tool marks
Fig. 5B — Face of suspected hammer

Exercise 6: Metal Cutters — Copper Wire
Fig. 6A — Photomacrograph of cut end of copper wire
Fig. 6B — Photomacrograph of copper wire cut with suspect's pliers

6.3 Machinist Dies, Typefaces, and Metal Punches
Exercise 7: Die
Fig. 7A — Photomacrograph of the number "5" stamped on automobile engine
Fig. 7B — Photomacrograph of suspected die

Exercise 8: Punchmark
Fig. 8A — Punchmark on spindle of safe
Fig. 8B — Enlargement of a section of Fig. 8A
Fig. 8C — Enlargement of a section of a test punchmark

6.1 Automobiles

*Exercise 1: Tire Sand Impression**

Figure 1A is a photograph of a portion of a tire impression in sand found at the scene of a crime. Figure 1B is a photograph of an inked impression of a section of a tire. The vehicle on which this tire was located was suspected of being involved in the case for other investigative reasons.

Examine the photographs in this exercise for details that would permit an answer to the detective's inquiry concerning whether the tire present on the suspected car was or was not responsible for the track at the scene.

** Case solution, p 415.*

6.2 Jimmies, Axes, Hammers, and Metal Cutters

*Exercise 2: Jimmy Mark in Wood**

Figure 2A is a photograph of a tool impression in wood. Figure 2B is a photograph of a suspected tool printed in reverse so that a direct comparison may be made with the impression; otherwise, one would be dealing with a mirror image and unnecessarily complicating the comparison.

Examine both photographs side by side and note any characteristics of manufacture of defect acquired through use that may serve to establish an identity.

** Case solution, pp 415, 417.*

Exercise 3: Jimmy

Figure 3A is a photograph of a door that had been pried open. Figure 3B is an enlarged photograph (ca. 9X) of a cast of the tool mark impression in the door, and Fig. 3C is an enlarged photograph (ca. 9X) of the tip of the tool taken from the suspect. Examine Figs. 3B and 3C to determine if an identity exists. Prepare a written report stating your conclusions and what you believe a qualified tool mark examiner would offer as testimony in court.

Exercise 4: Ax Chop Marks

In the case described in Chapter 6, §6.2, the burglar obtained the contents of a safe by chopping through the top of the safe. Figure 4A is a photograph of the top of the safe, and Fig. 4B is a photograph of a piece of the insulation material removed from the lining of that safe. Figures 4C and 4D are enlargements of the two separate ax marks in Fig. 4B.

Carefully examine the lines, i.e., the striations, and the dark areas in Figs. 4C and 4D. Can the furrows or lines in one be paired with those in the other, i.e., matched line for line?

Cut Fig. 4D and superimpose it on Fig. 4C. Can the striations now be aligned? Attention should be given to the minor scratch marks as well as to the more obvious ones.

Exercise 5: Hammer Impression

Figure 5A is an enlarged photograph of a section of a safe dial which was knocked off in preparation for a "punch job." Figure 5B is an enlarged photograph of the face of a hammer suspected of having been used to strike the dial. Note that the hammer print has been reversed in order to permit a direct side by side comparison.

Exercise 6: Metal Cutters—Copper Wire

Figure 6A is a photomacrograph of the end of a copper wire cut during the commission of a crime. Figure 6B is a photomacrograph of a wire cut with a pair of pliers found in the tool box of a suspect. Examine the two figures to determine if an identity exists.

6.3 Machinist Dies, Typefaces, and Metal Punches

Exercise 7: Die

This exercise involves a stamping die which was but one of a set suspected of having been used to alter an engine serial number. Figure 7A is a photomacrograph of a number stamped in the metal block of an automobile engine while Fig. 7B is a photomacrograph of the die which was suspected of having been used to produce the imprint in Fig. 7A.

Examine both figures. Are the obvious characteristics class or individual? How is this known? How could these ideas be verified? Incorporate your thoughts in the report to be prepared when the exercise is completed.

Exercise 8: Punchmark

Figure 8A is an enlargement of a safe spindle bearing superimposed punchmarks. Figure 8B is an enlargement of a section of Fig. 8A. Figure 8C is an enlargement of a section of a test punchmark made in lead using a punch found in the possession of a suspect. Compare the latter two figures to determine if Fig. 8B was made by Fig. 8C.

6.4 Weapons

Exercise 9: Bullet Comparison

Although the method of choice for the comparison of two bullets is examination under the comparison microscope, it is nevertheless possible to do a comparison through a side by side study of photomacrographs of the test and questioned bullets. Figure 9A is a recovered crime scene bullet and Fig. 9B is a test bullet fired through a suspected weapon. Examine the two figures to determine whether an identity exists.

Exercise 10: Firing Pin Impression

Figure 10A is a head of a cartridge found at a crime scene and Fig. 10B is the head of a test cartridge fired in a suspected gun. Examine both illustrations in the area of the firing pin impression, i.e., in the depression almost in the center of each photograph. Mark any matching characteristics which you are able to find in each impression.

*Exercise 11: Breech Face Marks**

Figure 11A is a photomacrograph of the breech face marks on the head of a cartridge found at the crime scene. Figure 11B shows breech face marks on a cartridge head after it was fired through the Polish Radom 9mm. automatic that was submitted. Is there an identity?

* *Case solution, p 422.*

Exercise 12: Powder Residue

Figure 12A is a photograph of the same shirt presented in Chapter 6, Fig. 6—49 (p 106). This photograph was taken to increase the contrast between the powder pattern and the cloth of the shirt. Figure 12B is a series of test photographs depicting the details of a powder pattern left on a similar shirt when a gun was fired at known, measured distances from the shirt.

Examine Fig. 12A and compare the powder residue pattern on it with the test shot distance patterns in Fig. 12B. Estimate the distance at which the shot was fired to leave the pattern in Fig. 12A.

*Exercise 13: Hose Knife Cut**

Figure 13A is the end of a hose found attached to an illicit still. It had been cut in haste as a prelude to flight from an invasion by law enforcement officers whose presence had been detected very shortly before the raid was to begin. Subsequently, a suspect was apprehended with a hose in his possession. One end of it had been cut with a knife (Fig. 13B). The investigators desired to learn if both ends could be matched to show that they were originally of one piece. Figure 13B has been reversed in printing to permit a direct rather than a mirror image comparison with Fig. 13A.

* *Case solution, pp 423-424.*

6.5 Shovels

Exercise 14: Shovel Marks

Examine Figs. 14A and 14B to determine if the same shovel was or was not used for both diggings.

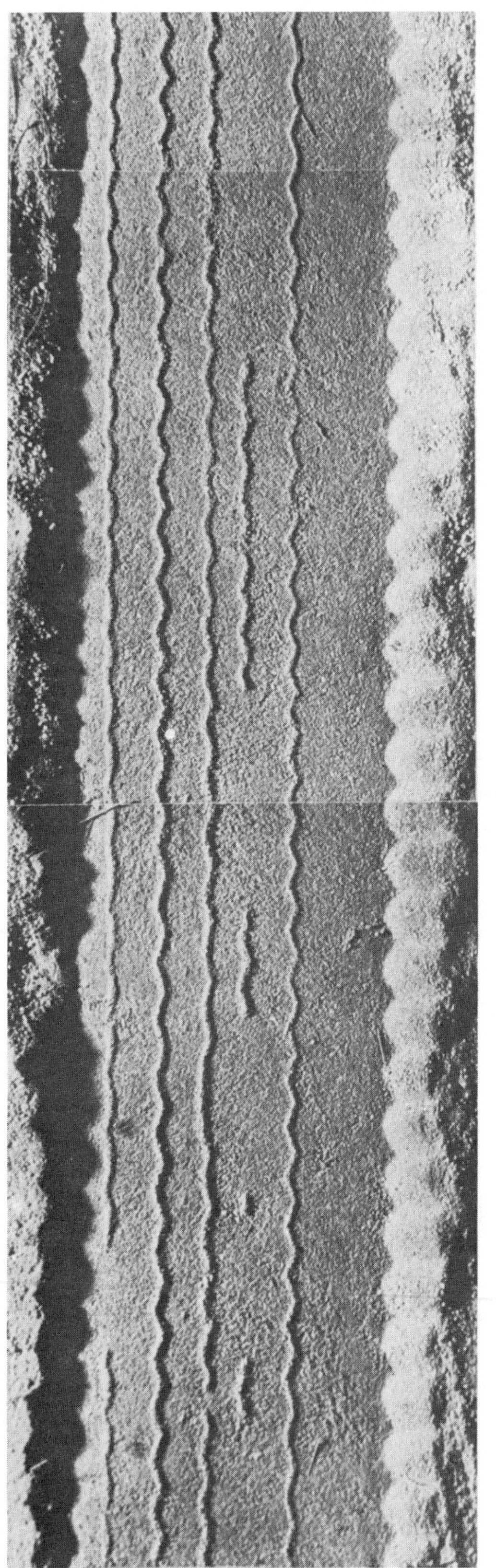

Fig. 1A
Tire impression left in sand at crime scene.

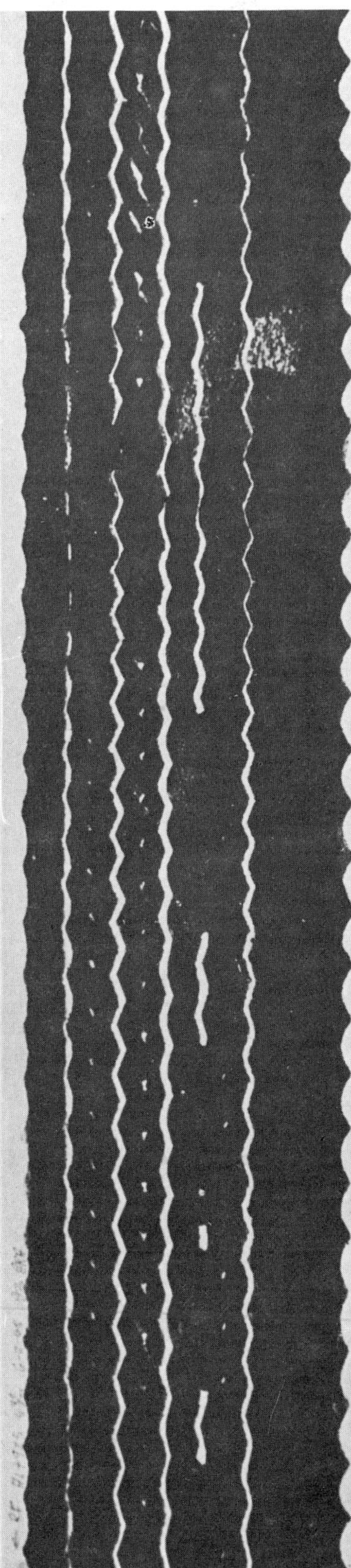

Fig. 1B
An inked impression of a suspected tire.
(Courtesy, Sheriff's Office, Kern County, California.)

Fig. 2A
Jimmy impression on edge of door.

Fig. 2B
Suspected tool.
(Courtesy, Orange County Sherriff's Department.)

Fig. 3A
Door that was pried open.

Fig. 3B
Cast of jimmy mark on door (enlarged 9X).

Fig. 3C
Tip of suspect's tool (enlarged ca. 9X).
(Courtesy, Santa Ana Police Department, California.)

Fig. 4A
Top of safe opened by "chop job."

Fig. 4B
Safe insulation material bearing several sets of "chop marks."

Fig. 4C
Enlarged portion of an area in Fig. 4B.

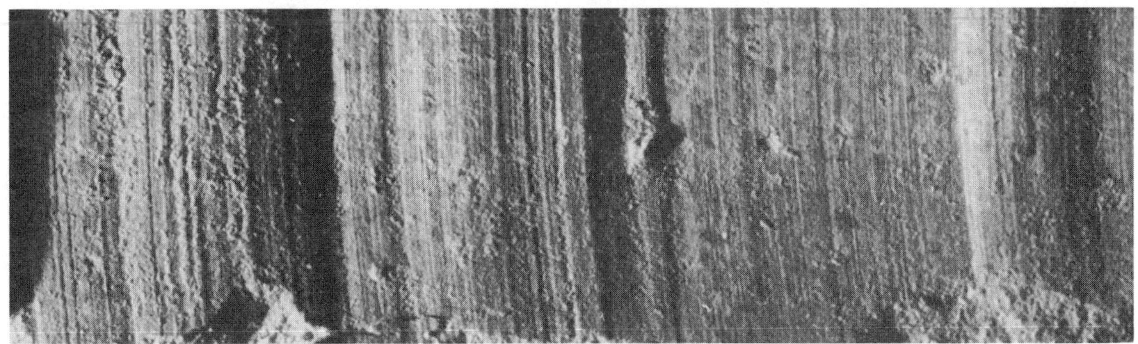

Fig. 4D
Enlarged portion of another area in Fig. 4B.
(Courtesy, Dansville Police Department, New York.)

Fig. 5A
Portion of the face of a dial (enlarged) which bears marks of a tool used to knock it off safe.

Fig. 5B
Face of hammer suspected of having been used in safe burglary case.
(Courtesy, Los Angeles County Sheriff's Department.)

Fig. 6A
Photomacrograph (ca. 30X) of the cut end of a copper wire found at crime scene.

Fig. 6B
Photomacrograph (ca. 30X) of copper wire cut with suspect's pliers.
(Courtesy, New York City Police Department.)

Fig. 7A
Photomacrograph (ca. 15X) of the number "5" stamped on the metal block of an automobile engine.

Fig. 7B
Photomacrograph of die (ca. 15X) suspected of having been used to alter an engine number. *(Courtesy, New York City Police Department.)*

Fig. 8A
Punchmark on spindle of safe.

Fig. 8B
Enlargement of a section of Fig. 8A.

Fig. 8C
Test punchmark in lead made by suspect's punch (enlarged to same size as Fig. 8B).
(Courtesy, Sheriff, San Bernardino County, California.)

Fig. 9A
Photomacrograph (ca. 14X) of fatal bullet recovered at crime scene.

Fig. 9B
Photomacrograph (ca. 14X) of test bullet fired through suspected weapon, a .38 caliber Iver Johnson revolver.
(Courtesy, Minnesota State Bureau of Criminal Apprehension.)

Fig. 10A
Head of cartridge found at scene of crime.

Fig. 10B
Head of test cartridge fired in suspected gun. *(Courtesy, Minnesota State Bureau of Criminal Apprehension.)*

Fig. 11A
Photomacrograph of breech marks on head of crime scene cartridge.

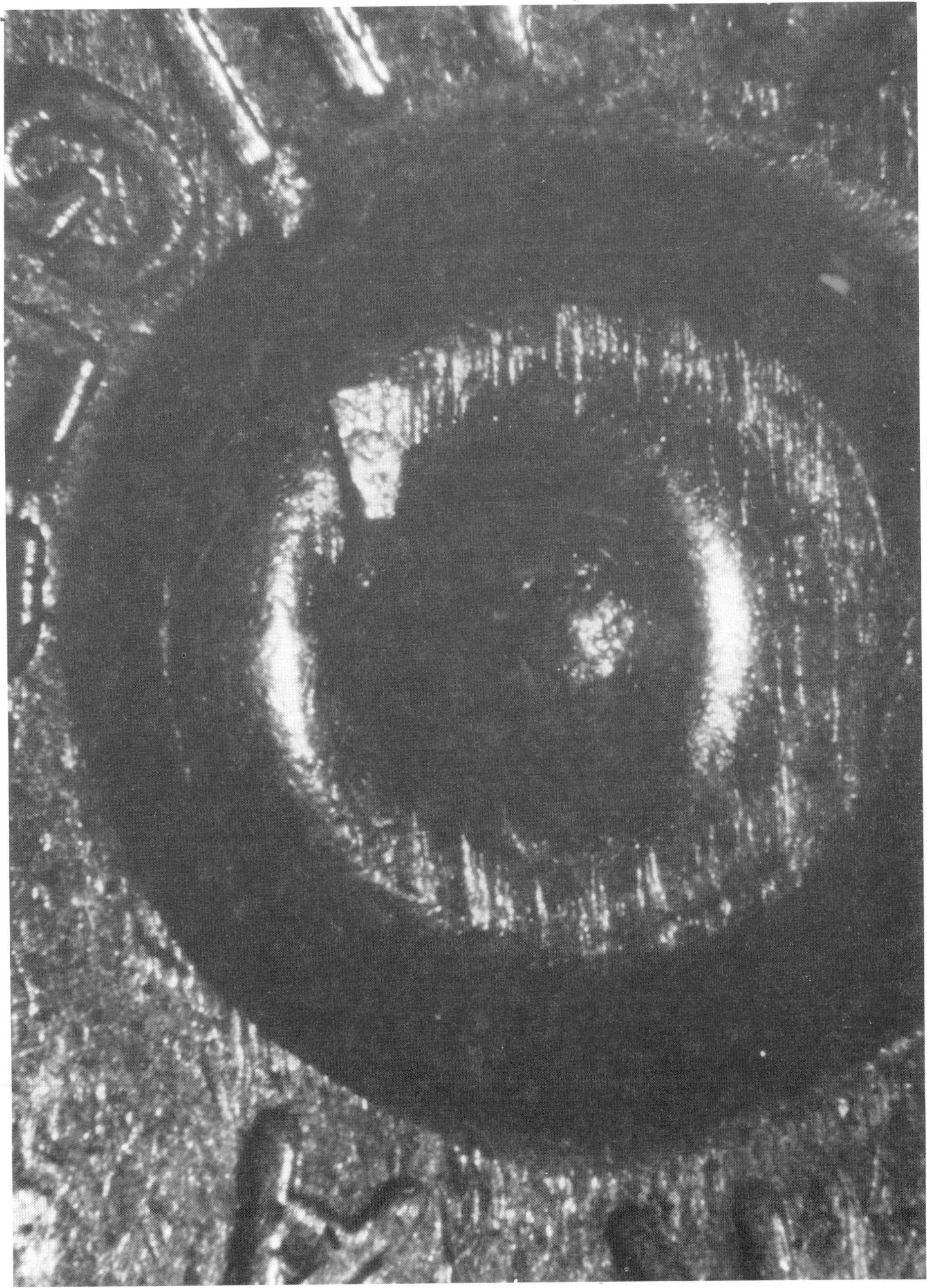

Fig. 11B
Mark on head of cartridge fired through suspected weapon.
(Courtesy, Joseph D. Nicol.)

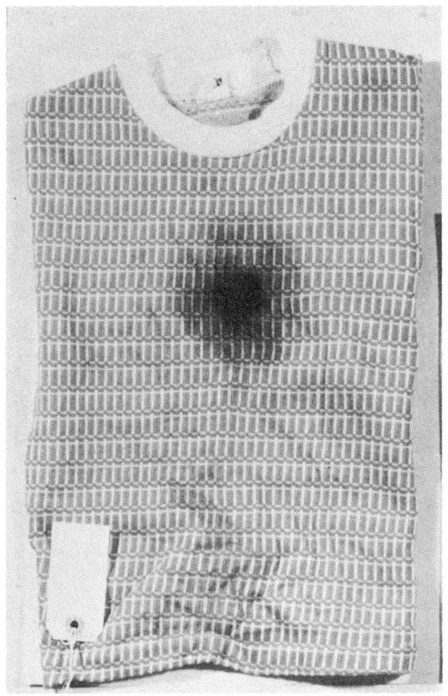

Fig. 12A
Same shirt as in Fig. 6—49, Chapter 6. Photographed to increase the details of the powder pattern.

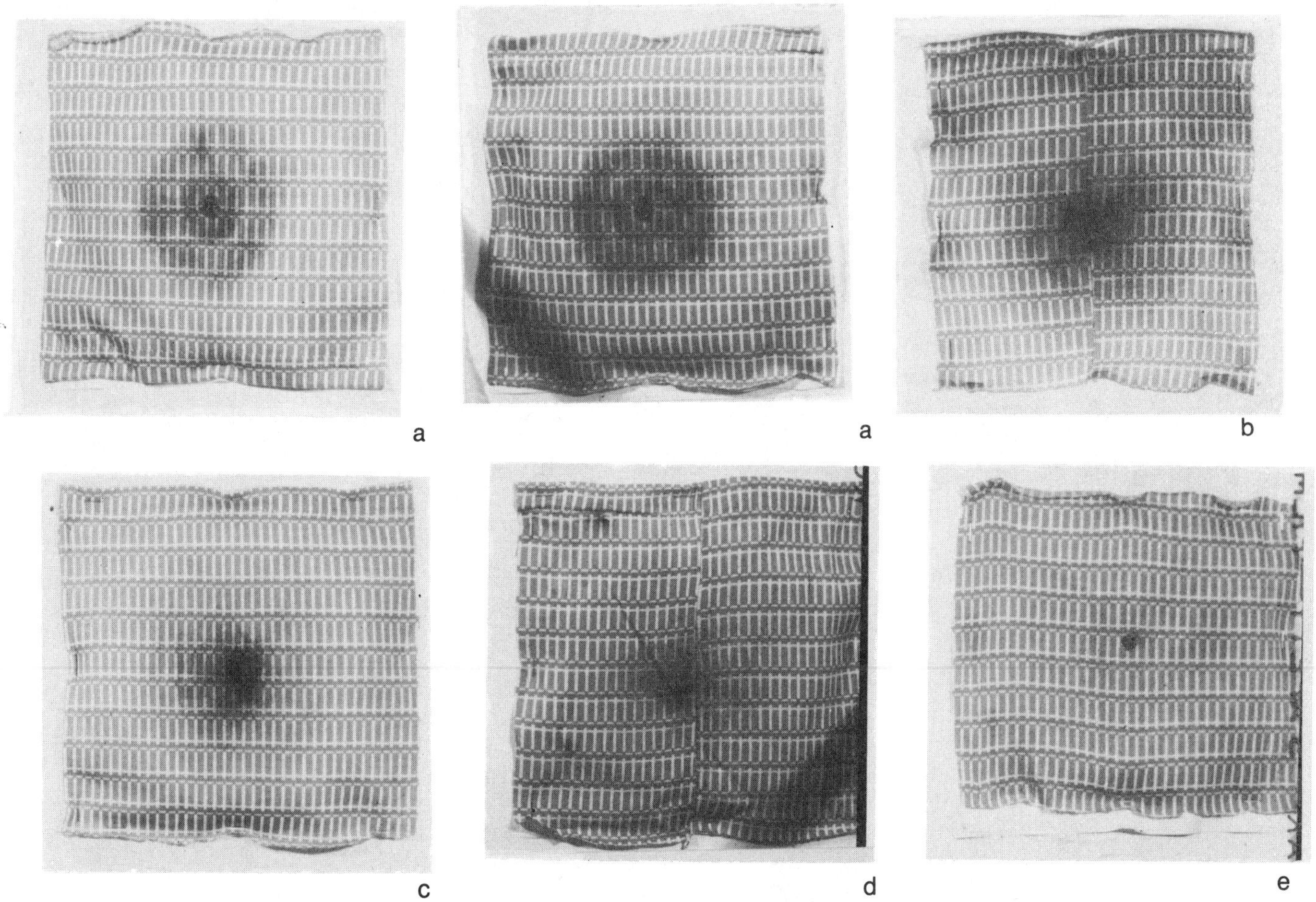

a a b

c d e

Fig. 12B
Test shot-distance patterns:
a. Contact shots
b. Shot at 3 inches.
c. Shot at 6 inches.
d. Shot at 9 inches.
e. Shot at 12 inches.
(Courtesy, Minnesota State Bureau of Criminal Apprehension.)

Fig. 13A
End of hose found attached to illicit still.

Fig. 13B
End of hose found in possession of suspect — reverse printed.
(Courtesy, Columbus Police Department, Ohio.)

Fig. 14A
Photographic enlargement (ca. 3X) of clod of earth bearing shovel marks found in soil of hole dug to bury evidence.

Fig. 14B
Soil near burial plot dug with suspected shovel.
(Courtesy, Michigan State Police.)

Miscellaneous Traces Case Exercises

7.1 Physical Matches

*Exercise 1: Wiper Blade Spot Weld**

Figure 1A depicts evidence found in a hit-and-run case. The windshield wiper blade was found at the crime scene and the activator part was removed from a suspected vehicle. The obvious request made to the laboratory concerned whether associative evidence could be developed through examination of these two parts. Figure 1B shows the respective areas involved if they had been spot welded together.

In this exercise the student should study the evidence in Fig. 1B to determine if there are any individual details present that would permit an identity to be established.

* *Case solution, p 429-430.*

*Exercise 2: Headlamp Rims**

In a hit-and-run homicide the metal rim of a headlamp was found at the scene. Subsequent investigation established the make and model of the vehicle. Local automative repair shops were canvassed and a vehicle was discovered with damage to the right front fender area and with its headlamp rim missing. The right headlamp mounting bracket and housing were removed and brought to the laboratory. As an example of a complete headlight the left headlight assembly was also removed and brought to the laboratory.

The bracket for the right headlamp was observed to have a scratched area adjacent to one corner of a slot designed to hold a tab protruding from the top of the headlamp rim. Figure 2A is a portion of a photomicrograph of this mark on the right headlamp bracket.

Figures 2B and 2C represent test marks made using the tabs which protruded from the headlamp rims. Can either, both, or neither be connected to Figure 2A?

* *Case solution, pp 431-432.*

Exercise 3: Mattress Stain — Sheet Stain

There are cases involving the matching of miscellaneous physical characteristics that are not quite as simple as Case Exercises 1 and 2 for Chapter 7. For example, when blood seeps through a sheet onto a mattress, some untoward difficulties for the usual comparison process may arise. In some areas the blood may not filter evenly through the sheet, or the mattress ticking may have been previously soiled and consequently the stain pattern on it will not be identical with that present on the sheet. This exercise was selected because both complications are possible.

Figure 3A is a photograph of a portion of a bed sheet found underneath the body of a homicide victim. Figure 3B is a photograph of a mattress that was located on the bed of a suspect who lived in a room near the victim. Examine these photographs to determine if the sheet and mattress were in intimate contact at the time the victim was bleeding.

7.2 Paint Chips

Exercise 4: Paint Chip Match

The following case involves the examination of a piece of a price tag (Fig. 4A) torn from an article sold by a hardware store. On the reverse side of the tag some paint chips were found clinging to the adhesive material used to attach it to the merchandise (Fig. 4B). This tag was found in an automobile which was believed to be the get-away car used in an attempted safe burglary. Two suspects were apprehended near the scene. They had a crowbar which was believed to have been used in the crime (Fig. 4C). The officers noted that the crowbar was new and an examination of the shaft revealed an area where a price tag had apparently been removed and chips of paint were missing.

Figure 4D is an enlarged photograph showing the area of the crowbar where a price tag was probably once attached. This illustration has been reversed in printing to permit a direct comparison with Fig. 4E, which is an enlarged photograph of the top end of the back of the price tag. Examine Figs. 4D and 4E to determine if this particular tag had been attached to the crowbar found in the possession of the suspect.

7.3 Broken Glass

Exercise 5: Broken Glass Strain Marks

Occasionally, a broken edge of glass clearly shows marks of the strain (other than rib marks) to which the glass was subjected during breakage. When they are present in both edges that fit together they may be used as a basis for establishing an identity. This case involves two pieces of automobile headlight glass. Figure 5A is a photographic enlargement showing the strain marks present in a glass fragment found at the scene of a hit-and-run accident. Figure 5B is a similar photograph of the edge of a glass fragment located on a suspected automobile. Examine the strain marks to determine if both fragments originally were joined as part of a single headlight lens.

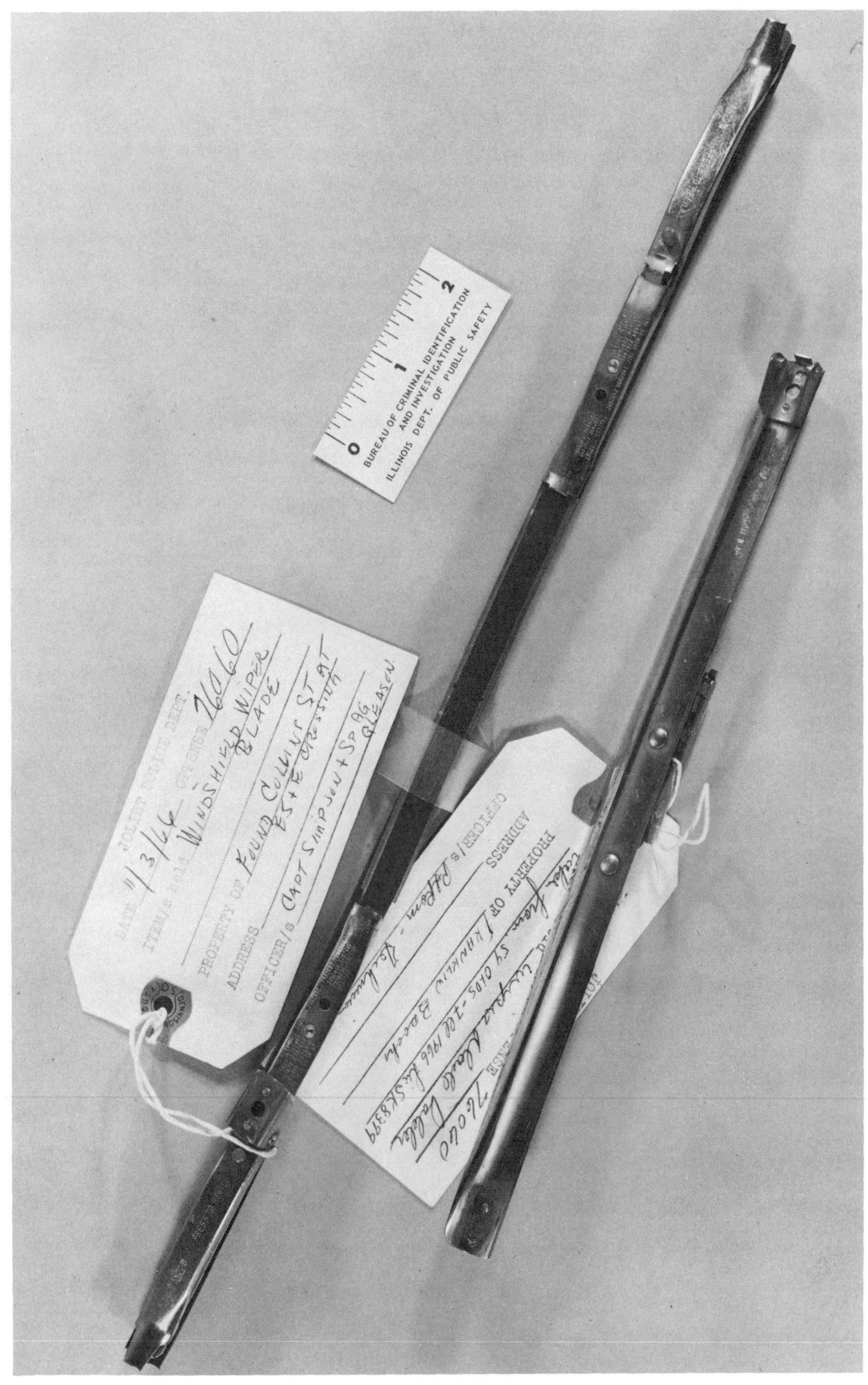

Fig. 1A
Hit-and-run evidence. Windshield wiper blade was located at scene. Activator part was removed from suspected vehicle.

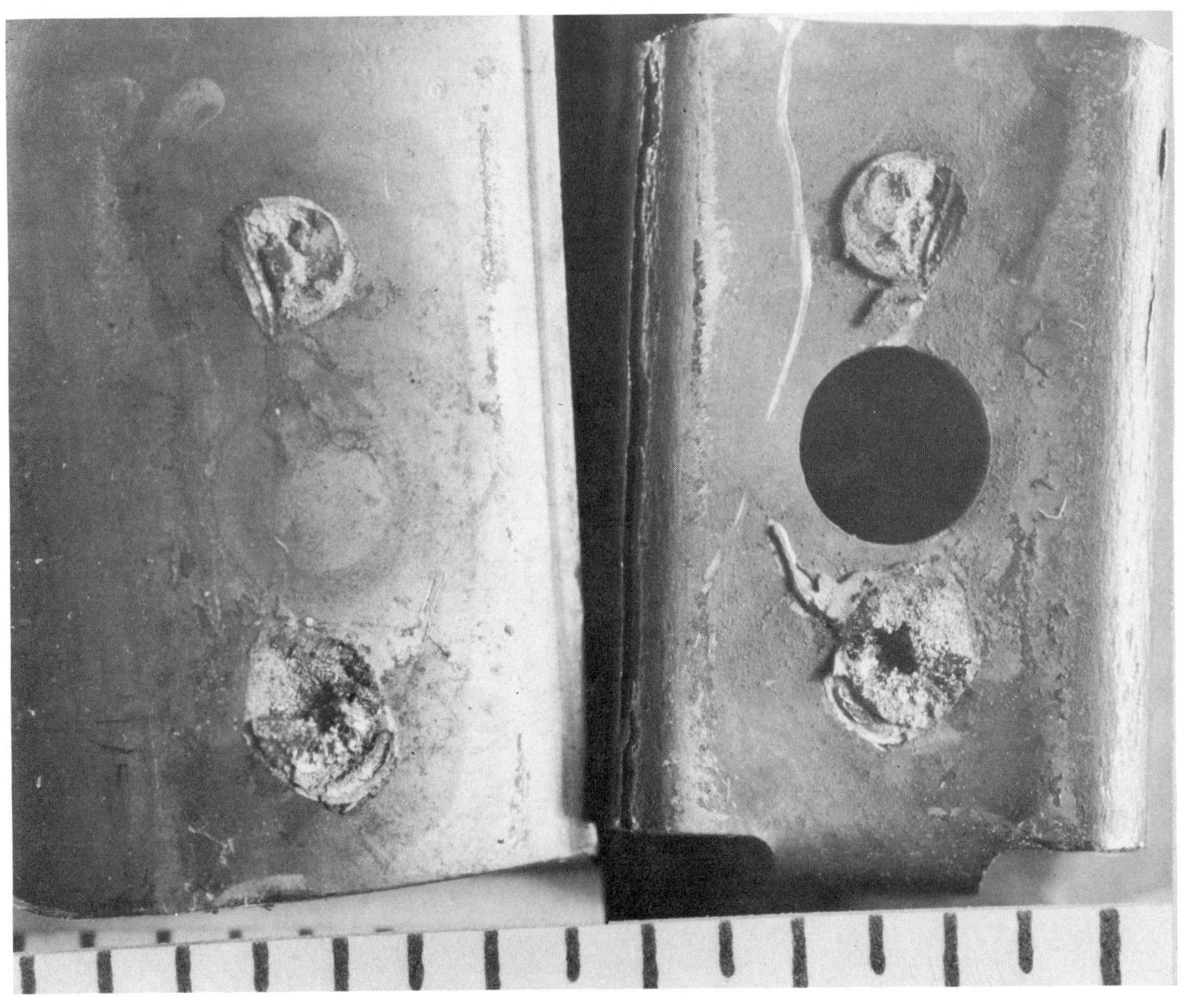

Fig. 1B
Spot weld areas: left, evidence from suspected vehicle; right, crime scene evidence.
(Courtesy, Illinois Bureau of Criminal Identification and Investigation)

Fig. 2A
Photomacrograph of mark on right headlamp bracket.

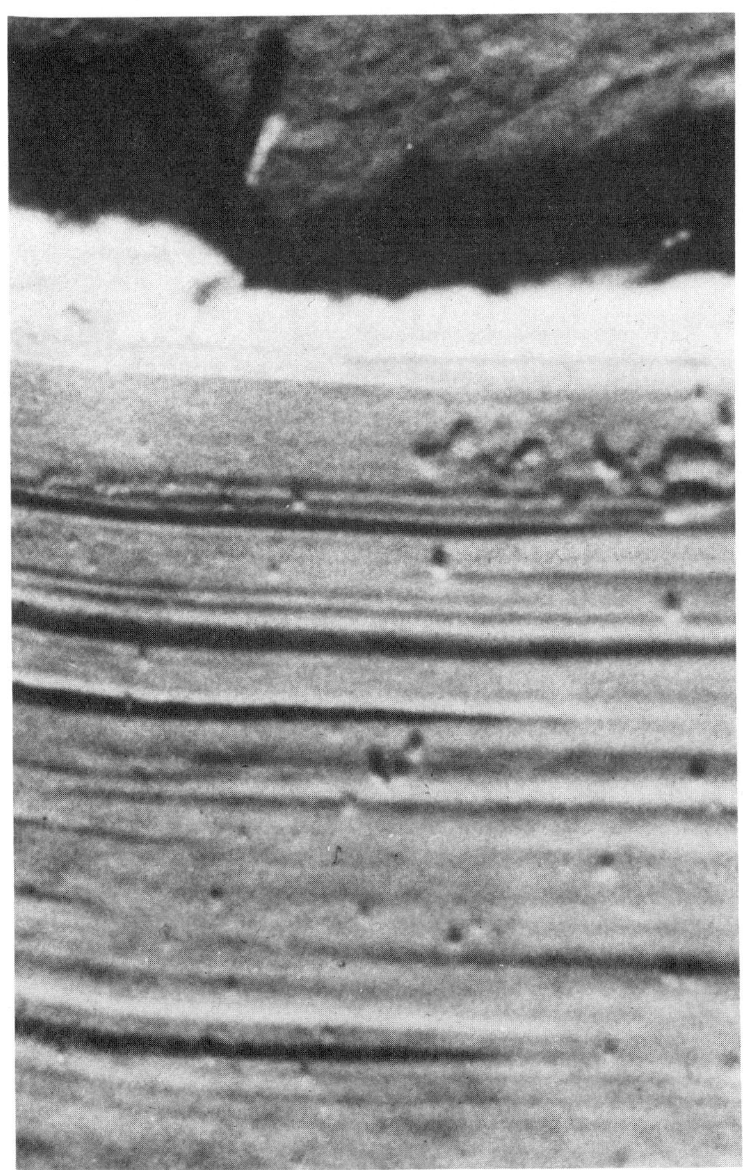

Fig. 2B
Test mark made with one protruding tab.

Fig. 2C
Test mark made with other protruding tab.
(Courtesy, Sheriff's Department, Contra Costa County, California.)

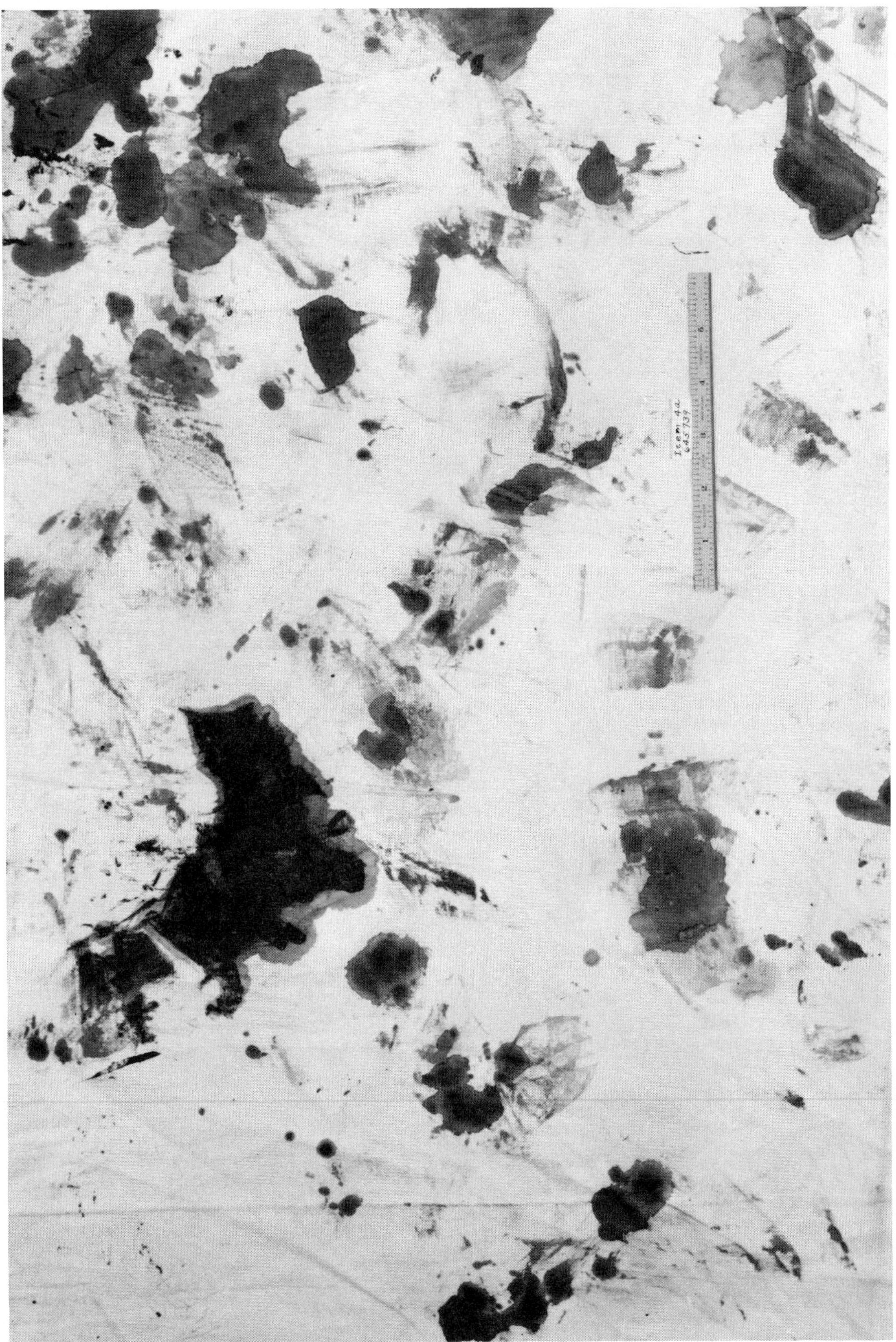

Fig. 3A
Bedsheet found under homicide victim.

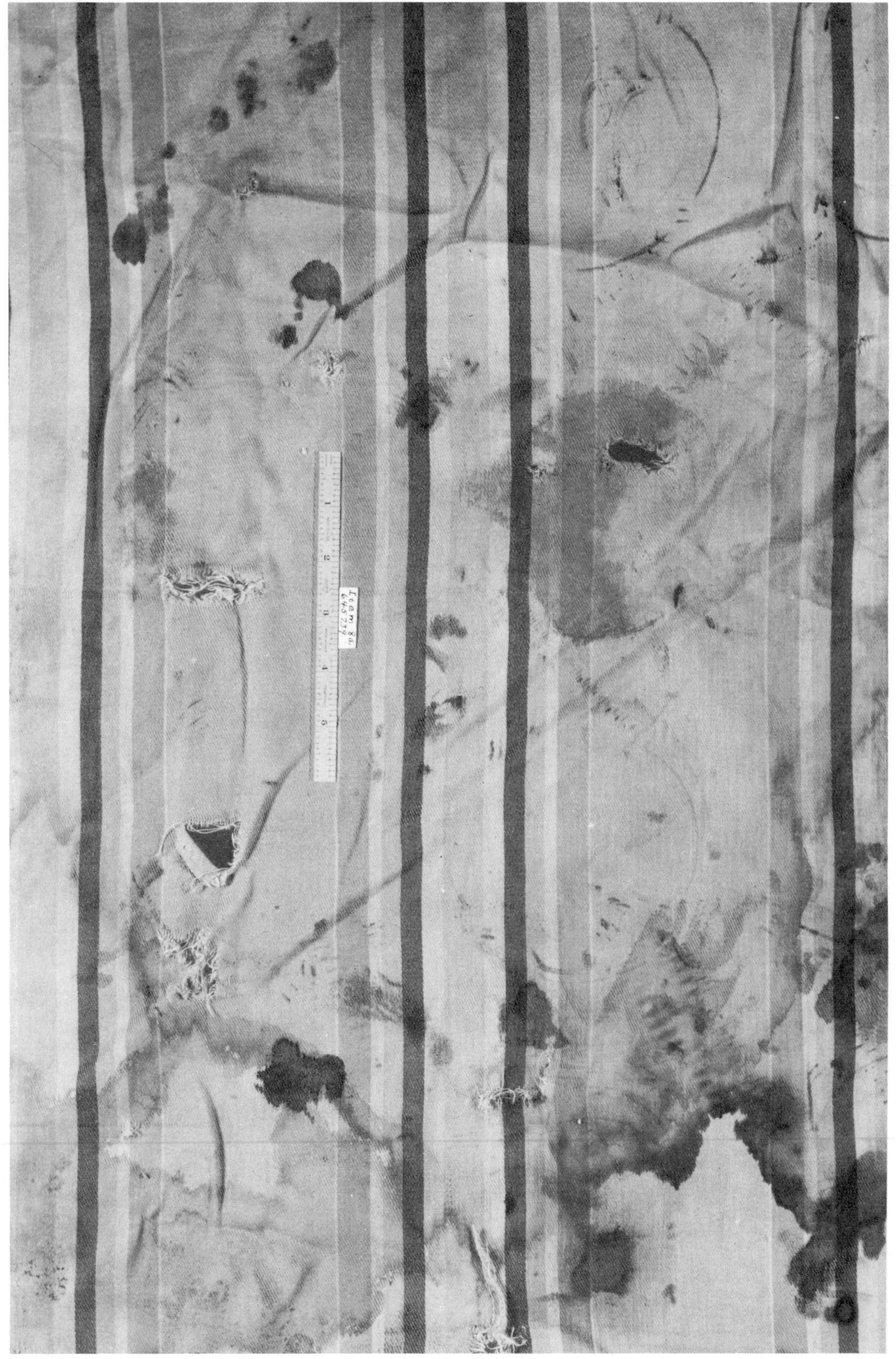

Fig. 3B
Mattress located on bed in room occupied by suspect.
(Courtesy, Minnesota State Bureau of Criminal Apprehension.)

Fig. 4A
Torn hardware store price tag.

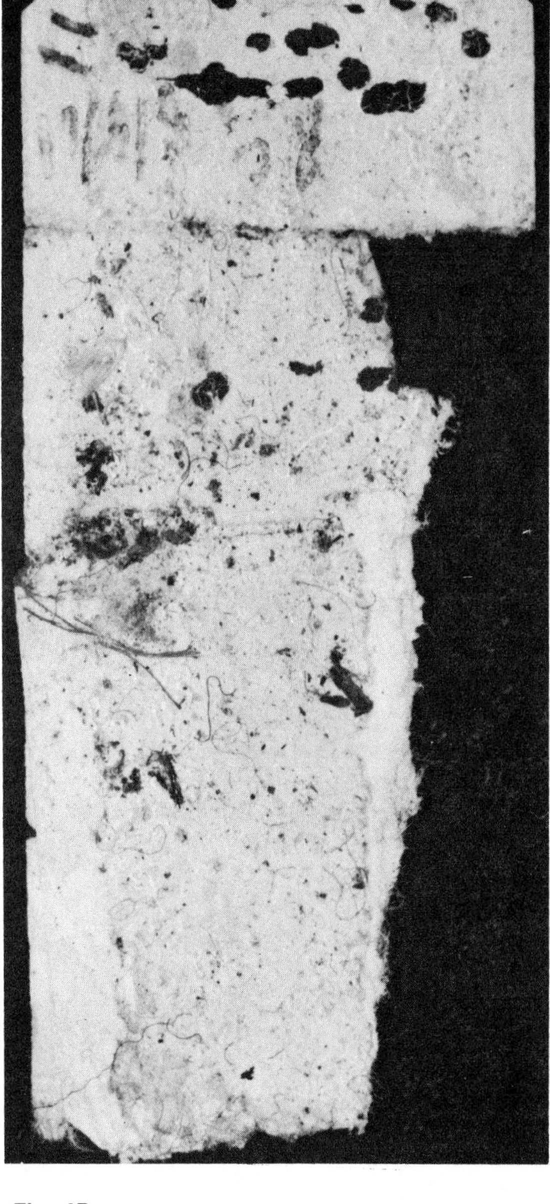

Fig. 4B
Reverse side of Fig. 4A.

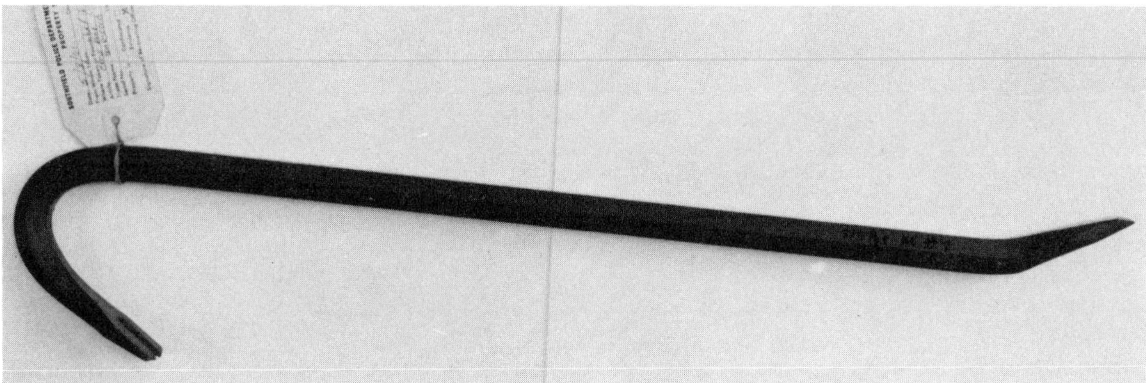

Fig. 4C
Crowbar found in possession of suspect.

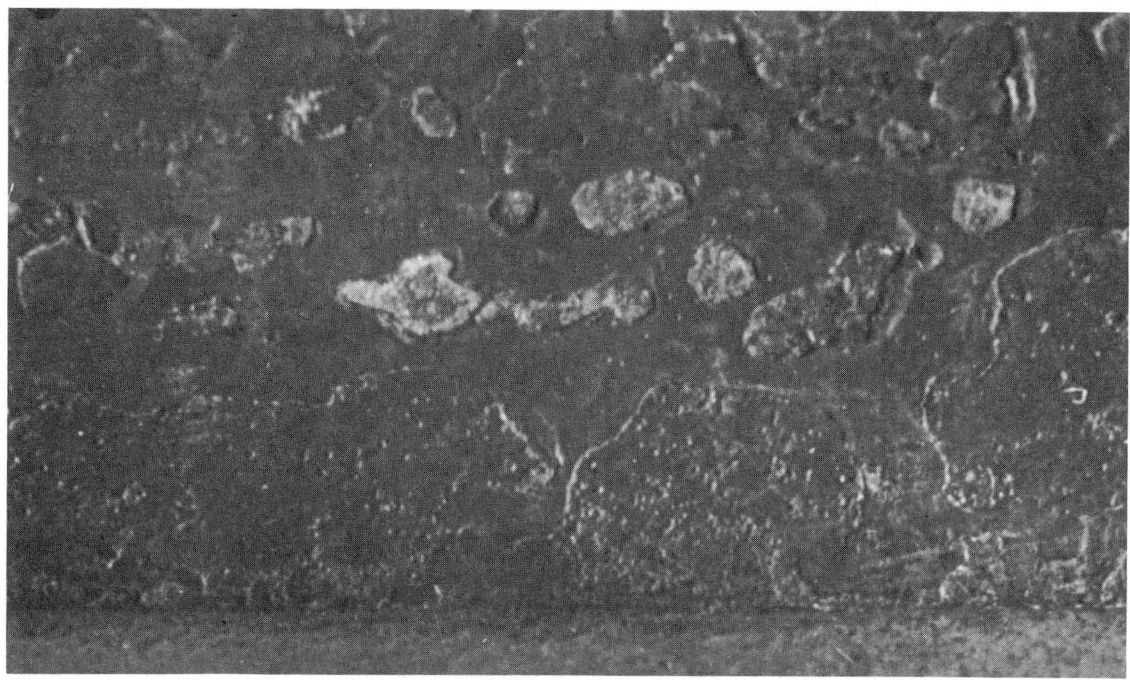

Fig. 4D
Enlargement of a small area of the crowbar shown in Fig. 4C.

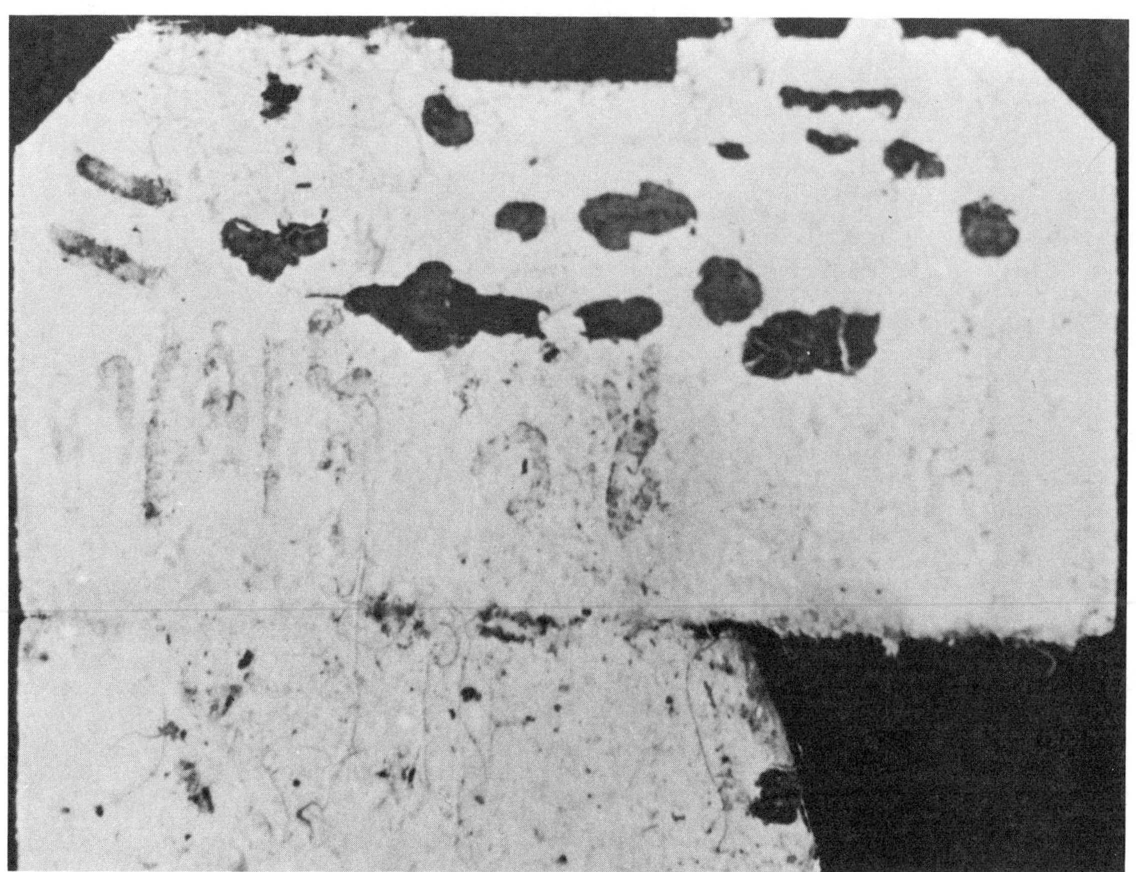

Fig. 4E
Portion of Fig. 4B (price tag, reverse side) enlarged to same size as Fig. 4D.
(Courtesy, Michigan State Police.)

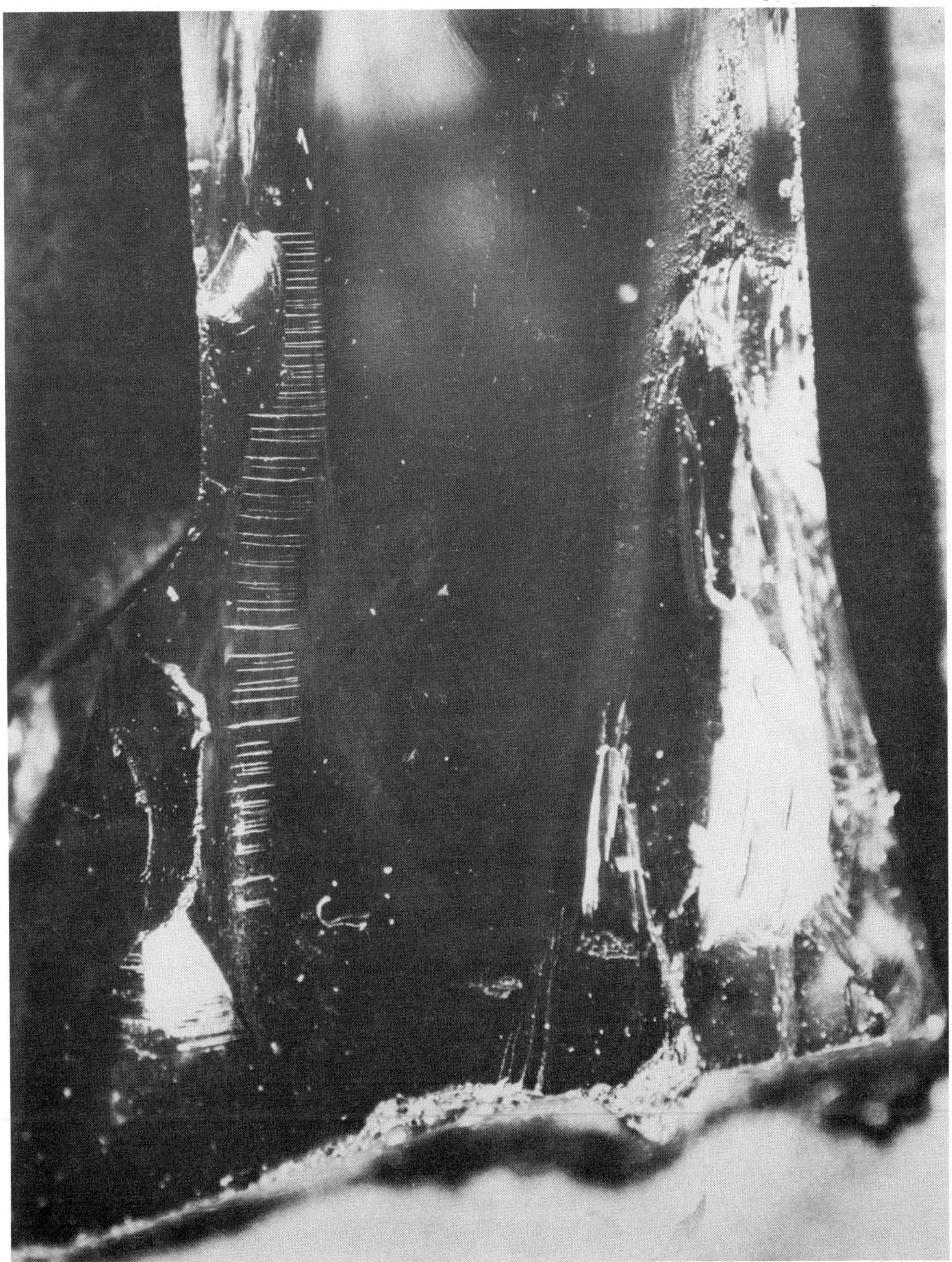

Fig. 5A
Enlarged edge of piece of glass found at scene of a hit-and-run accident showing strain marks.

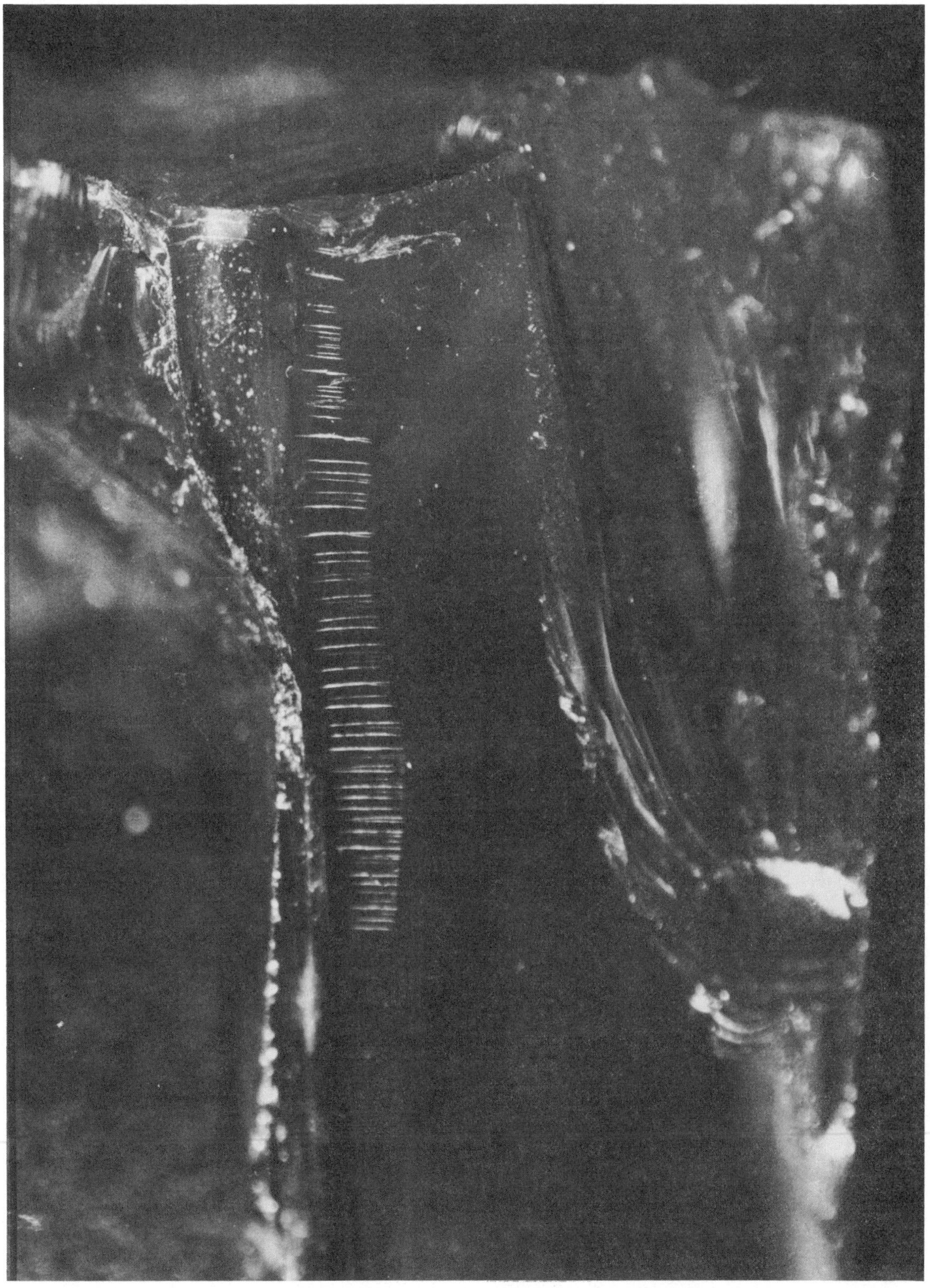

Fig. 5B
Enlarged edge of piece of glass removed from suspected automobile. Strain marks are visible. *(Courtesy, New York City Police Department.)*

Trace Evidence Sources Case Exercises

8.1 Traces Taken from the Scene

*Exercise 1: Wood Grain — Auto Hood**

The case selected for this exercise is rather difficult. The reader is referred to the discussion of wood traces on p 140 so he or she will be able to evaluate the significance of the points of identity noted during the examination of the case evidence.

In the exercise under consideration, Fig. 1A is a photograph of a portion of an indentation found on a curved section of the damaged hood of an abandoned car. Within this indentation an impression of some object was barely visible, but the source or nature of this trace impression was not obvious at first; however, investigators recalled that a wooden police barricade had been struck by an automobile. The question was then asked whether the impression on the hood was possibly that of a portion of the wooden barricade. Figure 1B is a photograph of an ovoid paint impression found on the wooden barricade. It has been printed in reverse, as indicated by the numbers on the ruler, so that a direct comparison between both photographs is possible.

Examine Figs. 1A and 1B carefully. First, attempt to locate similar areas; then mark those points in each area in the photographs which appear to be useful for comparison purposes. When the examination is complete, write a report and state the reasons for the conclusion given.

* *Case solution, pp 433-435.*

Exercise 2: Crimping Plier Tool Mark

Figure 2A is a photomicrograph (ca. 80X) of a mark that was present on one of the terminals of the searchlight suspected of being stolen. Figure 2B is a photomicrograph (ca. 80X) of a comparison test mark made with a crimping pliers obtained from the burglarized factory. Examine the questioned and exemplar photographs to determine if an identity exists.

8.2 Mutual Transfer Evidence

Exercise 3: Coat — Auto Lens

The material selected for this exercise involves mutual transfer evidence arising from a case in which a person was struck and killed by an automobile whose driver left the scene without stopping. Subsequently, a suspected car was recovered and a request was made by the detective that the clothing of the victim and the exterior of the vehicle be examined for any evidence to indicate or prove the two had been in contact.

Figure 3A is a photograph of the jacket worn by the victim at the time he was struck. It is to be examined for any trace evidence of the vehicle which may have been impressed on it. Figure 3B is a photograph of a headlight lens and guard shade on the suspected vehicle. Examine the photographs for any transfer evidence that might indicate the vehicle and the jacket were in contact.

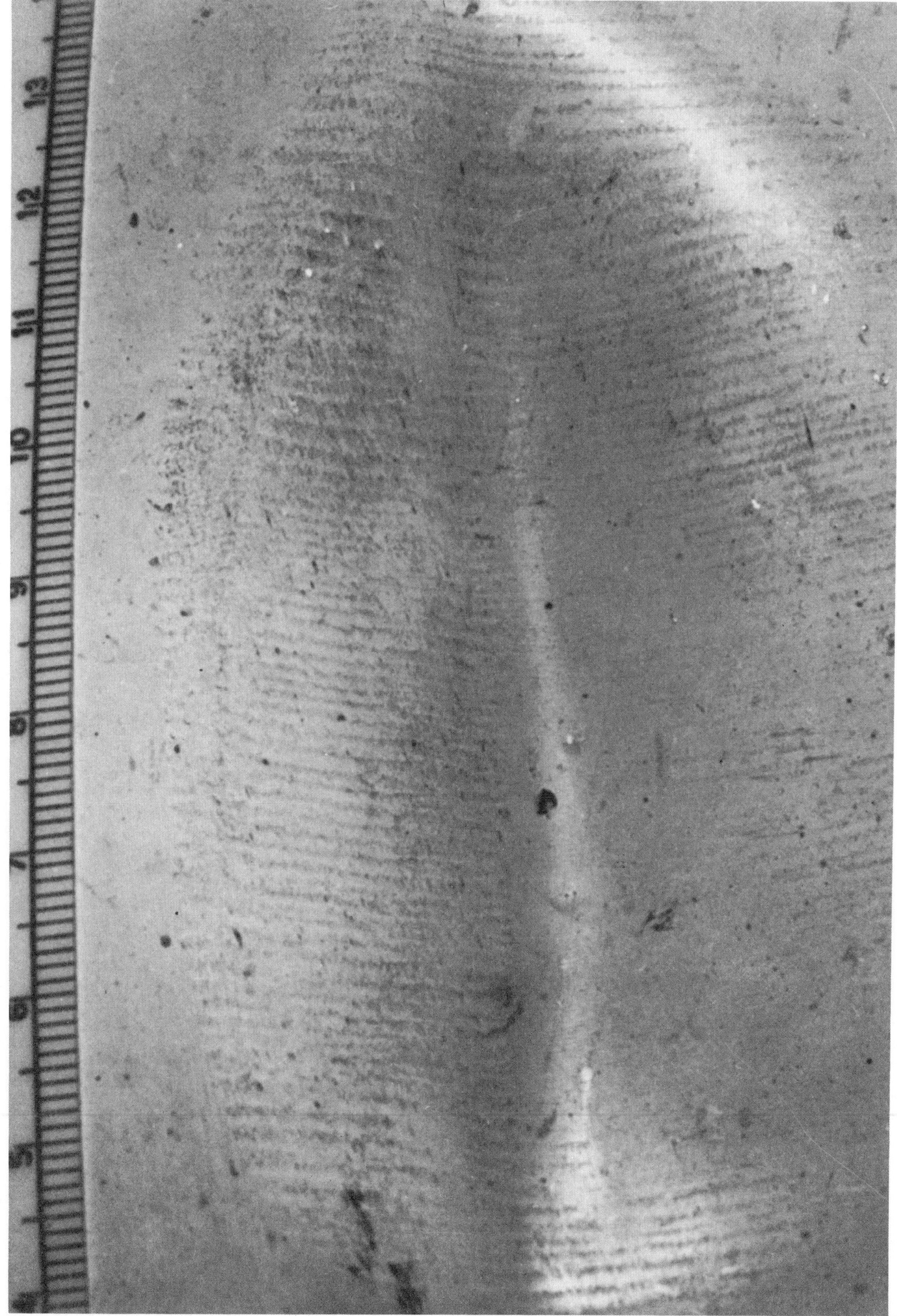

Fig. 1A
Imprint noted in a damaged area of the hood of an abandoned automobile.

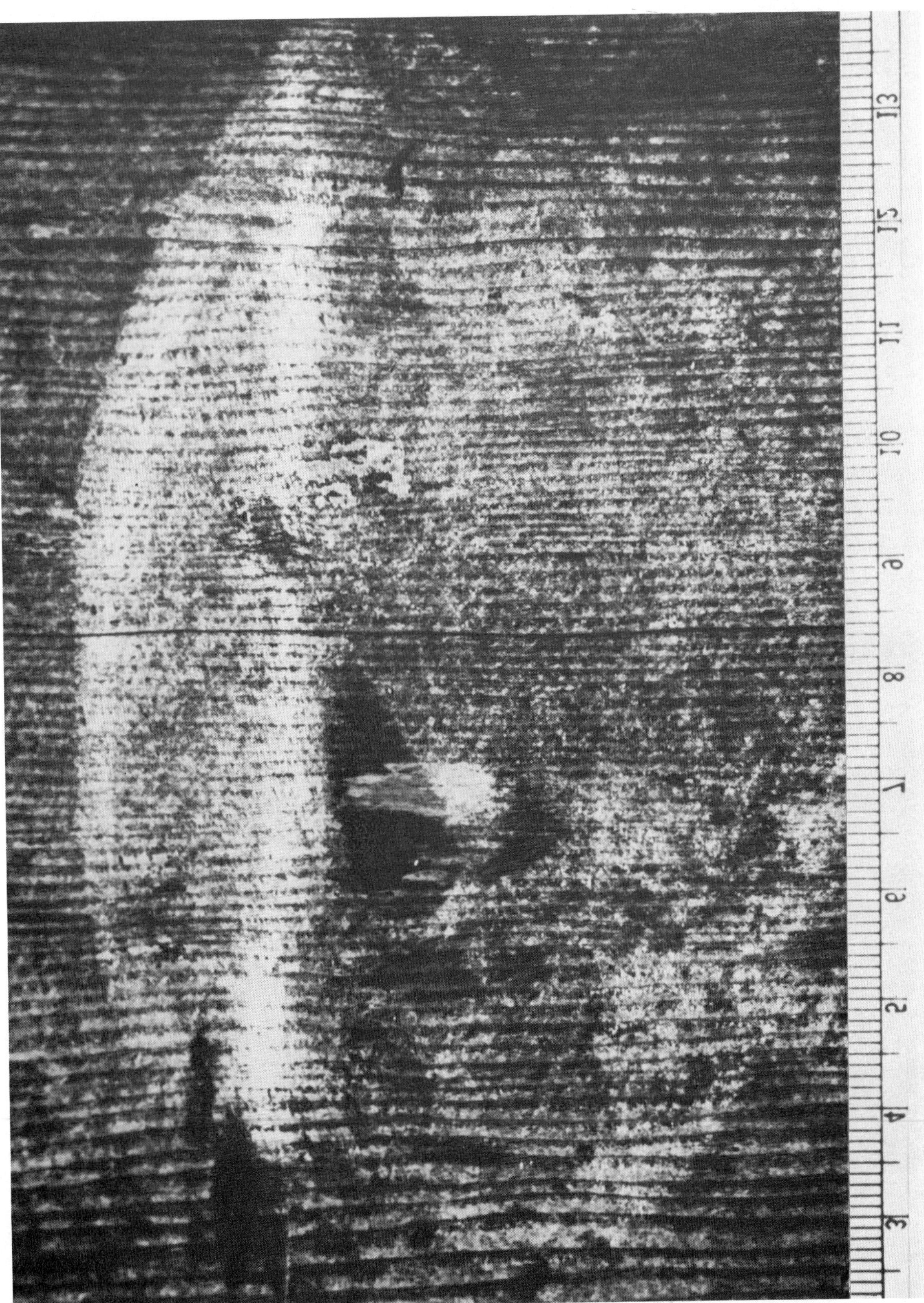

Fig. 1B
An egg-shaped paint impression found on a wooden barricade that had been struck by a fleeing automobile.
(Courtesy, Minnesota State Bureau of Criminal Apprehension.)

Fig. 2A
Tool mark on shaft of electrical terminal of searchlight suspected of being stolen (ca. 80X).

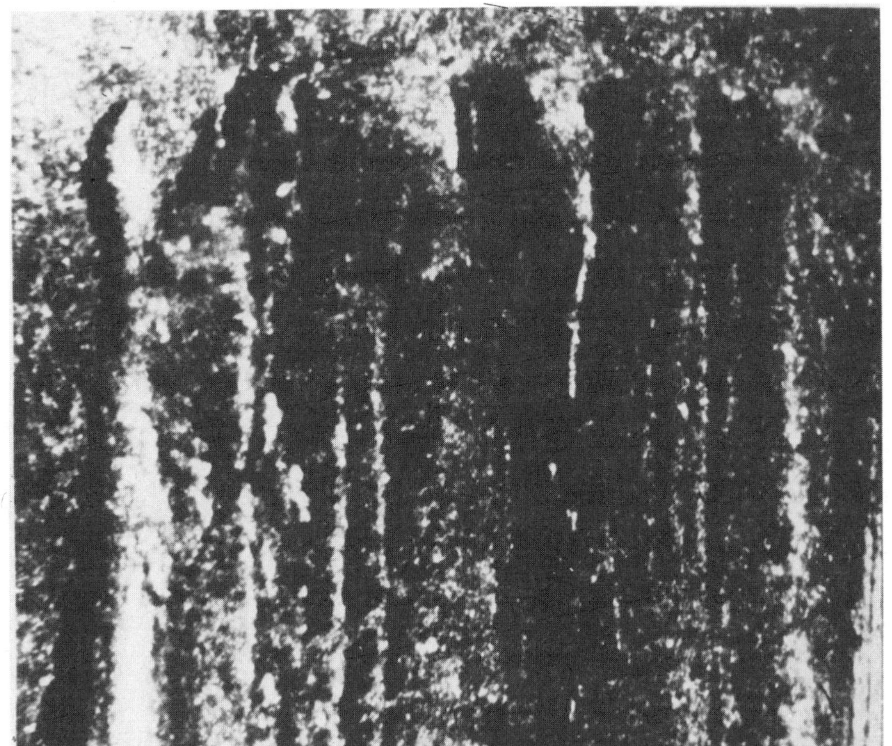

Fig. 2B
Test mark made with crimping pliers of known ownership (ca. 80X).
(Courtesy, Michigan State Police.)

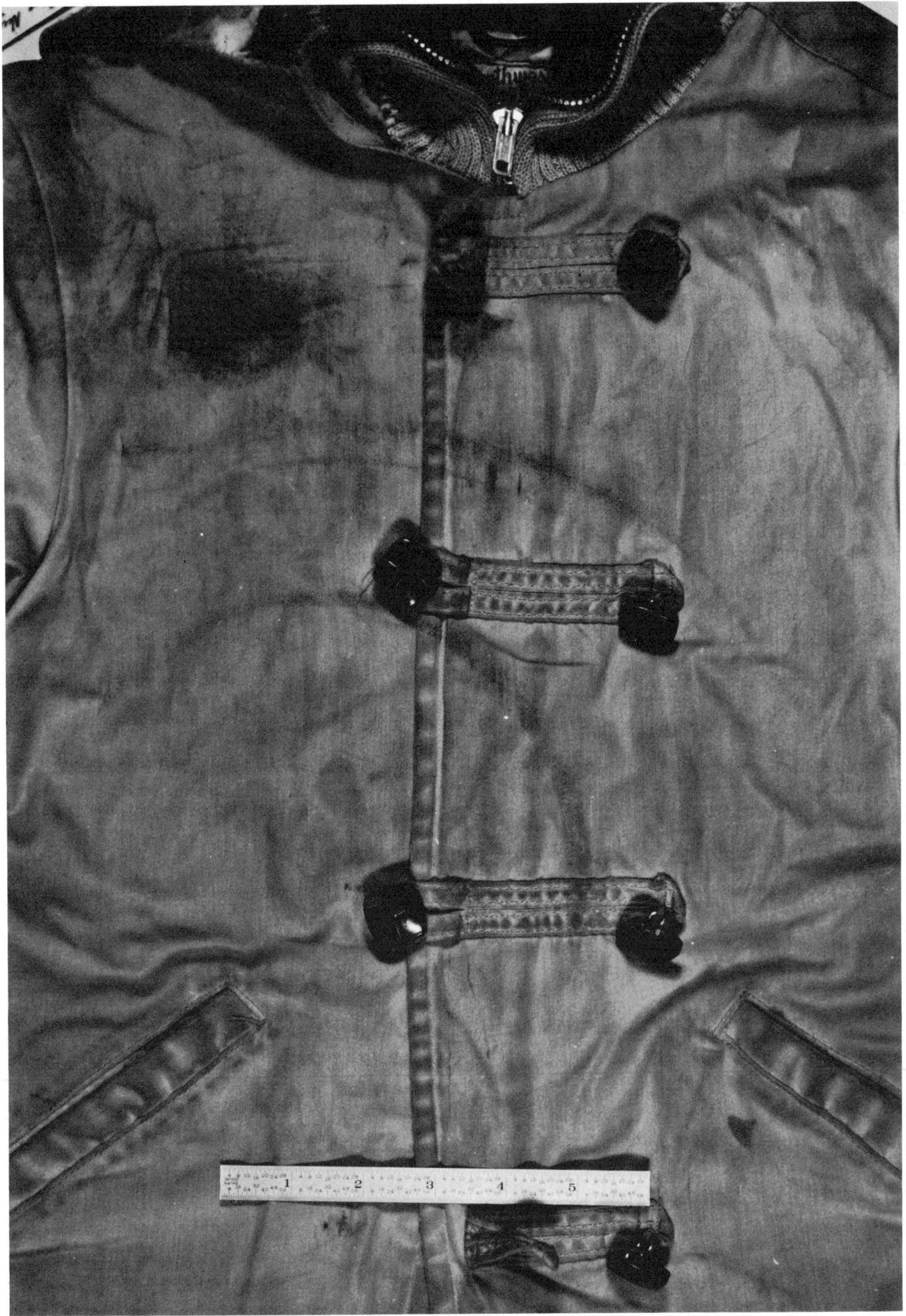

Fig. 3A
Outer jacket worn by victim in a hit-and-run motor vehicle homicide.

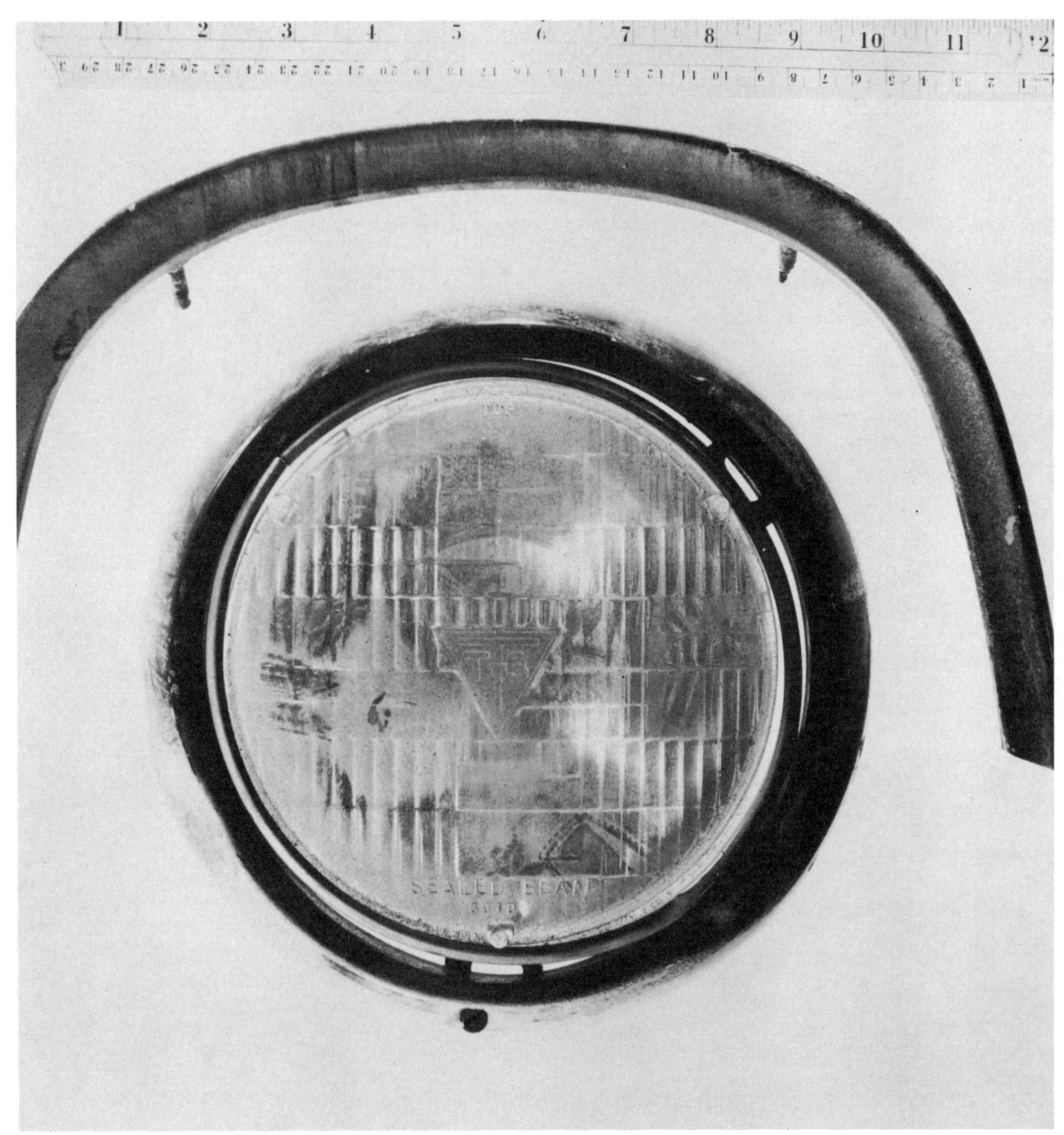

Fig. 3B
Photograph of a headlight lens and guard shade on a suspected vehicle.
(Courtesy, Minnesota State Bureau of Criminal Apprehension.)

Part 5

"Hands On" Laboratory Exercises

Introduction

In response to the requests of many instructors using the first edition of this text, a set of exercises that provides "hands on" experience has been developed. They require flat table space to perform. They do not involve any "wet" chemistry.

Based on police records, a scenario describing a crime situation and set of laboratory instructions relating to the physical evidence (simulating that which was found at the crime scene) are provided for each case that follows. The clue material needed for each student can be prepared by the instructor.* The Instructors Guide contains a description of the items needed, as well as the method of their preparation. Also included is a list of the points that a student should cover in the report which may be required by the instructor upon completion of each exercise. The exercises are listed below:

Exercise 1: *Selection of Comparison Specimens*

Exercise 2: *Recognition of Class Similarities through the Comparison of Wood Cuts*

Exercise 3: *Recognition and Value of Class and Individual Characteristics*

Exercise 4: *Cloth Comparison and Literature Research*

Exercise 5: *Broken Glass Problem (from Inside or Outside)*

Exercise 6: *Evaluation of Crime Scene Debris for Evidence*

Exercise 7: *Matchbooks, Matches, and Arson: The Concept of Taxonomy*

Exercise 8: *Comparison of Perforations: How Does One Become An Expert?*

Exercise 9: *Comparison of Cartridge Heads: The Concept of Photomacrography*

Exercise 10: *Student Preparation of a Simulated Case*

---

*If sufficient interest is shown by instructors, it may be possible to have course kits prepared by a commercial manufacturer. The author would welcome a written expression of interest (sent to Editor, Law and Society Series, Clark Boardman Company, Ltd., 435 Hudson Street, New York, New York 10014), since some evidence is needed to arrange for the kits to be manufactured.

Exercise 1: Selection of Comparison Specimens

Situation

Exhibit A is a wooden bludgeon found near the scene of a fatal beating. A suspect stated during interrogation that the club he used had been obtained from a tree at the scene of the homicide. A newly appointed detective was dispatched to obtain specimens of branches of the trees near or at the scene (Exhibits B - G). Examination of this evidence in the crime laboratory might provide corroboration of the statement of the suspect. Corroboration in a "murder one" case is required in some states.

Laboratory Instructions

In this exercise the student is asked to examine Exhibit A (the wooden club) and Exhibits B - G (known branch specimens) in order to ascertain which, if any, of the specimens (B - G) appear to be of a species similar to that of the weapon. Upon completion of the examination the student should prepare a short written critical commentary concerning the investigator's activity in selecting the comparison samples (Exhibits B-G). In addition, the student should write a short set of instructions to be given to an investigator to assist him in obtaining the most appropriate samples of branches upon visiting the alleged crime scene.

Exercise 2: Recognition of Class Similarities Through the Comparison of Wood Cuts

Situation

During the first week of a three week hunting season, two hunters had a quarrel after shooting a twelve point buck. At the end of the second week one of the hunters, who this time had gone hunting alone, was found shot in the woods. He had been buried in a shallow grave covered by some leaves.

During the investigation, which included a thorough examination of the local terrain, a decoy hunting blind was found nearby. Immediate consideration was given to whether or not this could have served as a means of ambushing the deceased.

Because of the dispute the other hunter, who had contested strenuously the deceased's claim to the twelve point buck, was considered as a possible suspect. Subsequent examination, with permission, of his automobile disclosed four tools: three wood saws (a coping saw, a crosscut saw, a pruning saw) and a pair of pruning shears. The suspect denied the shooting. He also denied that he had ever used a blind for hunting and certainly had not used any such means to ambush anyone.

Exhibit A is a typical cut end to a branch removed from the blind and used in its construction. Exhibits B through E are branches the ends of which were cut by the investigator with each of the tools found in the suspect's car.

Laboratory Instructions

The student is to ascertain which, if any, of the type of tools found in the car might have been used to produce cut ends similar to those found on the branches employed to construct the blind. In addition, a discussion should be prepared about the value of this evidence to the investigator.

Exercise 3: Recognition and Value of Class and Individual Characteristics

Situation

A small child was reported missing at 12:45 p.m. after his mother had come to the school to pick him up at noon. He had been last seen at about 11:50 a.m. in the school playground following a kindergarten party, at which cake, pie, and soft drinks were served. A housewife, who has been raking leaves in her front yard across the street from the school playground, reported seeing a man sitting in a turquoise Mustang near the playground. To the best of her recollection, he had been parked for about half an hour before she went into her house to prepare lunch for her child.

At 5:35 p.m. the same day, a turquoise Mustang was stopped for speeding by a police officer at the corner of Lincoln Avenue and 3rd Street. The officer, having been notified of a possible kidnapping and of the attendant circumstances, noticed Exhibit A, part of a broken plastic fork, in the front seat of the automobile. Exhibits B through J were retrieved subsequently from the waste basket in the room where the kindergarten party had been held.

Laboratory Instructions

The student is asked to examine Exhibit A and to compare it with Exhibits B through J in order to determine if a physical match exists between A and any of the other exhibits.

Exercise 4: Cloth Comparison and Literature Research

Situation

On the evening of November 6, the home of a wealthy merchant was robbed of several thousand dollars in cash, jewelry, and other valuables. According to Mrs. O'Brien, the merchant's wife, two men forced their way into the house at gun point at approximately 9:30 p.m., during her husband's absence. They demanded that she open a safe in which the family kept money, jewelry, and valuable documents. The men removed the contents of the safe, bound and gagged her and the maid, then departed hastily. Exhibit Q is one of the torn ends of the adhesive tape used to bind the wrists of Mrs. O'Brien. Exhibits R and S are pieces of cloth which were used to gag the victims.

Part I

A suspect was located who fitted one of the descriptions given by the victims. Two rolls of adhesive tape, Exhibits A and B, were found subsequently in a first aid kit in the glove compartment of the suspect's automobile. Exhibits C and D, two additional rolls of tape, were obtained (under warrant) from a medicine chest in the home of the suspect. Further rolls of tape, Exhibits E and F, were located at the suspect's place of employment. The ends of each roll of tape were removed and the proper ends were labeled Exhibit A_1, B_1, C_1, D_1, E_1, and F_1 respectively.

Part II

Additional evidence discovered by the investigator is Exhibit G, a cloth fiber which was lying on the front floor of the suspect's car. Exhibit H, a small piece of blanket, was also found and removed from beneath the seat of the automobile on the driver's side of the suspect's car.

Laboratory Instructions

Part I

The student is to examine the torn ends on each of the exhibits to determine if Exhibit Q could have been obtained from one of the known rolls of tape, Exhibits A through F.

Part II

The student is to compare Exhibits G and H with Exhibits R and S, to determine whether any similarities or dissimilarities exist. The written report should include a discussion of further techniques which could be used to increase the validity of the student's conclusion. A search of the literature — books and journals — will be necessary to prepare a satisfactory commentary in the report.

Exercise 5: Broken Glass Problem (from Inside or Outside)

Situation

At 7:15 p.m. on December 3, a woman reported to the police that her husband had been shot. She related the events of the evening as follows: She and her husband sat down to dinner at approximately 7:00 p.m. Shortly thereafter a shot was fired from outside the house through the dining room window fatally wounding her husband in the head. She immediately went to the side of her husband and then called the police for an ambulance. She had not seen or heard anyone near the house during this time.

The investigators at the scene collected fragments of broken glass from both inside and outside the house and reassembled these pieces together with fragments remaining in the window frame. This reassembled window was labeled Exhibit A and the letter "I" was placed on the pane denoting the inside surface.

Laboratory Instructions

The student is to examine the loose fragment removed from Exhibit A and labeled FA in order to determine the direction of travel of the bullet as it passed through the window pane. The conclusion should be supported by a description of the method of examination used and the references in the literature that describe the method (see §7.3).

Exercise 6: Evaluation of Crime Scene Debris for Evidence

Situation

On a Monday morning, August 9, the manager of a high rise office building discovered that many of the premises had been ransacked. Several thousand dollars in cash, office equipment, and merchandise were missing from some forty offices, suggesting that a group effort had been made in burglarizing the building over the weekend.

While searching the building and the surrounding area, investigators discovered what appeared to be a "campsite" on the roof of a tall building directly adjacent to the scene of the burglary. To an experienced detective it was obvious that a group of individuals had entered this building on the previous Friday, concealed themselves on the roof, and waited until both buildings were vacated. They apparently had brought food since a paper bag stuffed with waxed paper was located behind a ventilator. Several cigarette butts, burned and unburned matches, and empty cigarette packs were also found on the roof. After all offices in the high rise had closed for the weekend the burglars moved to the roof of the building, entered, and spent part of the weekend breaking into safes and removing other valuables from the premises.

Evidence Facts

The material collected from the roof was labeled as follows: Exhibits A_1 through A_5, five cigarette butts; Exhibits B_1 through B_4, four used paper cups; Exhibit C, an empty cigarette pack; Exhibit D, a paper sack; Exhibits E_1 through E_3, three pieces of waxed paper; F_1 and F_2, two unburned matches; Exhibits G_1 through G_7, seven burned matches.

Based on information provided by a witness, i.e., a person whose suspicions were aroused but who did not report his observations until he learned of the burglary, four suspects were developed. As a result, the following material was obtained from their persons, automobiles, and homes. Exhibits S-I-A_1 through S-I-A_4, four match books; Exhibit S-I-B, a paper cup; Exhibit S-I-C, a cigarette pack; Exhibits S-I-D_1 through S-I-D_3, three paper clips from suspect I. Exhibits S-II-A_1 through S-II-A_5, five match books; Exhibit S-II-B, a paper cup; Exhibit S-II-C, a cigarette pack from suspect II. Exhibits S-III-A_1 through S-III-A_3, three match books; Exhibits S-III-B_1 through S-III-B_4, four rubber bands; Exhibit S-III-C, a paper sack from suspect III. Exhibits S-IV-A_1 through S-IV-A_4, four match books, Exhibits S-IV-B_1 and S-IV-B_2, two paper cups; Exhibit S-IV-C, a piece of aluminum foil from suspect IV.

Laboratory Instructions

The student should describe the manner in which he would handle the crime scene evidence assuming that he was the investigating officer. Next, in his capacity as a student in a crime laboratory course, he should examine the crime scene evidence and the material obtained from the suspects to determine if any associative evidence is present. If there is, he should describe its nature and what a laboratory can do with it in order to turn it into associative evidence.

Exercise 7: Matchbooks, Matches, and Arson: The Concept of Taxonomy

Situation

Matches as evidence, while not common, are

sometimes found at scenes of such crimes as arson, burglary, and assault involving torture. The greatest potential for such evidence is the establishment of a connection between crime and suspect: to link the burnt match or matches found at the crime scene and the (partially) used book of matches found in the possession of a suspect.

The purpose of this exercise is to teach taxonomy: to demonstrate how a classification scheme is developed, in this instance, for matches. With matches, the class characteristics are sufficiently numerous, so that a classification scheme is fairly easy to produce. The student should understand initially that the aim is to establish as many classes as possible, so that only a few matches fall into each class. When a classification scheme is developed, a burned (crime scene) match can be examined and possibly placed in one of the classes. Then the used matchbooks of that class only need be examined to determine if the crime scene match came from one of them.

The following is an example of how the class characteristics of matches are useful to the detective.[1] A partially burned match was discovered near the origin of a forest fire. The match was not one distributed in that region, since its appearance (class characteristics) differed markedly from that of matches which were available locally. By tracing the source of the crime scene match to another section of the country, it was possible to check on the persons who were recent arrivals from that area. Since some of them were found to possess the same type of matches, the one responsible for the fire was, as a result, identified.

Laboratory Instructions

A set of used and unused matchbooks is provided. Excluding cover design of the matchbooks, the student is to examine the matches and list all significant differences. He should then classify those differences so that, if possible, each matchbook falls into its own class.

A second exercise requires the student to discover the matchbooks from which a partially burned match, Q_1, and an unburned match, Q_2, were removed. The use of the stereomicroscope is necessary in this determination.

Exercise 8: Comparison of Perforations: How Does One Become an Expert?

Situation

Postage stamps and blank checks are the most common perforated objects that may be involved in a criminal transaction. It is sometimes possible to fit the perforated edge of the postage stamp or check found as evidence with the perforated edge of its counterpart. A comparison of the torn edges requires, of course, that the roll or sheet of stamps, or the checkbook can be procured from the suspect.

Laboratory Instructions

A set of four code labelled stamps is provided. The problem is: Were any of these stamps connected to each other originally? None, one, or more connections are possible.

Exercise 9: Comparison of Cartridge Heads: The Concept of Photomacrography

Situation

Spent cartridges are a common clue material found at crime scenes. The breech face marks found on the head of a cartridge when it is fired in a weapon are impressed upon a relatively flat surface, thus simplifying the problem of photographing the breech impression. The details in such breech face marks must be enlarged if they are to be compared. Ordinarily a comparison microscope is used for this purpose; however, the same results may be achieved by means of a special type of photography called "photomacrography." Photomicrography is a relatively familiar term

[1]Kirk, Paul L. *Fire Investigation.* (New York: Wiley, 1969). P 91.

used to describe the process of taking photographs through a microscope. The less widely known term "photomacrography" refers to the procedure whereby the lens of the camera (instead of the microscope lens) is employed to create an enlarged image.

Laboratory Instructions

This exercise assumes that the student is familiar with the nomenclature of a camera and the process of taking a photograph. A 4x5 camera with a double extension bellows and a short focal length lens, about 2 inches, is required. The following formula states the relationship between magnification (M), bellows extension length (B), and the focal length of the lens (F).

$$M = \frac{B-F}{F}$$

Thus, with a bellows extension of 12 inches and a 2 inch lens, a magnification of 5X is achieved.

$$M = \frac{12-2}{2} = \frac{10}{2} = 5$$

This equation permits an understanding as to how a fingerprint camera produces a one-to-one or life-size image. By fixing the bellows extention length to twice that of the focal length, the equation would read:

$$M = \frac{2F-F}{F} = \frac{1F}{F} = 1$$

In other words, there is neither magnification nor reduction: one inch is reproduced as one inch, or life-size.

By fixing the bellows at 2F, and with the object to be photographed placed at this distance from the lens, an image will be formed and will be in focus at the same distance behind the lens. A one-to-one size image will be the result. Thus, with a wide-angle lens for a 4x5 camera, approximately 3.5 inches in focal length, the bellows must be extended 7 inches (from the front of the lens to the ground glass or film plane) to reproduce the object one-to-one. The object must also be placed 7 inches in front of the lens to achieve this result.

An example of the need for an investigator to be informed about photomacrography can be found in the famous Oakes/de Marigny case in the Bahamas. A fingerprint, which eventually was to prove of crucial importance as the case developed, was found on a Chinese screen in the bedroom of Sir Harry Oakes, the deceased. The police investigator did not bring a fingerprint camera. Accordingly, he claimed he was unable to record the fingerprint at the crime scene. A Speed Graphic, 4x5 camera was available, and had the investigator understood the use of its wide-angle lens and bellows (extension), the fingerprint could have been photographed on the object bearing this important evidence. Since the question of whether the latent print was found on the Chinese screen in the bedroom became one of the most important issues at the trial, the question as to its origin could have been answered convincingly by an examination of the photograph. The nature of the surface bearing the latent fingerprint could have been shown to be (or not to be) that of the Chinese screen. This is an example of an investigator falling slave to, rather than being master of, technical equipment, where mastery of the equipment through an understanding of the basic principles involved would have saved the day.

A photomacrograph is made by placing the object (such as a cartridge head) at a distance confined between 2F and F from the lens. The bellows must be extended beyond 2F to bring the object into focus.

Laboratory Instructions

Place the head of the known or exemplar cartridge labelled K parallel to the lens and at a distance less than twice its focal length, and more than its focal length. Extend the bellows of the camera beyond 2F and move the cartridge head very slowly forward or away from the lens until the face of the cartridge comes into focus.

Measure the image size on the ground glass. Next, measure the cartridge itself. Divide the former by the latter to calculate the magnification. Now calculate the magnification by using the formula above, after measuring the bellows extension. Remember to keep all measurements and focal lengths in inches (or millimeters). When the cartridge head fills the 4x5 plate, make a photograph of the image.

Repeat the above, using the cartidges labelled Q_1 and Q_2. When all photographs have been dried, compare them to determine if Q_1 or Q_2, or both or neither, were fired in the same weapon as K, the exemplar cartridge.

If an enlarger is available, the following exercise can be undertaken. Take a one-to-one photograph of the cartridge head, setting the bellows extension at 2F. Enlarge the negative to 5X and compare the photograph so made with the photomacrograph taken at 5X. Is there any difference in the details which are made visible by these methods?

Exercise 10: Student Preparation of a Simulated Case

The following exercise is intended to provide an opportunity for the student to reflect on both the case and laboratory exercises that have been completed. At this point it should be clear that there is often a unique set of characteristics which permits an identity to be established between two objects. A student may assume that this is a commonplace phenomena.

In order to examine more carefully whether a coincidence of individual characteristics is usual or unusual, the student is asked to select some readily available items, manufactured in large quantities, such as hammers, axes, typewriters, rubber heels, screwdrivers, and so on. Unused as well as used specimens should be examined for any differences that may be present. If possible, the same items after being used for some time should again be examined. For instance, documents prepared when a typewriter was new are available in business offices. If the machine is a few years old, specimens can be taken and examined for any changes in the type impression that have resulted. New and old hammer faces can be studied for the variety of nicks and other imperfections that accumulate there.

This exercise is best performed when a stereomicroscope and a capability for photomacrography are available to the student. Differences between new items and changes imparted through use and wear should be recorded photographically and presented as part of the report to be submitted to the instructor.

A potential community resource which students should not overlook is the experienced detective. This individual may be able to recall some unusual type of physical evidence encountered during his career. Based on this discussion, the student should prepare known and questioned specimens that stimulate the situation described by the detective. Photographs (8x10) of this evidence should be prepared, similar to those used in the case exercises in this text. There should also be prepared a set of photgraphs in which the individual characteristics are marked to show the solution to the identity, and submitted to the instructor.

Appendix

Selected Case Solutions by Contributing Laboratory Experts

Experience has shown that some cases, especially those attempted at the beginning of the case execises, require comment in order to provide the student with a better comprehension of the details which characterize physical evidence. Of course, those same types of details must be preserved by field officers in handling evidence if the criminalist is to make decisions concerning identity.

The case exercise solutions in this Appendix have been listed by chapter rather than in the order suggested in the Introduction to Part 4. The page on which each exercise may be found in Part 4 is indicated in the list that follows. The student should take great care in locating the appropriate pages and should avoid examining any exercise material not yet attempted.

Introductory Exercise A

Comment

Note the manner of marking for this exercise and use it as you perform each succeeding case exercise in Part 4. In doing the case exercises, when you conclude that the crime scene impression and the suspect impression have a common origin, mark the corresponding points of identification. There is no one acceptable way to do this; the main criteria are accuracy, simplicity, neatness, and clarity. However, the experts use certain general guidelines to make the task of marking easier; these are delineated as follows:

1. Make certain you are looking at the same areas of both photos before you attempt to mark; once you have established a common starting point it will be less difficult to identify subsequent details.
2. Number all your points, proceeding clockwise or counterclockwise. Be sure both photos are marked in identical fashion to eliminate confusion.
3. Mark your points lightly in pencil first, keeping them well separated and numbered as consecutively as possible. Rule your lines like spokes of a wheel without crossing them, so that they are distributed around the picture. After you are satisfied with your selection, go over your lines in readily discernible ink.
4. Use straight lines in marking, ending just short of the point in question so as not to destroy its clarity; do not terminate your lines with arrowheads. If the point is large, or there are numerous small points in the same area, e.g., periphery of blood drops, you may wish to encircle the area, or bracket it off to reduce the number of lines.
5. As a final word, it is quite possible, even probable, that the student will select more or different points of comparison than the actual expert did. This does not indicate inefficiency on the part of the expert, since he or she is only interested in establishing identity; once this has been accomplished the expert stops looking for more points of identity. The student, on the other hand, should exhaust his or her efforts to discover *all* points of identity beyond those actually required in a given case for courtroom testimony.

Introductory Exercise B

Comment

It may be interesting to learn that approximately 60 per cent of students find only three "f"s on the first try. About 30 per cent find four or five. Only 10 per cent find all six. The fs in the three "of"s are most commonly missed.

Youngsters while learning how to read are taught to scan, to instantly recognize words and groups of words. They certainly are not taught to look at individual letters in words. This exercise is intended to inform the student that a criminalist must change many habits acquired during the course of his education. Usually, we learn not to observe details, but rather to be concerned with the more general aspects of an object or phenomenon. For example, if our peripheral vision catches some movement as we cross a busy thoroughfare, we may quickly identify the movement as an automobile, and take proper precautions to avoid being struck. Seldom do we note the make of the car. Put another way, we look at the forest and not at individual trees. In criminalistics, we must look at both and with considerable more attention to the details.

Introductory Exercise A

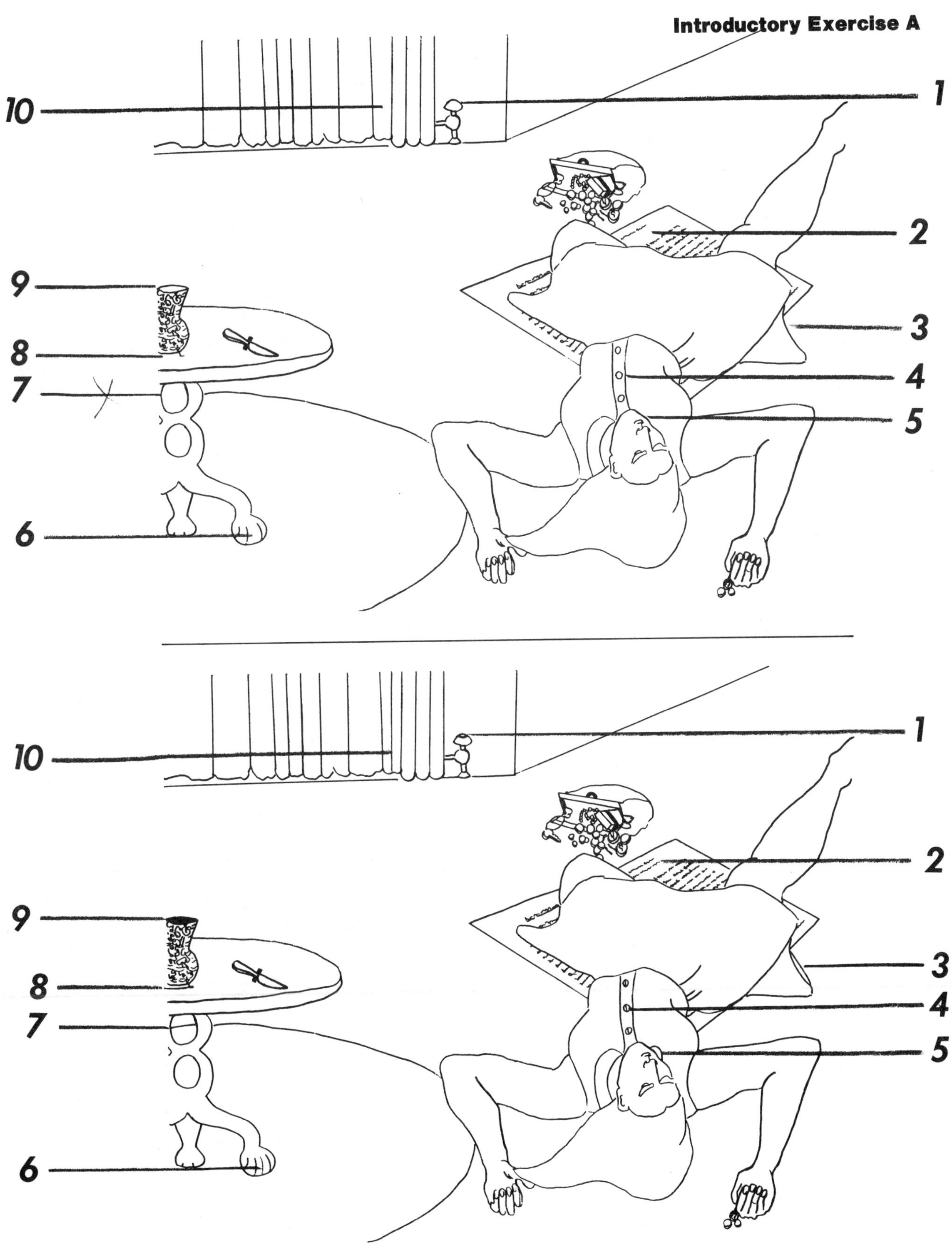

4

Exercises 2, 8, 9, 10, 13

Exercise 2: Inked Fingerprints

Comment I

The student should now refer to the marked set of prints, especially if he or she experiences any difficulty in locating points of comparison. After careful consideration of the marked set would you now change your report to that of an identity between the two prints? Would you consider an argument for identity if two more points of comparison, i.e., twelve in all, had been marked?

Comment II

This comparison was included to emphasize the importance not only of similarities but also of differences. For example, an uninterrupted ridge runs immediately to the left of point 10 in Fig. 2A while a bifurcation is present at the same place in Fig. 2B. This difference alone is sufficient to establish non-identity of the prints. Of course, there are many other differences that may be observed.

It is possible that differences will exist in two imprints arising from the same source; however, the differences must be understandable and rationally explained. Unequivocal differences as in the case above — a straight ridge versus a bifurcation — cannot be reasonably explained and hence an identity is impossible.

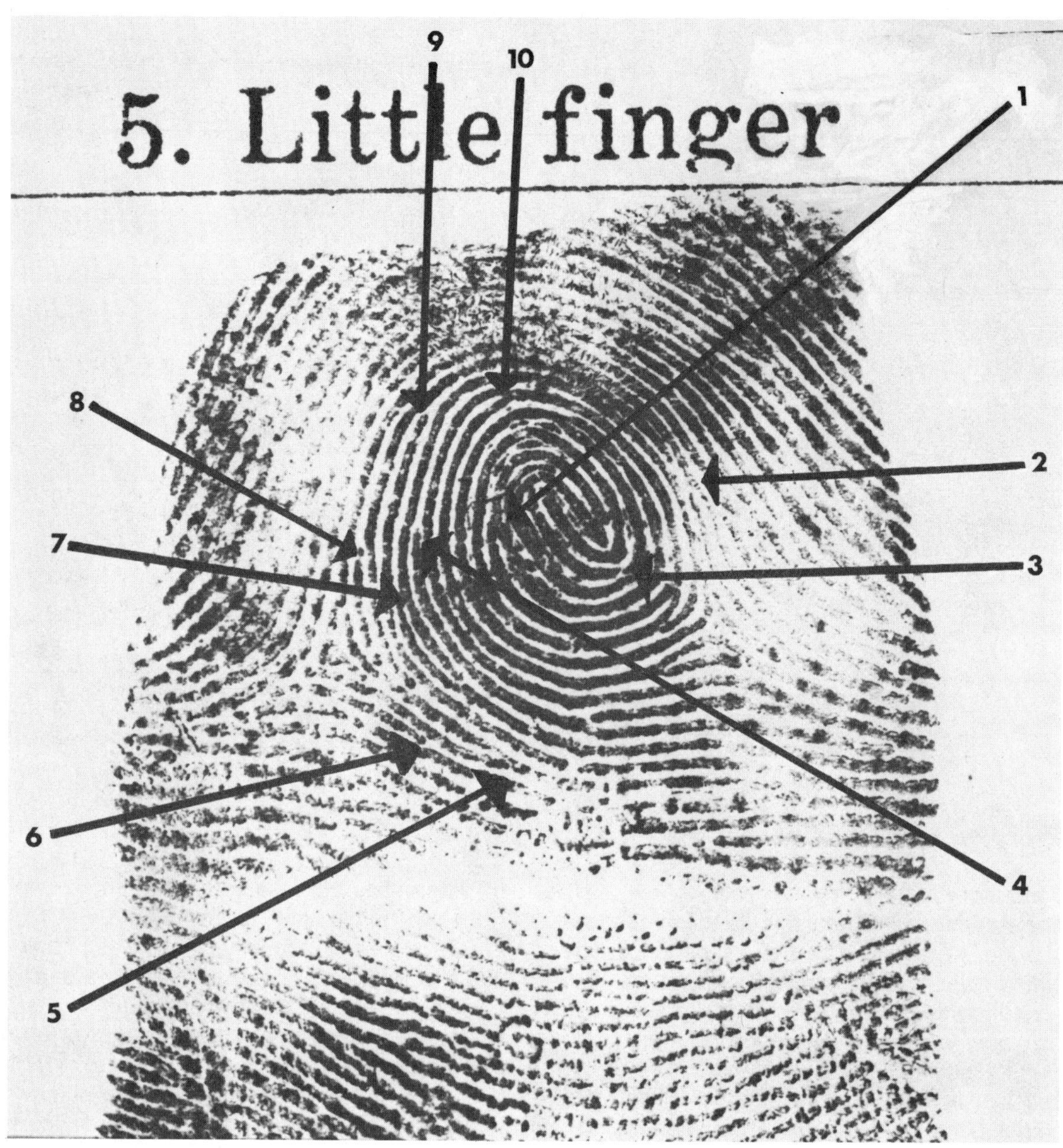

Fig. 2A
Inked fingerprint taken for record purposes.

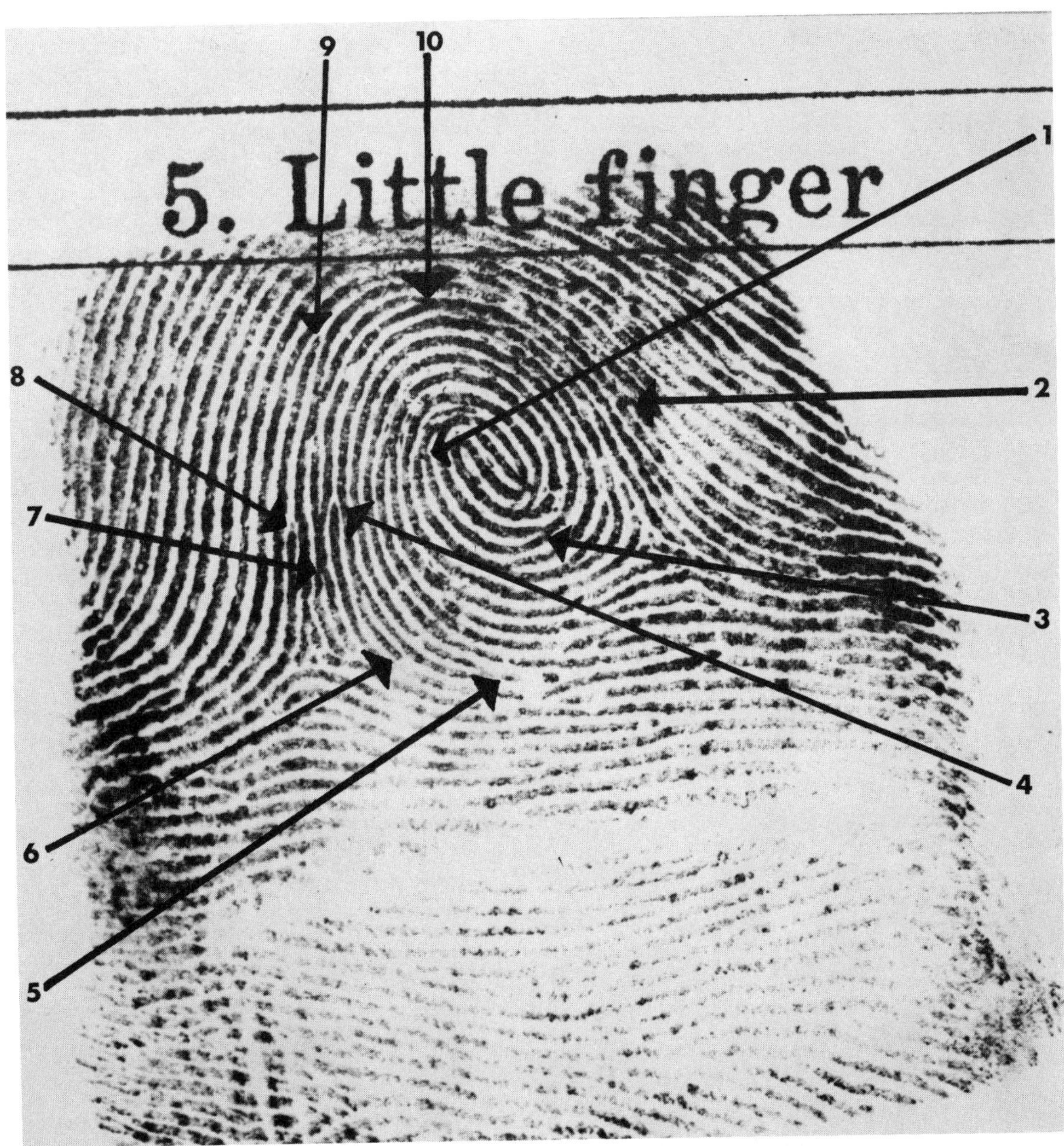

Fig. 2B
Inked fingerprint taken for record purposes. *(Courtesy, State Bureau of Investigation, Department of Justice, Raleigh, North Carolina.)*

Exercise 8: Kidnap Note Characteristics

Comment I

The student should mention the following in his or her report:

1. The ransom note should be dictated. The suspect should not be permitted to see the note before several specimens are obtained. Each specimen should be taken about fifteen (or more) minutes apart. A person who is trying to disguise his handwriting will forget rather quickly the changes he made in his normal writing if some time lapses between taking each specimen.
2. It is also good practice to eliminate as many variables as possible when a comparison is to be made in criminalistics. Accordingly, the same type of writing instrument and the same type and color of paper should be used in obtaining the exemplars, if possible.

Comment II

The characteristics brought to the attention of the field investigators by the document examiner are shown in Fig. 8A. The document which was finally discovered by an FBI agent is shown in Fig. 8B. The interest in this document arose out of the initial stroke and general information of the *M* in the last name of the man, i.e., *Marca,* the shape of the lower loop of the *g* in *Angelo,* the $\frac{00}{xx}$ and the lower loop of the *f* in *carfare.* After submission of the document, an expert quickly established the identity of the writer of the kidnap notes.

When requested, the suspect agreed to supply specimens of his handwriting. The material was dictated to him and several specimens were obtained. Had he not agreed to provide this known comparison material, additional investigative effort would have been required to locate known writing of the suspect. Signatures on election records, driver licenses, automobile registrations, and the like could serve this purpose.

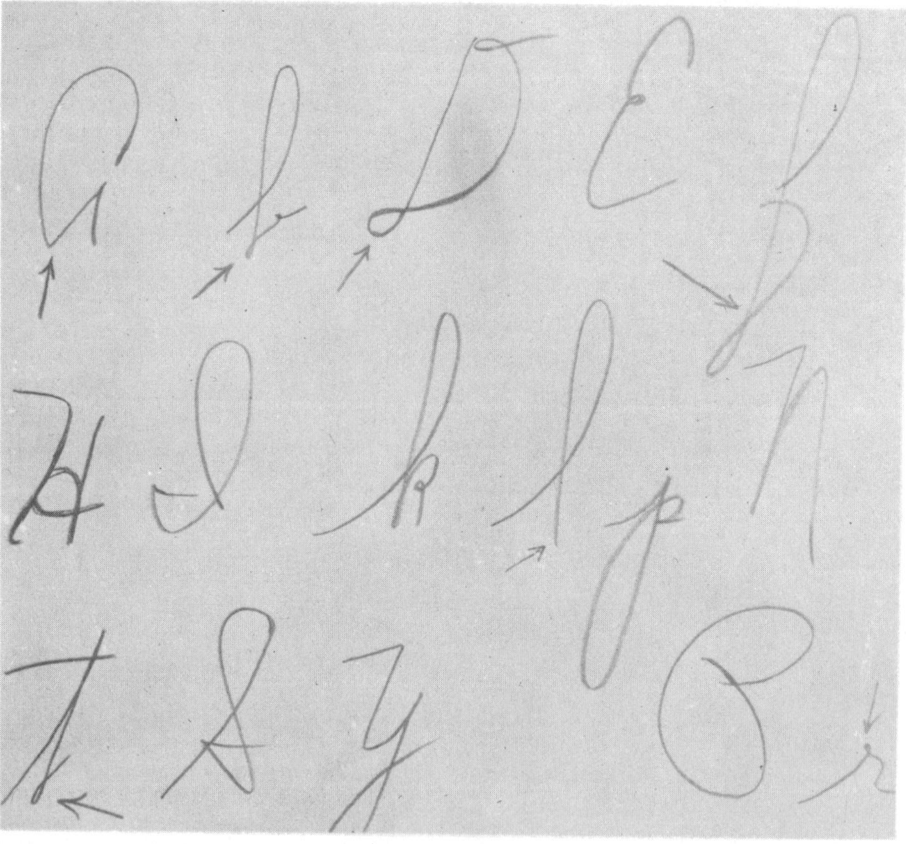

Fig. 8A
Chart of characteristics selected by FBI document examiner after an analysis of the original ransom note (Fig. 4—6).

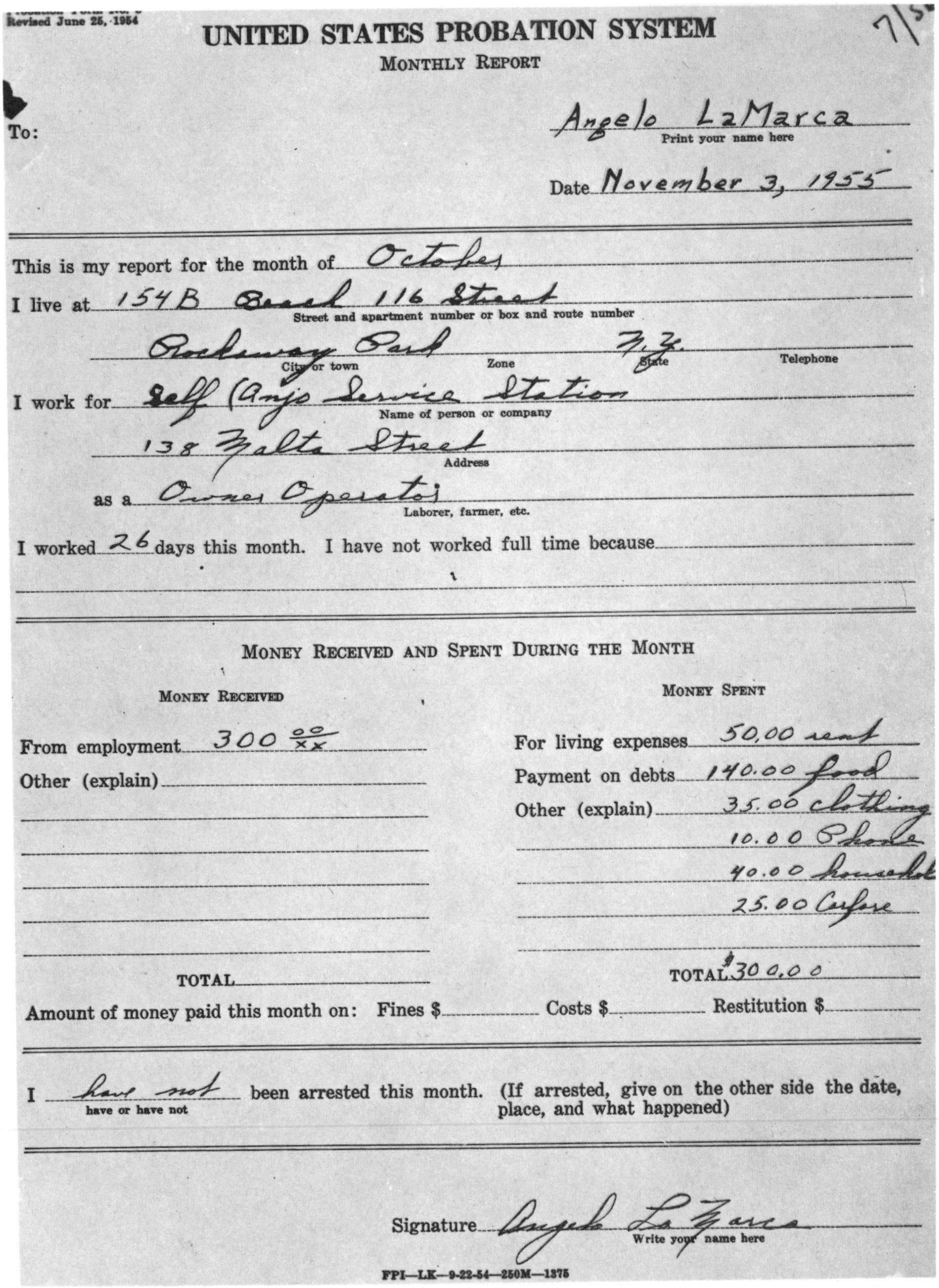

Probation Form No. 3
Revised June 25, 1954

7/5

UNITED STATES PROBATION SYSTEM

MONTHLY REPORT

To:

Angelo LaMarca
Print your name here

Date November 3, 1955

This is my report for the month of October

I live at 154B Beach 116 Street
Street and apartment number or box and route number

Rockaway Park N.Y.
City or town Zone State Telephone

I work for Self (Anjo Service Station
Name of person or company

138 Malta Street
Address

as a Owner Operator
Laborer, farmer, etc.

I worked 26 days this month. I have not worked full time because

MONEY RECEIVED AND SPENT DURING THE MONTH

MONEY RECEIVED		MONEY SPENT	
From employment	300 00/xx	For living expenses	50,00 rent
Other (explain)		Payment on debts	140.00 food
		Other (explain)	35.00 clothing
			10.00 Phone
			40.00 household
			25.00 Carfare
TOTAL		TOTAL	$300.00

Amount of money paid this month on: Fines $ Costs $ Restitution $

I have not been arrested this month. (If arrested, give on the other side the date, place, and what happened)
have or have not

Signature Angelo LaMarca
Write your name here

FPI—LK—9-22-54—250M—1375

Fig. 8B
Writing on a probation report selected by a field investigator as having characteristics similar to those illustrated in Fig. 8A.

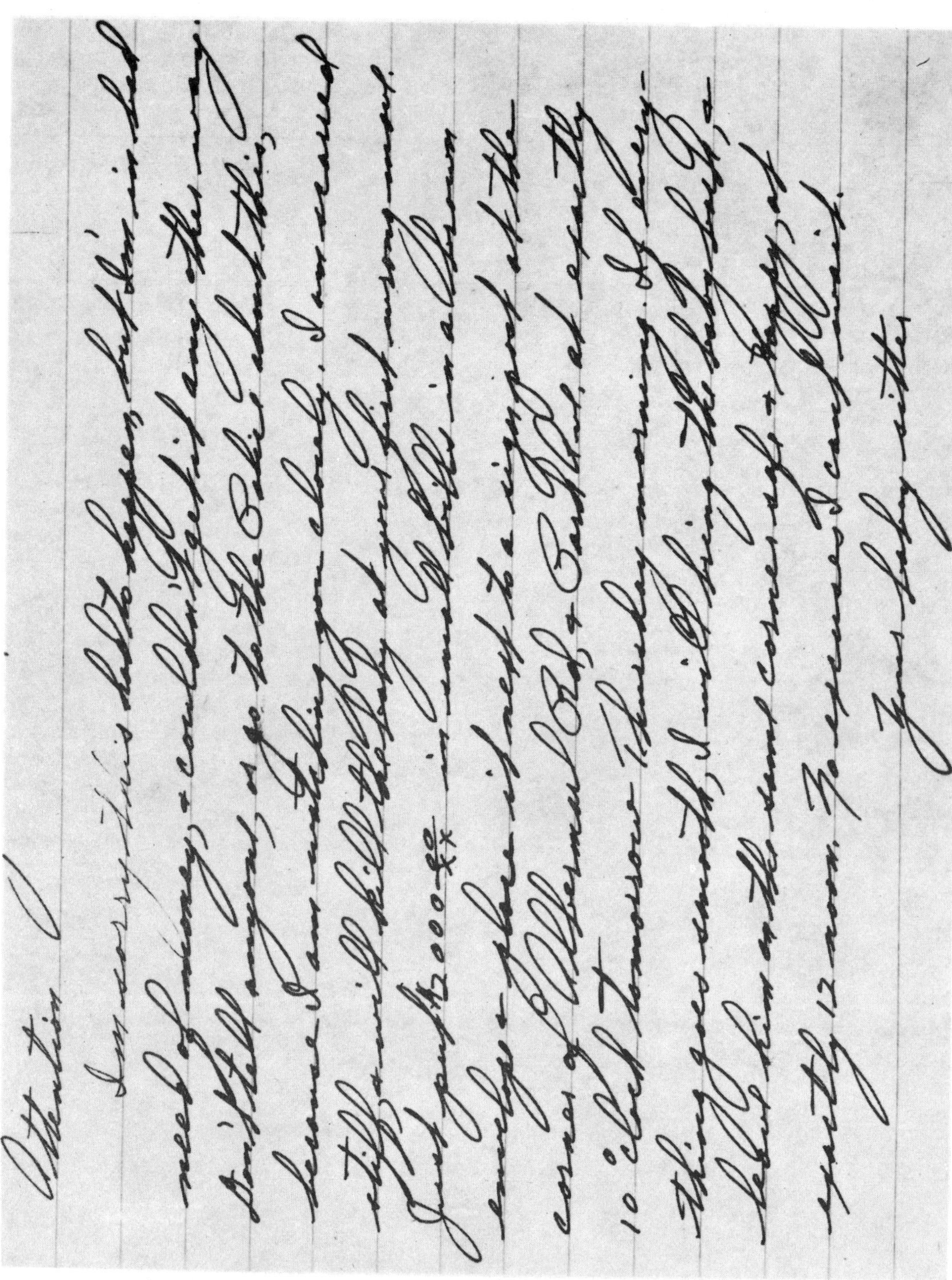

Attention

I'm sorry this had to happen, but I'm in bad
need of money, + couldn't get it any other way.
Don't tell anyone, or go to the Police about this,
because I am watching you closely. I am scared
stiff, + will kill the baby at your first wrong move.
Just put $2000.00/xx in small bills in a brown
envelope + place it next to a sign post at the
corner of Albermal Rd, + Park Ave, at exactly
10 o'clock tomorrow Thursday morning. If every-
thing goes smooth, I will bring the baby back, +
leave him on the same corner safe + happy, at
exactly 12 noon. No excuses I can't wait.

Your baby sitter

Fig. 8C
Known writing of suspect who was apprehended after the document presented in Fig. 8B was found. Suspect agreed to cooperate and wrote this version of the kidnap note when it was dictated to him.

Exercise 9: Questioned Printing*

Documents

QUESTIONED: Photographic print of crossword puzzle beginning with the word "DAM" and ending with the word "RES."

KNOWN: Photographic print of crossword puzzle beginning with the word "BOOT" and ending with the word "SEEM."

Opinion

Examination and comparison of these documents caused the opinion to be formed that the document in question was written by the author of the known writing.

Reasons

A study of the writing on the Questioned document shows that it is a melange of upper case hand-printed forms such as the "D," the "N," the "S," lower case hand-printed forms such as the "e" and "t," together with script capitals such as the "P," the "R," and the "B." Examination of the writing on the Known document discloses the same type of writing is employed. Note the use of the upper case hand-printed form of "D" and "N" and "S." Also used in the lower case hand-printed form of the "e" and the "t," plus the script capitals, "P" and "R" and "B."

The degree of skill employed by the author of the writing on the Questioned document is matched by the skill of the writing on the Known document. The only variation reflects the speed of the writing. Note that the writing of the letters on the Known document is more even and smoother than the writing of the letters on the Questioned document. The letters in question have been written slower and in a more deliberate fashion than the letters on the Known document. It is believed that this variation in the writing pattern was caused by the author's concentration on the word meanings rather than placement and design. The Known writing, though done more quickly, indicates that attention was paid to individual letter design and placement.

A more specific aspect of the examination was the side by side comparison of the individual letters which make up the words of these two documents. The letters of the Questioned writing were examined and compared with their counterparts in the Known writing. When these letters were compared and examined one with another, taking into consideration the design of the individual letter, the form of the letter, the proportions of its parts to each other, and the execution of the writing stroke or strokes making up the letter, it was found that the letters of the Questioned writing and the Known writing virtually duplicate each other. In brief, side by side comparison disclosed these similarities:

"A"—In both documents "A" is written in the same fashion — retraced loop staff at left side with a rounded top. Writing stroke in one continuous movement. Horizontal line placement in approximately same area.

"B"—Both documents have same type; script capital form with retraced loop staff at left. Relative size of top and bottom are similar in both. Degree of curvature of arc similar. Writing stroke is in one continuous movement.

"C"—Plain, unadorned form on both documents. Same design used on both documents. Deep semi-circle. Relative size, both width and height, used in both Questioned and Known documents.

"D"—Plain, hand-printed form on both. Curvature and relative size of arc agrees on both Q and K. Bottom of arc slightly flat in all instances.

"e"—In both Q and K the lower hand-printed form is utilized throughout. Curvature of arc agrees in both documents. Letter appears to be leaning slightly backward. Note that though this is the lower case form of the letter it takes up the same amount of space as upper-case and capital forms.

"F"—No comparison as a lower case "f" is used in the Known document.

"g"—In both documents an individualistic

*Solution provided by Joseph P. McNally, Questioned Document Examiner, and at the time a Captain in the New York City Police Department, Police Laboratory.

type of lower case hand-printed "g" is used. Circular part is similar in both documents with lower staff curving at the bottom to form a deep dish design. Note how this lower case form fills entire space.

"H"—No comparison.

"I"—In both documents a straight vertical line is used for this letter. No serifs and no diacritic serves to distinguish this form from a hand-printed "l" or the number "1." Though this line has no individuality in and of itself its use in this context serves as a point of identification.

"J"—No comparison.

"K"—No comparison.

"L"—The "L's" of the Questioned document are formed in a rather peculiar fashion. What should be the lower horizontal line of the letter is formed in a "stepping-stone" fashion with a spur extending upward at the right. It almost gives the appearance of the heel and toe of a shoe. All of the "L's" of the Known document, save two, are written in a rather normal fashion with a straight vertical and a straight horizontal stroke. However, the "L" of "Lead" in space 25 on the Known document is almost an exact duplicate of the "L's" as found on the Questioned document. The fact that this type of "L" unquestionably exists in the writing pattern of the author of the Known document is another added element in this identification.

"M"—Similar in design and form in both the Known and Questioned writing. All strokes making up the letter are written in a diagonal fashion and the letter is formed in one continuous movement.

"N"—Similar in design and form in both the Known and the Questioned writing. The center diagonal line extends from the top of the left vertical to the bottom of the right vertical at the base line of the writing. Letter formed in one continuous writing stroke.

"O"—There are variations of this letter in the Known and Questioned writings. Some of the "O's" in the Known are more circular than those of the Questioned. The bulk of the "O's" in the Questioned are flattened to some degree at the left and this characteristic does appear in some of the "O's" in the Known. Note "SOS" in Space 5 Across in the Known, plus "ADO" in Space 32 Across in the Known.

"P"—Written as a script capital form with a retraced loop staff at the left in both Questioned and Known writing. An exception appears in the word, "PUP" on the Known, Space 13 Across. The last "P" differs slightly as it has no looped staff. However, note overhang on the left of this letter. This is an indication of continuity of the writing stroke from the bottom of the staff to the top. It indicates that the writing instrument barely missed the surface of the paper. Actually this form could very well be considered an incompleted script form of a script capital "P."

"Q"—No comparison.

"R"—In both puzzles written like a script capital. Retraced loop at the left. Curvature of the upper arc and its placement is similar in the Questioned and Known writing. Terminal diagonal stroke is similar in both writings, agreeing in length and degree of slant. Entire letter written in one continuous movement.

"S"—Design and form of letter similar in both the Q and K documents. Curvature of arcs, both upper and lower, agrees in both the Q and K documents. This letter is broad and squat, filling in the entire space in both the Q and K documents.

"T"- This letter is written interchangeably as both a capital and a "t" in the Questioned and Known documents. Similar in design and proportions. Variation of upper and lower case forms in the Questioned documents is repeated in the Known documents.

"U"—Depth of this letter, lateral dimensions, and curvature of bottom arc similar in both the Q and K documents.

"V"—No comparison.

"W"—No comparison.

"X"—No comparison.

"y"—In both the Questioned and Known writings this is written as a small letter. In neither case is it strictly a script form, nor is it a hand-printed form. It has an individuality of its own and this individuality is apparent in both the Questioned and Known handwritings. The upper portion of this letter in both the Q and K is a deep "u" type bowl with the lower portion being a vertical line descending then turning in a right angle to the left. Note how this small letter fills the entire space.

"Z"—No comparison.

Summary

A number of factors should be considered in this analysis. The overall pictorial quality of the writing was taken into account. This is a general impression gained by a preliminary study of the writings to be considered. As is obvious even to a non-expert, the general appearance of the Questioned and the Known documents exhibits a great deal of similarity. This impression is gained from the recognition of a few obvious letter similarities plus the similarity of letter slope, rhythm, and shading. These general factors are also taken into consideration by the expert. It was found that the slope of the writing employed in the Questioned and the Known documents was the same. The fluency of the writing strokes and the rhythm of the writing pattern in both the Questioned and the Known documents agrees. Shading of letters is not pronounced in these documents but where it does appear in the Questioned document as in the letter "O," it also appears in the Known writing. The degree of skill employed by the author of the Questioned document is matched by the skill of writing on the Known document. Inconsistencies in the writing pattern exhibited on the Questioned document are matched by like inconsistencies in the writing pattern in the Known document.

But much more importantly, when the individual letters making up the words on these documents were subjected to a side by side examination and comparison, it was found that these individual letters matched each other in design, form, execution of writing stoke, proportions and relative size.

Therefore, since the general factors such as skill, slope, rhythm, fluency, shading and line quality coincided in the Questioned and Known documents and the specific factors such as the design, form, and execution of stroke of the individual letters making up the words in both the Questioned and Known documents also coincided, the conclusion was reached that the Questioned crossword puzzle was written by the author of the Known crossword puzzle.

Exercise 10: Questioned Handwriting (Cursive)

This case presents an opportunity to point out that a criminalist must look at the forest as well as the trees. Thus the style and form (the forest) of the threatening note can be as important as the details of letter and number formation and misspellings (the trees).

Style and Form

Use of a hyphen after the salutatory name. The "I'll Be Seeing You" is set on a line by itself and indented. Also note the use of capitals for the first letter of each word in the closing remark. Only Suspect 2 (Fig. 10C) used this style and form.

These characteristics permit one to discriminate among the possible writers.

Word Spelling, Letter and Number Formation

Error in the spelling of twenties (twentys)
The capital O in Oasis
The five and zeros of $1500
The g in night and again
The P in 8 PM

There are other characteristics present in the writing of Suspect 2 (Fig. 10C) that are left to students and instructors to discover. Conclusion: The writer of Fig. 10C also wrote the questioned note.

Exercise 13: Acoustic Patterns

Four frequency ranges are delineated by the horizontal lines in the acoustic spectrum patterns. While an overall impression may be significant in pattern recognition, in this case it is equally important to examine the four ranges individually. Inspection of the top two ranges eliminates Speakers III and IV and raises questions about Speaker I. Comparison of the two lower ranges and an examination of the details of the accoustic patterns of individual words leaves Speaker II as the only possibility.

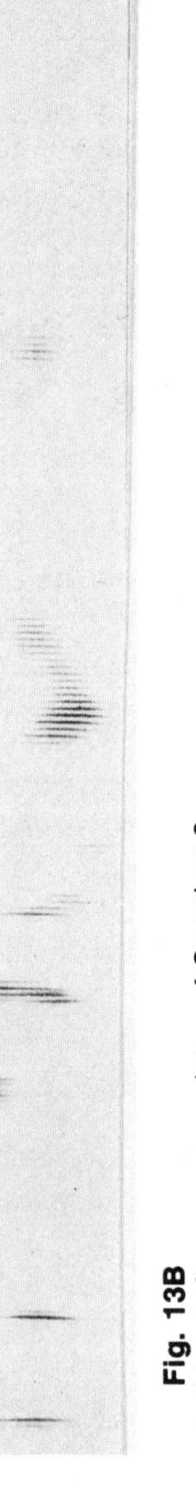

Fig. 13B
Upper frequency register of Speaker 2.

Unknown Speaker

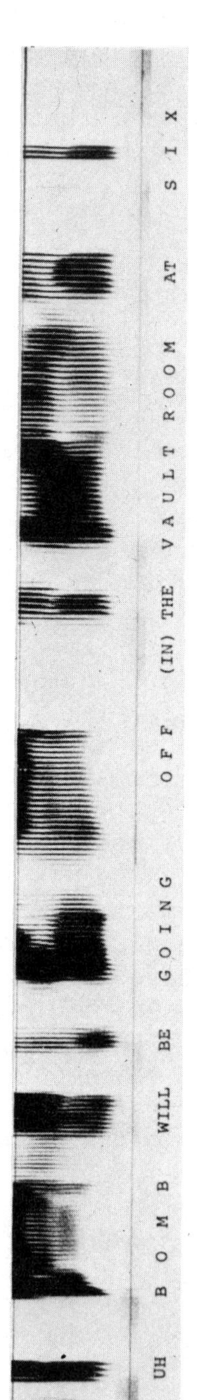

Fig. 13B
Lower frequency register of Speaker 2.
(Courtesy, Michigan State Police.)

5

Exercises 1, 4, 8

Exercise 1: Crepe Sole Print

Comment
In offering testimony the expert described to the jury the meaning of the points of identity as follows:

1. Peninsula
2. Small projection
3. Peninsula
4. Ridge ending
5. Scar
6. Peninsula and contour on either side
7. Island
8. Island
9. General contour — double depression
10. Island
11. Bulb with constriction on either side
12. Shape of bay

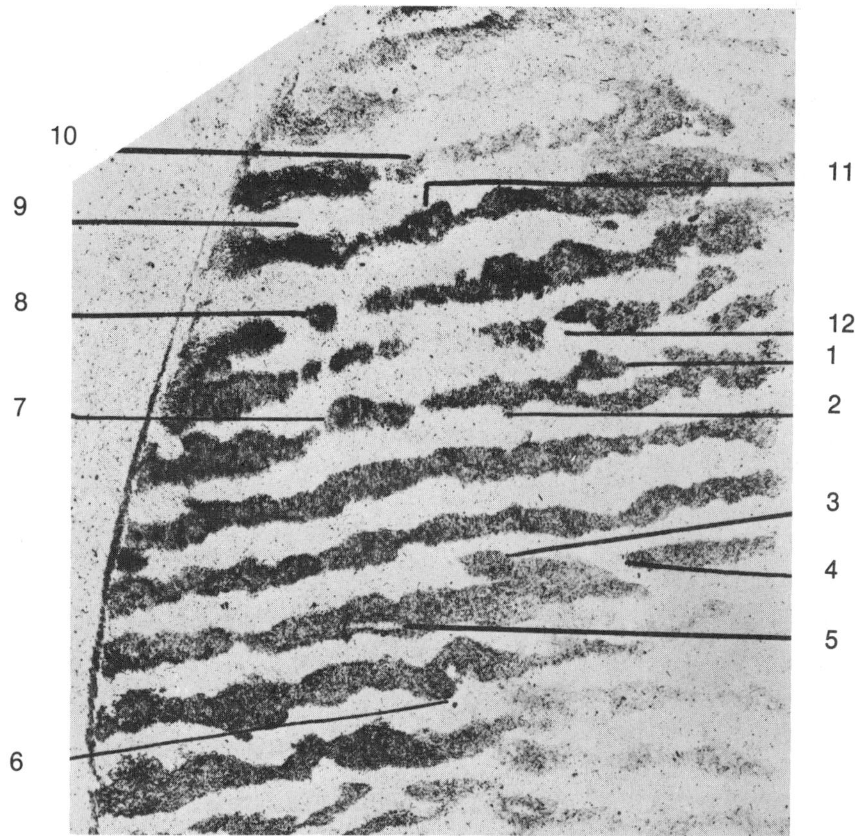

Fig. 1A
Crepe sole impression left by a burglar on a recently painted chair.

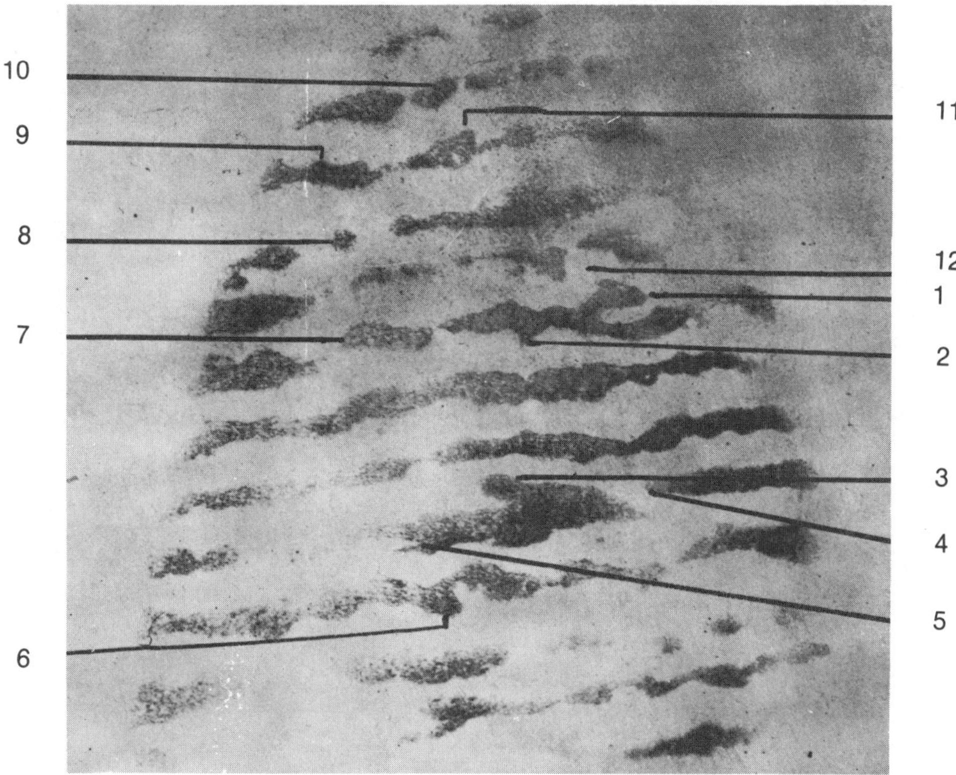

Fig. 1B
Known impression made by detective using suspect's shoe.
(Courtesy, New York City Police Department.)

Exercise 4: Heelprint in Sand

Comment

This exercise illustrates the simplicity of some identity problems. In this case the two gouges, labeled 1 and 3, and the general wear, labeled 2, are sufficient to establish an identity.

There is a tendency to strive for a large number of characteristics. This tendency is manifested in this case because of the few characteristics available. Groping for characteristics through a vivid use of the imagination

Fig. 4A
Impression of heelmark in dirt at scene of crime.

does not make them real. The decision of identity must be based only upon characteristics actually present. If it were possible in this exercise, the examination of the actual evidence in three dimensions would add to the confidence of the student in the identity and minimize the desire to stretch the number of characteristics. The marked but unnumbered points in Fig. 4A would be better examined in the original state than in the photograph. The depth and three dimensional aspects of these points are particularly important in their evaluation.

Fig. 4B
Heel found on shoe of a suspect in case.
(Courtesy, Sheriff's Office, Kern County, California.)

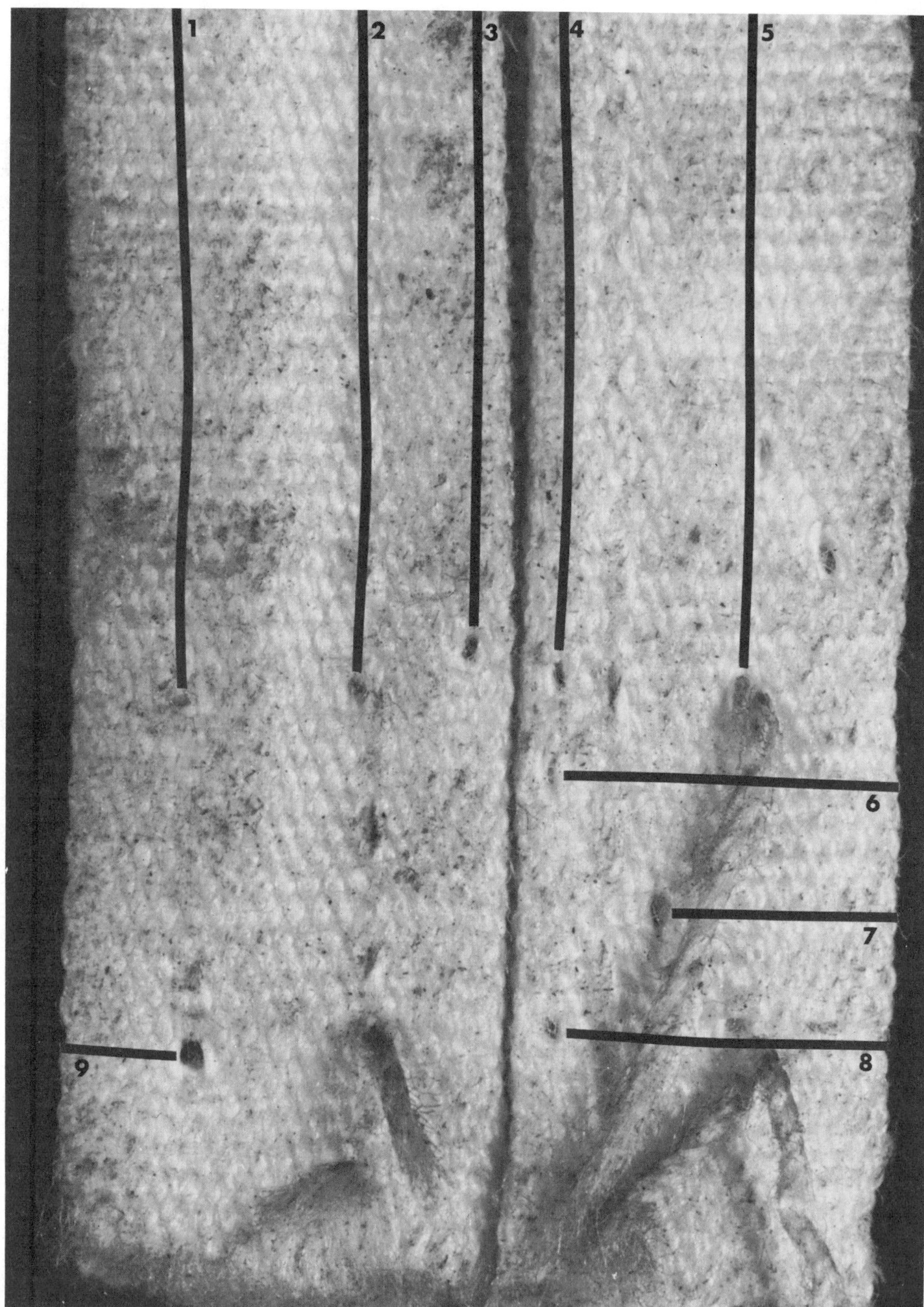

Fig. 8A
End of cloth garrote.

Exercise 8: Bra Strap

Comment

Another method of comparison that simplifies locating individual characteristics is to use a clear sheet of plastic material (or unexposed, clear photographic film). This is placed over the reproduction of the bra strap and a circle marked with a grease crayon, or felt tipped marking pen. The transparent sheet, so marked, is then placed over the other photograph and the points of identity should lie within the circles. Some latitude is permissible since the force used to rip the garment apart may cause distortion or dislocation in the size and position of the stitch holes. Of course, having the actual garments available for inspection allows any minor discrepancies to be understood.

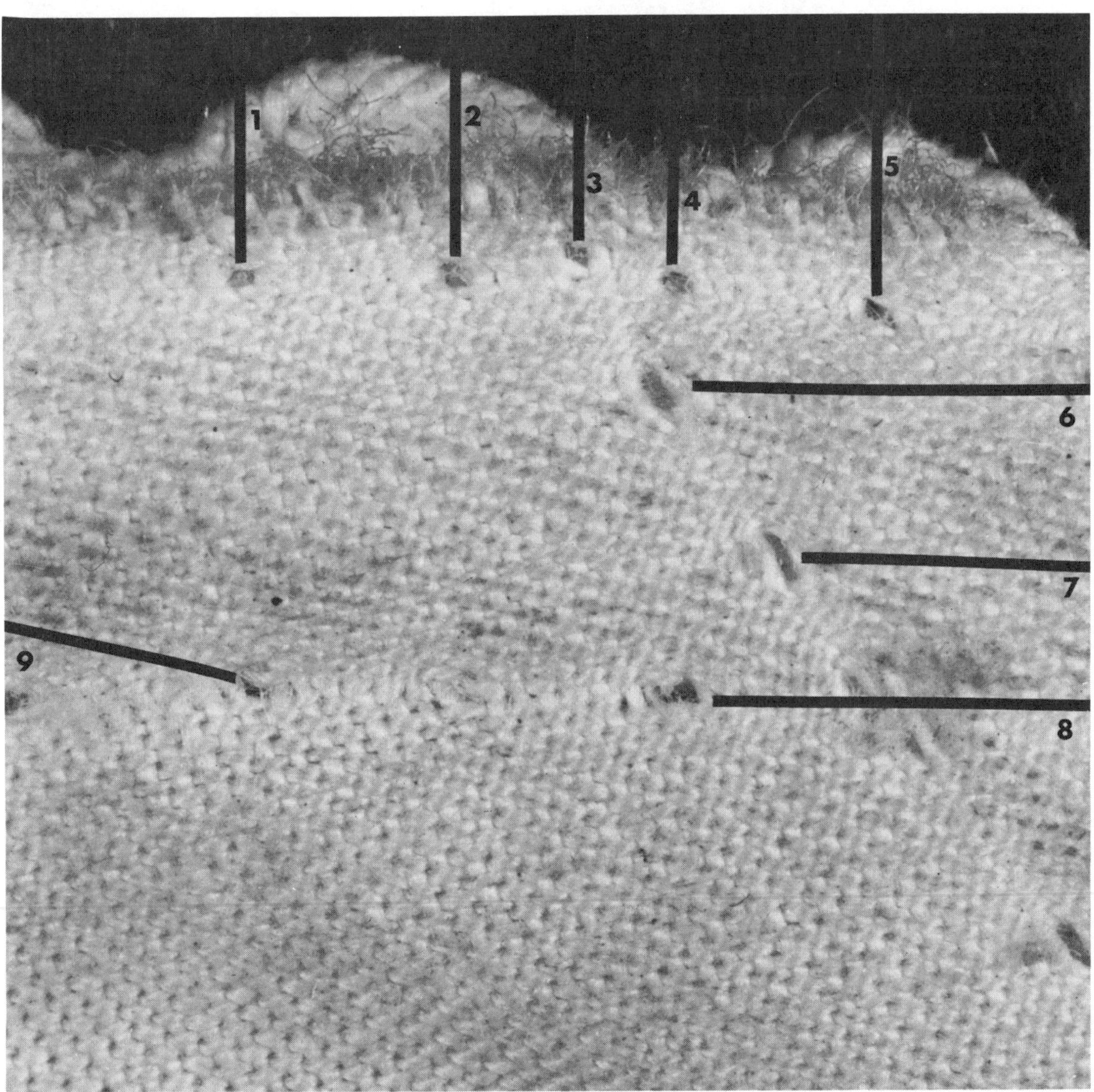

Fig. 8B
Portion of torn brassiere.
(Courtesy, Indiana State Police.)

6

Exercises 1, 2, 11, 13

Exercise 1: Tire Sand Impression (Part 1)

Comment 1
Figure 1A is the tire impression left in sand as presented in the case exercise. Figure 1B, the inked impression of a suspected tire, has been intentionally omitted to permit the student to test his initial conclusion regarding an identity between Figs. 1A and 1B against a further study here based on Fig. 1C, which is an inked impression of *another* tire on the suspected vehicle. Because it is important for the student to test his first conclusions, in light of his study of Fig. 1C, the reader is referred to Part 2 (pp 425-427) of this exercise upon completion of the analysis and written report.

Exercise 2: Jimmy Mark in Wood

Comment I
The usual student solution is shown in Figs. 2A and 2B but the greater effort and care employed by an expert who expects to testify in court and to withstand cross-examination is shown in Figs. 2C and 2D. In addition other photographs, silicone casts, and the actual evidence were available for comparative examination.

Students generally spend considerably less time in completing their examination than did the experts who furnished the cases. Any student who mistakenly believes himself to be an expert in criminalistics through use of this text is warned, here and now, of the dangers and pitfalls awaiting him at the hands of a

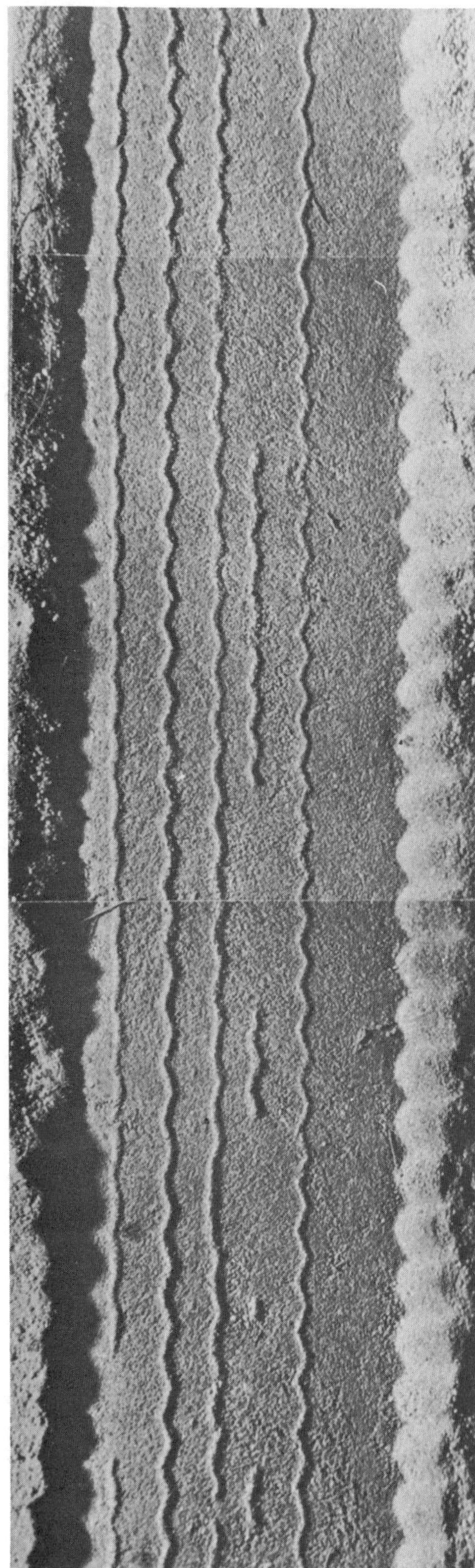

Fig. 1A
Tire scene impression left in sand at crime scene.

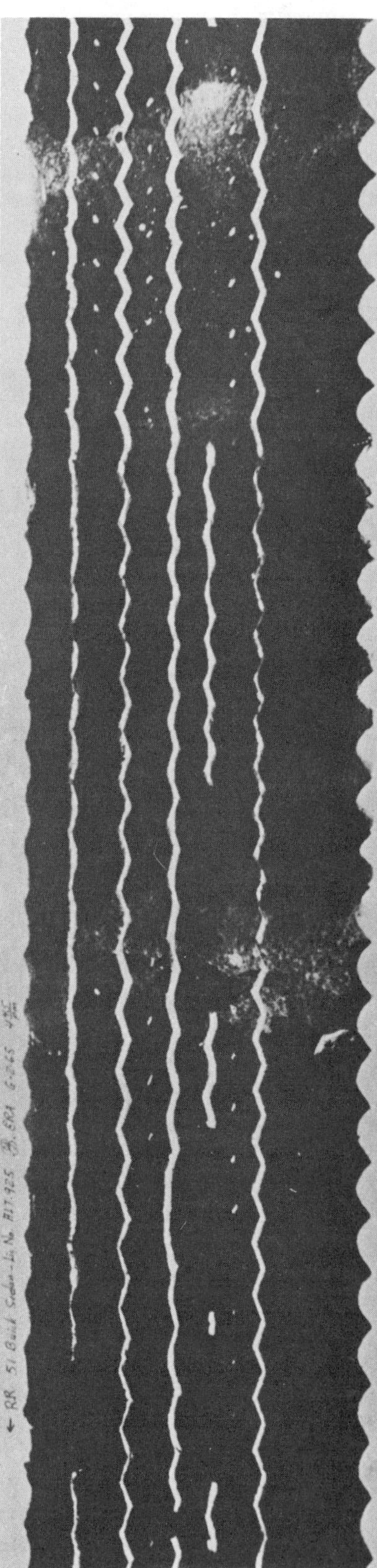

Fig. 1C
An inked impression of a suspected tire (other than that illustrated in Fig. 1B).
(Courtesy, Sheriff's Office, Kern County, California.)

competent defense counsel if he persists in his belief and attempts to testify as an expert.

Comment II

The following remarks (relative to Figs. 2C and 2D) were taken from a letter written to the author by the expert who furnished the case:

> The following notes regarding each of the numbers I have used to mark photographs may be of some assistance. It is quite obvious that the "make" was based on characteristics found in three dimensions. No single photograph in two dimensions can capture all of the information necessary to demonstrate this type of an identification. . . . Some of the characteristics by which the tool was identified were as follows:
>
> 1,2,3. These are file marks running diagonally across the level face of the tool tip as illustrated in . . . [Fig. 2D]. The corresponding embossed impressions appeared in silicone casts of the tool mark and in some other photos which were taken but not reproduced in this text.
>
> 4. The broad curve of the sharpened tool tip [Fig. 2D] was found to match the corresponding curve of the impression edge where it broke through the paint of . . . [Fig. 2C].
>
> 5. The slight angle between the opposite edges of the tool bevel [Fig. 2D] was similar to the corresponding impressions found in . . . [Fig. 2C].
>
> 6. The inner edge of the bifurcated tool [Fig. 2D] was represented in the impression [Fig. 2C].
>
> 7. The terminus of the bevel, at the inside of the tool bifurcation [Fig. 2D], was represented very accurately in angles and configurations by the impression [Fig. 2C].
>
> 8. The opposite inner edge of the bifurcated tool [Fig. 2D] was represented in the impression [Fig. 2C].
>
> 9. The terminus of the befel, at the inside of 9. The terminus of the bevel, at the inside of the tool bifurcation [Fig. 2D] was found to be represented accurately in the impression [Fig. 2C].
>
> 10. A relatively large defect due to damage subsequent to sharpening was noted on the leading edge of the tool [Fig. 2D]. The impression [Fig. 2C] showed evidence of a defect in the paint above where the tool edge had broken through and at the bottom of the impression where it had been carried.
>
> 11. A defect similar to (10) but smaller . . . . 12 through 31. These are diagonal file marks at the edge of the bevel of the tool [Fig. 2D]. The corresponding diagonal impressions are to be found in the silicone cast made as well as in one of the other photographs taken but not reproduced in this text.
>
> 32. This edge of the tool [Fig. 2D] has a slight ridge extending above the face. The impression in the corresponding position was found at the bottom of the questioned tool mark.
>
> 33. This edge of the tool [Fig. 2D] also has a ridge extending above the face. The ridge is markedly less pronounced than (32). The impression of the corresponding mark was found in . . . [Fig. 2C].
>
> The distance from edge (33) to (6) of the tool [Fig. 2D] was closely similar to the corresponding distance of the impression edge.
>
> The distance from edge (8) to edge (32) of the tool [Fig. 2C] was closely similar to the corresponding impression of the impression edge.
>
> In addition to the above points, there was a transfer of light tan paint adhering to several places on the tool. This paint was similar in all properties examined to the known light tan paint from the impression [Fig. 2C].
>
> In addition to the above, there was a transfer of blue paint adhering in micro fragments at several places on the surface of the impression [Fig. 2C]. This paint was similar in all properties examined to the original blue paint of the tool [Fig. 2D].

Fig. 2A
Jimmy impression on edge of door.

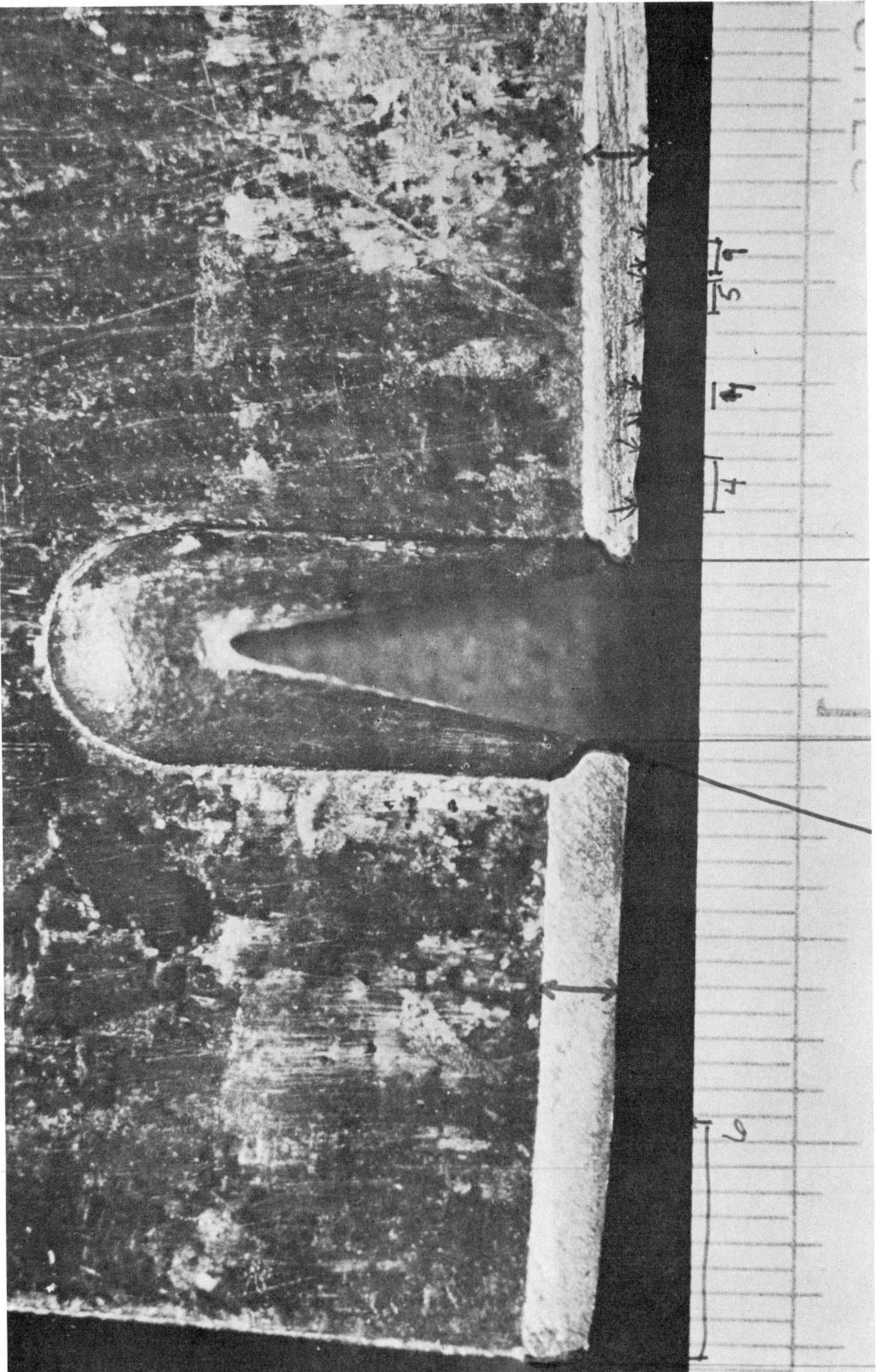

Fig. 2B
Suspected jimmy.

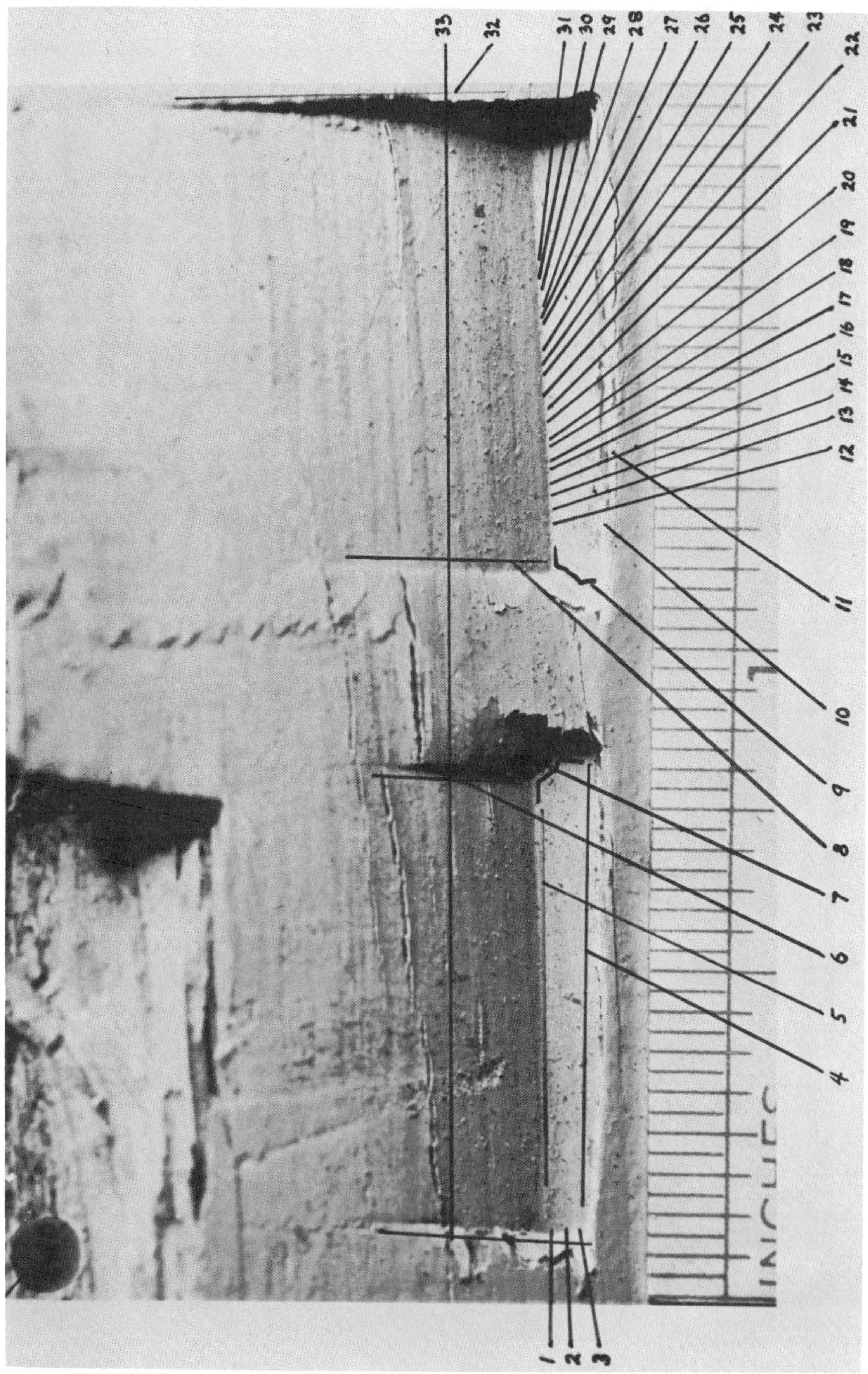

Fig. 2C
Jimmy impression on edge of door.

Fig. 2D
Suspected jimmy.
(Courtesy, Orange County Sheriff's Department, California.)

Exercise 11: Breech Face Marks

Comment

By cutting the breech face marks in Fig. 11B in two places, to the left and right of the firing pin impression, and sliding them along on Fig. 11A, it is possible to effect a match without the use of a comparison microscope.

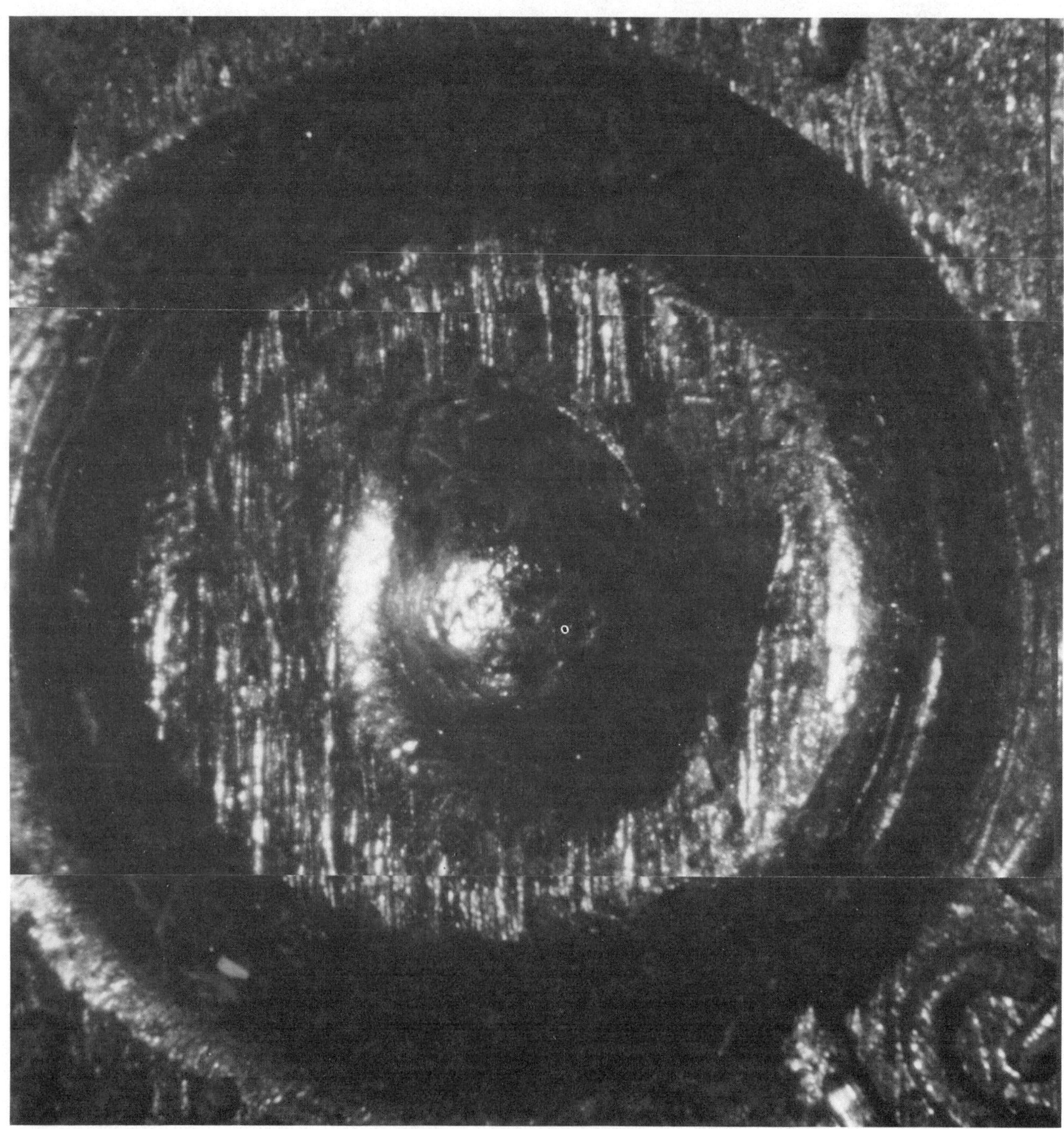

Fig. 11C
Composite of Figs. 11A (in the middle) and 11B (at top and bottom.)
(Courtesy, Joseph D. Nicol.)

Exercise 13: Hose Knife Cut

Comment
In addition to marking the striations as shown in the accompanying figure, the student can try the technique described on p 424.

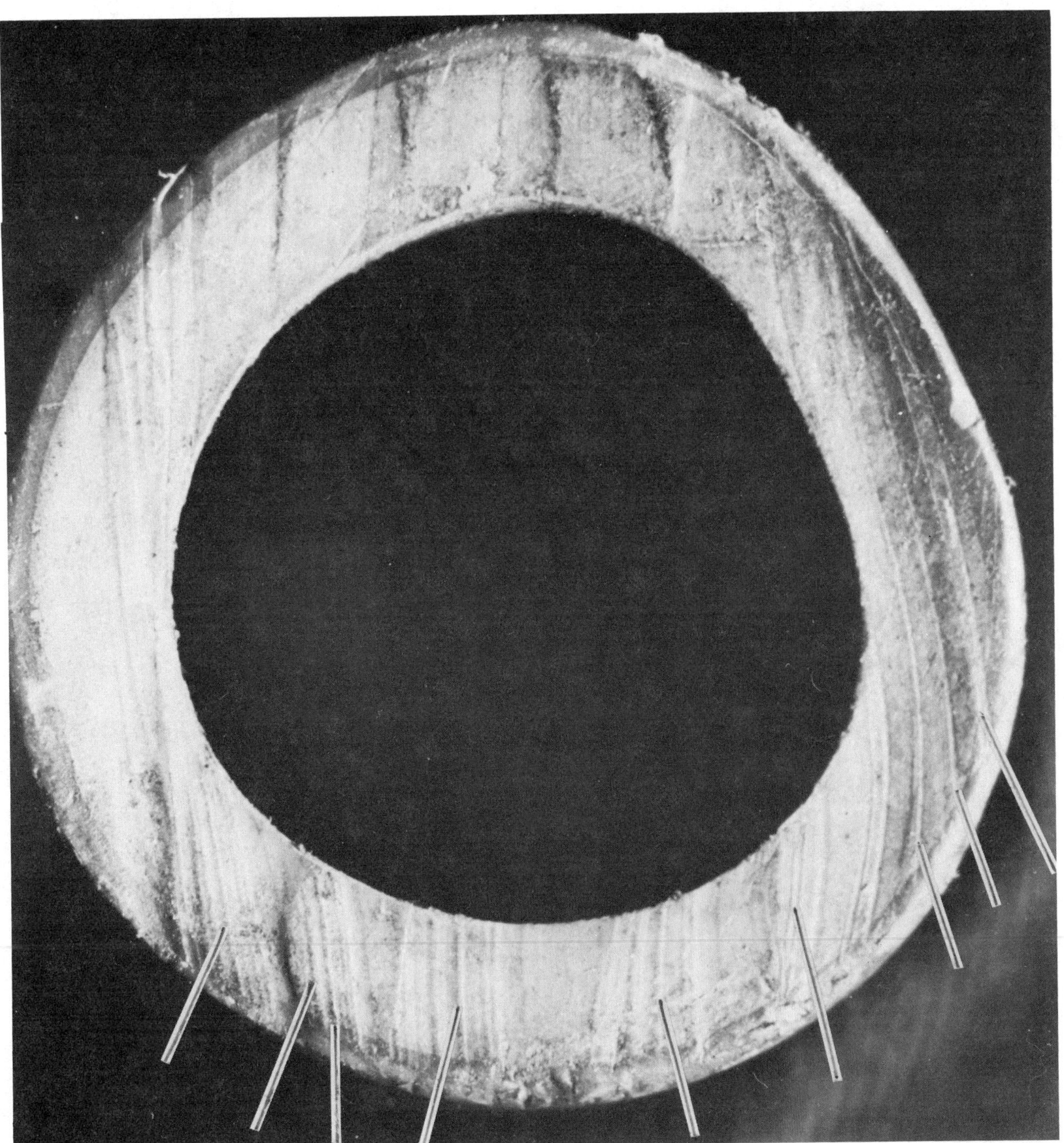

Fig. 13A
End of hose found attached to illicit still.

The crime scene evidence photography can be cut horizontally across the bottom part of the hose wall and superimposed on the same area in the other photograph. The alignment of the nick marks (striations) will become readily apparent. Which method of comparison do you prefer? Which would be more convincing to a jury?

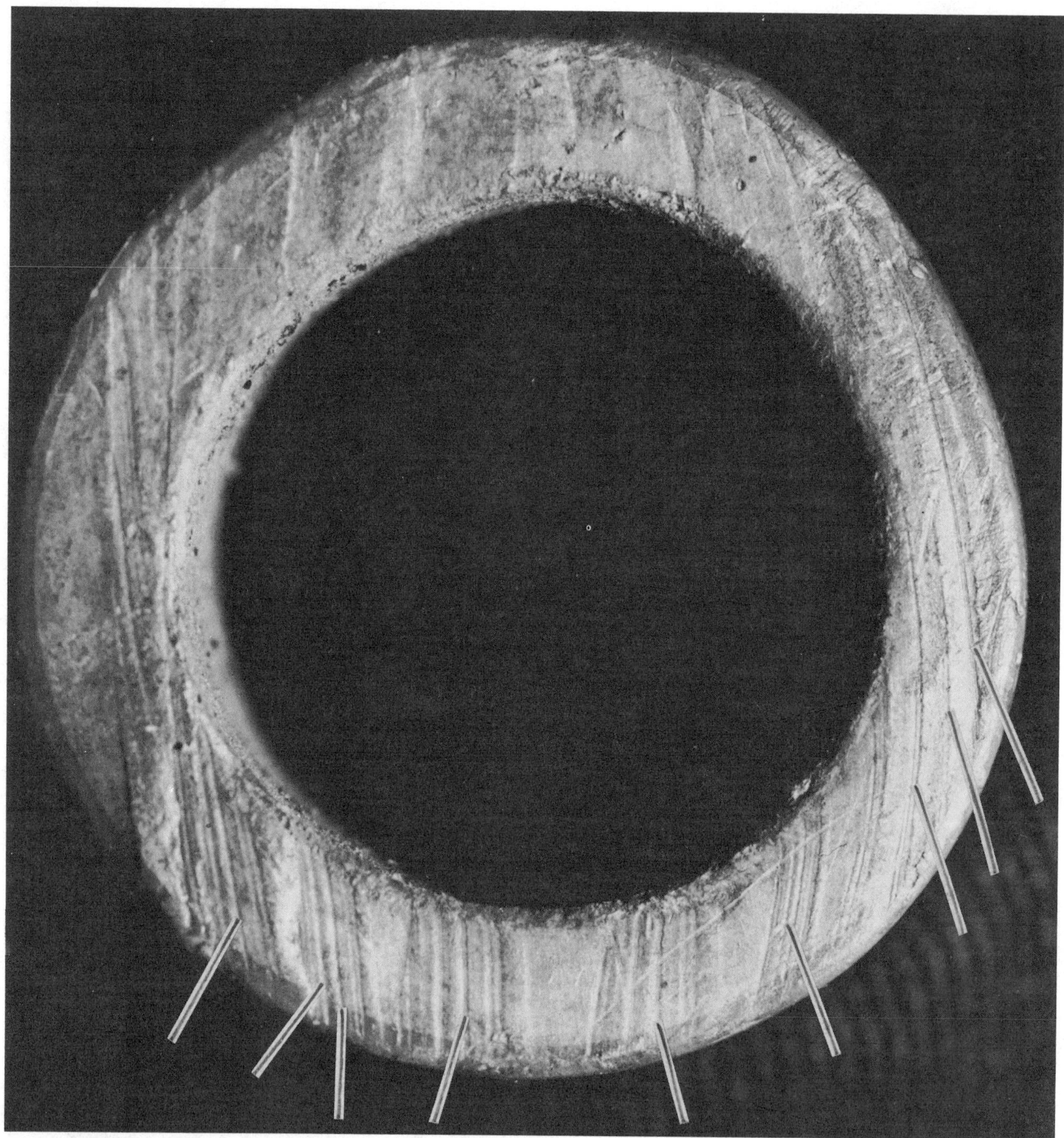

Fig. 13B
End of hose found in possession of suspect—reverse printed.
(Courtesy, Columbus Police Department, Ohio.)

Exercise 1: Tire Sand Impression (Part 2)

Comment II

Most students arrive at a conclusion of identity when the study of Figs. 1A and 1B is completed because the differences between the two impressions were either unobserved or ignored (see pp426-427). Although a previous exercise has stressed this matter of differences, this evidence graphically illustrates again their importance.

This exercise also permits further discussion of the meaning of class and individual characteristics. The distinction can be made by observing the same type of tire for signs of wear. If all such tires, when used for approximately the same mileage, have similar wear patterns, we are dealing with a class characteristic. On the other hand, if in fact the tires all show different types of wear, we may be dealing with an individual characteristic attributable to usage in a particular position on a particular motor vehicle. In other words, the alignment, balance, and load of a vehicle may cause individual wear on a tire. Rotation of the tires imposes no burden upon the examiner if the individual wear at the particular position is a characteristic of that position.

If the importance of the case warrants, it would be possible to demonstrate that usage in a particular position does, indeed, produce individuality. This case illustrates the need for, and importance of, research to provide data upon which a definite answer may be based.

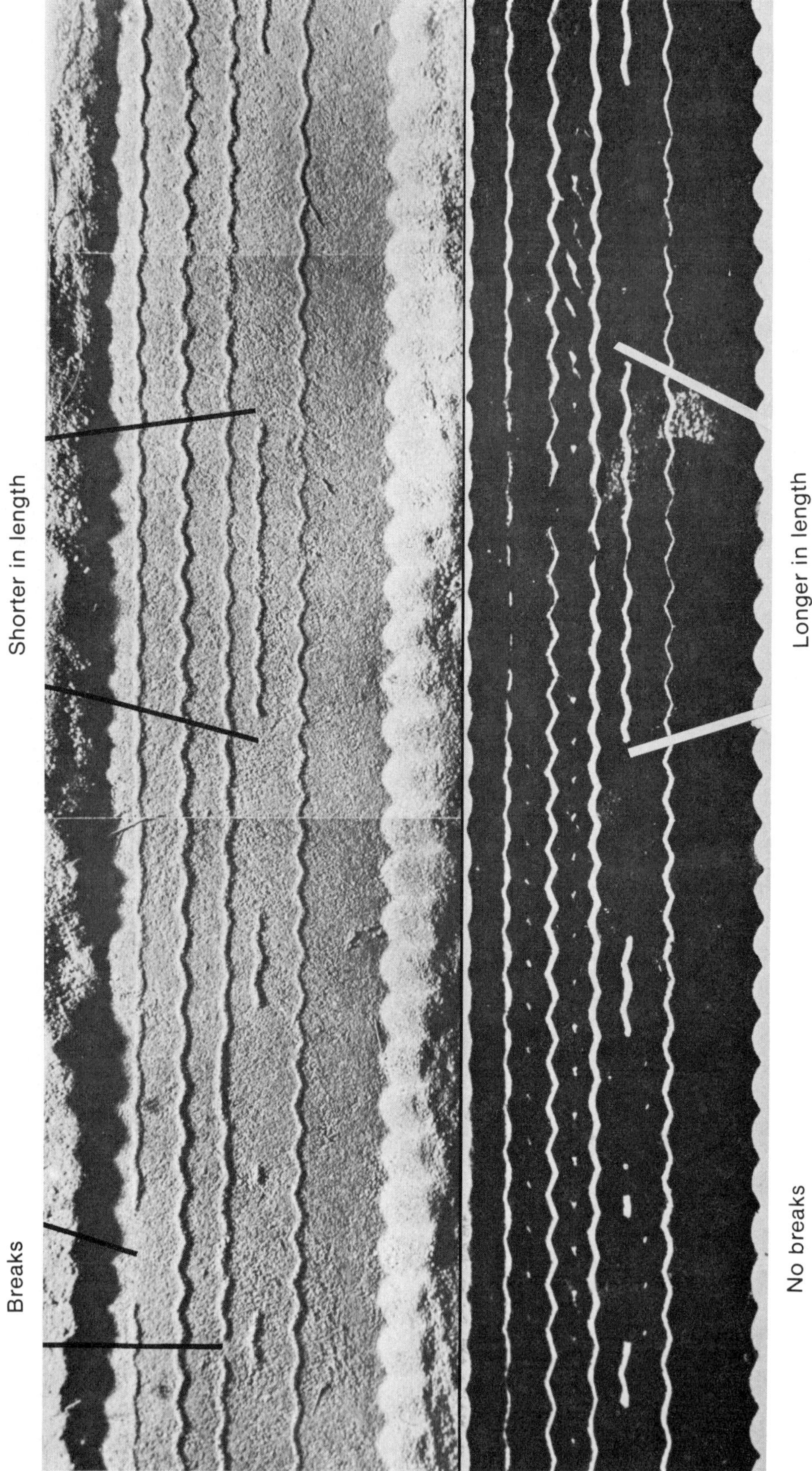

Fig. 1A
Tire impression left in sand at crime scene.

Fig. 1B
An inked impression of a suspected tire.

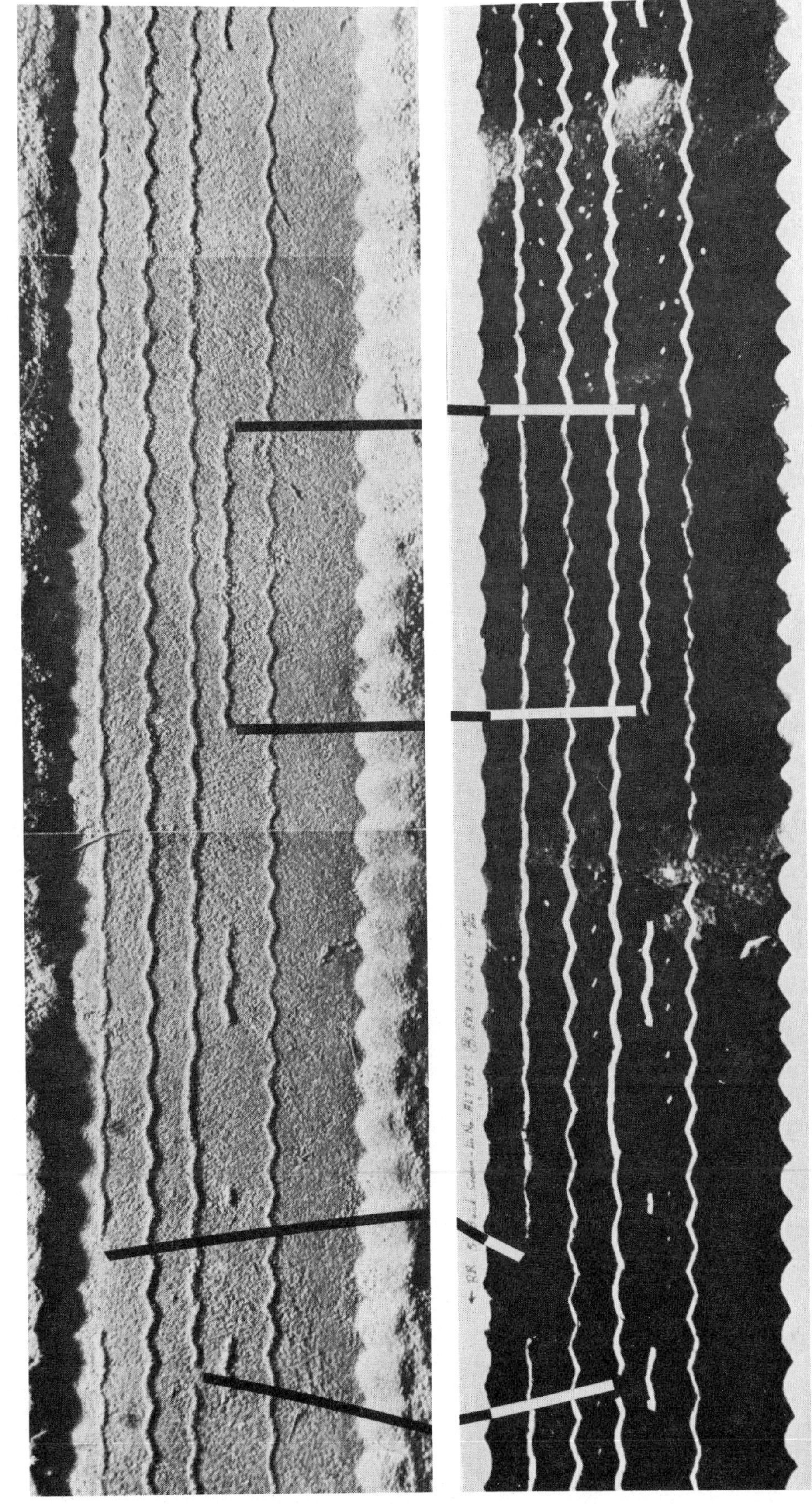

Fig. 1A

Fig. 1C

7

Exercises 1, 2

Exercise 1: Wiper Blade Spot Weld

Comment

In a letter sent with the marked case photographs, the expert commented as follows:

> I did not attempt to include all of the possible points of identification, leaving some to the ingenuity and discretion of the students. Since some of the areas of identification represent broad contours, it was not possible to point to any specific areas of identification. For example, in the circle marked "1", you can see a stain which has a positive-negative relationship on the two pieces and in the broad area of the line "2" and the fracture of the line "5" there is again broad correspondence without anything in specific detail. Obviously if these two pieces were reproduced at higher magnification, one could see some more matches in the fractures. I believe, however, it will be sufficient for your purpose to show how an investigator might at least get an idea of correspondence of some of this evidence just by common sense examination of visible points of identity.

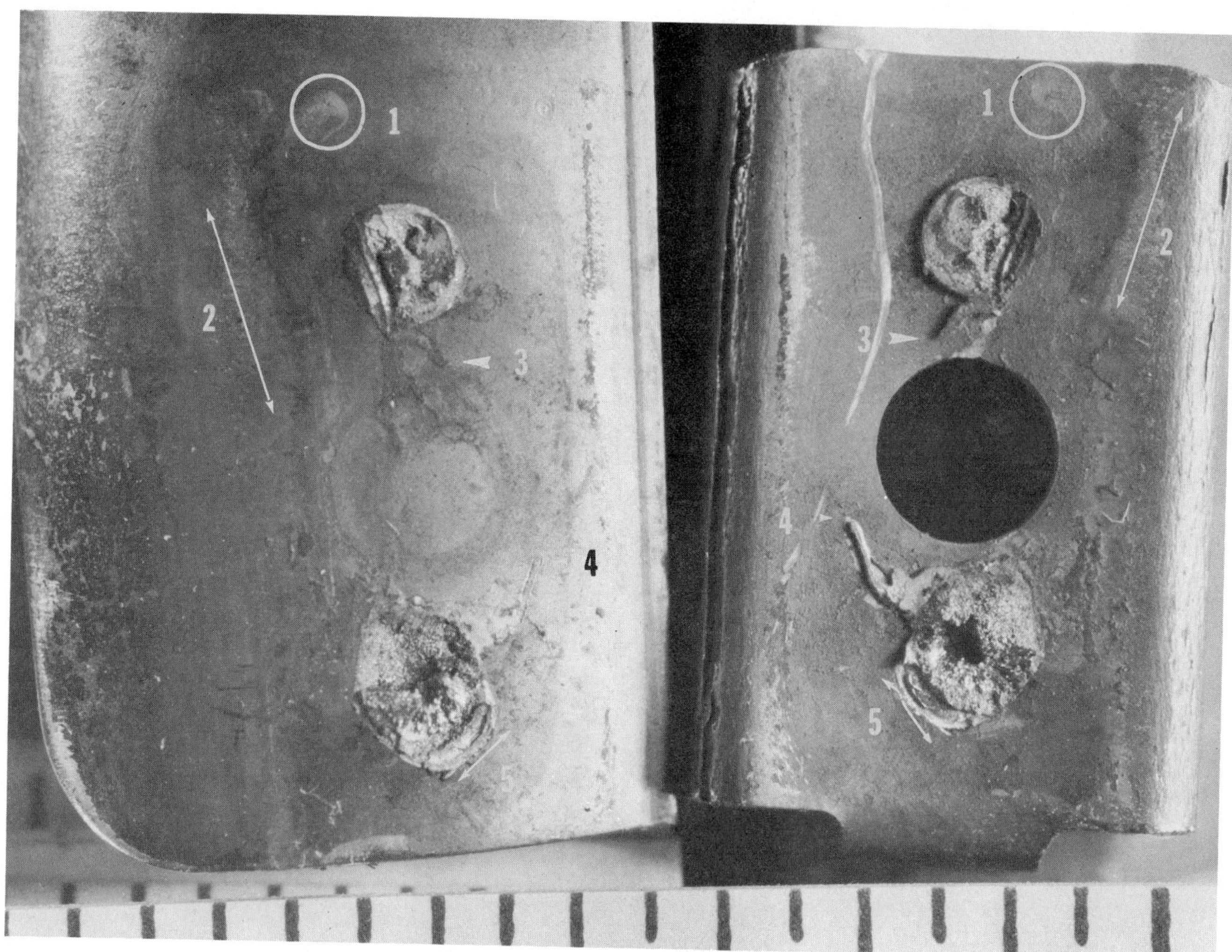

Fig. 1B
Spot weld areas: left, evidence from suspected vehicle; right, crime scene evidence.
(Courtesy, Illinois Bureau of Criminal Identification and Investigation.)

Exercise 2: Headlamp Rims

Comment

The photograph shown on p 432 depicts an apparent match in the upper portion that is mistakenly taken by some students as sufficient to establish an identity. However, the gross differences in the lower portion of the tool mark are enough to create doubt since they cannot be accounted for. Figures 2A and 2B do match.

The contributor in a letter to the author stated:

> During the course of this examination, the testmark from the left headlamp rim was first compared with the evidence mark on the headlamp housing. Substantial significant agreement was observed. When it was noted that the wrong headlamp rim had been used for comparison purposes, the testmark from the right headlamp rim was compared. Substantially more significant agreement was observed.
>
> This case was one of the earliest tool mark cases which I handled and occurred during a period of time when little consideration had been given in the literature or by examiners of the possible carryover of class characteristics which could give rise to striate markings on manufactured products in which the tool (die) used in the manufacturing processes possessed individualizing features and due to the hardness of its metal reproduced markings from item to item.

Figs. 2A and 2C
Composite of Figs. 2A and 2C (on the bottom). *(Courtesy, Sheriff's Department, Contra Costa County, California.)*

8

Exercise 1

Exercise 1: Wood Grain — Auto Hood

Comment

This exercise presents special difficulties. For example, note that the scale in the lighter picture, i.e., that of the imprint left on the hood of the automobile, is not linear. Thus the "inch" between 4 and 5 is larger than that between 13 and 14; both differ from the "inch" shown in the barricade wood grain photograph. *This is a case in which examination of the actual evidence (together with photographs) is necessary.* In addition, any paint that was transferred would be helpful in locating areas suitable for close examination.

Mention should also be made of the possible use of sophisticated, instrumental techniques of analysis, i.e., the spectrograph, electron microprobe, and X-ray diffraction. Of course, these are found only in well-equipped laboratories.

The laboratory that submitted this case marked general areas that have similar grain structure; however, the comparison was based on other techniques mentioned in the discussion above.

Fig. 1A
Imprint noted in a damaged area of the hood of an abandoned automobile.

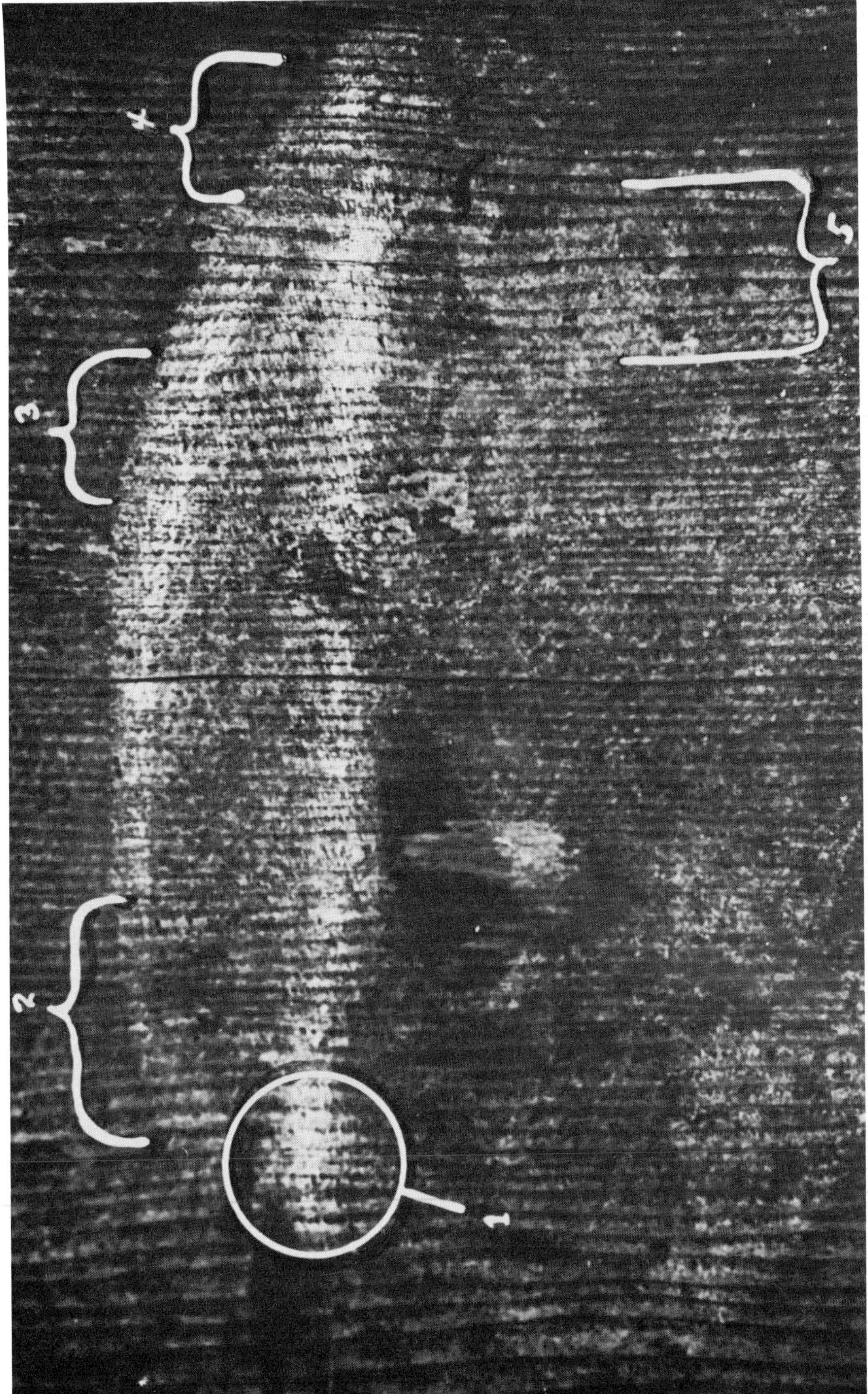

Fig. 1B
An egg-shaped paint impression found on a wooden barricade that had been struck by a fleeing automobile.
(Courtesy, Minnesota State Bureau of Criminal Apprehension.)

Glossary

Armprint: Impressions of the friction ridges, flexion creases, or texture patterns on the skin of the arm.

Associative evidence: Evidence that links the crime scene to the criminal.

Benzidine test: A nonspecific, preliminary chemical test to determine if a stain contains blood.

Chain of custody: Possession of physical evidence that can be accounted for from the time of its discovery to its presentation in court as evidence.

Class characteristics: The more obvious, general, or gross features distinguishable in an object that are repeated in other objects.

Comparison microscope: An instrument that permits a direct comparison (in a split field of the eyepiece) of two objects. Generally a series of lines or striations inherent in the evidence are compared at magnifications of 25X or less.

Comparison specimens: Samples used as the basis of comparison with a questioned item of physical evidence.

Continuity of possession: See *Chain of custody.*

Criminalistics: That profession and scientific discipline that is directed to the recognition, identification, individualization, and evaluation of physical evidence by application of the natural sciences in law-science matters.

Die marks: Stamped impressions placed on articles or products for purposes of identification.

Earprints: Impressions of the ridge patterns found on the ear.

Escobedo decision: A United States Supreme Court decision in which the right to counsel is constitutionally guaranteed to a suspect prior to arraignment, if he or she requests to see a lawyer. Escobedo v. Illinois, 378 U.S. 478 (1964).

Exemplar: A known standard of evidence obtained for comparison purposes.

Flexion creases: Folds in the skin that form distinctive patterns.

Forensic: Pertaining to, connected with, or used in courts of law.

Forensic pathologist: A medical specialist who, among other things, determines the cause of death in suspected homicide cases. This specialist's work is especially important in establishing whether death was the result of a criminal act.

Friction ridges: Crests on the extremities and skin that leave impressions upon contact with a surface.

Grooves: The spiral cuts in the interior surface of a gun barrel or on a bullet following its passage through the barrel of a gun.

Identification: The process of placing an entity in a predefined, restricted class.

Identity: The evaluation of the combination of conditions that uniquely characterize an entity.

Individual characteristics: Those characteristics that make possible an inference concerning the likelihood of a common source for crime scene evidence and a reference specimen of known origin.

Individualization: See *Identity.*

Jimmy: A lever-like tool a criminal uses to break into a home, business establishment, or safe.

Lands: The area between grooves in a gun barrel or on the surface of a fired bullet.

Latent print development: The chemical process employed to make fingerprints visible.

Magna Brush: A proprietary device for developing fingerprints with powder, yielding fine detail.

Metal punch: An instrument used to form tool impressions in the form of compression marks.

Miranda decision: A United States Supreme Court decision that established rules for custodial interrogation of a suspect, including the right to the presence of counsel during the questioning. Miranda v. Arizona, 384 U.S. 436 (1966).

Morphology: The study of structure, form, or shape.

Mutural transfer evidence: Physical traces interchanged between two objects. For example, when an automobile collides with a water hydrant or bicycle, paint traces of each are deposited on the other.

Neutron activation analysis: A method of measuring through induced radioactivity the quantitative and qualitative details of chemical trace element composition in physical evidence.

Palmprints: Impressions of the ridge patterns found on the palm.

Partial prints: Impressions of a portion of a whole print, such as a fingerprint, palmprint, or footprint.

Photomacrography: Photography whereby the camera lens increases the size and detail of an object.

Photomicrography: Photography using the microscope to increase size and detail of an object.

Physical match: Placing two objects in juxtaposition to determine if both pieces were originally one.

Powder patterns: Firearm powder residue patterns formed by burnt and unburnt powder granules.

Resolution: Disclosure of detail through magnification.

Ridge details: Linear series or patterns of crests on the skin that uniquely characterize an individual.

Smudge: A latent print left by sliding fingers along an object's surface.

Sound spectograph: An instrument that converts an accoustic signal recorded on tape into a visual image.

Striations: A series of microscopic lines, grooves, or ridges on a surface which, through juxtaposition, provide the basis for establishing an identity between two objects; characteristic marks found on a bullet after its passage through the barrel of a gun.

Texture lines: Texture patterns on the skin that form distinctive patterns.

Tool imprint: Impression of a tool mark.

Voiceprints: Accoustic signals recorded on tape and converted into a visual image.

Weave patterns: An aspect of textile fabrication that can be useful in the development of associative evidence.

Index

Index to Text Figures

NOTES

NOTES